Tony Cliff

Marxist Theory
After Trotsky

Tony Cliff

Marxist Theory
After Trotsky

SELECTED WRITINGS
VOLUME 3

BOOKMARKS

London and Sydney

Tony Cliff: Marxist Theory After Trotsky: Selected Writings Volume 3

First published 2003
Bookmarks Publications Ltd, c/o 1 Bloomsbury Street, London WC1B 3QE, England
Bookmarks, PO Box A338, Sydney South, NSW 2000, Australia
Copyright © Bookmarks Publications Ltd

ISBN 1 898876 93 2 (Paperback)
ISBN 1 898876 92 4 (Hardback)

Printed by The Bath Press, Bath
Cover by Ian Goodyer

Bookmarks Publications Ltd is linked to an international grouping of socialist
organisations:
Australia: International Socialist Organisation, PO Box A338, Sydney South. *iso@iso.org.au*
Austria: Linkswende, Postfach 87, 1108 Wien. *linkswende@yahoo.com*
Britain: Socialist Workers Party, PO Box 82, London E3 3LH. *enquiries@swp.org.uk*
Canada: International Socialists, PO Box 339, Station E, Toronto, Ontario M6H 4E3.
    iscanada@on.aibn.com
Cyprus: Ergatiki Demokratia, PO Box 27280, Nicosia. *wd@workersdemocracy.net*
Czech Republic: Socialisticka Solidarita, PO Box 1002, 11121 Praha 1. *socsol@email.cz*
Denmark: Internationale Socialister, PO Box 5113, 8100 Aarhus C. *intsoc@socialister.dk*
Finland: Sosialistiliitto, PL 288, 00171 Helsinki. *info@sosialistiliitto.org*
France: Socialisme par en bas, BP 15-94111, Arcueil Cedex. *speb@mageos.com*
Germany: Linksruck, Postfach 304 183, 20359 Hamburg. *info@linksruck.de*
Ghana: International Socialist Organisation, PO Box TF202, Trade Fair, Labadi, Accra
Greece: Sosialistiko Ergatiko Komma, c/o Workers Solidarity, PO Box 8161, Athens 100 10.
    sek@otenet.gr
Holland: Internationale Socialisten, PO Box 92025, 1090AA Amsterdam.
    info@internationalesocialisten.org
Ireland: Socialist Workers Party, PO Box 1648, Dublin 8. *swp@clubi.ie*
Italy: Comunismo dal Basso, Leeder, CP Bologna, Succ 5. *dalbasso@hotmail.com*
New Zealand: Socialist Workers Organisation, PO Box 13-685, Auckland.
    socialist-worker@pl.net
Norway: Internasjonale Socialisterr, Postboks 9226, Grønland, 0134 Oslo.
    sarbeide@online.no
Poland: Pracownicza Demokracja, PO Box 12, 01-900 Warszawa 118. *pracdem@go2.pl*
Spain: En Lucha, Apartado 563, 08080 Barcelona. *enlucha@hotmail.com*
United States: Left Turn, PO Box 445, New York, NY 10159-0445. *left-turn@left-turn.org*
Uruguay: Izquierda Revolucionaria. *ir@adinet.com.uy*
Zimbabwe: International Socialist Organisation, PO Box 6758, Harare. *isozim@hotmail.com*

This volume is one of a series devoted to the writings of Tony Cliff (1917-2000). Born in Palestine to a Zionist family, his development as a revolutionary Marxist was shaped by an extraordinary combination of influences. He came to hate all forms of oppression after witnessing the systematic exclusion of Arabs from Zionist society. Opposition to imperialism led to him being jailed by the occupying British power. He came to embrace Trotskyism when Stalin's disastrous international policies helped Hitler become German Chancellor in 1933.

Arriving in post-war Britain from an impoverished colonial country, Cliff was struck by the relative affluence here. This made him question the dogmatic followers of Trotsky who maintained the capitalist economy was collapsing. Above all, Cliff rejected their assertion that Red Army tanks, rather than workers' self-activity, could establish socialism in Eastern Europe. If the Eastern bloc was not socialist, and yet identical to Russia, that country was not socialist either. He concluded it was state capitalist.

This analysis preserved the central Marxist notion that workers' liberation (and therefore humanity's in general) comes from self-activity. This meant that theory and practice must be linked, which helped Cliff avoid the sterile abstractions of much of what passed for Marxism. Such insights guided him and others who formed successively the Socialist Review Group, the International Socialists and the Socialist Workers Party.

A wave of industrial militancy which peaked in the early 1970s enabled the SWP to intervene practically in the class struggle. The focus was in two areas: on rank and file action rather than union bureaucracy; and on the building of a revolutionary party which could offer political leadership in the fight for socialism.

The collapse of Stalinist regimes after 1989 confirmed the state capitalist analysis of 40 years before and cleared the way for the spread of the International Socialist Tendency in many countries.

Across seven decades of revolutionary activism, Cliff was a tireless writer and speaker who always combined theoretical rigour with practical action. We are pleased to be able to republish his writings, not as a monument to the past, but as tools to help build a future where humanity will no longer be threatened by the poverty, oppression, wars and environmental destruction that are inextricably part of capitalism.

Donny Gluckstein

Contents

Introduction

Chris Harman

This volume contains Tony Cliff's most important contributions to Marxist theory. They constituted a 'Copernican revolution' that was a precondition for revolutionary socialists consistently coming to terms with the central features of the second part of the 20th century—Stalinism in the USSR and Eastern Europe, the character of the independent states in the former European empires, and the 30 year long boom experienced by Western capitalism in the aftermath of the Second World War.

Like others of his generation who were on the left, Cliff grew up in the light cast by the 1917 revolution in Russia, and the shadow produced by what followed in the late 1920s. For hundreds of millions of people across the world, the mere existence of the Soviet Union was proof that an alternative to capitalism existed. But Cliff was already aware in his late teens of something that most people on the left did not grasp for another quarter of a century—that Russia under Stalin had turned against the goals of workers' democracy and internationalism that were proclaimed in 1917.

He accepted Leon Trotsky's increasingly stringent criticisms of the Stalinist regime and was an activist in the Fourth International founded by Trotsky in 1938. Like Trotsky, he believed there remained in Stalinism one element of continuity with the revolution of 1917. He accepted the argument that the nationalisation of all the means of production could only have come about as a result of a workers' revolution. Therefore he thought the USSR remained a 'workers' state', albeit an extremely degenerated one, ruled over by a monstrous counter-revolutionary bureaucracy.

But enormous holes were apparent in this argument after the end of the Second World War. Trotsky had held that the Soviet bureaucracy, as a thoroughly parasitic 'caste' without roots in production, would be unable to survive the world war. Instead it extended its rule to all of Eastern Europe. What was more, the Eastern European states had the same nationalised property as the USSR, but it was imposed from above, without workers' revolution. If Russia was a workers' state, so were they. But then workers' states could come about without revolution. The whole of Marxism had to be turned upside down in order to stick to the letter of Trotsky's analysis.

Argument raged over this issue within the Trotskyist movement internationally. Cliff set out in 1947 to defend the 'orthodox' view. In the process of doing so, he came to the conclusion that there was only one way to maintain the integrity of Marxism and analyse the dynamics of the USSR—to abandon that 'orthodox' view. But he did not turn his back on Trotsky. Cliff repeatedly said that Trotsky was a giant, but that it was necessary to sit on the shoulders of the giant and to see further than he. For Cliff this meant concluding that the Soviet Union, far from being any form of workers' state, was an extreme form of capitalism—bureaucratic state capitalism.

He came to this conclusion through a pathbreaking synthesis of an enormous mass of empirical material about the Soviet Union, using elements from Marxist analyses of the most recent trends in world capitalism carried out in the previous 40 years by Hilferding, Luxemburg, Lenin and Bukharin. It is this synthesis that forms the longest work in this volume, 'The Nature of Stalinist Russia'. It first appeared in print as a cyclostyled internal bulletin of the Fourth International's then British section—the Revolutionary Communist Party—and has been republished since in several different editions.

The main difference between the first version, republished here, and the subsequent editions lay in the order of the chapters. In the later editions Cliff started with the facts about material life and the priorities of production in the USSR, showing how the living standards of the masses were subordinated to a drive to accumulate means of production in a very similar way to that which prevails under capitalism. He then moved on to fit these into a theoretical framework. In this first version, by contrast, he starts with theoretical considerations before assembling his empirical data. In either case, the work was both a revelation, showing what life was really like in the USSR (long before Gorbachev's *perestroika* of the late 1980s, which forced the whole of the left to see things as they really were), and an important development on the insights of early Marxists. It is this theoretical development which makes it a work well worth reading and re-reading today.

Cliff was not the only activist within Trotskyism to reject the notion that Russia was a workers' state. Others had done so before him. Usually they drew the conclusion that the USSR was neither socialism nor capitalism but some completely new form of class society, often called 'bureaucratic collectivist'. In the third work in this collection, 'The Theory of Bureaucratic Collectivism: A Critique', first published in 1948, Cliff dissected this notion with reference to the writings of the Italian Bruno R and the American Max Shachtman. Cliff's central point is that such people gave a name to the form of production existing inside the USSR but did not provide any analysis of its dynamic. As a result, they were unable to provide any insight as to where the USSR was going. By contrast, Cliff insisted the analysis of the USSR as state capitalist saw its dynamic as lying in capital accumulation. Such accumulation would eventually lead the country into acute economic crisis, at the same time as giving rise to an exploited modern working class that would rebel against the system.

The analysis had important practical implications. Many 'workers' statists' ended up supporting the Stalinist states in the Cold War. Shachtman ended up supporting Western capitalism, even going so far as to support the US Bay of Pigs invasion of Cuba in 1961. Cliff by contrast held fast to the slogan 'Neither Washington nor Moscow but international socialism'.

The analysis of the USSR also fed into two other theoretical advances made by Cliff. One was the analysis of China, Cuba and various other countries which achieved their independence from Western colonial rule in the 1950s and 1960s, contained in the article 'Permanent Revolution' reprinted in this book. The existence of various degrees of state ownership in these countries led much of the left to baptise them as 'socialist' or as 'workers' states'. Cliff showed that specific historical circumstances, in which neither the existing bourgeoisie nor the working class had the confidence to act independently, had enabled a radical section of the middle class to take advantage of deep social crisis to establish a top-down control over society. Such regimes could be hostile to the old established imperialisms, but they were not in any sense based upon democratic control by the mass of people. They all too often ended up making an eventual peace with the imperialism against which they had once rebelled.

Again, Cliff's analysis served in practice to arm those who accepted it against easy illusions concerning the 'socialist' regimes in the Third World—and from easy disillusion when the truth about these regimes eventually came out.

This was particularly important in the case of China. Many people who turned against Stalinism in the 1960s and early 1970s believed China represented an authentic socialist alternative to Russia. Cliff wrote a major study, *Mao's China*, in the early 1950s, and then a series of articles analysing the course of the Maoist regime, two of which are printed here. He not only showed the similarities between state capitalism in China and Russia, but also pointed to the particular features of China that led its rulers to clash with Russia, and to run into the great crisis that almost tore the country apart in the decade between the 'Great Leap Forward' of 1958 and the 'Cultural Revolution' of 1966-68.

Cliff's analysis of state capitalism also led him to examine the impact of massive arms spending on the dynamics of capitalism (see pp110-112 in this volume) as early as 1947. By the early 1950s this had become a central issue for socialists in the Western states. Capitalism was undergoing the longest boom in its history, and it was easy for people to draw the conclusion that capitalist crisis was a thing of the past. Cliff did not agree. But he did recognise that something was producing a long spell of stability for the system, and located this in the historically high levels of peacetime arms expenditure. The article reprinted here, 'Perspectives for the Permanent War Economy', is a popular presentation of the argument (neglecting, for the sake of accessibility, some of the elements presented in 'The Nature of Stalinist Russia'). It had the great merit of allowing people who read it to understand the real boom that was taking place, and how the boom would, after a decade and a half, give way to a new period of worldwide crisis.

Most of the other pieces in this collection are more or less self-explanatory. 'Earthquake in the East' was written in the final days of Gorbachev's rule in

Russia in 1991, and prophesied the period of intense crisis which followed. 'Economic Roots of Reformism' challenges the view that the attraction of reformist ideas can be explained in terms the existence of a small 'labour aristocracy' bribed by the 'super-profits' of imperialism. 'The Family: Haven in a Heartless World?' and 'Why Socialists Must Support the Gays' show how Marxism can explain oppression in terms of the wider structures of capitalist society without simply reducing it to a matter of class and economics alone. 'Marxism and the Collectivisation of Agriculture' is an important challenge to much of the received wisdom among Marxists on how a socialist society should organise the vital task of actually feeding itself.

Cliff's writing was always characterised by a clarity and simplicity of phrase all too often missing from Marxist writers who are well known in academic circles. But one article in the collection does require a little explanation. 'All That Glitters is not Gold' was a polemic Cliff wrote in 1947 against Ernest Mandel (who then went under the pseudonym Germain). There was a bitter argument in the Fourth International at the time over whether the capitalist system was sinking into a deep slump (the view of Mandel) or experiencing at least a temporary boom (the view of Cliff and the majority of the British section). In the article, Cliff challenged not only Mandel's mistaken interpretation of the immediate economic situation, but also his tendency to substitute impressionism for analysis, and to be 'economical' with the facts. As Mandel became one of the best known Marxist authors in the second half of the 20th century, Cliff's comments retain a relevance they might not otherwise have had.

Cliff himself always insisted it was necessary to look reality in the face, however much this might clash with one's preconceptions. It was this that enabled him to produce theoretical work in the late 1940s and 1950s that remains relevant today. This volume contains much of the best of it.[1]

Notes

1   Editor's note: readers who are unfamiliar with the theories of Shachtman, Bruno R and other Marxists of the period will find it useful to read the chapter 'Permanent Revolution' and then 'The Theory of Bureaucratic Collectivism: A Critique' before reading 'The Nature of Stalinist Russia'.

The nature of Stalinist Russia

RCP internal bulletin, June 1948

Introduction

The Fourth International has constantly repeated that the Stalinist bureaucracy could not stand the trial of an imperialist war or a proletarian revolution. The Second World War rained hammer blows at the Stalinist regime;
and in its train, with the destruction of the German military machine, a vast
revolutionary wave swept over Europe. The Stalinist bureaucracy triumphantly
stood the trial of war, and then not only withstood the revolutionary wave,
but succeeded, with the aid of its agents the Red Army and the 'Communist'
parties, in suppressing it. This, and the rise of the 'New Democracies', impels
us to review the analysis of Russia as a degenerated workers' state. Research
into the question has led us inexorably to the conclusion that there is an un-
bridgeable antagonism between the definition of Russia as a degenerated
workers' state and fundamental elements of Marxism, such as, to take one
example, the self-mobilisation and self-conscious action of the masses as a necessary element for the socialist revolution. We have come to the conclusion
that the definition of Russia as a degenerated workers' state contradicts all the
fundamentals of Trotskyism itself—the theory of the permanent revolution,
the Marxist-Leninist theory of the state, the principles of the October
Revolution.

For more than ten years Lenin held to the slogan of 'the democratic dictatorship of the proletariat and peasantry', which to many Bolshevik leaders had
been the A to Z of Bolshevism, until the overriding historical event of the
February Revolution led him irrevocably to discard the slogan. Similarly, today
there are more than a few Trotskyists who see the A to Z of Trotskyism in the
definition of Russia as a workers' state and the political conclusions derived
therefrom. After probing into the problem we have come to the conclusion that
not only is this conception not the A to Z of Trotskyism, but, quite the contrary, is an element foreign to it. That it has been able for so long to remain
an integral part of the conceptions of the Fourth International results from the

1

fact that the historical experience of workers' states in general is very limited (only in Russia did the proletariat succeed in holding power for any length of time), that the overthrow of the Russian proletariat did not lead to the restoration of the old regime, and that the development of Russian economy and politics has been very complicated. Just as it became necessary to discard the slogan of 'the democratic dictatorship of the proletariat and peasantry' after the Bolshevik Party had existed for 14 years, so has it now become necessary to renounce the theory of Russia as a degenerated workers' state. This is a necessary prerequisite for the reorientation and rearming of the Fourth International. Indeed, without taking such a step the Fourth International loses its reason for existence.

In the following document some chapters are brought from the manuscript of a book on the Russian question. We hope that during 1948 a second document will be published which will deal with an analysis of the nature of the Stalinist parties, and the perspectives and tasks of the Fourth International. In the same document we shall try to evaluate the different tendencies existing inside the Fourth International.

If this document contains a large number of quotations, they have been brought in order to prove that the conclusions of the analysis are rooted in the teachings of the great Marxist teachers. They warn us against two dangers: firstly, the danger of frozen orthodoxy which is simply a repetition of some formulations that have already been thrashed to death; secondly, the danger in analysing a new phenomenon of losing the threads of Marxism altogether. The first approach cannot lead us through the labyrinth of reality as it has no dynamism and does not recognise its complexity; the second approach makes one lose one's way inside this labyrinth.

November 1947

Translator's note

This document was ready for translation in November 1947, but owing to technical difficulties it could not be finished until now. It is regrettable that this should have been the case as the document now appears too late to be circulated to the members before the World Conference. Since November only a few minor changes have been made to the document.

30 March 1948

Chapter 1: An examination of the definition of Russia as a degenerated workers' state

(1) Can a state not under workers' control be a workers' state?

In Trotsky's works we find two different and quite contradictory definitions of a workers' state. According to one, the criterion of whether a state is a workers' state is whether the proletariat has direct or indirect control, no matter how restricted, over the state power; that is, whether the proletariat can get rid of the bureaucracy by reform alone, without the need for revolution. In 1931 he wrote:

> The recognition of the present Soviet state as a workers' state not only signifies that the bourgeoisie can conquer power in no other way than by an armed uprising but also that the proletariat of the USSR has not forfeited the possibility of submitting the bureaucracy to it, of reviving the party again and of mending the regime of the dictatorship—without a new revolution, with the methods and on the road of reform.[1]

In a letter to Borodai, a member of the group of Democratic Centralists, he expresses this idea even more clearly. The letter is undated, but all indications show that it was written at the end of 1928. He writes:

> 'Is the degeneration of the apparatus and of the Soviet power a fact? That is the second question,' you write.
>   There is no doubt that the degeneration of the Soviet apparatus is considerably more advanced than the same process in the party apparatus. Nevertheless, it is the party that decides. At present, this means: the party apparatus. The question thus comes down to the same thing: is the proletarian kernel of the party, assisted by the working class, capable of triumphing over the autocracy of the party apparatus which is fusing with the state apparatus? Whoever replies in advance that it is *incapable* thereby speaks not only of the necessity of a new party on a new foundation, but also of the necessity of a second and new proletarian revolution.

Later in the same letter Trotsky says:

> If the party is a corpse a new party must be built on a new spot, and the working class must be told about it openly. If Thermidor is completed, and if the dictatorship of the proletariat is liquidated, then the banner of the second proletarian revolution must be unfurled. That is how we would act if the road of reform, for which we stand, proved hopeless.[2]

Trotsky's second definition has a fundamentally different criterion. No matter how independent the state machine be from the masses, and even if the only way of getting rid of the bureaucracy be by revolution, so long as the means of production are statified the state remains a workers' state with the proletariat the ruling class. Thus in *The Revolution Betrayed* Trotsky writes:

> The nationalisation of the land, the means of industrial production, transport, and exchange, together with the monopoly of foreign trade, constitutes the basis of the Soviet social structure. Through these relations, established by the proletarian revolution, the nature of the Soviet Union as a proletarian state is for us basically defined.[3]

Three conclusions are to be drawn from this:

(a) Trotsky's second definition of the workers' state negates the first.

(b) If the second definition is correct, *The Communist Manifesto* was incorrect in saying, 'The proletariat will use all its political supremacy to wrest, by degrees, all capital from the bourgeoisie, to centralise all instruments of production in the hands of the state'; and it was incorrect in saying, 'The first step in the revolution by the working class is to raise the proletariat to the position of the ruling class.' Furthermore, in this case, neither the Paris Commune nor the Bolshevik dictatorship were workers' states as the former did not statify the means of production at all, and the latter did not do so for some time.

(c) If the state is the repository of the means of production and the workers do not control it, they do not own the means of production, ie they are not the ruling class. The first definition admits this. The second avoids it, but does not disprove it.

(2) Russia's definition as a workers' state and the Marxist–Leninist theory of the state

The assumption that Russia is a degenerated workers' state must lead to conclusions in direct contradiction to the Marxist-Leninist concept of the state. An analysis of the role of what Trotsky called political revolution and social counter-revolution will prove this.

In *The Revolution Betrayed* Trotsky writes:

> In order better to understand the character of the present Soviet Union, let us make two different hypotheses about its future. Let us assume first that the Soviet bureaucracy is overthrown by a revolutionary party having all the attributes of the old Bolshevism, enriched moreover by the world experience of the recent period. Such a party would begin with the restoration of democracy in the trade unions and the Soviets. It would be able to, and would have to, restore freedom of Soviet parties. Together with the masses, and at their head, it would carry out a ruthless purgation of the state apparatus. It would abolish ranks and decorations, all kinds of privileges, and would limit inequality in the payment of labour to the life necessities of the economy and the state apparatus. It would give the youth the free opportunity to think independently, learn, criticise and grow. It would introduce profound changes in the distribution of the national income in correspondence

with the interests and will of the worker and peasant masses. But so far as concerns property relations, the new power would not have to resort to revolutionary measures. It would retain and further develop the experiment of planned economy. After the political revolution—that is, the deposing of the bureaucracy—the proletariat would have to introduce in the economy a series of very important reforms, but not another social revolution...

If—to adopt a second hypothesis—a bourgeois party were to overthrow the ruling Soviet caste, it would find no small number of ready servants among the present bureaucrats, administrators, technicians, directors, party secretaries, and privileged upper circles in general. A purgation of the state apparatus would, of course, be necessary in this case too. But a bourgeois restoration would probably have to clean out fewer people than a revolutionary party. The chief task of the new power would be to restore private property in the means of production... Notwithstanding that the Soviet bureaucracy has gone far towards preparing a bourgeois restoration, the new regime would have to introduce in the matter of forms of property and methods of industry, not a reform, but a social revolution.

Let us examine this. During bourgeois *political* revolutions, for instance the French revolutions of 1830 and 1848, the form of government changed to a greater or lesser degree, but *the type of state remained the same*—'special bodies of armed men, prisons, etc', independent of the people and serving the capitalist class. Hitler's victory in Germany certainly brought with it a large-scale purgation of the state apparatus, but the state machine as a whole was not smashed, remaining fundamentally the same. There is a much closer connection between content and form in a workers' state than in any other state. Even, therefore, if we assume that political revolutions can take place in a workers' state, one thing is clear: *the same workers' state machine as such must continue to exist after, as before, the political proletarian revolution*. If Russia is a workers' state, when the revolutionary workers' party comes to power, even though it may carry out a large-scale 'purgation' of the state apparatus, it must be able to use and will use the existing state machine; on the other hand, if the bourgeoisie comes to power, it will not be able to use the existing state machine but will be compelled to smash it and build another on its ruins.

Are these the conditions in Russia? To pose the question correctly goes halfway to answering it. It is surely self-evident that the revolutionary party will not use the NKVD[4] nor the bureaucracy nor the standing army. The revolutionary party will have to smash the existing state and replace it by Soviets, people's militia, etc.

As against this, if the bourgeoisie comes to power, it can certainly use the NKVD, the regular army, etc. Trotsky avoids the application of the Marxist theory of the state to the political revolution and social counter-revolution in Russia partly by saying that the revolutionary party 'would begin with the restoration of democracy in the trade unions and the soviets'. But actually there are neither trade unions nor soviets in Russia in which democracy can be restored. The question is not one of reforming the state machine, but of smashing it and building a new state.

Whether we assume that the proletariat must smash the existing state machine on coming to power while the bourgeoisie can use it, or whether we assume that neither the proletariat nor the bourgeoisie can use the existing state apparatus (the 'purgation of the state apparatus' necessarily involving such a deep change as would transform quantity into quality), on both assumptions we must come to the conclusion that Russia *is not* a workers' state. To assume that the proletariat and the bourgeoisie can use the same state machine as the instrument of their supremacy is tantamount to a vindication of the theoretical basis of social democracy and a repudiation of the revolutionary concept of the state expressed by Marx, Engels, Lenin and Trotsky. To assume that different layers, groups or parties of one and the same class cannot base themselves on the same state machine is equally a repudiation of the Marxist concept of the state.

(3) The form of property considered independently of the relations of production: a metaphysical abstraction

That the concept of private property in itself, independent of the relations of production, is a supra-historical abstraction is recognised by every Marxist. Human history knows the private property of the slave system, the feudal system, the capitalist system, all of which are fundamentally different from one another. Marx ridiculed Proudhon's attempt to define private property independently of the relations of production. What transforms the means of production into capital is the sum total of the relations of production. As Marx said:

> In each historical epoch, property has developed differently and under a set of entirely different social relations. Thus to define bourgeois property is nothing less than to give an exposition of all the social relations of bourgeois production.
>
> To try to give a definition of property as of an independent relation, a category apart—an abstract eternal idea—can be nothing but an illusion of metaphysics or jurisprudence.[5]

All the categories which express relations between people in the capitalist process of production—value, price, wages, etc—constitute an integral part of bourgeois private property. It is the laws of movement of the capitalist system which define the historical social character of capitalist private property, and which differentiate it from other sorts of private property. Proudhon, who abstracted the form of property from the relations of production, 'entangled the whole of these economic relations [the capitalist relations of production] in the general juristic conception of "property".' Therefore, 'Proudhon could not get beyond the answer which *Brisset*, in a similar work, had already, before 1789, given in the same words: "Property is theft".'[6]

That one private property can have a different historical character to another—can be the stronghold of a different class than the other—was made quite clear by Marx. That the same can apply to statified property also is not so evident. The main reason for this is that the known history of humanity has in the main been the history of the class struggle on the basis of private property. Cases of class differentiation not on the basis of private property are not very numerous and on the whole not very well known. Nevertheless they have existed.

As the first example let us take a chapter from the history of Europe: the Catholic church in the Middle Ages.

The church had tremendous tracts of land on which hundreds of thousands of peasants laboured. The relations between the church and the peasants were the same feudal relations as existed between the feudal manor owner and his peasants. The church as such was feudal. At the same time none of the bishops, cardinals, etc had individual rights over feudal property. It is the relations of production which define the class character of the church property, which was feudal notwithstanding the fact that it was not private.

It might be said that the Catholic church was only an appendage to the feudal system as a whole—hence its feudal character—but this argument is irrelevant, as we do not wish to explain why the Catholic church rose, concentrating in its hands tremendous tracts of land and entering into feudal relations with the peasants tilling it. We only wish to show that one and the same relations of production can be expressed in different forms of property, the one private, the other institutional.

From the history of the East we may draw numerous examples of systems of economy with deep class differentiations, based not on private property but on state property. Such systems existed in Pharaonic Egypt, Muslim Egypt, Iraq, Persia and India. That the state owned the land was, it seems, mainly due to the fact that agriculture depended entirely on the irrigation system in those countries, which in turn was dependent on the activity of the state. The following example is sufficiently instructive to warrant the deviation made.

(4) Arab feudalism: an example of class society based on state property

Let us examine the main characteristics of Arab feudalism under the Mamelukes. Here the subjugation of the peasants to the strong feudal state was much harsher than in medieval Europe, but the individual member of the ruling class had no individual property rights whatsoever. The sultan was the only landowner and he used to divide the right to collect the rent in the various regions among the different nobles (called multazims). While in Europe every feudal lord was the owner of a certain domain, which was handed down from father to son, in the Arab East the feudal lord had no permanent domain of his own, but was a member of a class that as a collective controlled the land and had the right to appropriate rent. In Syria and Palestine these feudal lords had the area from which they collected rent changed from year to year. In Egypt they received the right to collect the rent in a certain area for their whole lives, and their heirs had a preferential right in the appointment of the deceased's successor. While in Europe the feudal lord was an independent power as against the king, who was no more than the first feudal lord, in the Arab East only the feudal collective as such was a factor of any consequence; as individuals the Arab nobles were weak, because they were dependent on the state for their positions. This weakness of the feudal lord as against the state was clearly indicated in the way in which the fiefs were allocated: the sultan distributed them by lot among the emirs and knights, each getting a portion of land differing in size and quality according to his rank. The Arab nobles were thus divided into different groups with different incomes, the distinction between them being very great (thus, for instance, the 'emirs of the hundred' got 80,000 to 200,000 dinar jayshi a year, 'emir-al-tabl' 23,000 to 30,000, 'emirs of the ten' 9,000 and below, 'emirs of the five' 3,000 and so on). The form of appropriation was much more like that of a state official than that of the European feudal lord. As a result of this dependence of the nobles on the state, we find an exceptional phenomenon recurring in the Arab East. From time to time whole feudal strata were 'purged' and annihilated, others coming in their places. In place of the Arab feudal lords came the sultan's freed slaves—the Mamelukes—who were not of Arab origin and did not speak Arabic but Turkish. In the 13th and 14th centuries they mostly originated from the Mongolian state, the Golden Horde, whose centre was on the banks of the Lower Volga; in the 15th and 16th centuries they were mainly Caucasian. With the Tsar's increasing resistance to conscription in the Caucasus for the sultan, the Balkan elements (Albanians, Bosnians, etc) came to the fore.

The ownership of the land by the state not only prevented the rise of feudalism based on private property, but also of any layers with individualistic tendencies whatsoever. The town was a military camp; the majority of the artisans were not independent. Even when the guilds (Hirfeh) did arise, they did not attain any importance at all in the towns and did not become any serious, independent force. The government subordinated them to itself by appointing many of the heads of the guilds, making them its officials, and turning the guilds into government organisations.

The fact that the means of production—the land—belonged not to individuals, but to the state, and that the Arab nobles and the Mamelukes lacked juridical footholds and therefore did not have the right to inherit, did not improve the position of the masses of toilers. Nor did the plebeian origin of the Mamelukes effect any change. The concentration of the ruling class of the Arab East in the towns afforded them great military power over the peasants and, more than that, increased their appetites. In this too they were dissimilar to the European feudal lords in the Middle Ages. The produce which the European serfs gave to their feudal lords as rent was not sent out to be sold; the serfs therefore did not need to give their feudal lord more than he or his household needed for their daily use. 'The walls of his [the feudal lord's] stomach set the limits to his exploitation of the peasants' (Marx). The Arab feudals had different tastes, and their approach might best be summed up in the words used by Khalif Suliman to his emissary about the peasants: 'Milk till the udder be dry, and let blood to the last drop.'

The mode of production, the form of exploitation, the relation of the toilers to the means of production in the Arab East, was the same as in medieval Europe. The source of income of the ruling class was also the same; the only difference was in the mode of appropriation, and in the juridical expression of the right to exploit.[7]

From the form of property alone—whether private, institutional or state property—abstracted from the relations of production, it is impossible to define the class character of a social system. For this it is necessary to know the relation between people in the process of production, the relation between the toilers and the means of production. Or, to repeat what Marx said, 'to try to give a definition of property as of an independent relation, a category apart—an abstract eternal idea—can be nothing but an illusion of metaphysics or jurisprudence.'

(5) The Russian bureaucracy: a gendarme who appears in the process of distribution?

Trotsky writes that the Stalinist state's coercion of the masses is the result of:

…the fact that the present transitional structure is still full of social contradictions, which in the sphere of consumption—most close and sensitively felt by all—are extremely tense, and forever threaten to break over into the sphere of production.[8]

Therefore:

The basis of bureaucratic rule is the poverty of society in objects of consumption, with the resulting struggle of each against all. When there is enough goods in a store the purchasers can come whenever they want to. When there is little goods the purchasers are compelled to stand in line. When the lines are very long, it is necessary to appoint a policeman to keep order. Such is the starting-point of the power of the Soviet bureaucracy. It 'knows' who is to get something and who has to wait.[9]

Is it true that the bureaucracy appears as the 'gendarme' only in the process of distribution, or does it appear so in the process of reproduction as a whole, of which the former is but a subordinate part? This is of infinite theoretical and political importance.

Before attempting to answer this question, let us examine what Marx and Engels thought about the connection between the relations of production and distribution. Marx writes:

To the single individual distribution naturally appears as a law established by society determining his position in the sphere of production, within which he produces, and thus antedating production. At the outset the individual has no capital, no landed property. From his birth he is assigned to wage-labour by the social process of distribution. But this very condition of being assigned to wage-labour is the result of the existence of capital and landed property as independent agents of production.

From the point of view of society as a whole, distribution seems to antedate and to determine production in another way as well, as a pre-economic fact, so to say. A conquering people divides the land among the conquerors, establishing thereby a certain division and form of landed property and determining the character of production; or it turns the conquered people into slaves and thus makes slave labour the basis of production. Or a nation, by revolution, breaks up large estates into small parcels of land and by this new distribution imparts to production a new character. Or legislation perpetuates land ownership in large families or distributes labour as an hereditary privilege and thus fixes it in castes.

In all of these cases, and they are all historic, it is not distribution that seems to be organised and determined by production but, on the contrary, production by distribution.

In the most shallow conception of distribution, the latter appears as a distribution of products and to that extent as further removed from and quasi-independent of production. But before distribution means distribution of products, it is, first, a distribution of the means of production, and, second, what is practically another wording of the same fact, it is a distribution of the members of society among the various kinds of production (the subjection of individuals to certain conditions of production). The distribution of products is manifestly a result of this distribution, which is bound up with the process of production and determines the very organisation of the latter.[10]

This extract from Marx, the essence of which is repeated time and time again throughout his works, is sufficient as a point of departure for the analysis of the place of the Stalinist bureaucracy in the economy.

Let us pose these questions as regards the Russian bureaucracy:

Does the bureaucracy only administer the distribution of means of consumption among the people, or does it also administer the distribution of the people in the process of production? Has the bureaucracy a monopoly only over the control of distribution, or also over the control of the means of production? Is the rule of the bureaucracy connected only with a certain way of distribution of the means of consumption or also the distribution of the total labour time of society between accumulation and consumption, between the production of means of production and that of means of consumption? Does not the bureaucracy reproduce the scarcity of means of consumption, and thus certain relations of distribution? Do the relations of production prevailing in Russia not determine the relations of distribution which comprise a part of them?

(6) Trotsky's last book

As the working class in Russia was the only one which held power for any length of time, as its overthrow took an unpredictable form in the very complicated economic and political circumstances of Russia, it is no accident that even Trotsky with his encyclopedic knowledge and brilliant analytical faculties had to re-evaluate his basic analysis of the Stalinist regime from time to time. From the time that the acceptance of the theory of the degenerated workers' state was a condition for the membership of the Left Opposition to the time that, although opposing the anti-defencists, Trotsky did not propose their exclusion from the International, a tremendous shift took place in Trotsky's position, at least in emphasis. It is no accident that in his polemics with Shachtman at the end of 1939 and in 1940 he could say that, even though he might be in a minority against Shachtman and Burnham, he would oppose a split and would continue to fight for his position in the united party. This declaration was of immediate consequence as it was quite possible that Shachtman would have had a majority at the next SWP Convention.[11]

A clear step in the direction of a new evaluation of the bureaucracy as a ruling class finds expression in Trotsky's last book, *Stalin*. He writes:

> The substance of the Thermidor was, is and could not fail to be social in character. It stood for the crystallisation of a new privileged stratum, the creation of a new substratum for the economically dominant class. There were two pretenders to this role: the petty bourgeoisie and the bureaucracy itself. They fought shoulder to shoulder (in the battle to break) the resistance of the proletarian vanguard. When that task was accomplished a savage struggle broke out between them. The bureaucracy became frightened of its isolation, its divorcement from the proletariat. Alone it could not crush the kulak nor the petty bourgeoisie that had grown and continued to grow on the basis of the NEP; it had to have the aid of the proletariat. Hence its concerted effort to present its struggle against the petty bourgeoisie for the surplus products and for power as the struggle of the proletariat against attempts at capitalistic restoration.[12]

The bureaucracy, Trotsky says, while pretending to fight against capitalistic restoration, in reality used the proletariat only to crush the kulaks for 'the crystallisation of a new privileged stratum, the creation of a new substratum for the economically dominant class'. One of the pretenders to the role of the economically dominant class, he says, is the bureaucracy. Great emphasis is lent to this formulation when we connect this analysis of the fight between the bureaucracy and the kulaks with Trotsky's definition of the class struggle. He says:

> The class struggle is nothing else than the struggle for surplus-produce. He who owns surplus-produce is master of the situation—owns wealth, owns the state, has the key to the church, to the courts, to the sciences, and to the arts.[13]

The fight between the bureaucracy and the kulaks was, according to Trotsky's last conclusion, the 'struggle...for the surplus products'.

(7) The internal forces are not able to restore individual capitalism in Russia: what conclusion as regards its class character?

When Trotsky spoke about the danger of social counter-revolution in Russia, he meant the restoration of capitalism, based on private property. Stalinist Bonapartism is represented as a balancing factor between two forces on the national arena—the working class on the one side who support statified property and planning, and the bourgeois elements who drive towards individual property on the other. He writes:

> It [the bureaucracy] continues to preserve state property only to the extent that it fears the proletariat. This saving fear is nourished and supported by the illegal party of Bolshevik-Leninists, which is the most conscious expression of the socialist tendencies opposing that bourgeois reaction with which the Thermidorian bureaucracy is completely saturated. As a conscious political force the bureaucracy has betrayed the revolution. But a victorious revolution is fortunately not only a programme and a banner, not only political institutions, but also a system of social relations. To betray it is not enough. You have to overthrow it.[14]

This presentation exposes most clearly the juridical abstraction of the form of property, and it therefore also exposes most clearly the internal contradictions of the analysis. The Russian proletariat was not strong enough to keep its control over the means of production, and was ousted by the bureaucracy, but it is strong enough to prevent the promulgation of this relation in law! The proletariat was not strong enough to check the most antagonistic distribution of the product, to prevent the bureaucracy from brutally suppressing its standard of living and denying it the most elementary rights, to prevent the sentence of millions of its members to slave labour in Siberia; but it is strong enough to defend the form of property! As though there is any relation between people and property other than that based on the relations of production.

On the other hand, if the fear of the proletariat is the only factor preventing the restoration of private capitalism in Russia; if, as Trotsky said, the bureaucracy are conscious restorationists, his statement that the Stalinist regime is as stable as a pyramid standing on its head would have proved correct, and his prognosis of the fate of the statified economy during the war would have been realised. He summed up his position thus:

> In the heated atmosphere of war one can expect sharp turns toward individualistic principles in agriculture and in handicraft industry, toward the attraction of foreign and 'allied' capital, breaks in the monopoly of foreign trade, the weakening of governmental control over trusts, the sharpening of competition between the trusts, their conflicts with workers, etc. In the political sphere these processes may mean the completion of Bonapartism with a corresponding change or a number of changes in property relations. In other words, in case of a protracted war accompanied by the *passivity of the world proletariat* the internal social contradictions in the USSR not only might lead but would have to lead to a *bourgeois-Bonapartist* counter-revolution.[15]

That private capitalism could have been restored in Russia without its occupation by an imperialist power, even if an incorrect assumption, was understandable before the experience of the Second World War. The victory of the concentrated, statified Russian economy over the German war machine, however, shattered all talk of the possibility that the statified economy be overthrown by the kulak, who does not even own machinery or horses.

(This does not exclude the fact that external forces could restore individual capitalism, or even that a devastating war, accompanied by the annihilation of most of the Russian population, could cast Russian society back to a much lower level of historical development than private capitalism.)

When Trotsky defined Russia as a society in transition, he correctly emphasised that as such it must by its own immanent laws lead either to the victory of socialism, or the restoration of private capitalism. If the latter, as the outcome of the development of the internal forces, is out of the question, one of three things must happen:

(a) The internal forces in Russia lead in one direction only—towards communism. This is the point of view of the Stalinists (and also of Bruno R).[16]

(b) Russian society is neither capitalist nor socialist, and although the productive forces rise uninterruptedly it will not lead to communism; although the exploitation of the masses continues unabated, it will not lead to capitalism. This is the theory of the 'managerial revolution', and of bureaucratic collectivism in Shachtman's 1943 formulation.

(c) Russian society is either a transitional society which has two possible paths before it—state capitalism or communism—or it is already state capitalism.

To deny the possibility of the internal forces leading to private capitalism, and at the same time to denounce Stalinism, bureaucratic collectivism (according to both Bruno R and Shachtman) and Burnhamism, will leave us with the third alternative only.

Seeing that under state capitalism, as well as under a workers' state, the state is the repository of the means of production, the difference between the two systems cannot be in the form of property. Therefore the state ownership of the means of production which Trotsky uses as the basis for his definition of the class character of Russia must be dismissed as an unsound criterion.

(8) The 'new democracies' and the definition of Russia as a workers' state

The appearance of the 'new democracies' provided a testing stone of the definition of Russia as a workers' state. It is possible to adopt one of three assumptions regarding them:

(a) While Russia is a workers' state, the 'new democracies' are capitalist states.

(b) Russia is a workers' state and so are the 'new democracies'.

(c) Russia is not a workers' state, nor are the 'new democracies'.

The first assumption is subscribed to by the IS.[17] It should, however, not be difficult to disprove this by showing that Russia and the 'new democracies' have the same fundamental features. Already more than 60 percent of industry in the 'new democracies', consisting of large-scale, key enterprises, is statified. It would be illogical to suppose that the less than 40 percent which remains in private hands will subordinate the statified industry to its interests. On the contrary, there is every reason to assume that after a certain time those industries will be statified. Plans of production, as well as a monopoly of foreign trade, are in existence. The state structures of these countries are also becoming more and more like the totalitarian dictatorship in Russia. It needs just as high a degree of mental acrobatics to think that Mikolajcik and his ilk who flee abroad or waste away in prisons are the rulers in Poland as to consider that the rulers of Russia are the slave labourers in Siberia. Only such acrobats could assume that a degenerated workers' state would impose a different regime on its satellites than exists inside Russia itself; that the Stalinist bureaucracy which can successfully loot a considerable part of the industries in the 'new democracies' and statify over 60 percent of the industry should not be able to statify 100 percent; that a bureaucracy which overthrew German military might should not be able to smash the feeble bourgeoisie in the 'new democracies'.

If, then, Russia and the 'new democracies' represent fundamentally the same social system, we are left with the other two alternatives: that all of them are workers' states, or none of them are. Let us begin by analysing the first alternative.

If the state property form, planning and the monopoly of foreign trade define a country as a workers' state, then without doubt Russia, as well as the 'new democracies', are workers' states. This means that in the latter proletarian revolutions have taken place. These were led by the Stalinists on the basis of national unity, governmental coalitions with the bourgeoisie and chauvinism which led to the expulsion of millions of German toilers and their families. Such policies merely served to oil the wheels of the proletarian revolution.[18]

What, then, is the future of the Fourth International—what is its historical justification? The Stalinist parties have all the advantages over the Fourth International—a state apparatus, mass organisations, money, etc, etc. The only advantage they lack is the internationalist class ideology. But if it is possible to accomplish the proletarian revolution without this ideology, why should the masses come to us? To make an analogy, if a certain general has the confidence of the masses of soldiers because he leads them to many victories, the soldiers will on no account transfer their adherence to an unsupported general who claims to have a much better strategy. The mass of workers have tremendous loyalty towards their organisations, and they will not change a mass organisation for a tiny one unless they are convinced that the mass organisation does not solve their problems.

If a social revolution took place in the Eastern European countries without a revolutionary proletarian leadership, we must conclude that in future social revolutions, as in the past, the masses will do the fighting but not the leading. In all the struggles of the bourgeoisie it was not the bourgeoisie itself who did the fighting, but the masses who believed it was in their interests. The sans-culottes of the French Revolution fought for liberty, equality, fraternity, while the real aim of the movement was the establishment of the rule of the bourgeoisie. This was the case at a time when the bourgeoisie was progressive. In reactionary imperialist wars, the less the masses—who are the cannon fodder—know about the war's aims, the better soldiers they are. To assume that the 'new democracies' are workers' states means to accept that in principle the proletarian revolution is, just as the bourgeois wars were, based on the deception of the people.

If the 'new democracies' are workers' states, Stalin has realised the proletarian revolution; moreover he has carried it out quite speedily. Since the Paris Commune, 47 years passed by until the establishment of the first workers' state in a country of 140 million people. Less than 30 years passed until a number of additional countries became workers' states. In the West, Poland, Yugoslavia, Hungary, Romania, Bulgaria and Czechoslovakia added their 75 million people (and this does not include the Baltic states, Eastern Poland and Bessarabia, containing 20 million people, which were annexed to the USSR). In the East the state of Yenan in China with 150 million people was added. If these countries are workers' states, then why Marxism, why the Fourth International? We could only be looked upon by the masses as adventurists, or at best impatient revolutionists whose differences with the Stalinists are merely tactical.

If the 'new democracies' are workers' states, what Marx and Engels said about the socialist revolution being 'history conscious of itself' is refuted. Refuted is Engels' statement:

It is only from this point [the socialist revolution] that men, with full consciousness, will fashion their own history; it is only from this point that the social causes set in motion by men will have, predominantly and in constantly increasing measure, the effects willed by men. It is humanity's leap from the realm of necessity into the realm of freedom.[19]

Rosa Luxemburg, too, must have spoken nonsense in her summing up of what all the Marxist teachers wrote about the place of proletarian consciousness in a revolution:

In all the class struggles of the past, carried through in the interests of minorities, and in which, to use the words of Marx, 'all development took place in opposition to the great masses of the people', one of the essential conditions of action was the ignorance of those masses with regard to the real aims of the struggle, its material content, and its limits. This discrepancy was, in fact, the specific historical basis of the 'leading role' of the 'enlightened' bourgeoisie, which corresponded with the role of the masses as docile followers. But, as Marx wrote as early as 1845, 'as the historical action deepens the number of masses engaged in it must increase.' The class struggle of the proletariat is the 'deepest' of all historical actions up to our day, it embraces the whole of the lower layers of the people, and, from the moment that society became divided into classes, it is the *first* movement which is in accordance with the *real* interests of the masses. That is why the enlightenment of the masses with regard to their tasks and methods is an indispensable historical condition for socialist action, just as in former periods the ignorance of the masses was the condition for the action of the dominant classes.[20]

The IS writes:

To deny the capitalist nature of these countries [the 'new democracies'] amounts to an acceptance, in no matter what form of this Stalinist revisionist theory [of gradual transition from capitalism to socialism], it means seriously to consider the historical possibility of a destruction of capitalism by 'terror from above' without the revolutionary intervention of the masses.[21]

This is absolutely correct. But while denying that a revolution from above is possible, we cannot assume, as the IS does, that the 'new democracies' are capitalist while Russia is a workers' state. No. We are left with only the third possibility, that Russia is not a workers' state, nor are the 'new democracies'.

(9) The nationalisations in England and the definition of Russia as a workers' state

The nationalisations in England carried out by the Labour government bring us sharply to realise that the form of property alone is not the fundamental determinant of the class character of an economy and a state. The British Trotskyists correctly declare that, as in the nationalised industries there is no workers' control, and the state, even though headed by Labour leaders, is still the same old bourgeois machine—the nationalisations are only state capitalist measures. The question of compensation, as Marx and Engels showed, is not of decisive importance in determining the class relations in the nationalised economy, and the working class on coming to power would not on principle oppose the buying out of the capitalist class (although the tremendous increase of the bourgeois state machine in the defence of bourgeois property today virtually excludes such action being taken). What has brought us to decide that the nationalisations are state capitalist is the lack of workers' control in the nationalised industries, and the fact that the state is not a democratic workers' state in the form of, or in a similar form to, soviets, but is still a bureaucratic state which raises itself above the people.

According to this criterion, Russia is certainly not a workers' state. We cannot avoid this contradiction by saying that we define the nationalisations of the mines, railways, electricity, and steel as state capitalist measures only because they are carried out in the interests of the private capitalists in the other branches of industry. The present Labour government, it is true, intends to nationalise only 20 percent of the whole of industry (which makes up a very much larger percentage of large-scale industry alone). Supported by the workers, the government, in the interests of capitalism, nationalised the industries which are the most dangerous bottlenecks in the economy. Unless the social revolution circumvents it, international competition will continue, and with it the decline of British capitalism, in which case more far-reaching measures of coordination and amalgamation will be necessary. Under this pressure the British bourgeois state may nationalise all large-scale industry. Will the nationalisations cease to be state capitalist? Or if they continue to be state capitalist, is it because small-scale enterprises remain in private hands?

(10) Are Russia's war victories proof that Russia is a workers' state?

Whereas Trotsky, following up his analysis that Russia is a degenerated workers' state, predicted that the bureaucracy would not stand up to a war, many Trotskyists today, following Russia's victories in the war, conclude from these very victories that Russia is a workers' state. This post factum argument, however, cannot stand up to criticism.

The argument can be broken into two parts: (1) The enthusiasm of the masses in the war proves that they have something to lose besides their chains— that they are the ruling class; (2) The industrial-military strength of Russia proves the historical superiority of the Russian regime over capitalism.

The first part of the argument, which was prevalent in the press of the Fourth International in 1941-43, had the bottom knocked out of it by the march of events. For the German army, too, in the years when all hope of victory had already vanished, fought with all its strength until the very gates of Berlin. Had the German soldiers also something to lose besides their chains? Was the German working class also the ruling class?

As regards the second part of the argument, there is no doubt that large-scale enterprise has tremendous advantages over small-scale. This is the main explanation why, although both British and American production are based on the same social system, the latter is so superior to the former. Russian industry, newer and technically more modern, is built on an even larger scale than American. Besides this, the overlapping and lack of coordination prevalent in the countries of individual capitalism is avoided in Russia by the state ownership of the means of production. And yet another factor of advantage to Russia in a war, which many other countries cannot claim, is that its workers lack all democratic rights. In Russia, as in Nazi Germany, it is possible to produce guns instead of butter, to transfer millions of workers from the west to beyond the Urals, housing them in dugouts in the ground, etc. The authority of the state over the economy and over the workers—these are the two elements which are the strong points of Russia's industrial-military production. But the very same factors also explain Nazi Germany's military superiority over bourgeois-democratic France, which, as we know, collapsed before its advancing armies like a house of cards, and also over Britain—ex 'workshop of the world'—saved from invasion by the English Channel, American help from the West and the Russian threat to Germany from the East.

Germany's military victories at the beginning of the war fooled some people into believing that Germany was not a capitalist country, but represented a new and superior system of society. Burnham was notable among these.

The belief that the Russian military victories in themselves prove that Russia represents a new system of society has no more foundation than the same belief arrived at regarding Nazi Germany at the time of its victories.

Chapter 2: The economy of a workers' state

If Russia is not a workers' state, degenerated or otherwise, what is it, and how did it become what it is? We shall answer this by tackling the following questions: What are the relations of production in a workers' state? Why was it impossible to preserve such relations in a backward country under conditions of siege? What relations of production came in their place? How did the transition from one set of relations to another take place? What is common and different to these two sets of relations? Why do prevailing relations of production in Russia not express themselves in the traditional relations of property? What are the laws of motion of Russian economy? The following chapters will attempt an answer to these questions. We shall begin in this chapter by analysing the economy of a workers' state.

It is necessary, before considering the fundamental features of the economy of a workers' state, to mention one very important factor. As Marx and Engels expected the revolution to begin in the developed countries, they assumed that from its inception the new society would be materially and culturally more developed than the most advanced capitalist countries. Every prognosis, however, is conditional. History did not unfold exactly as Marx and Engels had expected. It was in Russia, one of the most backward capitalist countries, that the revolution first broke out and the workers took power, while the revolutions which followed in the more developed countries failed.

Marx and Engels' analysis of the economy of a workers' state in a developed country can serve as a norm with which we can compare the development in Russia, to show to what extent it conformed to it, then diverged from it, and finally contradicted it.

(1) The transformation of capitalist relations of production into socialist relations of production

The development of the productive forces under capitalism creates the material conditions necessary for socialism. There are two sorts of productive forces: the means of production and labour power. The centralisation of capital and the socialisation of the labour process under capitalism becomes the basis of socialist production.

Thus of the total relations of production which prevail under capitalism— relations between capitalists and capitalists, between capitalists and workers, between the workers themselves in the process of production, between technicians and workers, technicians and capitalists, etc—only one section is carried over into the socialist society, namely the relations between the workers in the process of production: the workers united in social production become the basis for new relations of production. At the same time, some elements of the relations of production existing under capitalism are abolished altogether by socialism through the abolition of the capitalists. Other elements, such as the present 'new middle class' (technicians, accountants, etc), will be fitted into a new context.

This 'new middle class' constitutes part of the productive forces, and as such is a necessary element of production, but their *place* in the hierarchy of capitalist society is a transitory one, just as capitalism is transitory. Socialism will entirely do away with their hierarchical position over the proletariat in the process of production. A new relationship will be created between the different elements necessary for the socialist mode of production, between mental and manual labour. The new relationship (which we shall deal with more fully later on) begins to take shape with the transition period.

The working class, which constitutes a part of the productive forces and a part of the capitalist relations of production at one and the same time, becomes the *basis* for the new relations of production and the point of departure for the development of the productive forces on the foundation of these relations. In the words of Marx:

> Of all the instruments of production, the greatest productive power is the revolutionary class itself. The organisation of revolutionary elements as a class supposes the existence of all the productive forces which could be engendered in the bosom of the old society.[22]

(2) The division of labour and the division into classes

Engels writes:

> In every society in which production has developed spontaneously—and our present society is of this type—it is not the producers who control the means of production, but the means of production which control the producers. In such a society each new lever of production is necessarily transformed into a new means for the subjection of the producers to the means of production. This is most of all true of that lever of production which, prior to the introduction of large-scale industry, was by far the most powerful—the division of labour.[23]

The division of labour, which is expressed in the separation of manual from mental labour, is of an historically transitory character; it has its roots in the separation of the workers from the means of production, and the juxtaposition of these two elements to each other. In the words of Marx:

> Intelligence in production expands in one direction, because it vanishes in many others. What is lost by the detail labourers is concentrated in the capital that employs them. It is a result of the division of labour in manufactures that the labourer is brought face to face with the intellectual potencies of the material process of production, as the property of another, and as a ruling power. This separation begins in simple cooperation, where the capitalist represents to the single workman the oneness and the will of the associated labour. It is

developed in manufacture which cuts down the labourer into a detail labourer. It is completed in modern industry, which makes science a productive force distinct from labour and presses it into the service of capital.[24]

The complete victory of communism means the complete abolition of the separation of mental and manual labour. It would be impossible to abolish this separation immediately after the revolution. But *workers' control over production will become an immediate bridge between mental and manual labour, and a point of departure for their future synthesis, the total abolition of classes.*

Here we come to a problem which is fundamental from the standpoint of the transformation of the relations of production, of the bridge between mental and manual labour.

(3) Workers and technicians

The technicians constitute a necessary element in the process of production, an important part of the productive forces of society, whether capitalist or communist. At the same time, as we have already said, under capitalism they form a layer in the hierarchy of production. They come into being as part and parcel of this hierarchy. Their monopolist position as regards the 'mental means of production' (as Bukharin terms it) is the result of the separation of the workers from the means of production on the one hand, and the socialisation of labour on the other. Communism will abolish this hierarchy. In the transition period it will in one sense continue to exist, but in another, be abolished. Insofar as mental labour remains the privilege of the few, the hierarchical relations will continue to exist in the factories, railways, etc, even after the proletarian revolution. But *seeing that the place of the capitalist in the hierarchy will be taken by the workers' state, ie by the workers as a collective, the technicians being subordinated to the workers, in this respect the mental hierarchy will be abolished. Workers' control over the technicians means the subordination of capitalist elements to socialist ones. The more efficient the workers' control, the higher the material and cultural level of the masses, the more will the monopolist position of the mental workers be undermined, till it is completely abolished and the full synthesis of mental and manual labour achieved.*[25]

(4) Labour discipline

Every form of social production needs the coordination of the different people participating in it; in other words, every form of social production needs discipline. Under capitalism this discipline appears to the worker as an external coercive power, as the power capital has over him. Under communism discipline will be the result of consciousness—it will become the habit of a free people. In the transition period it will be the outcome of the unity of the two elements—consciousness and coercion. The state institutions will be the organisation of the masses as a conscious factor. Collective ownership of the means of production by the workers, ie the ownership by the workers' state of the means of production, will be the basis for the conscious element in labour discipline. At the same time the working class as a collective, through its institutions—soviets, trade unions, etc—will appear as a coercive power as regards the disciplining of the individual workers in production. Individualistic consumption, the 'bourgeois right' as regards distribution, will serve as a weapon of coercive discipline.

The technicians, supervisors, etc have a special place in labour discipline. Under capitalism the supervisor is the transmission belt through which capitalist coercion of the worker is exercised. Under communism a supervisor will fill the same need as conductor of an orchestra. He will not fulfil any coercive function, as labour discipline will be based on consciousness and habit. In the transition period, whereas the workers, as regards themselves, will be both a disciplining and disciplined factor, a subject and an object, the technicians, even if they remain *formally* discipliners of the workers, in the same way as the conductor disciplines his orchestra, in reality will serve only as a transmission belt, this time of the workers' state.

(5) The worker and the means of production

The Communist Manifesto says:

> In bourgeois society, living labour is but a means to increase accumulated labour. In communist society, accumulated labour is but a means to widen, to enrich, to promote the existence of the labourer.
>
> In bourgeois society, therefore, the past dominates the present; in communist society, the present dominates the past. In bourgeois society capital is independent and has no individuality.[26]

In communist society accumulation will be conditioned by the needs of consumption of the people. In capitalist society accumulation determines the extent of employment and the rate of wages—ie the rate of consumption of the working people. Even as regards the capitalist himself the factor that makes him a capitalist is not consumption but accumulation. As Marx said:

> Accumulation for accumulation's sake, production for production's sake: by this formula classical economy expressed the historical mission of the bourgeoisie, and did not for a single instant deceive itself over the birth-throes of wealth.[27]

The process of capitalist accumulation determines, limits and undermines consumption. This is because the worker is dominated by the product of his labour. Communist consumption will determine the accumulation of means of production. This is because the labourer will dominate his product.

In every society, independent of the relations of production, the rationalisation of production generally involves a more roundabout way of production, ie an increase in the proportion of the total social labour to the production of means of consumption. This means an increase in the ratio of 'accumulation' relatively to the rate of consumption. Under communism this increase in the rate of 'accumulation' as against the rate of consumption would at the same time mean a large absolute increase in the consumption of the toilers.

Under capitalism, however, because of the antagonistic way of distribution, the rate of surplus value increases, and thus also the rate of accumulation, while the rate of consumption of the masses remains a subordinate factor.

The fact that under capitalism there is accumulation for accumulation's sake is the result of two factors: one the separation of the workers from the means of production, the other the existence of competition between the capitalists (no matter whether individual, monopolist or state). Socialism abolishes both these elements of the relations of production. Workers' control over production and the abolition of national boundaries—these are the two conditions for the full subordination of accumulation to consumption. Under such conditions society will accumulate in order to consume.

This subordination of accumulation to consumption, by raising the material and cultural conditions of the masses, will at the same time undermine the monopoly of the technicians over the 'mental means of production', and thus strengthen the workers' control over production.

(6) The relations of distribution in the transition period

The most exact and concise analysis of this question was given by Marx in his *Critique of the Gotha Programme*:

> What we have to deal with there is a communist society, not as it has *developed* on its own foundation, but, on the contrary, as it *emerges* from capitalist society; which is thus in every respect, economically, morally and intellectually, still stamped with the birthmarks of the old society from whose womb it emerges. Accordingly the individual producer receives back from society—after the deductions have been made [deductions in the interests of society as a whole]— exactly what he gives to it. What he has given to it is his individual amount of labour. For example, the social working day consists of the sum of the individual labour hours; the individual labour time of the individual producer is the part of the social labour day contributed by him, his share in it. He receives a certificate from society that he has furnished such and such an amount of labour (after deducting his labour for the common fund) and with this certificate he draws from the social stock of means of consumption as much as costs the same amount of labour. The same amount of labour which he has given to society in one form, he receives back in another.
>
> Here obviously the same principle prevails as that which regulates the exchange of commodities, as far as this is exchange of equal values. Content and form are changed, because under the altered circumstances no one can give anything except his labour, and because, on the other hand, nothing can pass into the ownership of individuals except individual means of consumption. But, as far as the distribution of the latter among the individual producers in concerned, the same principle prevails as in the exchange of commodity-equivalents—so much labour in one form is exchanged for an equal amount of labour in another form.

Hence *equal right* here is still in principle—*bourgeois right*, although principle and practice are no longer in conflict, while the exchange of equivalents in commodity exchange only exists on the *average* and not in the individual case.

In spite of this advance, this *equal right* is still stigmatised by a bourgeois limitation. The right of the producers is *proportional* to the labour they supply; the equality consists in the fact that measurement is made with an *equal standard*, labour.

But one man is superior to another physically or mentally and so supplies more labour in the same time, or can labour for a longer time; and labour, to serve as a measure, must be defined by its duration or intensity, otherwise it ceases to be a standard of measurement. This *equal* right is an unequal right for unequal labour. It recognises no class differences, because everyone is only a worker like everyone else; but it tacitly recognises unequal individual endowment and thus productive capacity as natural privileges. *It is therefore a right of inequality in its content like every right*. Right by its very nature can only consist in the application of an equal standard; but unequal individuals (and they would not be different individuals if they were not unequal) are only measurable by an equal standard insofar as they are brought under an equal point of view, are taken from one *definite* side only, eg in the present case are regarded *only as workers*, and nothing more seen in them, everything else being ignored. Further, one worker is married, another not; one has more children than another and so on and so forth. Thus with an equal output, and hence an equal share in the social consumption fund, one will in fact receive more than another, one will be richer than another, and so on. To avoid all these defects, right instead of being equal would have to be unequal.

But these defects are inevitable in the first phase of communist society as it is when it has just emerged after prolonged birth pangs from capitalist society. Right can never be higher than the economic structure of society and the cultural development thereby determined.

In a higher phase of communist society, after the enslaving subordination of individuals under division of labour, and therewith also the antithesis between mental and physical labour, has vanished, after labour has become not merely a means to live but has become itself the primary necessity of life, after the productive forces have also increased with the all-round development of the individual, and all the springs of cooperative wealth flow more abundantly—only then can the narrow horizon of bourgeois right be fully left behind and society inscribe on its banners: from each according to his ability, to each according to his needs.[28]

The bourgeois right of the transition period includes its negation. In order that the same amount of labour which every worker gives to society in one form he receives back in another, it is necessary that even if the workers are different from one another in respect of their skill, their needs and those of their families, etc, in one thing they will be *absolutely equal*: in respect of the ownership of the means of production. The advance of production, the increase of the amount of means of production belonging to society, ie owned equally by all the workers, will progressively undermine equal right in the distribution of the products. This will in turn progressively increase equality among the people.

Bourgeois right in the transition period, while it lays down that every worker will receive means of consumption from society according to the labour he gave it, is based on social equality as regards the means of production, and therefore will wither away of itself.

(7) In conclusion

The economy of a workers' state and a capitalist economy have many common characteristics. As the workers' state is a transition stage between capitalism and communism it inevitably includes some of the features of the society out of whose ruins it arises, and some of the nuclei of the future society. These elements, antagonistic as they are, are bound together, the former being subordinated to the latter. Common to both a workers' state and capitalism is the division of labour, primarily the division between mental and manual labour. The distinguishing feature is the existence or non-existence of workers' control over production. Workers' control forms the bridge, albeit a narrow bridge, to the abolition of the separation of manual and mental labour, which will be completely realised with the establishment of communist society. Common to both a workers' state and capitalism is the fact that the technicians form a hierarchy above the workers (although in a workers' state in essence it cannot really be called a hierarchy). The distinguishing feature lies in the fact that in a workers' state the technicians are not subordinated to capital, but to the will of the workers' state, to the proletariat as a collective. This is the point of departure to the abolition of any social hierarchy in production. Elements of coercion in labour discipline will exist in a workers' state as well as in capitalism. But in a workers' state, unlike in capitalism, they will not be the only elements, and they will be more and more subordinated to elements of consciousness until such time as social solidarity, harmonious relations between people and education, will altogether abolish the need of any coercion in the process of production at all. In a workers' state as well as in the capitalist commodity economy, equivalents are exchanged: a product containing a certain quantity of socially necessary labour is exchanged for another product containing an equivalent amount. But in a workers' state this result is achieved not through the action of blind forces but through the conscious direction of the economy; besides which all the workers have equal rights in the ownership of the means of production. Bourgeois right under the bourgeoisie means exploitation; the bourgeois right of distribution in a workers' state 'tacitly recognises unequal individual endowment and thus productive capacity as natural privileges', but at the same time it declares the equality of producers towards the means of production. The point of departure of the bourgeois right of distribution in a workers' state is the non-existence of any exploitation whatsoever, and the evolution towards the total abolition of all economic inequality, even that resulting from natural individual endowment.

Chapter 3: The material heritage of pre-October society

In the introduction to *The Critique of Political Economy*, Marx concisely formulates the main conclusions of historical materialism. Among other things he writes:

> No social order ever disappears before all the productive forces for which there is room in it, have been developed; and now, higher relations of production never appear before the material conditions of existence have matured in the womb of the old society.

The Mensheviks quoted this sentence in order to prove that capitalism in Russia was not yet ripe for the socialist revolution, and that it had a long future until it would reach this stage. This simple conclusion, however, neglects a whole series of factors which determine, limit or extend the possibilities of development of the productive forces.

What determined the development of Tsarist Russia was, on the one hand, the class relation of forces within Russia itself, and, on the other hand, Russia's relation of dependence on world capitalism. These two factors are dialectically knit together. If not for the unity of the world, the uneven, combined development of the different countries could not be explained—why the class struggle should take the deepest and most extreme form in such a backward country as Russia, how it was that the Russian proletariat under Tsarism was more concentrated in gigantic enterprises even than the proletariat of the US. These phenomena are evidence of the high level of social production which the *world economy* had reached, and the maturity of the *world* for the substitution of capitalist relations of production by socialist relations. The First World War which accelerated the downfall of Tsarism also was not evidence of the high level of the productive forces in *each* of the belligerent countries; but it did show that the material conditions were ripe for the socialist revolution on a world scale. The series of military defeats, in which the Russian army suffered disastrous losses, was clear testimony to the industrial-military backwardness of Russia in an advanced world. The fact that Marxism—the fruit of the synthesis of French socialism, English economic theory and German philosophy—was imported to Russia when the workers' movement was still in its cradle is evidence of the spiritual unity of the world. On the other hand, the fact that in Russia opportunism and revisionism struck much weaker roots than in the countries of the West is the outcome of the backwardness of Russia in a world ripe for socialism: the low standard of living of the workers which was kept down by the stream of peasant migration into the towns; the fact that the Russian bourgeoisie had no overseas investments, part of the superprofits from which were used in the West to bribe a layer of workers and improve the conditions of the masses as a whole for a period of time; the concentration of the workers in gigantic enterprises; the fact that the country was perched precariously on the powder barrel of the agrarian revolution.

This development of the productive forces within the framework of national and international social relations, and not, as the Mensheviks would have it, in a vacuum, entirely invalidated their dream of the tremendous possibilities of development before Russian capitalism. On the contrary, in the concrete national and international relations in which Russian capitalism found itself, its continued existence would have conserved the burden of feudalism; it would have involved the country in wars which might well have resulted in transforming backward Russia into a colony or semi-colony of the Western powers; it would have meant that the development of the national minorities, which made up about half the population of Russia, would have continued to be suppressed. The quotation from *The Critique of Political Economy* applies not to a country in isolation but to the world system. The very fact that the first proletarian revolution broke out in a backward country affirms this—it is the best evidence of the ripeness of the world for the socialist revolution.

The Russian Revolution is explicable by the law of uneven development, which is one facet of the unity of world development. But this law allows two possibilities of development: firstly, that the Russian Revolution, being evidence of the maturity of the world for socialism, would be the prelude to a series of new revolutions which would break out immediately or after a certain time; secondly, as a reformulation of the first possibility, that the 'certain time' lengthens into years, and leaves the Russian Revolution isolated in hostile world capitalism. It was impossible before October 1917 to determine which path humanity would follow by basing oneself simply on the law of universality of world history; one must take account of the contradiction this law contains within itself, the contradiction being the law of uneven development. Human practices alone can decide which way history will go. Now, looking back in retrospect, we may say that human practices—the main factor in them being the support social democracy gave to capitalism in Western and Central Europe—brought it about that no victorious revolution took place in other countries in the wake of the October Revolution.

The social order that existed under the Tsar had to disappear for the productive forces to be able to develop. But what social order was to come in its place? Seeing that the destruction of the social order of Tsarist Russia was the result of the maturity of the world for socialism, there is no doubt that, had the revolution spread, the social order that would have come in its place would have been the first stage of communist society. But as the October Revolution did not spread, what social order *could* come in Russia?

In seeking an answer to this question the first step to take is to analyse the material heritage handed down from the social order that existed before October:

> Men do not build themselves a new world with 'earthly goods' as vulgar superstition believes, but with the historical achievements of the old world which is about to go under. In the course of evolution they must begin entirely by themselves to produce the material conditions for a new society, and no effort of the human mind or will can release them from this fate.[29]

(1) The material heritage of the Tsarist period

In 1913 80 percent of the population of Russia earned their livelihood from agriculture, and only 10 percent from industry, mining and transport. These figures alone show up the backwardness of Russia. Of all the countries of Europe only Yugoslavia, Turkey, Romania and Bulgaria show a similar occupational distribution of the population.

Country	Year	Industy, mining and transport	Agriculture, fishing and forestry	All other occupations
Yugoslavia	1931	13	79	8
Turkey	1935	10	82	8
Romania	1930	9	78	13
Bulgaria	1934	8	80	12

The countries of Western and Central Europe and the US as far back as the middle of the 19th century showed a much higher percentage of their population occupied in industry, mining and transport and a much lower percentage occupied in agriculture than Russia in 1913. Thus in Britain in 1841 the percentage of population occupied in agriculture, fishing and forestry was 22.7, that occupied in manufacture, building, mining and transport, 47.3. France, which lagged a long way behind Britain, in 1837 had 63 percent occupied in agriculture; in 1866 it had 43 percent occupied in agriculture and 38 percent in industry. Germany in 1800 had nearly two thirds of the population occupied in agriculture; in 1852 it had 44.4 percent occupied in agriculture and 40.9 percent occupied in industry and handicrafts. The US, which was at the beginning mainly a country of agricultural settlement, in 1820 had 72.3 percent occupied in agriculture, forestry and fishing, and 12.3 percent occupied in manufacture, building and mining; in 1850 it had 64.8 percent and 17.8 percent respectively.

How poor was the material heritage the Bolsheviks acquired on taking power not only in comparison with contemporary developed capitalist countries, but even with those same countries in the infancy of their capitalist development will become even clearer from an analysis of the national income.

The most all-embracing calculation of the national income in different countries at different periods was undertaken by Colin Clark in his book *The Conditions of Economic Progress*.[30] Although we must accept a certain margin of error in a calculation of such magnitude and complexity, this on no account invalidates Clark's excellent calculations. In order to make an international comparison it is necessary to have a common measure, which Clark denotes in 'International Units' (IU). He defines the IU as 'the amount of goods and services which one dollar would purchase in the US over the average of the period 1925-34'.

Clark estimates the real income per occupied person in Russia in 1913 to be 306 IUs.

As against this the real income per occupied person in some developed countries was:

Great Britain		France		Germany		United States	
Year	IU	Year	IU	Year	IU	Year	IU
1688	378	1850-59*	382	1850	420	1850	787
1860-69*	638	1860-69*	469	1877	632	1880	1,032
1904-10*	999	1911	786	1913	881	1900	1,388
1937	1,275					1929	1,636
* = annual average						1937	1,407

Thus the average income per occupied person in Russia in 1913 was only 80.9 percent of the corresponding figure for Britain in 1688—nearly 100 years before the industrial revolution.

Similar figures to these for Russia are given for only these European countries (up to 25 percent above Russia, 1925-34 annual average): Finland 380 IUs; Hungary 359; Poland 352; Latvia 345; Italy 343; Estonia 341; Yugoslavia 330. Below Russia were: Bulgaria 259; Romania 243; Lithuania 207.

As regards Japan, Colin Clark calculates that its national income per occupied person for 1925-34 was 353 IUs. For Egypt in the same years he estimates that it was 300 to 350, for India 200, for China 100 to 120.[31]

(2) The rule of the working class where the material conditions for the abolition of capitalist relations of production do not exist

Marx and Engels more than once dealt with the question of what would happen if the working class took power before the historical requisites were present for the substitution of capitalist relations by socialist relations of production. They concluded that in such an event the working class would lose the power which would fall into the hands of the bourgeoisie. The taking of power by the working class would be only temporary and transitory, and would encourage the development of capitalism. Thus, for instance, Marx wrote in 1847:

> If it is true that the bourgeoisie politically, that is, through state power, 'maintains the injustice of property relations' [Heinzen's expression], then it is not less true that it does not create them. The 'injustice of property relations' is conditioned by the modern division of labour, the modern form of exchange, competition, concentration, etc, and does not owe its origin in any way to the political domination of the bourgeois class...the political domination of the bourgeois class flows from...the existing relations of production. Therefore, *if the proletariat overthrows the political domination of the bourgeoisie its victory will only be temporary, a point*

*in the process of the bourgeois revolution itself, and will serve its cause as it did in 1794,
so long as the 'movement' of history has not created the material conditions which make
it necessary to abolish the bourgeois mode of production and therewith definitively overthrow the political domination of the bourgeoisie.* The 'Reign of Terror' in France
therefore had to accomplish the cleansing of the surface of France from feudal ruins
by its terrible hammer blows. The timid, cautious bourgeoisie would not have
managed to complete this task in decades. The bloody acts of the people hence
merely served to level the path for this bourgeoisie.[32]

What Marx says about a revolution which brings the proletariat to power
before the historical premises for the transition from capitalism to communism
exist do not exactly fit the October Revolution. This is so not only because on
an international scale the material historical premises were present, but also because of the national conditions. Even under conditions where the revolution
did not spread, reality was more complicated than the above Marxian formulation. The Russian bourgeoisie was not only overthrown politically, but also
expropriated economically a few months after October. The rural bourgeoisie
that remained did not succeed in overthrowing the proletariat, and its social
weight, especially from the time of the Five-Year Plan, was almost negligible.
The isolation of October did not make it 'a point in the process' of the development of the Russian bourgeoisie, because the Russian bourgeoisie was annihilated. If so, what relations of production could come after October?

(3) Socialist relations of production?

The establishment of socialist relations of production demands a much higher
level of the productive forces than was the heritage of Tsarism. The way Engels
explains why in the past society was divided into classes, exploiters and exploited, entirely fitted Russia's conditions even after October:

> The division of society into an exploiting and an exploited class, a ruling and an
> oppressed class, was the necessary outcome of the low development of production
> hitherto. So long as the sum of social labour yielded a product which only slightly
> exceeded what was necessary for the bare existence of all; *so long, therefore, as all
> or almost all the time of the great majority of the numbers of society was absorbed in labour,
> so long was society necessarily divided into classes.* Alongside of this great majority
> exclusively absorbed in labour there developed a class, freed from direct produc-
> tive labour, which managed the general business of society: the direction of labour,
> affairs of state, justice, science, art and so forth. It is therefore the law of the di-
> vision of labour which lies at the root of the division into classes. But this does
> not mean that this division into classes was not established by violence and rob-
> bery, by deception and fraud, or that the ruling class, once in the saddle, has ever
> failed to strengthen its domination at the cost of the working class and to convert
> its social management into the exploitation of the masses.[33]

*In post-October, just as in pre-October Russia, the material conditions for the
abolition of the class division of society did not exist.*

(4) Capitalist function

The historical mission of the bourgeoisie is the socialisation of labour and the concentration of the means of production. On a world scale this task had already been fulfilled. In Russia the revolution got rid of the impediments to the development of the productive forces, put an end to the remnants of feudalism, built up a monopoly of foreign trade which defends the development of the productive forces of the country from the devastating pressure of world capitalism, and also gave a tremendous lever to the development of the productive forces in the form of the state ownership of the means of production. Under such conditions, all the impediments to the historical mission of capitalism—the socialisation of labour and the concentration of the means of production which are necessary prerequisites for the establishment of socialism, and which the bourgeoisie was not able to fulfil—are abolished. *Post-October Russia stood before the fulfilment of the historical mission of the bourgeoisie.*

Even in an advanced country there will be certain bourgeois tasks which a victorious proletarian revolution will have to accomplish. In certain parts of the US, for instance (mainly in the South), and in a certain sector of the economy (mainly agriculture) the development of the productive forces is impeded under the capitalist system, so that social production and the concentration of the means of production is not yet realised. But because the productive forces of the US as a whole are very well developed, these bourgeois tasks will be only accessories, subordinate to the work of building a communist society. Thus, for instance, the establishment of social production and the concentration of means of production where they do not yet exist, will not be achieved by the creation of a proletariat on the one hand and capital on the other; the labourers from the beginning will not be divorced from the means of production. As against this, in post-October Russia with its low level of national income, the fulfilment of the bourgeois tasks is the *central* problem. In the United States the addition of new means of production necessary for the socialisation of labour can be accompanied by a rise in the standard of living of the masses, by a strengthening of the element of conviction in production discipline, by the fortification of workers' control, by the continuous dwindling of the differences in income between manual and mental workers, etc. But can this be achieved in a backward country under conditions of siege? Can labour discipline based mainly on conviction prevail when the level of production is very low? Can a quick tempo of accumulation, necessitated by the backwardness of the country and the pressure of world capitalism, be accomplished without the separation of society into the managers of the general business of a society and the managed, the directors of labour and the directed? Could such a separation be put a stop to before those who directed production also directed distribution in their own interests? Can a workers' revolution in a backward country isolated by triumphant international capitalism be anything but 'a point in the process' of the development of capitalism, even if the capitalist class is abolished?

Chapter 4: Russia's transformation from a workers' state to a capitalist state

In this chapter we shall describe the transformation of the class character of the Russian state from a workers' to a capitalist state. We shall do this by dealing with the following points:

(1) Subordination of consumption to accumulation—subordination of the workers to the means of production.
(2) The accumulation of capital on the one hand and poverty on the other.
(3) The productivity of labour and the worker.
(4) Who controls production?
(5) Changes in the relations of distribution.
(6) The denial of any legal freedom to the worker.
(7) Forced labour.
(8) The expropriation of the means of production from the peasantry.
(9) The transformation of money into money capital—an important symptom of the system.
(10) The introduction of the turnover tax.
(11) From a workers' state with bureaucratic deformations to the complete liberation of the bureaucracy from popular control.
(12) Why the Five-Year Plan signifies the transformation of the bureaucracy into a ruling class.

(1) Subordination of consumption to accumulation— subordination of the workers to the means of production

Under capitalism the consumption of the masses is subordinated to accumulation. Sometimes consumption increases at the same time as accumulation, and at other times it decreases while accumulation rises, but always, in every situation, the basic relationship remains.

If we follow the history of Russia from October, we find that until the advent of the Five-Year Plan this subordination did not exist, but from then on expressed itself in unprecedented brutality. This will become clear from the following table:

DIVISION OF GROSS OUTPUT OF INDUSTRY INTO MEANS OF PRODUCTION AND MEANS OF CONSUMPTION

	1913	1928	1932	1937	1940	1942 (planned)
Means of production	33.3	32.8	53.3	57.8	61.0	62.2
Means of consumption	66.7	67.2	46.7	42.2	39.0	37.8

These official figures, nakedly as they show the decline in the weight of the production of means of consumption relative to that of means of production, if anything minimise the decline.

It is very difficult to check the *absolute* change in production of different means of consumption. Russian statistics practise a simple trick in order to describe the situation in rosier colours than is true. The production of the small factories, which as regards means of consumption was very important till 1928, is not included. Official statistics can therefore show a tremendous rise in output in the food industry between 1928 and 1932 (from 1,544 billion roubles to 3,485 billion roubles in 1926/7 fixed prices). And this increase—of more than 100 percent—took place at a time when the production of these very agricultural products which are the raw material of the food industry fell sharply! A similar phenomenon can be shown as regards shoe production, where a jump in shoe output (according to statistics) was accompanied by a steep decline in tanning. These statistical marvels are based not only on price falsifications where figures are given in prices, but also on the exclusion of the output of the small enterprises that were very important till 1928. There is one important means of consumption which even before the Five-Year Plan was produced almost only in big enterprises, and whose production can be measured in volume. This is textiles. Let us compare the output of this product over some years with the output of some means of production:

| | 1928 as percentage of 1913 | 1932 | 1937 | 1940 |
		as percentages of 1928		
Cotton goods	193.1	87.1	109.7	122.6
Woollen goods	86.1	124.8	128.5	–
Oil	122.1	192.2	262.9	294.9
Coal	124.9	178.1	352.6	456.2
Pig iron	78.6	187.9	439.4	451.5
Machines and manufactures of steel	181.8	470.0	1,375.0	2,420.0

It is not enough that the production of means of consumption lags badly behind that of means of production. The Russian government, relying on the 'short memory' of the masses, or more correctly on the oppressive machinery which ensures that past memories remain unuttered, adds insult to injury, and while promising a tremendous rise in the production of means of consumption with every Five-Year Plan, at the same time fixes the official target of the plan at a volume of production which does not exceed the target of former plans. This will be clear from the following table:

TARGETS OF PRODUCTION FOR THE END OF THE FIVE-YEAR PLANS

	First 1932–33	Second 1937	Third 1942	Fourth 1950
Some means of consumption				
Cotton goods (billion m)	4.7	5.1	4.9	4.7
Woollen goods (million m)	270.0	220.0	177.0	159.0
Sugar (million tons)	2.6	2.5	3.5	2.4
Some means of of production				
Electric current (million kwh)	22.0	38.0	75.0	82.0
Coal (million tons)	75.0	152.5	243.0	250.0
Pig iron (million tons)	10.0	16.0	22.0	19.5
Steel (million tons)	10.4	17.0	28.0	25.4
Oil and gas (million tons)	21.7	46.8	54.0	35.4

(2) The accumulation of capital on the one hand and poverty on the other

Until 1928, notwithstanding the increasing bureaucratisation, the accumulation of wealth in the statified economy was not accompanied by an accumulation of poverty. This will become clear from the following table:[34]

Year	Capital of large-scale industry (million roubles 1926–27)	Year (1913 = 100)	Real wages***
1921	7,930*		
1922	7,935*	1922–23	47.3
1923	7,969*	1923–24	69.1
1924	8,016*	1924–25	85.1
1925	8,105*	1925–26	96.1
1926	8,552**	1926–27	108.4
1927	9,151*	1927–28	111.1
1928	9,841*	1928–29	115.6

Thus even according to the calculation of Professor Prokopovich, ex-minister of the Kerensky government, whom no one would suspect of friendship for the Bolsheviks, the real wages of the Russian workers in 1928/29 were 15.6 percent higher than before the war. At the same time the working hours were cut by 22.3 percent. If we also take into account the social services which in 1928 made up about 32 percent of the wages, the rise will be even more pronounced. Another point that comes to light from this table is that in the last few years before the inauguration of the Five-Year Plan, as the bureaucracy strengthened itself, real wages almost ceased to rise and the tempo of their rise lagged a little behind the tempo of accumulation.

The situation changes radically with the inauguration of the plan. From now on accumulation leaps ahead with giant strides, while the standard of living of the masses not only lags far behind, but even declines absolutely compared with 1928. The following table gives an indication of the rate of accumulation:

INVESTMENT OF CAPITAL (BILLION CURRENT ROUBLES)

	Total	In industry
1923/4–27/8	11.1	5.2
1928/9–32	52.5	24.8
1933–37	114.7	58.6
1938–42 (plan)	192.0	111.9

Even if the value of the rouble declined in these years it is clear that a tremendous accumulation of capital took place in the three Five-Year Plans. According to the date of the Gosplan, the fixed capital of Russian industry in 1933 prices, which in 1928 was 10.5 billion roubles, rose in 1932 to 25.5 billion roubles, in 1937 to 75.1 billion roubles, and was in 1942 expected to exceed 150 billion roubles.

Seeing that from 1928 the Russian authorities stopped publishing the index of real wages and the cost of living and from 1931 wholesale or retail prices, it becomes very difficult to calculate the changes in the level of real wages. The following figures, however, will help towards an estimation of the changes in the standard of living:[35]

Year	Monthly wages*		Price of 'food basket'**		'Food baskets' per monthly wages	
	Roubles	Index	Roubles	Index	Number	Index
1913	25.4	100.0	6.57	100.0	3.7	100.0
1928	70.2	276.4	11.96	182.0	5.6	151.4
1932	115.4	454.3	24.07	366.4	4.8	129.7
1935	185.3	729.5	96.42	1,467.6	1.9	51.4
1937	241.8	952.0	99.90	1,520.5	2.4	64.9
1940	323	1,271.6	165.22	2,514.8	2.0	54.1

This tells the story of the changes in the workers' conditions as regards food. Clothing and housing conditions are, if anything, more difficult. In order not to expand too much, we shall suffice with some figures giving the *average* housing space per capita:

Year	Urban population (millions)	Housing area in towns	
		Total (million m²)	Per capita (m²)
1927/28	26.3	160.0	6.1
1932	35.6	185.1	5.2
1937	50.2	211.9	4.2

Is it necessary to give additional proof that the accumulation of wealth on the one hand means the accumulation of poverty on the other?

(3) The productivity of labour and the worker

In a workers' state the rise in the productivity of labour is accompanied by an improvement in the conditions of the workers. As Trotsky said in 1928, real wages 'must become the main criterion for measuring the success of socialist revolution'. The 'criterion of socialist upswing is constant improvement of labour standards'. Let us see what the relation between the rise in the productivity of labour and the standard of living of the workers was in Russia. The following table gives an indication of this:

Year	Productivity of labour Index	Number of 'food baskets' per average monthly wages Index
1913	100.0	100.0
1928	106.0	151.4
1937	196.6	64.9

Thus till 1928 not only were wages above pre-war, but they rose much more than the productivity of labour. Between 1928 and 1937, while the productivity of labour nearly doubled,[36] real wages not only did not rise correspondingly, but were actually cut by more than 50 percent.

The same point can be arrived at from a different angle, by comparing the level of productivity in Russia with that of other countries on the one hand, and the standard of living of the Russian workers with that of workers in other countries on the other hand.

In 1913 the average productivity of labour in Russian industry was about 25 percent of that in the US, 35 percent of that in Germany, and 40 percent of that in Britain. A committee of the Gosplan specially appointed in 1937 to investigate the productivity of labour in Russian industry found that it was 40.5 percent of that in industry in the US, and 97 percent of that in Germany. There is ground for the assumption that this calculation is exaggerated, and that the productivity of labour in Russian industry in 1937 was about 30 percent of that in the US, 70 percent of that in Germany, or about the same percentage of that in Britain. It would take too long to explain how we arrived at this conclusion. But to accept the conclusions of the Gosplan committee will even further strengthen the arguments we put forward. While the Russian worker produces about 70 percent as much as a British worker, his standard of living is very much lower.

In the following table we assume that the Russian worker earns 500 roubles per month, which is the average of all employed by the state (the bureaucracy included), planned for the end of the Fourth Five-Year Plan in 1950. On the other hand, we have taken as the basis of the price calculation the prices from Zone 1, in which prices are the lowest in Russia.[37] For Britain we have taken the workers' average weekly earnings of £5 3s 6d.[38] The basis of the price calculation is the official figures published by the Board of Trade.

NUMBER OF UNITS AVERAGE WEEKLY WAGES CAN BUY

Item	Unit	Russia	Britain
Wheat bread (first grade)	lbs	41.7	480.7
Wheat bread (second grade)	lbs	63.3	–
Rye bread	lbs	91.0	
Beef	lbs	9.0	79–127
Butter	lbs	4.1	77.2
Milk	pints	57–81	247.2
Sugar	lbs	18.5	412.0
Eggs	number	82–115	706.3
Tea	lbs	1.6	36.4
Coffee	lbs	3.4	41.2
Beer	pints	14.4	88.2
Cigarettes	number	464.0	618.0
Men's shoes	pairs	0.4	2–4.5
Women's shoes	pairs	0.4	1–4
Women's jackets, semi-wool	number	0.6	1.1–2.3
Stockings, women's cotton	pairs	16.2	25–27
Crepe-de-chine	yards	1.4	23–25
Men's suits, single-breasted, semi-wool	number	0.3	0.6–1.5

Item	Unit	Russia	Britain
Men's suits, wool	number	0.1	0.2-0.3
Rubber overshoes	pairs	2.6	9.5
Women's cotton dresses	number	0.2	3.5-6
Women's woollen dresses	number	0.6	0.8-2.1
Matches	boxes	577.0	824.0
Combs, women's toilet	number	28.8	103-154
Gramophones	number	0.12	0.6
Radio receiving sets (5 valve)	number	0.2	0.17
Wrist watches	number	0.12	0.3-0.5

If the productivity of labour of a worker in Russian industry is about four fifths of that in Britain, while his standard of living is about a third of that of the British worker, can we conclude otherwise than that, if the British worker is exploited, his Russian brother is much more so?

(4) Who controls production?

Immediately after the revolution it was decided that the management of every plant would be in the hands of the trade unions. Thus the programme of the Communist Party of Russia adopted at the Eighth Party Congress (held 18 to 23 March 1919) declared:

The organised apparatus of social production must primarily depend upon the trade unions... They must be transformed into huge productive units, enrolling the majority of the workers, and in due time all the workers, in the respective branches of production.

Inasmuch as the trade unions are already (as specified in the laws of the Soviet Republic and as realised in practice) participants in all the local and central organs administering industry, they must proceed to the practical concentration into their own hands of the work of administration in the whole economic life of the country, making this their unified economic aim. Thus protecting the indissoluble union between the central state authority, the national economy, and the broad masses of the workers, the trade unions must in the fullest possible measure induce the workers to participate directly in the work of economic administration. The participation of the trade unions in the conduct of economic life, and the involvement by them of the broad masses of the people in this work, would appear at the same time to be our chief aid in the campaign against the bureaucratisation of the economic apparatus of the Soviet power. This will facilitate the establishment of an effective popular control over the results of production.[39]

Participating in the running of industry, together with the workers' plant committees, were the party cells. Together with these, and under their control, worked the technical manager. These three together formed the Troika.

With the strengthening of the bureaucracy in the party and the trade unions, the Troika became more and more a mere label, more and more raised above the mass of workers. Nevertheless, fundamentally the control was still vested in its hands, until the advent of the Five-Year Plan. A Baykov, who is no supporter of workers' control, but praises Stalin's activities, says:

> De facto, during that period [before the Five-Year Plan] the director was largely dependent on the works' trade union organ, the 'Zavkom' [the factory trade union committee] and on the party cell, the organ of the Communist Party at the enterprise. Representatives of these organisations considered it their duty to supervise the director's activities, and usually interfered with his decisions.[40]

In addition, and as a last resort against the actions of the bureaucracy in the party, the state and the unions, the workers could take to strike action, which was legal. Despite the weariness after long years of war and civil war, despite the dilution of the proletariat by the influx from the villages, despite the exodus of a large part of the best workers into the ranks of the bureaucracy and, above all, despite the fact that the state was a workers' state, strikes were declared which embraced sometimes thousands of participants. In 1925 there were 196 strikes with 37,600 workers participating; in 1926 there were 337 strikes with 43,200 workers participating; in 1927 there were 396 strikes with 25,400 participants. More than 90 percent of the participants in these strikes were workers employed by the state.

With the complete victory of Stalin over the Left Opposition and with the inauguration of the Five-Year Plan a general attack began on workers' control. Thus a resolution of the Central Committee of the party decided that the workers' committee of the plant:

> ...may not intervene directly in the running of the plant, or endeavour in any way to replace plant management. They shall by all means help to secure one-man control, increase production, plant development, and, thereby, improvement of the conditions of the working class.[41]

The manager is in full and sole charge of the plant. All his economic orders are unconditionally binding on all the workers. He alone shall select, promote and remove personnel 'taking into consideration' 'the opinions of the party and the trade union organisations', but is not to be bound by them.

The Troika was officially buried in 1937. In the plenum of the Central Committee, Stalin's second in command, Zhdanov, declared:

> The Troika is something quite impermissible... The Troika is a sort of administrative board, but our economic administration is constructed along totally different lines.[42]

The new management of industry was very clearly defined by the official manual, Economics of Socialist Industry:[43]

> Each plant has a leader endowed with full power of decision, hence—fully responsible for everything: the plant manager.

Further:

One-man control implies strict demarcation between the administration on the one hand, and party and trade union organisations on the other. This strict demarcation must be applied on all levels of industrial management. Current operations in fulfilment are the tasks of the administration. The chief of a workshop, the manager of the plant, the head of the Glavk, have full powers, each within his field, and the party and trade union organisations may not interfere with their orders.

(5) Changes in the relations of distribution

The Russian Communist Party in 1919 stated its wages policy in these terms:

While aspiring to equality of remuneration for all kinds of labour and to total communism, the Soviet government cannot consider as its task the immediate realisation of this equality at the present moment when only the first steps are being made towards the transition from capitalism to communism.[44]

But as a matter of fact, in the time of military communism there was an equalisation of rewards. According to data given by the Soviet statistician Strumlin, the wages of workers of the highest category, which in 1917 amounted to 232 percent of those of the lowest category, were in the first part of 1921 only 102 percent, ie they were practically equal. The situation changed with the introduction of the NEP. The Bolsheviks were then compelled to retreat from nearly full equality. In 1921-22 a unified scale of wages was introduced in which there were 17 grades, from the apprentice to the highest specialist. According to this, the most highly skilled worker received three and a half times the wages of the lowest paid unskilled worker. Specialists earned a maximum of eight times as much as the unskilled worker.

These differences, however, were mitigated until the introduction of the First Five-Year Plan, by some factors. First of all, no member of the Communist Party was allowed to earn more than a skilled worker. This provision had great importance, as the majority of directors of enterprises, departments of industry, etc were party members. In 1928, of the personnel of the managing boards of the trusts 71.4 percent were party members, of the syndicates 84.4 percent were, and of those of individual enterprises 89.3 percent were.

An additional factor which made the differences much smaller than they seem from the unified scale of wages was that the *total* number of specialists (a section of whom were party members who thus did not earn more than skilled workers) was very small. In 1928 they constituted only 2.27 percent of all those engaged in industry.

A general picture of the income differentiation in Russia was given by *Statisticheski Spravechnik SSSR 1926*.[45] According to it, in 1926-27 the annual average income of manual workers in pre-war roubles was 465. At the same time the maximum allowed to specialists was 1,811. Excluding the bourgeoisie, the Nep Men and the kulaks, there were only 114,000 people who earned this maximum. They made up 0.3 percent of all earners, and their income made up only 1 percent of the national income.[46]

The situation changed radically with the introduction of the Five-Year Plan. The law of maximum income for party members was abolished. The 'general law of wages' promulgated on 17 June 1920, which laid down that anyone exceeding the norm in piecework was never to receive more than 100 percent above the normal rate, was cancelled. So was the other clause to the law laying down that a worker was never to receive less than two thirds of the established norm. At the same time the bureaucracy's rate of salaries was raised sharply. And in addition to salaries they received bonuses, shares in the 'Director's Fund' (introduced in 1936), and different services (such as private cars, villas, etc). From 1935 Russian statisticians stopped publishing any figures concerning the division of workers and employees according to their income. The only figure they did publish was the *average* income of all workers and employees—a figure arrived at by averaging the incomes of charwomen, unskilled labourers, skilled workers, specialists, chief engineers, managers, etc.

Despite the fact that Russian statisticians are doing their best to hide the income differentiation prevailing, we can get a picture of the situation from various factors.

In 1937 the maximum salary of a director was 2,000 roubles per month, unless the government gave special permission for it to go beyond this. Skilled workers received 200 to 300 roubles. In the same year the government introduced a minimum wage of 110 roubles per month for *piecework*. There were certainly many time-workers, who, even after this decree, received less than 110 roubles per month. That even the pieceworkers who received less than this amount were quite considerable in number is clear from the fact that this decree necessitated an additional government expenditure of 50 million roubles. Two thousand roubles is therefore no mean salary.

The director's main income, however, is not his fixed salary. More important than this are the bonuses. These are dependent on the overfulfilment of the economic plan. Thus, for instance, for every decrease of 1 percent of the real cost of production below the planned cost, the manager, his assistant, the chief engineer and his assistant receive a bonus of 15 percent of their salary except in the iron and steel industries, where the percentage is ten. For every percentage of increase of output above the plan, a manager of a mine and his close assistants receive 4 percent of their salaries.[47] If the output of pig iron exceeds the plan by 5 percent, the top administrators receive a bonus of 10 percent of their salary for every percent above the plan; if the output exceeds the plan by 6 to 10 percent, the bonus is 15 percent of the every percent above the plan. Thus, if the output is 10 percent above plan, the top administrators receive a bonus of 125 percent of their salary.

The third source of income is the Director's Fund. Its official aim is to build houses for the workers and employees, clubs, canteens, creches, kindergartens, to give bonuses for outstanding achievements at work, etc. From what sources is this fund drawn? The profits of the plant are divided between the plant itself and the higher state administration of industry. The proportion is determined by the state at intervals. The share of the state cannot be less than 10 percent in any enterprise. In 1937 industry as a whole gave 48 percent of all its profit to the state. The part which remains in the hands of the director of the plant is divided into two. A part goes to develop the plant—the rest remains in the hands of the director and is called the Director's Fund. According to a decree of 19 April 1936, 4 percent of the planned profit and 50 percent of the profit above the plan are to go to the Director's Fund. One Russian economist has given the figures of the size of this fund:[48]

	Realisation of plan in percent	Director's Fund in millions of roubles	Director's Fund per worker
Petroleum industry	104.1	21.7	344.92
Meat industry	118.6	51.9	752.69
Spirit industry	108.8	86.0	1,175

As has already been mentioned, the average wage of all workers and employees was 250 roubles per month in 1937. The above figures show that by exceeding the plan only a few percent the Director's Fund per annum in the petroleum industry comes to more than one monthly average income, in the meat industry to three, and in the spirit industry to more than four and a half. Other industries present the same picture. The table shows how huge are the sums concentrated in the hands of directors of industries numbering thousands of workers.

We have no statistical data on how the Directors' Funds are distributed. The only indication we have is from Yvon in *L'URSS telle qu'elle est*.[49] He writes that in the paper *Za Industrializatsiya* of 20 April 1937 figures were published concerning the distribution of the Director's Fund in the enterprise Porchen in Kharkov:

> Of the 60,000 roubles constituting the Director's Fund, the director appropriated 22,000 for himself, the secretary of the party committee 10,000, the chief of the production office 8,000, the chief accountant 6,000, the president of the trade union committee 4,000, the head of the workshop 5,000.

The distribution of the other 5,000 roubles is not indicated. They doubtless served to compensate the thousands of workers. This example is no doubt more glaring than many another, but the fact that such an excess can occur indicates the degree to which the industrial bureaucracy is independent of the masses; and it indicates that one-man management, together with the Director's Fund, are certainly excellent conditions for the increasing prosperity of the directors.

As is well known, some professional people in Russia receive very high incomes too. The only professional group about which we have detailed, even though not full, statistics of income distribution, is that of authors. According to Alexei Tolstoy, in 1937 the authors were divided according to their incomes thus: 14 authors receiving over 120,000 roubles a year; 11 authors receiving 72,000 to 120,000 a year; 39 authors receiving 24,000 to 36,000 a year; 114 authors receiving 12,000 to 24,000 a year; 137 authors receiving 6,000 to 12,000 a year; and 4,000 authors receiving less than 6,000 a year.

As regards the high status of officials, with the abolition of the Law of Maximum which said that no state official could receive more than a skilled worker, their incomes sky-rocketed. According to a decision of the Supreme Soviet of the USSR of 17 January 1938, the salary of the President of the Supreme Soviet of the RSFSR and his deputies was fixed at 150,000 roubles per annum; that of the president and vice-presidents of the Soviet of the Union and Soviet of Nationalities was fixed at 300,000 roubles per annum. Members of the Supreme Soviets were to receive 12,000 roubles a year in addition to 150 roubles per day of session.[50]

At the same time the unskilled worker was getting 100 to 150 roubles per month![51]

The difference between the income differentiation before the Five-Year Plan and that after its introduction necessarily leaves the realm of quantity alone and becomes a qualitative difference also. If a specialist or factory manager receives four, five, eight times more than the unskilled worker, it does not necessarily mean that there is a relation of exploitation between the two. A skilled worker, specialist or manager produces more values than an unskilled worker in one hour of work.

Even if the specialist receives more than the difference in the values that they produce, it still does not prove that he exploits the unskilled worker. This can be simply demonstrated. Let us assume that in a workers' state the unskilled worker produces his necessities in six hours a day, and that he works eight hours, the other two hours being devoted to the production of social services, to increasing the amount of means of production in the hands of society, etc. As these two hours of work are not labour for someone else, but for himself, it would be wrong to call it surplus labour. But to avoid introducing a new term, and to distinguish them from the first portion of the labour time (the six hours), let us call it 'surplus labour', while the six hours we shall call 'necessary labour'. For the sake of simplicity let us say than an hour of unskilled labour produces the value embodied in one shilling. The unskilled worker thus produces 8s, and receives 6s. Let us assume that the specialist produces five units of value, or 5s, in an hour of his labour. If the specialist earned five times more than the unskilled worker, ie 30s, then it is clear that no relation of exploitation exists here.

Even if he earned six times more than the unskilled worker, while he produces only five times more, there still would not exist a relation of exploitation, as the specialist would be earning 36 shillings a day, while he produces 40s. But if the specialist earned 100s or 200s the situation is fundamentally changed. In such a case a large part of his income *necessarily* comes from the labour of others.

The statistics we have at our disposal conclusively show that, although the bureaucracy had a privileged position in the period preceding the Five-Year Plan, it can on no account be said that it received surplus value from the labour of others. It can just as conclusively be said that with the introduction of the Five-Year Plans the bureaucracy's income consisted to a large extent of surplus value.

(6) The denial of any legal freedom to the worker

Until the First Five-Year Plan every worker could freely change his place of work and could migrate unhindered from one place in the country to another.

As regards the right to change the place of work at that time, the Labour Code said:

> The transfer of a hired person from one enterprise to another, or his shipment from one locality to another, even when the enterprise or institution moves, can take place only with the consent of the worker or employee concerned.[52]

As regards the freedom of movement, the *Small Soviet Encyclopedia* of 1930 severely criticises the hindrance to the free movement of people under the Tsar. It wrote:

> The custom of internal passports, instituted by the autocracy as an instrument of police oppression of the toiling masses, was suppressed by the October Revolution.[53]

But already in 1931 no worker was allowed to leave Leningrad without special permission, and in 1932 this system was adopted in all parts of Russia. An internal passport system much worse than under the Tsar was introduced. Now no one could change his place of residence without permission.

As early as September 1930 all industrial enterprises were prohibited from employing people who left their former place of work without permission. In 1932 labour books were introduced. Every worker must give his labour book to the director when he receives employment, and the director can write whatever remarks he likes in it when the worker leaves the job. No worker can be accepted in a new place of work without showing his labour book.

Serge writes:

> The passport is visaed at the place of work. With each change of employ, the reason for the change is entered into the passport. I have known of workers discharged for not having come on the day of rest to contribute a 'voluntary' (and, naturally, gratuitous) day of work, in whose passports is written, 'Discharged for sabotage of the production plan'.[54]

On 4 December 1932 the bureaucracy issued another decree designed to subjugate the workers. Plant supplies of food and other necessities were put under the sole control of directors 'in order to strengthen the powers of directors of enterprises' (*Pravda*).

On 26 June 1940 a new law prohibited any worker from leaving his job, unless he was physically unfit to work, was accepted into an institution of learning, or was given special permission by higher authorities. Any absence without a satisfactory excuse, even for a day, makes the culprit liable to six months correctual labour—which means a cut of 25 percent in his earnings during that time. It is symptomatic that a few months after the promulgation of this law a few women wrote a letter to *Izvestia* suggesting that domestic servants also be subject to this law. *Izvestia*, in its comment on this question (30 December 1940), although disagreeing with this suggestion, showed no astonishment as to its content in this period of the 'transition from socialism to communism'!

As far as strikes are concerned, not only are workers prohibited from calling strikes, but strikers are liable, according to law, to be sentenced to death for such an offence.[55]

A very important factor in the subjugation of the working class was the creation of the forced labour camps, which contained millions of people.

(7) Forced labour

Until the First Five-Year Plan, the labour of prisoners had scarcely any significance. Till then not only was the number of prisoners in camps very small (1928: 30,000), but the authorities opposed compelling them to work. The head of the prison system wrote in 1927:

> The exploitation of prison labour, the system of squeezing 'golden sweat' from them, the organisation of production in places of confinement, which while profitable from a commercial point of view is fundamentally lacking in corrective significance—these are entirely inadmissible in Soviet places of confinement.[56]

At that time the total production of all prisoners made up only a small percentage of their upkeep.

The situation changed fundamentally, as Dallin proves by a wealth of facts, with the inauguration of the Five-Year Plan. We shall first of all give some figures regarding the number of prisoners in labour camps:

> Kiseliov-Gromov, himself a former GPU official in the northern labour camps, states that in 1928 only 30,000 men were detained in the camps... The total number of prisoners in the entire network of camps in 1930 he gives as 662,257... A GPU official who escaped to Finland in 1930 said in a sworn statement that '734,000 prisoners were employed under the OGPU in the autumn of 1929'.

Dallin comes to the conclusion on the basis of available evidence that the number of people in labour camps in 1931 was nearly 2 million. In 1933-35 the figure was about 5 million. He says that in 1942 there were from 8 to 15 million. Ante Ciliga estimates that the number of prisoners is between 10 and 15 million.[57]

Another calculation having a solid basis is that of S Schwarz.[58] He calculates as follows: in 1939 the number of inhabitants of the USSR was 107.5 million. If not for the war, this population should have increased by 3 million in a year, which means that in seven years it would have increased by 21 million. In the regions annexed to Russia there were, before the war, 24.5 million. If not for the war, the number of inhabitants in these regions should have reached 25.5 million. All the population of the USSR in its present boundaries should have been, if not for the war, 217 million at the beginning of 1946. Now all of the people of 18 years and over, except those in concentration camps, have the vote. From the census of population in 1939 we learn that people aged 18 and over made up 58.4 percent of the population. Let us assume that the percentage in the annexed regions was the same. This means that the adult population would at the beginning of 1946 have amounted to 126.7 million. But the number allowed to vote amounted to only 101.7 million, ie 25 million less than there should have been.

The war caused a great loss of life and a sharp decrease in the birth rate. The birth rate is not important for the calculation as it does not affect the number of adults today. What were the war losses? A short time ago, in an interview with the correspondent of *Pravda*, Stalin said that the number of deaths in the war against Germany amounted to 7 million.[59] It seems that the natural deaths in Russia were not included in this figure. If we assume that the number of adults who died during the war amounted to 7 million above the normal death rate taken according to former years, and we add 1 million—an exaggerated number—for Russians who did not return to their country, there remain 10 million who must exist but have not the right to vote. This must be at least the number in the concentration camps.

If we take a minimum figure of 8 to 10 million people in the forced labour camps, 90 percent of whom are men, we see that they constitute about 16 percent of all adult men.

Forced labour is suitable mainly for manual labour which does not require modern industrial equipment. Lumber work, road and rail constructions, large-scale industrial construction, and irrigation work are undertaken by the camps. The maintenance of a prisoner is much cheaper even than that of a Russian worker. Dallin writes:

> Soviet authorities have never indicated precisely how great the cost differential is as between free and forced labour. It has been officially stated, however, that in 1932-33 'the cost of upkeep per prisoner was over 500 roubles a year'. During the same period the average wage in the Soviet Union, according to official statistics, amounted to 1,496 roubles a year. This differential, multiplied by the millions of prison workers and the years of work, is an important element of the government's industrialisation fund. General workers' wages rose 174 percent between 1926 and 1933 (due in part to the inflationary rise of prices); during the same period the cost of food per prisoner increased by only 90 percent.[60]

Notwithstanding its cheapness, the labour of prisoners, suiting as it does mainly manual labour not using modern techniques, can, because of this, be only secondary to the labour of 'free' workers. But seeing that Russia is in the process of primitive accumulation, that it suffers from a lack of capital much more than from a lack of labour power, which makes the life of a toiler in the eyes of

Russia's rulers much cheaper than that of a machine, slave labour is very widespread in the construction of factories, roads, etc. To conclude that slave labour will disappear with time is an oversimplification. A cataclysmic destruction of capital, which could result from a war, might cause the bureaucracy to make a new effort to tap its tremendous resources of cheap human lives. The annexation of backward areas with large populations (such as China) will bring the same result. The difficulties of raising the productivity of labour without improving the conditions of the workers, and the social danger the bureaucracy would face if it raised the self-confidence of the masses by improving their conditions, are also factors tending towards the increase of the number of slaves. Too many factors are involved in this question, however, to be able to predict whether the percentage of people in camps compared with the industrial proletariat will rise or not in the future.

The slave system, which as a prevailing mode was a special stage in human history, reappears in every exploitative society to one extent or another. Slavery existed in the Middle Ages when serfdom was the prevailing form of exploitation. It appeared in the US as part of an economic system which was capitalist par excellence. With the decline of capitalism, especially under conditions of war, the reappearance of slave labour is not excluded. Nazi Germany, which, Dallin writes, sent its experts at the beginning of the war to study forced labour in Russia, applied slave labour to construction works which needed mainly manual labour,[61] although of course the main products of the German war industry were produced by 'free' workers.

(8) The expropriation of the means of production from the peasantry

The October Revolution expropriated the big landlords, the church and the monarchy. The rural bourgeoisie—the kulaks—were not expropriated, and during the NEP not only did the old kulaks thrive, but many new ones rose out of the middle peasantry. The kulaks, together with the private merchants, exploited the rural poor. In addition, because industrial production lagged so far behind the demand, 'scissors' opened between the prices of industrial and agricultural goods, to the disadvantage of the agriculturists. Private capitalism continued to rule agriculture until 1928.

Collectivisation changed the situation fundamentally. Here we shall not discuss how the collectivisation influenced the class differentiation *among* the agriculturists, but shall deal with only the following question: what is the *total* balance of incomes agriculture receives as the result of the collectivisation? The most important factor to deal with in answering this question is the influence collectivisation had on the state's cut out of agriculture, which takes the form of obligatory deliveries: taxes, payment for work done by Machine Tractor Stations (MTS) and government flour mills.

Year	Total yield (million centners)		Obligatory Deliveries			Retained by agriculturists after obligatory deliveries	Index
	Gross	Net[62]	quantity (million centners)	Gross	Net		
1927/28	728.0	605.9	112.2	15.4	18.5	493.7	100.0
1932/33	698.7	570.1	185.2	26.5	32.5	384.9	77.9
1933/34	808.2	677.1	228.7	28.3	33.8	448.4	90.8
1934/35	804.6	669.5	226.6	28.1	33.8	442.9	89.7
1935/36	810.9	677.5	249.3	30.7	36.8	428.2	86.7
1936/37	744.6	612.5	260.0	34.9	24.4	352.5	70.1

Thus from 1927/28 till 1936/37 the quantity of obligatory deliveries taken by the state from agriculture rose from 112.2 million centners to 260 million (ie by 131.8 percent). The portion of the obligatory deliveries in the gross yield of agriculture rose from 15.4 percent to 34.9 percent, and its portion in the net yield from 18.5 percent to 42.4 percent.

Nearly half the obligatory deliveries consist of direct agricultural taxes while the remainder is made up of payment for the services of MTS and flour mills, over which the government has a complete monopoly.

It is interesting to note that in his book *The Agrarian Question in Russia at the End of the Nineteenth Century* (1908) Lenin writes:

> The horseless and one-horse peasants [ie the very poor peasants] pay in the form of taxes *one seventh and one tenth* respectively of their *gross* expenditure. It is doubtful whether serf dues were as high as that.[63]

The agricultural toilers in the 'Socialist Fatherland' pay much more than that!

Although the total quantity of products retained by the agriculturists in 1936/37 was lower than in 1927/28 (352.5 million centners and 493.7 million centners respectively) the quantity per household did not decline, and per capita of agricultural population even rose. This happened because the number of households declined from 25 million in 1927/28 to 20.4 million in 1936/37, ie by 24 percent, and the agricultural population decreased from 122.4 million to 78.6 million, ie a decline of 35.8 percent.[64]

Collectivisation not only transformed those who came into industry into proletarians, but also those who remained in agriculture. The overwhelming majority of agriculturists are in reality, if not in theory, people who do not own means of production—they are compelled to work an ever increasing number of days on the kolkhozes for very low payment. The constant rise in the number of days that every household works in the kolkhoz compared with the quantity of grain per household remaining to it after the obligatory deliveries is shown in the following table:

Year	Average number of 'labour days'[65] per household		Grain retained per household after obligatory deliveries	
	Number	Index	Centners	Index
1932	257	100.0	15.8	100.0
1933	315	122.5	19.3	122.1
1934	354	133.4	20.1	127.2
1935	378	147.1	20.5	129.7
1936	393	152.8	17.3	109.5

To add to the difficulties of the poor agriculturists, not everyone has to give the same number of labour days. The higher stratum of kolkhozniki give far fewer labour days than the poor kolkhozniki. The results of their labours, however, are in inverse proportion to the time contributed.

We should have less justification in calling the Russian agriculturists of today owners of the means of production than the serfs of the 19th century.

Collectivisation has resulted in the freeing of agricultural products for the needs of industrial development, the 'freeing' of the peasantry from the means of production, the transformation of a section of them into reserves of labour power for industry, and the transformation of the rest into semi-workers, semi-peasants, semi-serfs in the kolkhozes.

Similar general results, even though different in some important particulars, were achieved by the English bourgeoisie in the 16th and 17th centuries with the eviction of the peasantry from the land. Marx called this process 'primitive accumulation'.[66] He wrote, 'The history of this…is written in the annals of mankind in letters of blood and fire'.[67]

Much more blood flowed during the primitive accumulation in Russia than in Britain. Stalin accomplished in a few hundred days what it took Britain a few hundred years to do. The scale on which he did it and the success with which he carried it out completely dwarfs the actions of the Duchess of Sutherland. They bear stern witness to the superiority of modern industrial economy concentrated in the hands of the state, under the direction of a ruthless bureaucracy.

Engels made a prognosis about the future of primitive accumulation in Russia which has been completely realised, although in different circumstances than he ever imagined. In a letter to Danielson of 24 February 1893 he wrote:

> The circumstance of Russia being the *last* country seized upon by the capitalist *grande industrie*, and at the same time the country with by far the *largest peasant population*, are such as must render the *bouleversement* [upheaval] caused by this economic change more acute than it has been anywhere else. The process of replacing some 500,000 pemeschchiki [landowners] and some 80 million peasants by a new class of *bourgeois* landed proprietors cannot be carried out but under fearful sufferings and convulsions. But history is about the most cruel of all goddesses, and she leads her triumphal car over heaps of corpses, not only in war, but also in 'peaceful' economic development.[68]

Till 1928 the Stalinist bureaucracy vacillated between the Russian proletariat and bourgeoisie—among whom the kulaks played an important part. With the collectivisation the struggle became one between the bureaucracy and the kulaks over the surplus product created by the agricultural toilers. He who controls the surplus product is the ruling class.

(9) The transformation of money into money-capital: an important symptom of the system

In another place in this document we deal with the scope of state bonds,[69] which are the main form of money-capital in the hands of individuals. The fact that the relations of production prevailing in Russia make place for the appearance of a form of property which is traditionally capitalist, and which allows for the appropriation of surplus value, is an important symptom of these relations of production themselves. Changes in the quantity of state bonds and deposits in savings banks held by individuals can serve as a barometer of changes in the relations of production:

| Date | Total national debt (billion roubles) | Part owing to individuals | | Personal deposits in savings banks (billion roubles) | Total personal savings (billion roubles) |
		Sum (billion roubles)	Percentage		
1928	1.2	0.4	33.0	0.2	0.6
1933	9.8	5.4	55.7	1.0	6.4
1936	22.1	14.9	67.5	2.5	17.4
1937	26.3	18.0	68.5	3.5	21.5
1938	28.5	20.9	73.3	4.5	25.4
1941	46.9				
1943	73.6				
1944	99.6				

We have no figures showing the distribution of the national debt between individuals and institutions (factories, kolkhozes, etc) since the outbreak of the Second World War. But according to the minister of finance, Zverev, Russian citizens subscribed 76 billion roubles in the war years to state bonds. If we add to this the state bonds owned by individuals before the war, and their deposits in the banks, we should not be overestimating to say that the total personal savings today amount to 100 billion roubles. In 1928 they amounted to 0.6 billion (a considerable part of which was owned by Nep Men), in 1938 to 25.4 billion— today they amount to 100 billion!

The Five-Year Plan appeared as a turning point between the period that opened up in 1917-18, when all private debts on sums of more than 10,000 roubles were abolished, and the beginning of the period when Soviet millionaires appeared.[70]

(10) The introduction of the turnover tax

The most important source of state income is the turnover tax, which is an indirect tax. Its rate is fixed not by being added to the existing selling price, but by being included in it in advance. Thus for instance a turnover tax of 20 percent means that the tax makes up 20 percent of the selling price. If the selling price of a commodity is 100 roubles, the government will take 20 roubles of this. This is an addiion of 20 roubles over and above the cost of production, the profit of the industrial enterprise, the trading organisation, etc, which comes to 80 roubles. An addition of 20 roubles to 80 is an addition of 25 percent. A turnover tax of 30 percent raises the price by 42.8 percent, a turnover tax of 40 percent by 66.7 percent, a turnover tax of 50 percent by 100 percent, a turnover tax of 60 percent by 150 percent, a turnover tax of 75 percent by 300 percent, a turnover tax of 80 percent by 400 percent, a turnover tax of 90 percent by 900 percent.

The rate of turnover tax rose sharply with the introduction of the Five-Year Plans, as the following table shows:

Year	Gross retail turnover (billion roubles)	Turnover tax (billion roubles)	Net retail turnover (billion roubles)	Rate of turnover tax (percent)	Turnover tax as percentage of net retail turnover
1928	15.5	2.4	13.2	15.5	17.9
1932	40.4	19.5	20.9	48.2	93.6
1935	81.7	52.0	29.7	63.6	175.3
1938	138.6	80.4	58.2	58.1	138.2
1940	174.5	105.9	68.7	60.7	154.2

If we assumed that the turnover tax placed an equal burden on all the commodities produced,[71] that the industrial enterprises themselves did not get any profits directly from the sale of their products, that there were no other costs of production except wages, and that there were no other taxes except the turnover tax, the rate of exploitation of the workers would then have been *at least* equal to the ratio of the turnover tax to the net retail turnover, ie in 1940 154.2 percent. In reality, of course, it is very much higher than this.

(11) From a workers' state with bureaucratic deformations to the complete liberation of the bureaucracy from popular control

Because of the backwardness and isolation of Russia, the workers' state there never corresponded with the conception of the dictatorship of the proletariat elaborated by Lenin in *State and Revolution*. In the very first years after October Lenin constantly repeated this. Thus, for instance, in the Eighth Soviet Congress, 30 December 1920, he said:

> From our party programme it follows that our state is a workers' state with bureaucratic deformations. We have to paste this—how shall we call it?—sorry label on it. That it the reality of the transition!... Our present state is such that the organised proletariat must defend itself and we must utilise these workers' organisations for the defence of the workers against their state and for the defence of the state by the workers.

Two years later his tone became even more admonitory. At the Eleventh Party Conference on 29 March 1922 he said:

> This mass of bureaucrats—who is leading whom? The 4,700 responsible communists the mass of bureaucrats, or the other way around? I do not believe you can say that the communists are leading this mass. To put it honestly, they are not the leaders, but the led. Something has happened here that recalls the historical events we heard of in our childhood. We were taught: once upon a time a certain people conquered the country of another people and subjected this people. The conquering people was the victor and the people whose country was conquered was the vanquished. That's obvious. But what happens with the culture of these peoples? Now the question is not so simple. If the culture of the victorious people is higher than that of the vanquished, it imposes its culture on the vanquished. But if the contrary is the case, the vanquished people imposes its culture on the victor. Has not something similar happened in the capital of the RSFSR? Have not the 4,700 communists in this city (almost a whole division, and only the very best comrades) been vanquished by an alien culture? This might give rise to the impression that the conquered possessed a higher culture. Nothing of the kind. Their culture was miserable, paltry, but nevertheless higher than that of our communist militants, inasmuch as they are capable of managing.

This strengthening of the bureaucracy which brought about the partial victory of Stalin in 1923 led at a certain point to a change in the quality of the state—from a workers' state with bureaucratic deformations to a bureaucratic state independent of the workers and oppressing them. A survey of the change will be facilitated if we sketch the main lines of this development in a basic part of the state apparatus—the army. We have chosen this sector, as 'the army is a copy of society and suffers from all its diseases, usually at a higher temperature'.[72]

The organisation and structure of the army reflect the relations of production and the productive forces of society. The Red Army reflected the backwardness of the productive forces in Russia, the low cultural level, the fact that the proletariat was a small minority of the population, etc. It was therefore never a militia, but was built from the beginning as a compromise between the militia and the regular army, the emphasis being on the latter. Smilga clearly explained at the Tenth Congress of the Bolshevik Party why a militia was impossible in Russia. He said:

The militia system, of which the basic characteristic is the territorial principle, is faced with an insuperable obstacle in the path of its introduction in Russia. Given the numerically weak proletariat in Russia, we would not be able to ensure proletarian guidance in these units. Even greater objections to the introduction of the militia system arise from the viewpoint of strategy. With the weakness of our railroad system, we should not be able, in case of war, to concentrate forces on the threatened directions... Furthermore, the experience of the Civil War has incontrovertibly shown that territorial formations *were entirely unsuitable*, and that the soldiers deserted. Therefore, the return to this organisational form would be a crude, unjustifiable error.[73]

The resolution at the Tenth Congress against building the Red Army in the pattern of a militia was passed in this spirit.

The material and cultural backwardness of Russia revealed itself also in the relations between soldiers and officers.

From the beginning the Bolsheviks found it an unavoidable necessity to appoint ex-Tsarist officers, notwithstanding their previous agitation for the substitution of all appointed officers by those elected by the soldiers. It was impossible to wage the war against the White armies without tried commanders, and if the choice were left to the soldiers they would not have elected ex-Tsarist officers.

From the beginning there was a struggle between the political commissars on the one hand, and the party collectives in the army on the other. This conflict intersected with another between centralist and decentralist tendencies. Out of these two struggles the political commissars emerged victorious over the party collectives, and the centre overcame the guerrilla tendencies. The intersection of these two struggles reflected a strengthening bureaucratic tendency in the army.

It did not take long before the ex-Tsarist officers began to influence the new commanders of proletarian origin. The Bolshevik Petrovsky states:

Within the walls of the military school we encountered the old-regime view of the peasant about the role of the officer with respect to the mass of the private soldiers. We had also noticed a certain trend to the upper class traditions of the cadets of the Tsarist military schools. Professionalism is the scourge which lashed morally officers of all times and in all countries... They [the Red Army commanders] became members of the new officers' group, and no agitation whatsoever, nor beautiful speeches about the necessity of contact with the masses would be of any avail. The conditions of existence are stronger than kind wishes.[74]

The commanders, the political commissars in the army, etc, began to use their position in the hierarchy in order to gain some material advantages. Trotsky attacked them severely for this. On one occasion he wrote to the Revolutionary Military Councils of fronts and armies condemning the use of government automobiles by those in authority for 'gay parties right before the eyes of the tired Red Army soldiers'. He spoke angrily about 'commanders dressed with extreme elegance, while the fighters go half-naked'. He pointed an indignant finger at drinking bouts which were organised by commanders and political commissars. And he concluded, 'Such acts cannot but provoke exasperation and discontent among the Red Army soldiers.' Trotsky's realistic revolutionary conception throws light on the difficulties of the situation. In the same letter he expounds his aim: 'Without setting the immediate goal of immediate elimination of all and sundry privileges in the army, to endeavour to reduce these systematically to the actually necessary minimum'.[75]

Despite these abuses, however, the existence of the Bolshevik Party with its cells in all sections of the army and the presence of Trotsky at its head, together with the revolutionary enthusiasm and self-sacrifice of the mass of soldiers, ensured the proletarian character of the Red Army at the time of the civil war.

With the partial victory of the bureaucracy in 1923 the debauchery of commanders, their bourgeoisification, their commandeering approach to the soldiers, was transformed from a limited and exceptional phenomenon to a normal one. A further factor began to appear at this stage which weakened the control over the commanders. The central positions in the party cells in the different units began to be occupied by the commanders themselves. Thus the Political Department of the Republic notes in the autumn of 1926 that two thirds of all positions in the party apparatus in the army were in the hands of commanders. The same people, therefore, who commanded the soldiers had simultaneously to be the political leaders of their defence against these very commanders.

Even so, we still cannot speak of an *absolutely independent* officers' caste. We shall give three facts to prove this:
(1) The living conditions of the commanders were arduous and not in any fundamental different from that of the soldiers. Thus White writes:

In 1925 only 30 percent of the commanding personnel were housed in a manner regarded by Frunze at all as tolerable. Seventy percent had housing facilities below that level. Frunze spoke of various localities where several commanders with their families had only one room among them. In other words, each family had only a part of a room at its disposal.

The reserve commanders, when called for retraining outside of the ranks of the army, were remunerated for their work on a basis which would not look attractive to a Chinese coolie. Those employed or belonging to the peasantry were paid five kopeks per hour, while the unemployed among them were paid nine kopeks per hour, for the time they were engaged in their studies.[76]

Wollenberg, who was a commander in the Red Army, writes:

In 1924 the pay of a corps-commander was 150 roubles a month, corresponding to that earned by a well-paid metal worker. It was thus 25 roubles a month below the 'party maximum', ie the largest monthly salary that a party member was allowed to accept in those days... There was at that time no special officers' mess. The meals of officers and men were prepared in the same kitchens. Communist officers seldom wore the badges of the rank when off duty, and frequently dispensed with them even when on duty. At that time the Red Army acknowledged a relationship of superior and subordinate only during the performance of military duty, and in any case every soldier knew his commanding officer with or without badges of rank.

Officers' servants were abolished.[77]

(2) The soldiers were allowed to and did protest against their commanders. Their complaints were submitted to the Military Prosecutor's Office. The number of such complaints was: in 1925 (average per month) 1,892; in 1926 1,923; in 1927 2,082.[78]

(3) Wollenberg, who was at that time in the Red Army, says that only in 1931-33 did the 'natural and free relations between officers and men' disappear. He brings a number of facts to prove this.

White, on the basis of numerous data, came to the same conclusion, although he puts the turning point a little earlier—the Army Statutes of 1928. He writes that this 'was the real dividing line, and…what followed was the development of a trend already well established'.[79] The statutes made the army command a life career, and White justifiably speaks of them as the 'Magna Carta of the commanding personnel', 'something akin to the Petrine Table of ranks'.[80]

Already in 1929 there began the 'gradual transformation of Red Army Houses into Officers' Clubs'.[81] The officers' salaries started rising while the soldiers' continued to be a mere pittance.

	1934 (roubles)	1939 (roubles)	Percent increase
Platoon commander	260	625	240
Company commander	285	750	263
Battalion commander	335	850	254
Regimental commander	400	1,200	300
Division commander	475	1,600	337
Corps commander	550	2,000	364

In this period the value of the rouble declined very sharply, but this affected the officers much less than the ordinary citizens. One of the reasons for this was the establishment for the officers of the Voentorg, a co-operative consumers' system. It created retail shops, organised communal feeding, barber shops, laundries, and tailoring and bootmaking establishments. In 1935 it had 1,700 stores, about 1,000 industrial establishments, and 800 restaurants with a turnover of one and a half billion roubles.[82]

Special houses with all conveniences were built for the officers. A decree of 22 September 1935 restored the personnel ranks: lieutenant, captain, major, colonel, brigadier, marshal, etc. Permanent orderlies were assigned to the officers. Fraternisation between officers and soldiers was prohibited. The soldiers had to salute not only the commissioned officers, but also the non-commissioned officers (June 1940). To assure the permanence of the military hierarchy, even people in the reserves are divided into the same ranks as the army has, and they have the right to wear their military uniforms. Privates and non-commissioned officers have to give up their seats to officers in buses, tubes and trams. The disciplinary rights of the officers go further than any army, except perhaps the Prussian, has known. V Ulrich, who was president of the Moscow frame-up, describes the character of the disciplinary statutes of 12 October 1940 in these words:

> The disciplinary statutes considerably extend the right of commanders as regards the use of force and firearms. Comradely relations between soldiers and officers are no more. The 'hail fellow well met' spirit in the relationships between a commander and a subordinate can have no place in the Red Army. Discussion of any kind is absolutely prohibited among the subordinates.[83]

An article in *Pravda* of 6 October 1940 throws light on another aspect of these statutes:

> Grievances may be introduced only personally and individually. Submission of group grievance for others is prohibited. No more group declarations, no more joint discussions—whether concerning an order or bad food, or any other topic—all this comes under the heading of 'insubordination' and it a soldier may be shot on the spot without so much as a court-martial, hearing or investigation, if a superior officer solely and personally so decides.[84]

The hierarchy in the army has reached a stage where the officers are absolutely independent of the soldiers.

Again the Five-Year Plan marks the turning point. Then the organisation and structure of the army began to change fundamentally. From a workers' army with bureaucratic deformations it became the armed body of the bureaucracy as a ruling class.

(12) Why the Five-Year Plan signifies the transformation of the bureaucracy into a ruling class

We have seen that the inauguration of the Five-Year Plan has been a turning point in the development of the relations of distribution, in the relations between accumulation and consumption, between the productivity of labour and the standard of living of the workers, in the control over production, in the legal rights of the workers, in the institution of forced labour, in the relation of agriculturists to the means of production, in the function of money as money capital, in the tremendous swelling of the turnover tax and, finally, in the structure and organisation of the army, which is a main sector of the state machine. The reality of industrialisation and collectivisation turned out to be in absolute contradiction to the hopes the masses had in them, and even to the illusions which the bureaucracy themselves held. They thought the Five-Year Plans would take Russia many strides forward to the building of socialism. This is not the first time in history that the results of human actions are in outright contradiction to the wishes and hopes of the actors themselves.

Why was the First Five-Year Plan such a turning point?

For the first time the bureaucracy now sought the rapid creation of the proletariat and accumulation of capital, in other words, as quickly as possible to realise the historical mission of the bourgeoisie. A quick accumulation of capital on the basis of a low level of production, of a small national income per capita, must put a burdensome pressure on the consumption of the masses, on their standard of living. Under such conditions the bureaucracy, transformed into a personification of capital, for whom the accumulation of capital is the be-all and end-all, must get rid of all remnants of workers' control, must substitute conviction in the labour process by coercion, must atomise the working class, must totalitarianise all social-political life. It is obvious that the bureaucracy, which became necessary in the process of capital accumulation, and which became the oppressor of the workers, would not be tardy in making use of its social supremacy in the relations of production in order to gain advantages in the relations of distribution. Thus industrialisation and a technical revolution in agriculture ('collectivisation') in a backward country under conditions of siege transforms the bureaucracy from a layer which is under the direct and indirect pressure and control of the proletariat, into a ruling class, into a manager of 'the general business of society: the direction of labour, affairs of state, justice, science, art and so forth'.

Dialectical historical development, full of contradictions and surprises, brought it about that the first step the bureaucracy took with the subjective intention of hastening the building of 'socialism in one country' became the foundation of the building of state capitalism.

Chapter 5: The common and different features of state capitalism and a workers' state

None of the Marxist theoreticians doubted that if the concentration of capital could reach such a stage that one capitalist, a collective of capitalists or the state concentrated the total national capital in its hands, while competition on the world market continued, such an economy would still be a capitalist economy. At the same time, *all* the Marxist theoreticians emphasised that long before the concentration of capital could reach such a level either the antagonism between the proletariat and the bourgeoisie would bring about a victorious socialist revolution, or the antagonisms between the capitalist states would drive them into such a destructive imperialist war that society would totally decline. While state capitalism is possible *theoretically* it is indubitable that individual capitalism through evolutionary development will in reality never arrive at the concentration of the entire capital in one hand. Trotsky clearly explained why this would not happen:

> Theoretically, to be sure, it is possible to conceive a situation in which the bourgeoisie as a whole constitutes itself a stock company which, by means of its state, administers the whole national economy. The economic laws of such a regime

would present no mysteries. A single capitalist, as is well known, receives in the form of profit, not that part of the surplus value which is directly created by the workers of his own enterprise, but a share of the combined surplus value created throughout the country proportionate to the amount of his own capital. Under an integral 'state capitalism', this law of the equal rate of profit would be realised, not by devious routes—that is, competition among different capitals—but immediately and directly through state bookkeeping. Such a regime never existed, however, and, because of profound contradictions among the proprietors themselves, never will exist—the more so since, in its quality of universal repository of capitalist property, the state would be too tempting an object for social revolution.[85]

The last two factors—the 'contradictions among the proprietors themselves', and the fact that if the state were the 'universal repository of capitalist property the state would be too tempting an object for social revolution'—explain why it is most improbable that traditional individual capitalism will develop gradually till it reaches 100 percent state capitalism. But do these two factors exclude the possibility that, after a ruling working class is overthrown, not traditional capitalism, but state capitalism, is restored? The revolutionary proletariat has already concentrated the means of production in the hands of one body, and so eliminated the first factor. As regards the second factor, in any case, any oppression and exploitation of the workers by the state makes the state a 'tempting…object for social revolution'; the political expropriation of the working class is thus identified with the economic expropriation.

The only argument that could be given against the possibility of the existence of state capitalism is that if the state becomes the repository of all capital the economy ceases to be capitalist; in other words, *theoretically* state capitalism is impossible. This argument, indeed, has been given by Burnham, Dwight MacDonald and others. Thus, for instance, Burnham writes:

> The term 'state capitalism' seems to be due to a misunderstanding… When the state owns only a part, and a minor part, of the economy, with the rest of the economy remaining capitalist private enterprise, we might correctly speak of 'state capitalism' in connection with that minor state-owned part: since, as we have seen, the economy remains in its balance capitalist and even the state-owned part may be directed primarily to the benefit of the capitalist party. But the 'capitalism' in 'state capitalism' is derived not from the state-controlled part. When the latter disappears, or becomes negligible, then the capitalism has disappeared. There is no paradox in saying that ten times 10 percent state capitalism, far from equalling 100 percent capitalism, equals 0 percent capitalism. The multiplication is of state, not of capitalism. Though the mathematics would be much more complex, it would be nearer an analogy to say that, just as 10 percent state capitalist economy equals only 90 percent capitalist economy, so 100 percent (or even 80 percent or 70 percent) state economy would have eliminated capitalism altogether.[86]

Of course if state capitalism is a contradiction in terms, the name of such a society in which the competition on the world market, commodity production, wage labour, etc prevail will be quite arbitrarily chosen. One may call it managerial society, or bureaucratic collectivism, arbitrarily determining its laws. Bruno R tells us that bureaucratic collectivism leads automatically to communism. Burnham tells us that in managerial society production will rise uninterruptedly (pp115-116), that a capitalist crisis of overproduction will not break out (p114), that unemployment will never exist, that managerial society will develop the backward countries (pp154-155), that it will become more and more democratic (pp145-147), and because of all this it receives the enthusiastic support of the masses (p160). As against this, Shachtman tells us that bureaucratic collectivism is barbarism.

If Adam Smith came to life today, he would have found great difficulty in discovering the similarity between the economy of, let us say, Nazi Germany—with its tremendous monopoly organisations, state regulation of the distribution of raw materials, state purchase of more than half the national product, state regulation of the labour market, etc—and the manufacture of the 19th century, based on the employment of a few or at most a few score workers, free competition between the enterprises, the active participation of the capitalists in organising production, the non-existence of the capitalist crisis of overproduction, etc. A perusal of the gradual development of capitalism from one stage to the next makes it easier to see what is common to both economies, and that the laws of both are capitalist. The difference between the Russian economy and the Nazi economy is much smaller than the difference between the Nazi economy and the economy of Adam Smith's time. It is only the absence of the gradualness of development through the stage of monopoly capitalism which makes it difficult to grasp the similarities and differences between the Russian economy and traditional monopoly capitalism, and the dissimilarity of state capitalism and traditional capitalism on the one hand, and similarity of state capitalism and a workers' state on the other.

Seeing that state capitalism is the extreme theoretical limit which capitalism can reach, it necessarily is the furthest away from traditional capitalism. It is the negation of capitalism on the basis of capitalism itself. And at the same time, seeing that a workers' state is the lowest stage of the new socialist society, it must necessarily have many features in common with state capitalism. What distinguishes between them categorically is the *fundamental*, the *essential* difference between the capitalist system and the socialist system. The comparison of state and traditional capitalism on the one hand, and a workers' state on the other, will show that state capitalism is a transition stage to socialism, this side of the socialist revolution, while a workers' state is a transition stage to socialism the other side of the socialist revolution.

If one said that this abstract analysis is far from the concrete Russian reality, we would answer with Lenin's excellent formulation about the relation between abstraction and contemplation (taken from the posthumous papers of Lenin):

> By proceeding from the concrete to the abstract, thought...provided it is correct...*does not depart from the truth but comes closer to it*. The abstraction of matter, of natural law, the abstraction of value, etc...in short, all scientific abstractions mirror nature more profoundly, more completely. From vivid contemplation to abstract thinking and from this to practice...that is the dialectical road to the knowledge of truth.

(1) State capitalism: a partial negation of capitalism

The state as a regulator of economic functions, even if it is not yet the repository of the means of production, partially negates the law of value.[87]

According to the law of value, the regulation of economic functions takes place in an anarchical way, and the relations between people therefore appear, not as direct, crystal-clear relations, but as indirect, mystical relations. The law of value determines the exchange relations between the different branches. Now, the law of value holds absolute sway only under conditions of free competition, when there is a free movement of capital, commodities and labour power. Therefore, even the most elementary forms of monopolist organisation already partially negate the law of value. When the state regulates the allocation of capital and labour power, the price of commodities, etc, it is most certainly a partial negation of capitalism. This is even more the case when the state becomes an important buyer of products. On this question Lenin said:

> When capitalists work for the defence, ie for the government, it is obviously no more 'pure' capitalism—it is a special form of national economy. Pure capitalism means commodity production. Commodity production means work for an *uncertain* and free market. But the capitalist 'working' for the defence does not work for the market at all—he fills the orders of the government, and money is invariably advanced to him by the treasury.[88]

Banking capital receives a social form long before industrial capital. As Marx noted, 'The banking system presents indeed the form of common bookkeeping and distribution of means of production on a social scale, but only the form'.[89]

This is even more the case when the state becomes the main field of investment for money-capital. It reaches its extreme when the capitalist state takes the banking system into its own hands.

Capitalist private property is also partially negated. While under the capitalism of free competition, the capitalist was the absolute owner of a private property, under monopoly capitalism, and especially its higher stage, state capitalism, the individual capitalist no longer has absolute ownership of the means of production. In the share companies capital becomes 'directly endowed with the form of social capital… It is the abolition of capital as private property within the boundaries of capitalist production itself'.[90]

This is more the case when the state regulates the stream of capital. In this case private property, as endowed with freedom of contract, is abolished. Private capital disappears, while individual appropriation continues. This reaches its extreme when the state takes the means of production into its own hands. In this case the bondholder as an individual has no control whatsoever over his part of the social capital.

State capitalism is a partial negation of labour power as a commodity. In order that labour power appear as a 'pure' commodity in the market, two conditions are necessary: first of all that the worker be 'free' of the means of production; and secondly, that he be free of any legal impediments to selling his labour power. Under state regulation of the labour market, and in its most extreme form, under fascism, the worker ceases to be free to sell his labour power. If the state becomes the actual possessor of the means of production, then the choice of employer is entirely abolished, while the choice of place of work is much restricted. And if state capitalism is accompanied by a freezing of the labour power, compulsory mobilisation, etc, this freedom is even more negated.

The partial negation of the law of value does not free the economy from this law but, on the contrary, subordinates it as a whole even more. The difference is only in the form in which the law of value expresses itself. When one monopoly increases its rate of profit as against other industries, it simply increases its part in the total surplus value, or it increases the rate of exploitation of the workers at the same time, they being compelled to produce more surplus value. When one industry receives subsidies from the state and thus sells its commodities below its cost of production, it is only a transference of part of the cost of production from one branch to another. When the state regulates prices, the point of departure is the cost of production. Under all these conditions wage labour continues its antagonism to capital, surplus value continues to be produced, and it continues to be converted into capital. The total labour time of society and the total labour time directed to the production of the necessities of life of the workers as a collective determine the rate of exploitation, the rate of surplus value. The total labour time allotted to the production of new means of production determines the rate of accumulation. While the price of every commodity does not exactly express its value (this did not happen, except accidentally, even under individual capitalism), the division of the total product of society among the different classes, as also its allotment to accumulation and consumption is dependent on the law of value. Where the state owns all the means of production and the workers are exploited while *internationally* world economy is disunited, this dependence receives its purest, most direct and absolute form.

(2) State capitalism: a transition to socialism

Everything that centralises the means of production centralises the working class. State capitalism brings this concentration to the highest stage possible under the capitalist system.

The partial negation of capitalism on the basis of capitalist relations of production means that the productive forces which develop in the bosom of the capitalist system so overgrow it that the capitalist class is compelled to use 'socialist' measures, and manipulate them in its own interests: 'In spite of themselves, the capitalists are dragged, as it were, into a new social order, a transitional social order from complete free competition to complete socialisation'.[91]

The productive forces are too strong for capitalism, and 'socialist' elements therefore enter into the economy (Engels called this 'the invading socialist society'). *But they are subordinated to the interests of the preservation of capitalism.* In a workers' state, because of the insufficiently developed productive forces for socialism, the working class is compelled to use capitalist measures (eg the capitalist law applied to distribution) in the interests of building socialism.

State capitalism and a workers' state are two stages in the transition period from capitalism to socialism. State capitalism is the extreme opposite of socialism—they are symmetrically opposed, and they are dialectically united to one another.

Whereas under state capitalism wage labour is partially negated in that the worker is not free to choose his employer, under conditions of the dictatorship of the proletariat wage labour is partially negated from the angle that the workers as a collective cease to be 'free' of the means of production. At the same time, wage labour ceases to be a commodity. The content of the 'selling' of labour power is different from that of the selling of labour power under capitalism, because under a workers' state the workers as individuals do not sell their labour power but put it at their own service as a collective. As a commodity is something given in exchange by one to another, this ceases really to be one—as the exchange takes place here between the workers as individuals and these same workers as a collective. Whereas state capitalism means the fusion of the unions with the state until they are ultimately annulled as unions, the workers' state raises the influence of the trade unions to the maximum. Whereas state capitalism signifies historically the totalitarianism of the state, a workers' state gives the highest degree of democracy society has ever known. State capitalism signifies the extreme subjugation of the working class by the capitalist class which controls the means of production. A workers' state means the suppression of the capitalist by the working class which controls the means of production.

Lenin clearly formulated the relation between state capitalism and socialism in these words:

> The measure called 'war socialism' by the German Plekhanovs (Scheidemann, Lensch and others) is in reality wartime state monopoly capitalism. Or to speak more plainly and clearly, it is military penal labour for the workers, military defence of the capitalists' profits.
>
> But try and substitute for the Junker-capitalist, for the landowner-capitalist state, a *revolutionary-democratic* state, ie such as would destroy *all* privileges in a revolutionary way without being afraid of introducing in a revolutionary way the fullest possible democracy—and you shall see that, in a truly revolutionary-democratic state, state monopoly capitalism inevitably and unavoidably means progress towards socialism...
>
> For socialism is nothing but the next step forward from state capitalist monopoly. In other words, socialism is nothing but state capitalist monopoly *made to benefit the whole people*; by this token it *ceases* to be capitalist monopoly.[92]

Bukharin, who dealt extensively with the question of state capitalism, clearly formulated the relation between state capitalism and the dictatorship of the proletariat in these words:

In the system of state capitalism the economic subject is the *capitalist state*, the collective capitalist. In the dictatorship of the proletariat, the economic subject is the *proletarian* state, the collectively organised working class, 'the proletariat organised as the state power'. Under state capitalism, the production process is that of the production of surplus value which falls into the hands of the capitalist class, with the tendencies to transform this value into surplus product.

Under the dictatorship of the proletariat the production process is a means for the planned satisfaction of social needs. The system of state capitalism is the completest form of exploitation of the masses by a handful of oligarchs. The system of the dictatorship of the proletariat makes any exploitation whatsoever altogether unthinkable, as it transforms collective capitalist property and its private capitalist form into collective proletarian 'property'! Thus according to content, notwithstanding their formal similarity, they are diametrical opposites. This antagonism determines also the antagonism of all the functions of the systems under discussion, even if formally they are similar. Thus, for instance, the general labour duty in the system of state capitalism means the enslavement of the working class; as against this, in the system of the dictatorship of the proletariat it is nothing but the self-organisation of labour by the masses; in the former case the mobilisation of industry is the strengthening of the power of the bourgeoisie and the strengthening of the capitalist regime, while in the latter it is the strengthening of socialism. All the forms of state compulsion represent under the state capitalist structure a pressure which will assure, broaden and deepen the process of exploitation, while state compulsion under the dictatorship of the proletariat represents a method of building up communist society. In short, the functional contradictoriness of the formally similar phenomena is here wholly determined by the functional contradictoriness of the systems of organisation, by their contradictory class characteristics.[93]

Much earlier than Lenin or Bukharin fundamentally the same ideas were put forward by Engels in *Anti-Dühring*:

The more productive forces it [the state] takes over, the more it becomes the real collective body of all the capitalists, the more citizens it exploits. The workers remain wage-earners, proletarians. The capitalist relationship is not abolished; it is rather pushed to an extreme. But at this extreme it changes into its opposite. State ownership of the productive forces is not the solution of the conflict, but it contains within itself the formal means, the handle to the solution.[94]

Chapter 6: A further consideration of Stalinist society, economy and politics

(1) The Stalinist bureaucracy is a class

If we examine the definitions of a social class given by different Marxist theoreticians, we shall find that according to all of them we should have to call the Stalinist bureaucracy a class. Thus, for instance, Lenin writes:

> Classes are large groups of people which differ from each other by the place they occupy in a historically definite system of production, by their relation (in most cases fixed and formulated in laws) to the means of production, by their role in the social organisation of labour, and, consequently, by the dimensions and method of acquiring the share of social wealth that they obtain. Classes are groups of people one of which may appropriate the labour of another owing to the different places they occupy in the definite system of social economy.[95]

Bukharin gives a very similar definition:

> A social class...is the aggregate of persons *playing the same part in production, standing in the same relation toward other persons in the production process, these relations being also in things* (instruments of labour).[96]

If there is any doubt left about whether the Stalinist bureaucracy is a class or not, we need to peruse Engels' analysis of the merchant class which did not even take a *direct* part in the process of production. He writes:

> A third division of labour was added by civilisation: it created a class that did not take part in production, but occupied itself merely with the exchange of products—the merchants. All former attempts at class formation were exclusively concerned with production. They divided the producers into directors and directed, or into producers on a more or less extensive scale. But here a class appears for the first time that captures the control of production in general and subjugates the producers to its rule, without taking the least part in production. A class that makes itself the indispensable mediator between two producers and exploits them both under the pretext of saving them the trouble and risk of exchange, of extending the markets of their products to distant regions, and of thus becoming the most useful class in society: a class of parasites, genuine social ichneumons, that skim the cream of production at home and abroad as a reward for very insignificant services; that rapidly amass enormous wealth and gain social influence accordingly; that for this reason reap ever new honours and ever greater control of production during the period of civilisation, until they at last bring to light a product of their own—periodical crises in industry.[97]

In the light of this definition it is clear why Marx could designate the priests, lawyers, etc as 'ideological classes', as the classes which have, according to Bukharin's apt expression, a class monopoly over the 'means of mental production'.

We think it would be wrong to call the Stalinist bureaucracy a caste for the following reasons: While a class is a group of people who have a definite place in the process of production, a caste is a judicial-political group. The members of a caste can be members of different classes, or in one class there can be members of different castes. A caste is the outcome of the relative immobility of the economy, of the division of labour and the productive forces. The Stalinist bureaucracy was transformed into a ruling class on the crest of the *dynamism* of the economy.

(2) The Stalinist bureaucracy: the extreme and pure personification of capital

Marx wrote:

> Except as personified capital, the capitalist has no historical value, and no right to that historical existence... But, so far as he is personified in capital, it is not values in use and the enjoyment of them but exchange value and its augmentation that spurs him into action. Fanatically bent on making value expand itself, he ruthlessly forces the human race to produce for production's sake... So far, therefore, as his actions are a mere function of capital—endowed as capital is, in his person, with consciousness and a will—his own private consumption is a robbery perpetrated on accumulation... Therefore save, save, save, ie reconvert the greatest possible portion of surplus value, or surplus product into capital! Accumulation for accumulation's sake, production for production's sake.[98]

The two functions of the extraction of surplus value and its transformation into capital, which are fundamental to capitalism, become separated with the separation of control and management. While the function of management is to extract the surplus value from the workers, control directs its transformation into capital. For capitalist economy actually these two functions alone are necessary; the bondholders appear more and more only as consumers of a certain part of the surplus value. The function of the consumption of a part of the surplus product by the exploiters is not specific to capitalism, but existed under all class systems. What is specific to capitalism is accumulation for accumulation's sake, with the object of standing up to competition.

In capitalist corporations the majority of the accumulation is institutional, the corporation financing itself internally, while the great majority of the dividends disbursed among the shareholders is used for consumption. Under state capitalism which evolves gradually from monopoly capitalism, the bondholders would appear mainly as consumers, while the state would appear as the accumulator.

The more the relative part of the surplus value devoted to accumulation increases as against the part consumed, the more purely does capitalism reveal itself. The more the relative weight of the factor of control increases as against that of bondholding, in other words, the more dividends are subordinated to the internal accumulation either of the corporation or of the state which owns the means of production, the more purely does capitalism reveal itself. If as a result of financial manipulations Morgan were to reduce the dividends disbursed among the hundreds of thousands of shareholders in the corporations he controls till they were completely eliminated as a factor, or if the state succeeded in doing this by cutting the rate of interest down to nothing (which in fact would mean the expropriation of the whole of the capitalist class), then capitalism would reveal itself in its purest form.

(Everyone knows that those who have the control of capital in their hands, who are the extreme personification of capital, do not deny themselves the pleasures of this world, but the significance of their spending is much smaller than that of accumulation, and of much less historical importance.)

We can therefore say that the Russian bureaucracy, 'owning' as it does the state and controlling the process of accumulation, is the personification of capital in its purest form.

At the same time, Russia is different from the norm, the concept, of state capitalism.

Every concept is the result of abstraction. And the manifold factors which in reality are active—the criss-crossing of different chains of causes, their clashing, etc—inevitably make it impossible for concept and reality to be congruent.[99]

The divergence of Russian economy from the state capitalism which evolves gradually, organically, from monopoly capitalism, does not relegate the question of the concept of state capitalism to unimportance. Far from this, it is of great importance to find that Russian economy approaches this concept much more closely than the state capitalism evolved gradually on a capitalist foundation could. The fact that the bureaucracy fulfils the tasks of the capitalist class, and by this transforms itself into a class, makes it the purest personification of this class. Although different from the capitalist class, it is at the same time nearest to its historical essence. *The Russian bureaucracy as a partial negation of the capitalist class makes it at the same time the truest personification of the historical mission of this class.*

To say that a bureaucratic class of bureaucratic collectivism or managerial society rules in Russia is to circumvent the cardinal issue—the capitalist relations of production prevailing in Russia. To say that Russia is state capitalist is perfectly correct, but not sufficient; it is necessary also to point out the differences in the juridical relations between the ruling class in Russia and that in state capitalism which evolved gradually from monopoly capitalism. Therefore the most precise name for Russian society is bureaucratic state capitalism.

(3) The form of appropriation of the bureaucracy is different to that of the bourgeoisie

In Russia the state appears as an employer, the bureaucrats as managers only. There is an absolute separation between the function of ownership and that of management. This, however, is only formally so. In essence ownership is in the hands of the bureaucrats as a collective—it is vested in the state of the bureaucracy. But the fact that the individual manager appears to lack all ownership of means of production, and that the appropriation of his part in the national income is in the form of a salary, may deceive one into believing that he receives only the reward for his labour power in the same way as the worker receives the reward for his labour power. The difference between the function of the worker and that of the manager is befogged because both are included under the heading of the social process of production; the labour of management is necessary for every process of social production, and as such has nothing to do with relations of exploitation. Antagonistic class relations may thus appear to be harmonious. The labour of the exploited and the labour of organising exploitation both appear as labour. The state appears to stand above the people, as personified ownership, while the bureaucrats, who direct the process of production and are therefore historically in essence the personification of capital, appear as labourers, and as such as producers of values by *their labour itself*.

But what appears superficially to be the case is not the objective truth.

The best way to make the difference clear between the 'labour' of the manager and that of the worker, to see the connection between the position of the former and the separation of the latter from the means of production, will be by comparing it with the relations between the workers in a capitalist enterprise, the manager of the same, and the owner of capital.

Let us assume that the owner of capital is not an active capitalist, but is only a lender of his capital, while the active capitalist does not own the capital. (For the sake of the question being dealt with here, it is not important that this separation should be complete.) Marx explains that in such a case the profit is divided into two parts: firstly, the interest; secondly, the 'profit of enterprise'. The interest seems to be a payment for the mere ownership of capital, and the profit of enterprise a payment for the functions which the active capitalist fulfils. Seeing that capitalist ownership is already represented by one man (the lender) and is expressed in one form of payment (interest), it seems that profit of enterprise has nothing to do with ownership and capitalist exploitation, as if it is simply the active capitalist's reward for his participation in the social process of production. Marx said:

> The industrial capitalist as differentiated from the owner of capital does not appear as a functionary of capital, but as a functionary separated from capital, as a simple agent of the labour process, as a labourer, and specifically as a wage-labourer.[100]

In this way the labour of exploitation and the exploited labour both appear as labour, as identical. The labour of exploitation is labour just as well as the labour which is exploited. It is the interest which represents the social form of capital, but it does so in a neutral and indifferent way. It is the profit of enterprise which represents the economic function of capital, but it does so in a way which takes no cognisance of the definite capitalist character of this function.[101]

Compared to the money-capitalist the industrial capitalist is a labourer, but a labouring capitalist, an exploiter of the labour of others. The wages which he claims and pockets for this labour amount exactly to the appropriated quantity of another's labour and depend directly upon the rate of exploitation of this labour, so far as he takes the trouble to assume the necessary burdens of exploitation.[102]

If in traditional capitalism the concentration of ownership in one person and the function of capitalist in another person befogs the real character of the latter, then in Russia the fact that the state is the official owner of the means of production while the bureaucrats 'only' manage production even more befogs the function of the bureaucrats as 'active producers'.

However, the difference between what the function of the bureaucracy and its remuneration seem to be on the one hand, and their real character on the other, is much deeper than the difference between what the profit of enterprise seems to be and is in reality.

Although interest seems to be *qualitatively* different from profit of enterprise, they are at the same time very similar to each other. In Russia the state which owns the means of production does not receive its part of the surplus value in the form of interest, and the bureaucracy does not receive its part in the form of profit of enterprise. There is therefore even more confusion between the character of the function of the bureaucracy as the extractor of surplus value from the workers, and its function simply as part of the social process of production (and as such as value producer). Seeing that the workers as well as the bureaucracy receive wages, one could easily believe on the one hand that the bureaucracy receives the reward for its value producing alone, and on the other hand—as a corollary to this—that the whole surplus value goes into the hands of the state.

It is clear, however, that the income of the bureaucracy has a direct ratio not to its work but to that of the workers. The quantity itself reveals the *qualitative* difference between it and the wages of the workers. Otherwise, to take a corresponding example in Britain, we should have to say that Lord McGowan, who receives the highest director's salary in Britain, does no more than sell his labour power. Besides this the state, which is the employer and appears to rise above all the people, is in reality the organisation of the bureaucracy as a collective.

What are the laws which determine the division of surplus value between the state and the bureaucrats as individuals?

While the *quantitative* division of the total value produced between wages and surplus value is dependent on two elements *qualitatively* different—labour power and capital—the division of the surplus value between the bureaucracy as a collective (the state) and individual bureaucrats cannot be based upon a qualitative difference between them. One cannot therefore speak of *exact*, general laws of the division of the surplus value between the state and the bureaucracy or the division of the latter part between the different bureaucrats. (Similarly one cannot speak about exact general laws regulating the distribution of profit between profit of enterprise and interest, or between the owners of different sorts of shares in capitalist countries.[103]) It would be wrong, however, to assume that absolute arbitrariness governs this division. The *tendencies* can be generalised. They are dependent on the pressure of world capitalism which demands an acceleration of accumulation, the material level which production has already reached, the tendency of decline of the rate of profit which relatively decreases the sources of accumulation, etc. Taking these circumstances into account, we can see why a constantly increasing part of the surplus value is accumulated. At the same time the bureaucracy which administers the process of capital accumulation does not overlook the gratification of its own personal desires, and the quantity of surplus value consumed by it rises absolutely. These two processes are possible only if there is a continuous increase in the rate of exploitation of the masses, and if new sources of capital are constantly found. Hence the process of primitive accumulation in which the Russian peasantry is pillaged, and the plunder of the countries of Eastern Europe.

(4) Relations of production and law

The overwhelming majority of the means of production in Russia is in the hands of the state. Bonds or other forms of legal claim cover so small a part of the means of production as to be of only minor significance.

Why is this so? Is there a tendency to introduce such a form of private claim on a large scale? Why is there a difference between the law of property prevailing in Russia and that in the rest of the world? We have already seen how Trotsky explains the fact that the bureaucracy did not restore capitalist private property. He says, 'It [the bureaucracy] continues to preserve state property only to the extent that it fears the proletariat.' But as we have said, the Russian proletariat has no contact with the form of property as such except as regards their relation to the state which is the repository of the means of production. It is therefore impossible for the proletariat, after losing control over the state and instead being oppressed by it, to keep control over the form of property.

Trotsky's explanation of the non-emergence of shares and bonds being unsatisfactory—and the war experience during which the bureaucracy was tremendously strengthened confirms this—we are still left with the same question: why does the bureaucracy not assure the permanent right to surplus value and the right of testament by issuing shares and bonds on a large scale? In order to give the answer to this question let us analyse the relationship between the relations of production and the law of property.

Law is based on the economy. Property relations are the juridical expressions of relations of production. But there is no exact and absolute parallelism between the relations of production and the development of law, in the same way as there is no exact and absolute parallelism between the economic basis and the other elements of the superstructure. The reason for this is that law does not express the relations of production directly, but indirectly. If it reflected the relations of production directly, every gradual change in the relations of production being accompanied by an immediate and parallel change in law, it would have ceased to be law. The function of law is, so to say, to bring harmony between the antagonistic interests of the classes, to fill up the gaps which tend to break in the economic social system. In order to achieve this, it must rise above the economy, while basing itself upon it.

From the standpoint of its content, law is the indirect reflection of the material basis on which it is erected, but from the standpoint of its form, it is but the assimilation and completion of the law inherited from the past. There is always a lapse of time between the change in the relations of production and the change in law. The deeper and quicker the change in the relations of production, the more difficult it is for law to keep pace and still formally preserve the continuity from its past development. Thus there are some historical examples of the rise of a new class which has been reluctant to publicise its coming to power and has accordingly tried to adapt its existence and rights to the framework presented by the past, even though this framework has stood in absolute contradiction to it. Thus, for instance, for a very long time the rising bourgeoisie endeavoured to prove that profit and interest are but some sort of rent—at that time the rent of the landlord was justified in the eyes of the ruling classes. The English capitalist class tried to base its political rights on the Magna Carta, the charter of rights of the feudal class, which from the standpoint of content and form is fundamentally in contradiction to bourgeois right. The attempt of the ruling class to hide its privilege under the cloak of the law handed down from the past is most strongly made in the case of a counter-revolution which dare not declare its existence.

The revolutionary proletariat does not hide its aims, and the law it dictates on taking power is therefore revolutionary both in content and form. Had the armies of intervention been victorious after the October Revolution, their bloody rule would have been accompanied by the restoration of most of the old laws scrapped by the October Revolution. But, as the bureaucracy in Russia transformed itself gradually into a ruling class, the changes in the relations of production were not expressed immediately in the complete change of the law. For various reasons, the main being the need Stalinist foreign policy has of pseudo-revolutionary propaganda among the workers all over the world, the Russian bureaucracy did not openly declare that a counter-revolution had taken place.

This alone, however, is insufficient to explain why the bureaucracy does not restore private property in the form of bonds or shares covering the whole economy in such a way that every member of the bureaucracy should be able to bequeath a safe economic position to his son. Other factors must be taken into account in explaining this. The desires of a class, a caste or a social layer are moulded by its material conditions of life. Not only has each class its own special place in the process of production, but each owning class has a different stronghold in the social wealth. If simply the desire for the maximum material and cultural benefits in the abstract had been the driving force of humanity, then not only would the working class would have desired socialism, but also the petty and middle bourgeoisie, and even the big bourgeoisie; the more so as this generation lives under the shadow of atomic warfare. But this is not the case. When people make history, they make it according to the external, objective reality in which they find themselves, which moulds their desires. The feudal lord thus strives to increase the area of his and his son's domains; the merchant endeavours to give his sons security by bequeathing them a large quantity of

money; the physician, the lawyer and the other members of the free profes-
sions attempt to pass their privileges on to their sons mainly by giving them
'mental means of production'; as there is no Chinese wall between the different classes and layers, the latter will, of course, try to bequeath more than
'mental means of production', but material means of production also.

The state bureaucracy, as Marx said in his 'Critique of Hegel's Philosophy of
Law', possesses the state as private property. In a state which is the repository
of the means of production the state bureaucracy which is therefore the ruling
class has forms of passing on its privileges which are different to those of the
feudal lords, the bourgeoisie or the free professionals. If co-optation is the prevailing mode of selecting the directors of enterprises, heads of departments,
etc, every bureaucrat will try to pass on to his son not so much, let us say, a million roubles (even though this has importance) as his 'connections'. Obviously
he will at the same time try to limit the number of competitors for the position
in the bureaucracy by restricting the possibilities the masses have of getting a
higher education, etc.

(5) Are government bonds the harbingers of a transformation of the form of property?

The last few years have witnessed a big increase in Russia's national debt, a big
increase in the amount of state bonds owned by the higher layers of Russian society. Does this herald the beginning of a general transformation of the form of
property?

In traditional capitalist economy, the process of accumulation of capital has
two aspects—the material aspect expressed in the production of means of production, and the monetary aspect which reflects this process in additional fictitious capital. For example, a corporation which wants to buy additional
machinery can get the necessary money from one of two sources—either from
the surplus value of the corporation, or by issuing new shares, bonds etc to the
public. In the second case, it is clear that the increase in the total real capital
in the hands of the corporation is accompanied by a corresponding (although
far from exactly corresponding) increase in the total fictitious capital. When the
corporation does not issue new securities the increase in real capital still reflects
itself (other conditions being the same) in an increase in fictitious capital as the
price of its shares on the market rises.

In Stalinist Russia the increase in the real capital need not necessarily be accompanied by an increase in the fictitious capital, for the following reasons:
Firstly, the state is the industrial capitalist and the banker at one and the same
time, so that accumulation is not financed in the main by individuals.
Secondly—this factor being the converse of the first—almost only that part of
the surplus value used for consumption reaches private hands, while the part used
for accumulation remains from the beginning in the hands of the state, so that
individuals have not sufficiently abundant monetary means to finance the state
economy. If the state has decided to finance the economy *wholly* internally, the

accumulation of capital would not have been accompanied by bonds at all despite the great improvement in the position of the bureaucracy.

Only in the measure that the economy diverges from pure state capitalism, from the absolute separation of accumulation and consumption, does the appearance of bonds seem explicable. And indeed, the existence of elements of individual capitalism, cracks in the planning of the state capitalist economy—the importance of which very much increased during the war, when the accumulation of *real* capital in the hands of the state was in general very restricted and even negative (the destruction of whole regions, the wear and tear of machinery, etc)—very much spurred on the appearance of bonds. It is also not accidental that among the Soviet millionaires a prominent part is played by the rural rich who accumulated big sums of money from the sale of their products on the free market.

Nevertheless, whatever the future may show, the appearance of Soviet millionaires, owning bonds worth millions of roubles, the decreeing of the new inheritance law, etc—all these have very great importance in themselves. They are important, if not as harbingers of the anchoring of the bureaucracy's privileges in the traditional forms of private property, then as a proof that the function fulfilled by the bureaucracy is a capitalist function. The fact that without any change in the relations of production there appears a form of property which no one will deny is typical of capitalist economy (bonds, money-capital, interest) serves as additional proof of the capitalist character of the relations of production. These relations accord the class which controls the means of production the privilege of controlling the surplus value produced by others. One of the forms of appropriating surplus value is the taking of interest on money-capital.

But, whether there were bonds and shares covering the whole economy or not, the fundamental laws of the economy—the plan and its limits, the antagonistic way of distribution of the products of production, the tempo of accumulation and consumption, etc—would not be changed, nor would the relation of the masses to the means of production. The position of the bureaucracy as regards the process of production would still be the same; so would the degree of stability or instability of the bureaucracy as a collective (although it is true that as individuals it would have changed very much). There is therefore no fundamental reason *why* the form of property in Russia should have changed.

If shares and bonds covered the whole economy, no Marxist would deny that there was state capitalism. But if their existence changes nothing in the laws of motion of Russian economy as long as the relations of production remain as they are, what ground is there for denying that there is state capitalism there?

Because in the state capitalism which is an organic, gradual continuation of the development of capitalism, a form of private property would prevail in the ownership of shares and bonds, we must not conclude that the same will apply to state capitalism which rose gradually on the ruins of a workers' revolution. History often leaps forward or backward. When it leaps backward, it does not return directly to the same position, but goes down a spiral, combining the elements of the two systems from which and to which society passed. Historical continuity in the case of state capitalism which evolves from monopoly capitalism is shown in the existence of private property (bonds). Historical continuity in the case of state capitalism which evolves from a workers' state that degenerated and died is shown in the *non-existence of private property*.

(6) The synthesis of the extremities of development

Russia presents us with the synthesis of a form of property born of a proletarian revolution and relations of production born of the poor national forces of production and the pressure of world capitalism. The content of the synthesis shows historical continuity from the pre-revolutionary period; the form shows historical continuity from the revolutionary period. In the retreat from the revolution the form does not move right back to its point of departure. Despite its subordination to content, it yet has considerable importance.

The spiral development of the combination of content and form brings about the synthesis of two extremes of capitalist development in Russia, a synthesis of the highest stage which capitalism can ever reach, and which probably no other country will reach; and of such a low stage of development as has yet to experience the preparation of the material prerequisites for socialism. The defeat of the October Revolution serves as a springboard for Russian capitalism which at the same time lags well behind world capitalism.

The synthesis reveals itself in an extremely high concentration of capital, in an extremely high organic composition of capital; and on the other side, taking the level of technique into account, in a low productivity of labour, in a low cultural level.

The synthesis explains the speed of the development of the productive forces in Russia, a speed far outstripping what youthful capitalism experienced, and the very opposite of what capitalism in decay and stagnation experiences.

Youthful capitalism practised inhuman brutality on the toilers, which is shown in the struggle against 'vagabonds', the poor laws, the forcing of women and children to work 15 to 18 hours a day, etc; aged capitalism recommits many of the brutalities of its childhood, with the difference that it is able, as fascism has shown, to carry them out much more effectively. Both periods are characterised by the use of measures of compulsion in addition to the activity of the automatism of economic laws. The synthesis of state capitalism and the task of capitalism in its youth gives the Russian bureaucracy an unlimited appetite for surplus value and capacity for inhuman brutality, while at the same time it provides it with the ability to practise the highest efficiency in carrying out its oppression.

When Engels said that 'humanity, descended from animality, has needed to use barbarous, almost animal, methods in order to escape from barbarism', he certainly was not describing the socialist revolution, when history becomes 'conscious of itself'. But he well described the prehistory of humanity. Peter the Great will go down in history as one of the fighters against barbarism using barbaric methods. Herzon wrote that he 'civilised with a knout in his hand and knout in hand persecuted the light'.[104]

Stalin will go down in history as the oppressor of the working class, the power which could have advanced the productive forces and culture of humanity without the knout, as the world was mature enough to break it, but which nevertheless advanced the productive forces 'knout in hand', and at the same time endangering all humanity with the threat of decline through imperialist wars.

The proletarian revolution pushed all the impediments to the development of the productive forces out of its path and abolished a lot of the old barbarities. But being isolated, and taking place in a backward country, it was vanquished, leaving the field free for the fight against barbarism by barbaric methods.

(7) Economics and politics

The state is 'special bodies of armed men, prisons, etc', a weapon in the hands of one class to oppress another class or other classes. In Russia the state is a weapon in the hands of the bureaucracy for the oppression of the mass of toilers. But this alone does not describe all the functions of the Stalinist state. It represents also the direct needs of the social division of labour, of the organisation of social production. A similar task was fulfilled, mutatis mutandis, by the states of ancient China, Egypt and Babylonia. There, because of the vital necessity of big irrigation works, the organisation of which could be carried out at all only if done on a large scale the state came into being not only as a result of the appearance of class divisions, and so *indirectly* as a result of the social division of labour, but also *directly*, as part of the process of production. There are thus such mutual relations of dependence and influence between the class divisions and the emergence and strengthening of the state as make any separation of economics and politics impossible. In Russia, similarly, the Stalinist state did not rise only as a result of the widening abyss between the masses and the bureaucracy and the need for 'special bodies of armed men', but also as a direct result of the needs of the productive forces themselves, as a necessary element of the mode of production.

One of the Chaldean kings said:

> I have mastered the secrets of the rivers for the benefit of man... I have led the waters of the rivers into the wilderness. I have filled the parched ditches with them... I have watered the desert plains. I have brought them fertility and abundance. I have formed them into habitations of joy.

Plekhanov, who cites this, remarks, 'For all its boastfulness, this is a fairly accurate description of the role of the oriental state in organising the social process of production'.[105]

Stalin could similarly claim that he built the industries, drove the productive forces of Russia forward, etc (although of course the tyranny of the Chaldean king was historically necessary and progressive in its time, while that of Stalin is historically superfluous and reactionary). As in ancient societies, so in Russia today, because of the double function of the state, as a guardian of the ruling class and as organiser of social production, there is a total fusion of economics and politics. This is out of accord with vulgar materialism, but to a dialectical materialism entirely valid.

The fusion of economics and politics is characteristic of capitalism in its highest stage, as well as of a workers' state. But while under a workers' state this fusion means that the workers, being politically dominant, advance ever closer to a situation in which the 'government of persons is replaced by the administration of things and the direction of the process of production',[106] under capitalism in its highest stage it means that political coercion is added to the automatism of the economy in oppressing the toilers.

> The special feature of the capitalist order is that all the elements of the future society appear in it in such a form as do not draw nearer to socialism but draw further away from it.

Thus, for instance:

> As regards the army, development brings general obligatory military service...that is, an approach to the people's militia. But it is realised in the form of modern militarism, which brings the domination of the military state over the people, which pushes the class character of the state to the extreme.[107]

This proves that our period is so ripe for socialism that capitalism is compelled to absorb more and more elements of socialism into itself. As Engels said, this is the invasion of socialist society into capitalism. This absorption, however, does not lighten the burden of exploitation and oppression; on the contrary, it makes it bear down much the more heavily.

Wherever there is a fusion of economics and politics it is theoretically wrong to distinguish between political and economic revolution, or between political and economic counter-revolution. The bourgeoisie can exist as the bourgeoisie, owning private property, under different forms of government: under a feudal monarchy, a constitutional monarchy, a bourgeois republic, the Bonapartism of Napoleon I and III, a fascist dictatorship and for a certain time even under a workers' state (the kulaks and Nep Men existed till 1928). In all these cases there is a direct relation of ownership between the bourgeoisie and the means of production. Even, therefore, if the state is independent of the control of the bourgeoisie, the bourgeoisie does not cease to be a ruling class. As against this, where the state is the repository of the means of production, there is an *absolute* fusion between economics and politics—political expropriation also means economic expropriation. If the above-mentioned Chaldean king were politically expropriated, he would necessarily also have been economically expropriated. The same applies to the Stalinist bureaucracy and, mutatis mutandis, also to a workers' state. Seeing that the workers as individuals are *not* owners of means of production even in a workers' state, and their ownership as a collective is expressed through their ownership of the state which is the repository of the means of production, therefore *if they are politically expropriated they are also economically expropriated.*

(8) Can there be a gradual transition from a workers' state to a capitalist state?

The proletariat cannot take over the bourgeois state machine but must smash it. Does it not follow that the *gradual* transition from the workers' state of Lenin and Trotsky (1917-23) to the capitalist state of Stalin contradicts the basis of the Marxist theory of the state? This is one of the pivots of defence of the theory that Russia today is still a workers' state. Those who hold to this theory quote Trotsky in 1933 (but omit to quote his opposite statement of a later date). He wrote in 'The Soviet Union and the Fourth International', the thesis adopted by the First International Conference of the Fourth International in Geneva in July 1936:

> The Marxian thesis relating to the catastrophic character of the transfer of power from the hands of one class into the hands of another applies not only to revolutionary periods, when history madly sweeps ahead, but also to the period of counter-revolution when society rolls backwards. He who asserts that the Soviet government has been changed *gradually* from proletarian to bourgeois is only, so to speak, running backwards the film of reformism.

The question at issue is the validity or otherwise of the last sentence.

Capitalist restoration can come about in many ways. Political restoration may precede economic restoration: this would have been the case if the White Guards and armies of intervention had succeeded in overthrowing the Bolsheviks. Or economic restoration, even if not complete, may precede political restoration: this would have been the case if the kulaks and Nep Men who entrenched their economic privileges until 1928 had succeeded in overthrowing the regime. In both cases the transition from a workers' state to a capitalist state would not have been gradual. Indeed, to say that it might have been gradual could justifiably be branded as 'only, so to speak, running backwards the film of reformism'. But where the bureaucracy of a workers' state is transformed into a ruling class economic and political restoration are indissolubly interwoven. The state becomes gradually further divorced from the workers, the relations between it and the workers thus becoming more and more like the relations between a capitalist employer and his workers. In such a case the bureaucratic clique that first appears as a distortion gradually transforms itself into a class which fulfils the tasks of the bourgeoisie in capitalist relations of production. The gradual revolutionary divorcement of the bureaucracy from the control of the masses, which continued until 1928, reached the stage of a revolutionary qualitative change with the First Five-Year Plan.

The question, however, still stands: does this not contradict the Marxist theory of the state?

From the standpoint of formal logic it seems irrefutable that if the proletariat cannot gradually transform the bourgeois state into a workers' state, but must smash the state machine, the bureaucracy on becoming the ruling class also cannot gradually transform the workers' state into a bourgeois state but must smash the state machine. From the standpoint of dialectics, however, we must pose the problem differently. What are the reasons why the proletariat cannot gradually transform the state machine, and do these reasons exist as an immovable impediment to the gradual change of the class character of a workers' state?

Marx and Engels said that the smashing of the state machine as the first step in the proletarian revolution did not apply to England, but only to the continent of Europe. They said that in England the 'social revolution might be effected entirely by peaceful and legal means'. On this Lenin says, 'This was natural in 1871, when England was still the model of a purely capitalist country, but without militarism and, to a considerable degree, without a bureaucracy'.[108]

It is, then, the bureaucracy and the standing army that constitute the impediment to the workers' peaceful accession to power, for the workers' state has no bureaucracy or standing army. Thus, where these institutions do not exist, a peaceful transition can be accomplished.

Let us now see whether what excludes a gradual social revolution excludes a gradual counter-revolution.

If the soldiers in a hierarchically built army strive for decisive control over the army, they immediately meet with the opposition of the officer caste. There is no way of removing such a caste except by revolutionary violence. As against this, if the officers of a people's militia become less and less dependent on the will of the soldiers, which they may do as they meet with no institutional bureaucracy, their transformation into an officers' caste independent of the soldiers can be accomplished gradually. The transition from a standing army to a militia cannot but be accompanied by a tremendous outbreak of revolutionary violence; on the other hand, the transition from a militia to a standing army, to the extent that it is the result of tendencies inside the militia itself, can and must be gradual. The opposition of the soldiers to the rising bureaucracy may lead the latter to use violence against the soldiers. But this does not exclude the possibility of a gradual transition from a militia to a standing army. What applies to the army applies equally to the state. A state without a bureaucracy, or with a weak bureaucracy dependent on the pressure of the masses may gradually be transformed into a state in which the bureaucracy is free of workers' control.

The Moscow trials were the civil war of the bureaucracy against the masses, a war in which only one side was armed and organised. They witnessed the consummation of the bureaucracy's total liberation from popular control. Trotsky, who thought that the Moscow trials and the 'constitution' were steps towards the restoration of individual capitalism by legal means, then withdrew the argument that a gradual change from a proletarian to a bourgeois state is 'running backwards the film of reformism'. He wrote, 'In reality, the *new constitution*…opens up for the bureaucracy 'legal' roads for the economic counter-revolution, ie the restoration of capitalism by means of a 'cold stroke'.[109]

(9) Stalinism—barbarism?

The word 'barbarism' denotes different things. On the one hand we say the barbaric exploitation of the workers, the barbaric oppression of the colonial peoples, the barbaric murder of the Jews by the Nazis, etc. 'Barbaric' here does not denote a stage in the history of humanity, a certain content of social relations, but a certain aspect of the actions of a class, which may even be a rising, progressive class: for instance, we say the barbaric eviction of the peasantry in Britain in the time of rising capitalism, or the barbaric looting of the population of South America, etc. On the other hand 'barbarism' may denote something which, even though it has common features with the former meaning, is yet entirely different. It may denote the total abolition of civilisation by the decline of society into an ahistorical era. This makes it a whole stage in the history of humanity. A particular event may be barbaric from both standpoints. For instance, a third world war would be barbaric as it describes the activity of the ruling classes (the first meaning), and as it is the cause of the total decline of society (the second meaning). Essentially, however, the meanings are different and must be distinguished between. Barbarism used with the first meaning as regards our epoch signifies the price humanity is paying for the *belatedness* of the socialist revolution. Used with the second meaning it signifies the loss of all hope in society which has decayed and declined. According to this it would be wrong to define Nazism as barbarism with the second meaning, as 'renewed feudalism', as the 'state of the termites', as an ahistorical period, etc, as the Nazi system was *based* on the labour of proletarians, who are historically its gravediggers and the saviours of humanity. It would be even less justified to designate the Stalinist regime as barbarism with the second meaning, as this regime, in the face of Russia's backwardness and fear of annihilation in international competition, is rapidly increasing the numbers of the working class.

This question is not a matter of philological hair-splitting, but a matter of prime importance. To use the word barbarism with its second meaning would be as wrong as to use the word slave to designate the Russian workers, if slave is used as something different and opposite to proletarian. Slavery, like barbarism with its first meaning, used to denote one aspect of the condition of the Russian worker under Stalin as well as of the German worker under Hitler— his lack of legal freedom, his partial negation of himself as a worker—would be a correct term. We must therefore strongly oppose the use of the word barbarism with its second meaning to denote the Stalinist regime. As a matter of fact we must oppose its use in general to denote the stage society has reached today, and can only condone its use with the first meaning, that is, used to describe certain aspects of declining capitalism as a whole, whether American, Russian, British or Japanese.

(10) Is the Stalinist regime progressive?

If a certain social order is necessary to develop the productive forces and prepare the material conditions for a higher order of society, then it is progressive. We must emphasise the *material conditions*, as if we speak of all the conditions (class consciousness, the existence of mass revolutionary parties, etc, etc) then any social order by its very existence proves that *all the conditions* for its overthrow are not there, ie it is progressive.

It does not follow from this definition that when a social order becomes reactionary, becomes an impediment to the development of the productive forces, the productive forces cease to advance, or the rate of advance falls absolutely. There is no doubt that feudalism in Europe became reactionary in the 13th to 18th centuries, but this does not mean that the productive forces developed more slowly in this period than before. The very opposite is the case. Similarly, while Lenin said that the period of imperialism (beginning with the last decades of the 19th century) signified the decline and decay of capitalism he at the same time said:

> It would be a mistake to believe that this tendency to decay precludes the possibility of the rapid growth of capitalism. It does not. In the epoch of imperialism, certain branches of industry, certain strata of the bourgeoisie and certain countries betray, to a greater or lesser degree, one or another of these tendencies. On the whole, capitalism is growing far more rapidly than before. But this growth is not only becoming more and more uneven in general; its unevenness also manifests itself, in particular, in the decay of the countries which are richest in capital (such as England).[110]

At the same time as Lenin spoke of the decay of capitalism, he said that the democratic revolution in Russia, by sweeping away the remnants of feudalism, would give tremendous possibilities of development to Russian capitalism, which would stride forward at an American tempo. And this view he held at the time that he believed that the 'democratic dictatorship of the proletariat and peasantry' would perform in Russia the tasks of the bourgeois revolution.

If we look at the figures for world industrial production since 1891 we can see that in the period of imperialism the productive forces of the world are far from absolute stagnation:[111]

WORLD INDUSTRIAL PRODUCTION (1913 = 100)	
1891	33
1900	51
1906	73
1913	100
1920	102
1928	148

As regards the capacity of production, we need but take into account the control of atomic energy to see what strides have been made.

If we abstracted the backward countries from the world, we could certainly say that capitalism would be progressive. For instance, if the countries of the West declined and disappeared, Indian capitalism would have no less long and glorious a future than British capitalism had in the 19th century. The same is true of Russian state capitalism. But as revolutionary Marxists we take the world as our point of departure, and therefore conclude that capitalism, wherever it exists, is reactionary. For the problem humanity must solve under pain of annihilation is not how to develop the productive forces, but to what and under what social relations to utilise them.

This conclusion as regards the reactionary character of Russian state capitalism, *notwithstanding* the rapid development of the productive forces, might have been refuted if one could prove either that world capitalism did not prepare the material conditions necessary for the establishment of socialism, or that the Stalinist regime prepared further conditions necessary for the establishment of socialism than the world at large prepared. The former alternative leads one to the conclusion that we are not yet in the period of the socialist revolution. Of the latter, the most one may say is that the heritage Stalinist Russia will bequeath will be a higher concentration of capital and the working class than in any other country. But this is only a *quantitative* difference: if we compare the economies of the US and England, we find that a concentration of capital and socialisation of labour is much higher in the former than in the latter, but this does not make present-day capitalism in the US historically progressive.

One may claim that the planning inside Russia is an element which transforms the Russian economy into a progressive one in comparison with the capitalism of other countries. This is a totally unsound claim. So long as the working class has no control over production, the workers are not the subject of planning but its object. This applies just as well to the planning within the gigantic enterprise of Ford as to the whole economy of Russia. And so long as the workers are the object, planning is important for them only as an element of the material conditions necessary for socialism—as an aspect of the concentration of capital and workers. In a factory employing 100,000 workers there is more elaborated, developed planning than in a factory employing 100 workers, and still more in state capitalism which employs 10 million workers. This does not make the relations of production in the big enterprise progressive relative to those in the smaller one. The plan in each is dictated by the blind external force of competition between independent producers.

The very fact of the existence of the Stalinist regime declares its reactionariness, as without the defeated October Revolution the Stalinist regime would not have existed, and without the maturity of the world for socialism the October Revolution would not have broken out.

Chapter 7: The Russian economy and the law of value

There is no aspect of the problem of Russia about which so much confusion has been spread as whether the economy is moved by the law of value or not. The main reason for this confusion lies in the lack of clarity as regards the definition of the law of value which leads to mistakes in the effort to locate it in the body-economy. Many of the Marxists who have dealt with Russia have 'found' the source of activity of the law of value even where it does not exist, while others have not found it even where it does exist. Even though we shall repeat some of the ABC of Marxism, it is necessary to sketch the essence of the law of value as a prelude to determining whether it acts in the Russian economy and, if so, how. In order to avoid a number of the confusions prevailing about the law of value, we shall formulate the law as far as possible in the words of Marx himself.

(1) The law of value

Under capitalism, and only under capitalism, 'all or even a majority of the products take the form of commodities'.[112] For products to become commodities it is necessary that there should exist a social division of labour. But this alone is not sufficient. Inside primitive tribes there was a division of labour without commodities being produced. The same thing applies to the latifundia based on slave labour and self-sufficiency. *Within* the capitalist factory too there is a division of labour without the fruit of each one's labour being a commodity. Only on the boundary between primitive tribes and latifundiae, or between one capitalist factory and another, are products exchanged, thus receiving the form of commodities. As Marx said, 'Only such products can become commodities with regard to each other, as result from different kinds of labour, each kind being carried on independently and for the account of private individuals'.[113]

Value is the common characteristic of commodities on the basis of which exchange is realised. Only as commodities have they exchange value. Exchange value is the form of expression of the social relations existing between producers of commodities, of the *social* character of labour of every producer. It is the *only expression* of the social character of labour in a society of independent producers. Marx says:

> Since the producers do not come into social contact with each other until they exchange their products, the specific social character of each producer's labour does not show itself except in the act of exchange. In other words, the labour of the individual asserts itself as a part of the labour of society only by means of the relations which the act of exchange establishes directly between the products, and indirectly, through them, between the producers.[114]

The only form of appearance of value is in the process of exchange itself. When we say that a commodity is value we mean that it is materialised abstract labour, that it is the fruit of a certain portion of the total productive labour of society: 'Magnitude of value expresses a relation of social production; it expresses the connection that necessarily exists between a certain article and the portion of the total labour time of society required to produce it'.[115]

Why is exchange value the only expression of 'the connection that necessarily exists between a certain article and portion of the total labour time of society required to produce it'? Why is this relation not expressed directly instead of through the medium of things? The reason is that the only social connection between independent producers can be through things, through the exchange of commodities.

The law of value in a society of independent producers determines (a) what will be the exchange relation between different commodities, (b) the total volume of commodities of one kind produced in comparison with commodities of another kind, and therefore (c) the division of the total labour time of society among different industries.

One aspect of (a) is the selling and buying of labour power. The law of value determines the relation of exchange between labour power and other commodities, and through this the division of the labour day of the worker into the portion of necessary labour, in which he reproduces the value of his labour power, and the portion of surplus labour, in which he produces surplus value for the capitalist.

One aspect of (b) is the proportion between the production of means of production and the production of means of consumption, the relation between accumulation and consumption. This is, of course, dependent on (a).

In order to get a clear picture of the activity of the law of value, let us quote Marx on the relation between the division of labour which is expressed in the appearance of values, of commodities, and the division of labour which is not thus expressed, that is, between the division of labour in capitalist society as a whole, and the division of labour in an individual capitalist factory. He writes:

> Division of labour in a society is brought about by the purchase and sale of the products of different branches of industry, while the connection between the detail operations in a workshop are due to the sale of the labour power of several workmen to one capitalist, who applies it as combined labour power. The division of labour in the workshop implies concentration of the means of production in the hands of one capitalist; the division of labour in society implies their dispersion among many independent producers of commodities. While within the workshop, the iron law of proportionality subjects definite numbers of workmen to definite functions, in the society outside the workshop, chance and caprice have full play in distributing the producers and their means of production among the various branches of industry. The different spheres of production, it is true, constantly tend to an equilibrium: for, on the one hand, while each producer of a commodity is bound to produce a use value, to satisfy a particular social want, and while the extent of these wants differs quantitatively, still there exists an inner relation which settles their proportions into a regular system, and that system one of spontaneous growth; and, on the other hand, the law of the value of commodities ultimately determines how

much of its disposable working time society can expend on each particular class of commodities. But this constant tendency to equilibrium, of the various spheres of production, is exercised only in the shape of a reaction against the constant upsetting of this equilibrium. The a priori system on which the division of labour, within the workshop, is regularly carried out, becomes in the division of labour within society, an a posteriori, nature-imposed necessity, controlling the lawless caprice of the producers, and perceptible in the barometrical fluctuations of the market prices. Division of labour within the workshop implies the undisputed authority of the capitalist over men, that are but parts of a mechanism that belongs to him. The division of labour within the society brings into contact independent commodity-producers, who acknowledge no other authority but that of competition, of the coercion exerted by the pressure of their mutual interests.[116]

Thus the action of the law of value brings order into disorder by its continual disturbance of the equilibrium, by the continuous movement of demand and supply, by competition. Therefore, despite the lack of a central deciding authority in a society of commodity producers, a certain order is established by the law of value alone, and certain proportionalities are reached in the production of different products, in the division of the total labour time of society between the different branches of the economy, etc. Within the individual factory, on the other hand, it is not impersonal anarchy that prevails, but the despotic will of the capitalist which decides the division of labour in the process of production and the quantity of different goods to be produced.

Now in all the different forms of society—from the primitive communism of the ancient past to the future communist society—the needs of society demand a certain proportionality in the production of different products, and therefore a certain division of the labour time of society among the different branches of the economy. But every form of society has a special mode in which this division of the total labour time is carried out. As Marx writes in a letter to Kugelmann on 11 July 1868:

> Every child knows that if a country ceased to work, I will not say for a year, but for a few weeks, it would die. Every child knows too that the mass of products corresponding to the different needs require different and quantitatively determined masses of the total labour of society. That this necessity of distributing social labour in definite proportions cannot be done away with by the *particular form* of social production, but can only change the *form it assumes*, is self-evident. No natural laws can be done away with. What can change in changing historical circumstances is the form in which these laws operate. And the form in which this proportional division of labour operates, in a state of society where the interconnection of social labour is manifested in the *private exchange* of the individual products of labour, is precisely the *exchange value* of these products.[117]

A necessary condition for exchange value to be the *form* of the division of the total labour time of society between the production of different products is that the activity of people in the process of production should be 'purely atomic', so that the relations between them are 'independent of their control and conscious individual action'. This means that there is completely free competition between the independent producers, between the different owners of commodities, including the sellers of labour power.

(2) Capitalist monopoly: a border case of the activity of the law of value

As the existence of value is conditioned by the non-existence of a conscious regulation of production, the concept of value itself assumes that the price of a commodity is not identical with it, except as an exception, but oscillates around it. In reality, as Marx explains in the third volume of *Capital*, this statement needs modification: the price of a commodity oscillates not round its value but round its price of production. The relation of exchange between two commodities is therefore not congruent with the labour time ratios incorporated in them. But as the price of production itself is derived—by means of the tendency towards an equal rate of profit—from the total value produced, under conditions of free competition prices are derived, even if not directly, from labour time ratios.

The appearance of monopolies changes this picture. The price of one commodity rises relative to another, so that the exchange relations not only do not conform to their labour time ratios, but not even to their prices of production. Monopoly, by altering the exchange relations between different commodities, also alters the exchange relation between the commodity labour power and other commodities, ie it changes the relation between wages and profits. Monopoly restricts the production of certain commodities in order to raise their price, so that the relation between the quantity of commodities produced by different industries is not exactly the same as that which would have existed under conditions of free competition. Thus monopoly also alters the division of the total labour time of society among the different branches of the economy.

The first Marxist who dealt extensively with the question of monopoly was Hilferding. His book *Finance Capital* is perhaps the most important book on Marxist economics since *Capital* itself. In one chapter he deals with the price determination of capitalist monopoly. He explains why it is impossible to draw any general law which will explain what is the *quantitative* influence of monopoly on the relations of exchange between commodities. He writes:

> What is undetermined and immeasurable under the rule of monopolies is demand. How this reacts on the raising of prices cannot be ascertained. Monopoly prices can be determined empirically, but their level cannot be determined theoretically. Classical economy [in this Hilferding includes Marx] conceives prices as the form of appearance of anarchical social production, their level as dependent on the social productivity of labour. The objective price law is realised only through competition. When the monopolist associations abolish competition, they remove with this the only means by which an objective price law can be realised. Price ceases to be an amount determined objectively, and becomes a problem of calculation for those who determine it with will and consciousness, instead of a result it becomes an assumption, instead of being objective it becomes subjective, instead of being

inevitable and independent of the will and consciousness of the actors it becomes arbitrary and accidental. The realisation of the Marxian theory of concentration—the monopolistic merger—seems to lead to the invalidation of the Marxian theory of value.[118]

Just as it is impossible to determine theoretically what will be the relations of exchange between different commodities under conditions of monopoly, so is it impossible to determine what quantity of different commodities will be produced, and what will be the division of the total labour time of society between different branches of the economy.

But it is possible to determine what the *tendency* of these three factors will be in comparison with the conditions that would have existed under free competition. Under conditions of equilibrium the exchange value of monopoly commodities will rise in relation to non-monopolised commodities, the quantity of monopolised commodities produced will be smaller relative to the non-monopolised commodities, and the portion of the total labour time of society absorbed into the monopolised industry will likewise be smaller. The exchange relations of the commodities, the quantity produced, and the division of the total labour time of society under conditions of monopoly are thus modifications of the same factors under free competition. The law of value under monopoly conditions is partially negated, but in essence it continues to exist: the division of the total labour time of society is derived, even if with certain deviations, from the law of value.

Competition continues, even if it is not absolutely free, and therefore, despite certain changes, it is still valid that 'the behaviour of men in the social process of production is purely atomic. Hence their relations to each other in production assume a material character independent of their control and conscious individual actions'.[119]

The competition between different monopoly groups, in the same branch or in different branches, makes the exchange relations between different commodities, even if they are not congruent with labour time ratios or cost of production ratios, not entirely independent of them. Even if the general division of labour in society is not absolutely independent of the conscious actions of individuals or groups (such as monopolies), they can change the division of the labour time of society from what it would have been under absolute free competition only within relatively limited boundaries. Notwithstanding the 'planning' of monopolies, therefore, the anarchical character of the division of labour among the different enterprises in society as a whole continues to exist. The division of labour among monopolistic groups thus continues to be different from the division of labour *within* the factory, 'not only in degree, but also in kind'. We see then that monopoly means a partial negation of the law of value but on the basis of the law of value itself. As Spinoza said, 'Determinatio est negatio.' The *partial* negation of the law of value therefore *borders* on the total negation. *We should be correct in describing capitalist monopoly as a border case of the activity of the law of value.*

Does the intervention of the capitalist state in the regulation of the price of commodities, its appearance as the buyer of an important part of the products of the economy, as the allocator of raw materials and regulator of capital investment negate the law of value entirely, or only partially negate it? Let us first re-quote Lenin on this question:

> When capitalists work for the defence, ie for the government, it is obviously no more 'pure' capitalism, it is a special form of national economy. Pure capitalism means commodity production. Commodity production means work for an *uncertain* and free market. But the capitalist 'working' for the defence does not work for the market at all, he fills the orders of the government, and money is invariably advanced to him by the treasury.[120]

This does not mean that the supply of products by capitalist enterprises to the state is outside of the law of value, of the automatism of the market. When in Nazi Germany the state began to buy half the total national product, when it concentrated in its hands the allocation of raw materials, regulated the flow of capital into the different branches of the economy, fixed the prices of commodities, and regimented the labour market, it did not leave the exchange-relation of different commodities, the relative quantity of different goods produced and the division of the total labour time of society among the different industries, to be regulated by the blind, automatic activity of the market. But the Nazi state did not take all the decisions as regards production. The law of value was not negated *altogether*, but only partially—it was negated on the basis of itself.

(3) The law of value in the Russian economy

In seeing whether the Russian economy is subordinated to the law of value or not, we shall look into two aspects of the problem. First we shall consider the Russian economy as a closed unit, abstracted from the world economy; we shall see in how far such an abstraction is permissible, and what importance it has. Then we shall examine the mutual relations between world economy and Russian economy. As far as the first aspect is concerned, the main problem to be tackled is whether the division of labour among the enterprises in Russia itself is *basically, in essence*, the same as exists within one workshop in capitalist society, or whether it is like the division of labour in the interior of society as a whole. As far as the second aspect is concerned, the problem to be tackled is whether the relations between Russian economy and world economy make for the existence of the law of value as the regulator of production in Russia.

(4) The division of labour within Russia

As first sight it seems that the relations among different enterprises in Russia are the same as among different enterprises in the traditional capitalist countries, which is the opposite of the relations within each enterprise. But this is only formally the case. The fundamental criterion in a society of private producers which distinguishes between the division of labour within the workshop and the division of labour inside society as a whole is that in the former the means of production are concentrated in one hand. The workers are subordinated to one will which decides the quantity to be produced, etc. In society as a whole there is no deciding authority, but only 'blindly working average' to determine the proportionality of workers employed in different enterprises, the quantity of commodities produced, etc. This criterion certainly does not distinguish between the division of labour within the factory and among the factories in Russia. Both are submitted to the planned regulation of production. The difference between the division of labour in, let us say, a tractor factory in Russia and the division of labour between this factory and the steel plant supplying it is a difference only in degree, but not in kind. It is a technical-administrative difference, but not a difference in the *working of the laws of the economy. The division of labour within Russian society is therefore in essence a species of the division of labour in the interior of a workshop.*

Formally the distribution of products among the different branches is made through the medium of exchange. But as the ownership of all the enterprises is vested in one body, the state, we cannot really speak of an exchange of commodities. The above-quoted passage from Marx makes this clear: 'Only such products can become commodities with regard to each other, as result from different kinds of labour, each kind being carried on independently and for the account of private individuals [or] groups of individuals.'

In a society of private producers where the only connection between them is exchange, the medium of regulating the division of labour in society as a whole is the monetary expression of their exchange value, in other words, their price. As in Russia there is direct connection between the enterprises through the medium of the state which directs production in nearly all of them, price is not the only expression of the social character of labour or regulator of production.

If in a traditional capitalist country the demand for shoes exceeds the supply, the blind action of the market will raise the price of shoes relative to the prices of other commodities; the result will be increased profits in the shoe industry into which a stream of capital and workers will flow, and an increase in the portion of the total labour time of society devoted to shoe production. The law of value works towards an equalisation of supply and demand, a position in which price is equal to value or, more correctly, is equal to the price of production. If a similar situation existed in Russia, the demand for shoes exceeding the supply, the result would be a rise in the price of shoes either officially or on the black market. But there will be no increase in the production of shoes, in the labour time of society directed to their production.

Let us take another example. In the traditional capitalist countries the proportionality between the production of means of production and the production of means of consumption is achieved (and also disrupted) by the activity of the law of value. If the supply of shoes is lower than the demand, while the supply of machinery is higher than the demand, the price of shoes will rise while the price of machinery will decline; a stream of capital and workers will flow from one branch to another, until the proportionality between the two departments is restored. In Russia the state owns both departments of industry. A high rate of profit in the production of means of consumption will not attract a stream of capital and workers into this department and out of that of means of production. Here the proportionalities existing between the two departments are not derived from the blind activity of the Russian internal market.

The relationship between the production of the two departments is directly dependent on the relationship between accumulation and consumption, between C and V. While in the traditional capitalist countries the competition between different factory owners causes them to accumulate and increase the organic composition of capital, in Russia, as all the factories are owned by one authority, this factor does not exist. Accumulation and technical improvement in Russia are not adopted, as they are in the traditional capitalist countries, as a defence-attack measure of one enterprise against another.

We have seen that the price is not the medium through which Russian production and the division of labour in society as a whole is regulated. The regulator here is the government plan. Price appears only as one of the weapons of the state in its regulation of production. It is not the motor, but the transmission belt.

This does not mean that the price system in Russia is arbitrary, dependent on the whim of the bureaucracy. The basis of price here too is the costs of production. If price is to be used as a transmission belt through which the bureaucracy directs production as a whole, it must fit its purpose, and as nearly as possible reflect the real costs, that is the socially necessary labour absorbed in the different products. Notwithstanding this, however, there is a fundamental difference between this price and the price of commodities in traditional capitalism. The latter expresses the autonomy of the economy (which is broadest under free competition, more canalised under monopoly); the former expresses its non-existence. The difference between these two kinds of prices will become clearer if we make an analogy with another historical period, the Pharaonic.

As we have said, in every society the total labour time must be divided among the production of different products, and in every society labour time is the real cost of production. Pharaoh had to distribute his slaves between the production of food and luxury products, the construction of the irrigation system, the building of the pyramids, etc. His calculation was direct: a certain number of slaves were devoted to one work, a certain number to another. As the process of production was relatively simple, there was no necessity for additional checks beyond seeing that the number of slaves was apportioned according to plan. In Stalinist Russia, as in Pharaonic Egypt, the state directly makes an almost[121] complete plan of the division of the total labour time of society, but as the process of production is much more complicated than a few thousand years ago, simply to check the number of workers engaged in the different branches is not sufficient for the economy to run according to plan. Certain proportions must be fixed between the use of machinery and workers, between the use of machinery of one sort and machinery of another sort, between the quantity produced and the raw material and fuel used, etc. For this it is necessary to have a measure common to all costs of production and all the fruits of production. The bureaucracy has adopted the price system to serve as this common measure. The difference between the division of labour under Pharaoh without a price system, and the division of labour between the enterprises under Stalin with a price system, is a difference in degree, but not in essence. Similarly, whether Ford directs all his enterprises as one administrative technical unit, or he breaks them up into smaller units which make it easier to calculate and direct, so long as the same will directs production, the difference between the two is only in degree.

One thing in Russia seems to fulfil all the requirements of a commodity. This is labour power. If it is a commodity, the means of consumption that the workers receive in exchange for their labour power are also commodities, being products produced for exchange. We should therefore have, if not a highly developed circulation of commodities, a huge truck or barter system comprising all the consumption of the workers. But first of all, Marx writes, 'The circulation of commodities differs from the direct exchange of products (barter), not only in form, but in substance'.[122]

Under the circulation of commodities:

> ...exchange...breaks through all local and personal bounds inseparable from direct barter, and develops the circulation of the products of social labour...it develops a whole network of social relations spontaneous in their growth and entirely beyond the control of the actors.[123]

Is labour power in Russia really a commodity as it is under traditional capitalism? Marx explains that labour power becomes a commodity only when two conditions exist: firstly, the labourer *must* sell his labour power as he has no other means of subsistence; secondly, the labourer *can* sell his labour power as he is the untrammelled owner of it, ie he is free to do so. The freedom of the worker on the one hand, his bondage on the other, are shown by the 'periodic sale of himself, by his change of masters, and by the oscillations in the market price of labour power'.[124]

Marx therefore says that in order that labour power become a commodity it is necessary:

> ...that the owner of the labour power should sell it only for a definite period, for if he were to sell it rump and stump, once for all, he would be selling himself, converting himself from a free man into a slave, from an owner of a commodity into a commodity. He must constantly look upon his labour power as his own property, his own commodity, and this he can only do by placing it at the disposal of the buyer temporarily, for a definite period of time. By this means alone can he avoid renouncing his rights of ownership over it.[125]

If there is only one employer, a 'change of masters' is impossible, and the 'periodic sale of himself' becomes a formal thing only. The contract also becomes only a formality when there are many sellers and only one buyer. (That even this formal side of the contract is not observed in Russia is clear from the system of fines and punishments, the 'corrective labour', etc.) 'Oscillations in the market price of labour power' take place in Russia, perhaps more so than in other countries. But here too the essence contradicts the form. We shall elaborate this point somewhat, as it will throw light on the central point we intend to prove, that in the economic relations *within Russia itself*, one cannot find the autonomy of economic activity, the *source* of the law of value, acting.

In traditional capitalist economy, where there is competition between the sellers of labour power, between the buyers of labour power, and between the sellers and the buyers, the price of labour power is a result of anarchic activity. If the rate of accumulation is high, there is extensive employment which under normal conditions raises the nominal wages. This increases the demand for means of consumption whose production duly increases, raising the real wages. (Under normal conditions of free competition this is absolutely true; less true under conditions of monopoly.) This rise of real wages reflexly influences the rate of profit, which influences the rate of accumulation, and so on recurrently. As against this, in Russia the total amount of real wages and salaries is fixed in advance in the quantity of means of consumption planned. It may happen, of course, that because of defects in the planning and its realisation, the quantity of money distributed as wages and salaries is larger than the total price of the means of consumption produced. If the difference is not taken by the state, it will cause a rise in prices (in the official market or the black market) but not a rise in real wages. The only way it could cause a rise in real wages is by the rise in prices in a certain branch of the economy causing the state to increase the production of that branch. But the state does not do this.[126] (There is a point below which real wages cannot fall for any length of time. This is the physical minimum, which applies to Russia just as much as to every other society, whether based on slave labour, serf labour or wage labour. The fact that real wages are not distributed equally among the Russian workers is, in connection with the problem we are discussing, of secondary importance to the fact that the total real wages are directly fixed by the state.)

Hence if one examines the relations within Russian economy, abstracting them from their relations with world economy, one comes to the conclusion that the source of the law of value as the motor and regulator of production is not to be found. In essence the laws prevailing in the relations between the enterprises and between the labourers and the employer-state would have been *no different* if Russia was one big factory managed directly from one centre, and if all the labourers received the necessary products directly in natura.[127]

Abstracting Russian economy from world economy, it is logical that Hilferding should write:

> A capitalist economy is governed by the laws of the market (analysed by Marx) and the autonomy of these laws constitutes the decisive symptom of the capitalist system of production. A state economy, however, eliminates precisely the autonomy of economic laws. It represents not a market but a consumers' economy. It is no longer price but rather a state planning commission that now determines what is produced and how. Formally, prices and wages still exist, but their function is no longer the same; they no longer determine the process of production which is now controlled by a central power that fixes prices and wages. Prices and wages become means of distribution which determine the share that the individual

receives out of the sum total of products that the central power places at the disposal of society. They now constitute a technical form of distribution which is simpler than direct individual allotment of products which no longer can be classed as merchandise. Prices have become symbols of distribution and no longer comprise a regulating factor in the economy. While maintaining the form, a complete transformation of function has occurred.[128]

At the same time he says:

In Germany, too, the state, striving to maintain and strengthen its power, determines the character of production and accumulation. Prices lose their regulating function and become merely means of distribution. The economy, and with it the exponents of economic activity are more or less subjected to the state, becoming its subordinates.[129]

From this he draws the conclusion that Russia is neither capitalist nor socialist, but 'represents a *totalitarian state economy*, ie a system to which the economies of Germany and Italy are drawing closer and closer'.[130]

(5) The relations between Russia and world economy

Let us now find out what importance the analysis of the internal relations in Russia has when abstracted from the influence of world economy.

The abstraction has solved one fundamental question: *that the source of the activity of the law of value is not to be found in the internal relations of the Russian economy itself.* In other words it has brought us so far nearer solving the problem of whether Russian economy is subordinated to the law of value by showing us *where not to look* for its source.

This point has great importance. Nearly all those who say that Russian economy is not subordinated to the law of value (such as Hilferding, Bruno R, Shachtman) do so on the basis of the relations within the Russian economy as abstracted from world economy. Some of the few who say that Russian economy is subordinated to the law of value 'find' its *source* in the internal relations.

After eliminating the internal relations in Russian economy as the source of the law of value, we must now examine the relations between the Russian and the world economy. It is here that we do find the source of the activity of the law of value to which Russian economy as a whole is subordinated, and to which, therefore, the internal relations of the economy are also subordinated.

We have said that the relations between the Stalinist state and the total labour time of Russian society are the same as between the factory owner and the amount of labour that he acquires through buying the labour power of a certain number of workers. The division of labour is thus consciously, and not anarchically, realised in Russia. We have yet to see, however, why the Russian state carries out a certain division of the total labour time of Russian society, and not another sort of division. The division of labour in Russia, done independently of competition with other countries, would be absolutely arbitrary. In reality Stalin decides on the division of labour inside Russia in the same way as the individual capitalist decides on the division of labour in his factory. But the decision itself is derived from powers over which he has no control whatsoever—it is derived from the autonomy of world economy, from world competition.

The rate of exploitation, which is the ratio between surplus labour and necessary labour (s/v) is not dependent on the arbitrary will of the Stalinist bureaucracy, but is dictated by the pressure of world capitalism, which compels Russia to undertake a quick accumulation. The same applies to the rise in the organic composition of capital (c/v), and therefore also to the division of the total labour time of Russian society between the two departments of production—the department of means of production and the department of means of consumption (Dept I/Dept II). Thus now, on an international scale, the basic feature of capitalism appears: 'Anarchy in the social division of labour and despotism in that of the workshop are mutual conditions the one of the other.'

Russia would achieve the same result as regards the tendencies of s/v, c/v and Dept I/Dept II if the pressure of international competition took the form of direct commercial competition or military pressure. If Russia made an effort to flood the world market with its products, or other countries flooded the Russian market with their products, the commercial competition ensuing would drive the Russian bureaucracy to cut the costs of production by cutting wages relative to the productivity of labour, or even absolutely (increasing s/v), advancing the technique (increasing c/v), and increasing Dept I/Dept II.

If the international division of labour did not exist, and there were no commercial competition, but competition revealed itself purely in the field of military preparedness and war, the results would be exactly the same.

Hitherto Russia's backwardness has ruled out any question of flooding foreign markets with Russian goods. On the other hand, Russian markets are kept from being flooded with foreign goods by the monopoly of foreign trade which only military might can smash. The combination of these two facts *till now* relegates the commercial struggle to a place of secondary importance,[131] and gives the military struggle pride of place.

The circumstance that the internal competition takes mainly a military form brings about a very interesting result. Because of it the law of value expresses itself in its opposite—the striving after use values. Let us elaborate on this point.

As value is the only expression of the social character of labour in a society of independent producers, a capitalist tries to strengthen his competitive position by increasing the sum of values he owns. As value expresses itself in money, it makes no difference to the capitalist whether he invests his million pounds in shoe production and receives £100,000 profit, or whether he invests it in cannon production and receives £100,000 profit. To get the profit, his product must be sold, therefore it must have use value, but what the use value is is of no account to the capitalist. The aim is value, the means to the aim use value. In the formula of the circulation of capital, M_1-C-M_2, C appears only as a bridge between M_1 and M_2 (M_2, if everything runs smoothly for the capitalist, being larger than M_1).

If there were extensive trade between Russia and other countries, the Stalinist bureaucracy would aim at the production of such commodities as would fetch a high price on the world market, and the purchase of the cheapest commodities possible. It would then strive, as individual capitalists do, to increase the sum of values at its disposal by producing one or another use value, indifferent to which is produced, as long as it serves its end. But if the competition with other countries is mainly military, the state as a *consumer* is interested not in values for their own sake, but in certain definite use values, such as tanks, aeroplanes, etc. Value expresses the existence of competitive relations between independent producers. The results of Russia's standing in competition are expressed by the elevation of use values to an end, the end being victory in this competition. Use values, therefore, while being an end, still remain a means.

This dialectical transformation of means into end, while subordinating the means-end fundamentally to the same end, takes place in the traditional capitalist countries also, although in a more veiled manner. Whereas it makes no difference to the individual Krupp whether he invests his capital in the production of guns or butter, that is, he cares not what use value he produces as long as it brings him the maximum profit, to the state of the Krupps, the use value of the product is very important. The relations of seller and buyer are preserved between Krupp and the state, the former being interested only in value while the latter is interested only in use value. But in reality the relations of exchange are purely formal. The state is no more than the organisation of the Krupps as a collective, and it does not give another commodity in exchange for the guns, but pays for them from the taxes and loans extracted from the whole German economy. Although formally the relation of exchange remains, in essence a certain technique of distributing the war effort over the whole economy is practised. (This would have been absolutely clear if the state, instead of collecting taxes and taking loans in order to buy the guns from Krupp's factory, had produced the guns itself.) The slogan 'Guns before butter' means that the competitive relations between the capitalist powers have reached the stage where the international division of labour is disrupted, where competition through selling and buying is replaced by direct military competition. Thus use values become the aim of capitalist production precisely because they *are not* its aim.

Russia's striving for certain use values in the form of guns, in order to strengthen its position in international competition, does not advance its economy nearer to a socialist economy, which is also motivated by a striving for use values, but on the contrary, makes it its extreme opposite. Obviously, if an increasing rate of exploitation, an increasing subordination of the workers to the means of production, is accompanied only by a greater production of guns, but not of butter, the mode of production will not be less oppressive of the Russian masses, but on the contrary, much more.

(6) Can there be world state capitalism?

From what has been said above in this chapter, it follows that if world production were under one authority, that is, if the Stalinist bureaucracy could unite the world under its rule, and the masses suffered such a regime, we should have a class order with a system of exploitation free of the law of value and all the implications thereof. Bukharin comes to this conclusion in his book *Imperialism and World Economy*. He explains that if the national state organises the national economy, commodity production nevertheless remains 'in the first place [in] the world market'. The economy is therefore state capitalist. But if 'the organisation of all world economy as one gigantic state trust' took place (which Bukharin does not believe is possible):

> ...we would have an entirely new economic form. This would be capitalism no more, for the production of *commodities* would have disappeared; still less would it be *socialism*, for the power of one class over the other would have remained (and even grown stronger). Such an economic structure would, most of all, resemble a slave-owning economy where the slave market is absent.[132]

There is no ground to assume that such a system could exist. If history proves us mistaken, we can only conclude that Marxism was wrong, and that the contradictions within the capitalist system do not lead to socialism, but to a new class system. We should have to contradict Marx's statement that 'the bourgeois relations of production are the last antagonistic form of the social process of production', that they are 'the closing chapter of the prehistoric stage of human society'. To know whether out of the renewed slavery of 'bureaucratic collectivism' a communist society will arise or not, one could not then look to Marxian political economy, which analyses the contradictions of *capitalist* society. Out of the new conditions a new science will have to be developed, even though its roots be embedded in dialectical historical materialism.

Up to now, however, Marxism has not been refuted, but has affirmed itself more surely with every historical development. The revolutionary potentialities of the proletariat in its striving to be the bearer of human history are yet far from being exhausted. We are far from 'the organisation of all world economy as one gigantic state trust'.

As all truth is concrete, the truth about Russia must be seen in the actual tendencies present within it and in its relations to the world. Such an analysis has shown that even if the *form of activity* of the law of value in Russian economy is very complicated and full of deep internal contradictions, *the law of value is nevertheless the central decisive factor in the movement of Russian economy.*

Engels writes in *Anti-Dühring*, 'In the value form of the commodity there is already concealed the whole form of capitalist production, the opposition between capital and labour, the industrial reserve army, the crisis'.[133]

Now, we have dealt with the connection between the law of value and the 'opposition between capital and labour'. But we have not yet dealt with its connection with the 'industrial reserve army, the crisis'. The complicated form which the activity of the law of value takes in Russia warns us in advance against a simplification of the analysis of the industrial reserve army and the crisis (a simplification that has been the disease of the majority of those who have characterised Russia as state capitalist).[134] The analysis of the law of value and Russian economy dealt with in this chapter will serve as an introduction to the analysis in the following chapter of the capitalist crisis and Russian economy.

Chapter 8: Russian economy and the capitalist crisis

(1) The tremendous tempo of development of the productive forces in Stalinist Russia

The tempo of development of the productive forces in Stalinist Russia is greater than it has been in any other country at any time. According to Soviet statistics the industrial production in the years 1928-40, measured in 1926/7 prices, multiplied 7.5 times. This is undoubtedly highly exaggerated. Thus, for instance, while the *value* of machinery and steel products multiplied 13 times, the *volume* of the coal, iron and steel output multiplied only three to five times. As volumes are much more difficult to falsify than price calculations, we may assume that production really multiplied about five times between 1928 and 1940. Even this figure shows that extraordinarily rapid progress was made. Let us compare it with the peak periods of the rise of industrial output in some important countries: in the United States between 1880 and 1890, when industrial production rose relatively quickest, it multiplied 2.2 times; in England between 1860 and 1870 it multiplied 1.29 times; in Germany between 1914 and 1923 it multiplied 1.81 times; in France between 1920 and 1930 it multiplied 2.2 times; in Tsarist Russia between 1890 and 1900 it multiplied 2.5 times and between 1910 and 1913 1.68 times.

(2) How can we explain this extraordinary tempo of development?

The first reason is that a clean sweep was made of feudalism by the October Revolution.

The second reason is the tremendous natural wealth of Russia.

Thirdly, the fact that world technique has advanced much beyond what it was at the time of the industrialisation of England, France, Germany and the US made it possible for Russia to adopt the last word in technique, and in this way to stride very rapidly forward. This factor is connected with the fourth.

The fact that Russian industry was built, so to say, from scratch, meant that the introduction of modern methods of production did not meet the obstacle produced by the existence of old means of production, which was and is a great hindrance in many countries (particularly Britain).

The fifth reason is that there are no monopolist organisations (cartels, syndicates or trusts) which are interested in a 'policy of scarcity' as a means of raising the rate of profit.

The sixth reason is the control of the state over the different elements of the process of reproduction—consumption and accumulation, the movement of workers in the labour market, etc, etc. This control of the state over the economy as a whole makes it possible to depress the standard of living of the masses to a very low level, to produce a very small quantity of means of consumption, and to divert capital and labour power to the production of new means of production. This is indeed the most important factor explaining Russia's quick tempo of industrialisation.[135]

As we shall see below, the last reason, together with the fact that Stalinist Russia began to develop its industry at a time when its productive forces were very much lower than those of the capitalist world as a whole, explain the non-existence hitherto of crises or stagnation. This constitutes the seventh reason for the great expansion of the productive forces in Stalinist Russia. The question of Russian economy and the trade cycles, however, needs special elaboration.

Before doing this, let us first of all summarise the Marxian interpretation of the crisis of overproduction, and then we can tackle the question of whether state capitalism can avoid such crises and, if so, how.

(3) The causes of capitalist crisis

In contradistinction to the pre-capitalist forms of production, accumulation, that is reproduction on an enlarged scale, is an inner necessity of the capitalist form of production. But reproduction on an enlarged scale meets with two obstacles which, although complementary, are yet contradictory. They both arise out of itself, and oppose themselves to it. The one is the decline of the rate of profit which means the decline of the sources of accumulation for reproduction on an enlarged scale. The other is the increase of production above and beyond the market. If not for the first contradiction, the 'underconsumptionist' concept of how to overcome the crisis—by raising the wages of the workers—would have been a simple and excellent method. If not for the second contradiction, fascism, by a continuous cutting of wages, could have saved capitalism from the crisis for at least quite a long period.

Let us begin with the first side of the dilemma of capitalism: the low purchasing power of the masses as a cause of overproduction.

Marx writes:

> The entire mass of commodities, the total product, which contains a portion which is to reproduce the constant and variable capital as well as a portion, representing surplus value, must be sold. If this is not done, or only partly accomplished, or only at prices which are below the prices of production, the labourer has been none the less exploited, but his exploitation does not realise as much for the capitalist. It may yield no surplus value at all for him, or only realise a portion

MARXIST THEORY AFTER TROTSKY

of the produced surplus value, or it may even mean a partial or complete loss of his capital. The conditions of direct exploitation and those of the realisation of surplus value are not identical. They are separated logically as well as by time and space. The first are only limited by the productive power of society, the last by the proportional relations of the various lines of production and by the consuming power of society. The last named power is not determined either by the absolute productive power or by the absolute consuming power, but by the consuming power based on antagonistic conditions of distribution, which reduces the consumption of the great mass of the population to a variable minimum within more or less narrow limits. The consuming power is furthermore restricted by the tendency to accumulate, the greed for an expansion of capital and a production of surplus value on an enlarged scale.[136]

And he adds:

The stupendous productive power developing under the capitalist mode of production relatively to population, and the increase, though not in the same proportion, of capital values (not their material substance) which grow much more rapidly than the population, contradict the basis, which, compared to the expanding wealth, is ever narrowing and for which this immense productive power works, and the conditions, under which capital augments its value. This is the cause of crises.[137]

Marx formulated the same idea in another place thus:

The last cause of all real crises always remains the poverty and restricted consumption of the masses as compared to the tendency of capitalist production to develop the productive forces in such a way that only the absolute power of consumption of the entire society would be their limit.[138]

In the *last analysis*, the cause of the capitalist crisis is rooted in the fact that a greater and greater part of the income of society falls into the hands of the capitalist class, and a greater and greater part of this is directed not towards buying means of consumption, but means of production—is directed towards the accumulation of capital. But, seeing that all means of production are *potentially* means of consumption—ie that after a certain lapse of time the value of the means of production becomes incorporated in means of consumption—therefore the relative increase of the part of the national income directed towards accumulation, as against that part directed towards consumption, must necessarily bring with it overproduction.

And this is a cumulative process. The increase in accumulation is accompanied by rationalisation, and therefore brings in its wake an increase in the rate of exploitation—the greater the rate of exploitation, the greater the fund from which accumulation is drawn, as against the wages of the workers and the revenue of the capitalist directed to consumption; the greater the accumulation, the greater the drive towards additional accumulation.

If 'the poverty and restricted consumption of the masses' were the only cause of the capitalist crisis, the crisis would exist as a permanent phenomenon, as the wages of the workers *always* lag behind the rise in the productivity of labour. We should then not have known the one-time catastrophic equation of different elements.

Before seeing why the crisis is not permanent, let us first of all deal with the second side of the dilemma of capitalism: the decline of the rate of profit. The process of capital accumulation is accompanied by a rise in the organic composition of capital, in other words the substitution of living labour by dead labour. The former produces surplus value, the latter not. This causes the tendency of the decline of the rate of profit. The decline of the rate of profit on its side sharpens the competition between the capitalists, each of whom tries to increase his profit at the expense of his rival. This competition pushes ahead the rationalisation of production, which causes the organic composition of capital to rise even more, which causes the rate of profit to decrease even more, and so the vicious circle begins again.

This tendency alone does not directly explain the cyclical movement of revival, boom, crisis and depression. Marx explains that the decline of the rate of profit which results from the raising of the organic composition of capital is a *very slow* process,[139] which comes up against many counteracting forces. It constitutes the background of the economic cycle. The *immediate* causes of the cycle must be sought in changes in the wage rate which result from changes in the demand for labour power accompanying the process of accumulation. Marx writes clearly about the decline of the rate of profit:

> It promotes overproduction, speculation, crises, surplus capital along with surplus population.[140]

> The barrier of the capitalist mode of production becomes apparent: (1) in the fact that the development of the productive power of labour creates in the falling rate of profit a law which turns into an antagonism of this mode of production at a certain point and requires for its defeat periodical crises.[141]

As regards the rise of the wage level in the wake of the increased employment during a boom, he writes that if it were said:

> ...that the working class receive too small a portion of their own product, and the evil would be remedied by giving them a larger share of it, or raising their wages, we should reply that crises are precisely always preceded by a period in which wages rise generally and the working class actually get a larger share of the annual product intended for consumption.[142]

On the connection between (1) the trade cycle, (2) the rate of profit, (3) the level of wages, and (4) the extent of employment, when the last factor takes on decisive importance in the ending of the boom and the heralding of the crisis, Marx writes:

> The whole form of the movement of modern industry depends, therefore, upon the constant transformation of a part of the labouring population into unemployed or half-employed hands... As the heavenly bodies, once thrown into a certain definite

action, always repeat this, so is it with social production as soon as it is once thrown into this movement of alternate expansion and contraction. Effects, in their turn, become causes, and the varying accidents of the whole process, which always reproduces its own conditions, take on the form of periodicity.[143]

The causal connection between the rate of profit, capital accumulation, the extent of employment and the level of wages may be described thus: the rate of profit determines the rate of accumulation, the rate of accumulation determines the extent of employment, the extent of employment determines the level of wages, the level of wages determines the rate of profit, and so on in a vicious circle. A high rate of profit means a quick accumulation which means an increase in employment and a rise in wages. This cumulative process proceeds to a point where the rise in the wage rate so adversely affects the rate of profit that accumulation either declines catastrophically or ceases altogether.

The *material basis* which unites the cycle of the rate of profit with the cycle of accumulation and the cycle of employment, Marx says, is the life and death of fixed capital (ie machinery, buildings, etc):

> To the same extent that the volume of the value and the duration of the fixed capital develop with the evolution of the capitalist mode of production, does the life of industry and of industrial capital develop in each particular investment into one of many years, say of ten years on an average. If the development of fixed capital extends the length of this life on the one side, it is on the other side shortened by the continuous revolution of the instruments of production, which likewise increases incessantly with the development of capitalist production. This implies a change in the instruments of production and the necessity of continuous replacement on account of virtual wear and tear, long before they are worn out physically. One may assume that this life-cycle, in the essential branches of great industry, now averages ten years. However, it is not a question of any one definite number here. So much at least is evident that this cycle comprising a number of years, through which capital is compelled to pass by its fixed part, furnishes a material basis for the periodical commercial crises in which business goes through successive periods of lassitude, average activity, overspeeding and crisis. It is true that the periods in which capital is invested are different in time and place. But a crisis is always the starting point of a large number of new investments. Therefore it also constitutes, from the point of view of society, more or less of a new material basis for the next cycle of turnover.[144]

This explains why, despite the antagonistic mode of distribution and the tendency of the rate of profit to decline, there is not a permanent crisis of overproduction, but a cyclical movement of the economy. During the period of the renewal of and addition to fixed capital, there is no direct relationship between the immediate introduction of new means of production and the addition to the supply of finished goods. After a certain lapse of time, running into a few years, however, the value of the new means of production begins to be incorporated in new products (means of production and means of consumption alike); this takes place without any, or with only a relatively small, capital investment taking place at the time. Thus capitalism experiences a period of a few years in which investments in the construction of new industries, or the expansion of existing ones, are very large when compared with the rise in the output of finished goods. These are the years of boom. Following this there is a period in which the output of finished goods expands considerably almost simultaneously with a decline in the rate of accumulation. This is the crest of the boom and the harbinger of the coming crisis. Then comes the crisis: production declines catastrophically while investments disappear or even give place to disinvestment.

Bound up with the declining rate of profit in its two aspects (the general tendency towards the decline of the rate of profit and its cyclical movement) and with the 'restricted consumption of the masses'—both as a cause and a result— is another important factor: the disproportionality between different industries.

The disproportionality between different industries may be the direct result of the anarchic character of capitalist production. In this case the capitalists of one industry overestimate the demand for its products and therefore overexpand the production capacity of the industry. As the number of capitalists is large, it is only *after* production has taken place that the capitalist becomes aware through the market that the supply has exceeded the demand. Overproduction in one branch of industry thus causes a decline in prices, a decline in profits, a restriction in production, and a decline in the demand for labour power, raw materials and machinery produced by other factories, etc. This restriction is not necessarily compensated for by the expansion of production in other industries. On the contrary, the contraction of production in one industry can bring in its wake a contraction of production in other industries directly or indirectly dependent on it. If the industry which suffers initially from overproduction is sufficiently important, the cumulative result of the disproportionality between this industry and the rest of the economy can be a *general crisis*. Marx said, 'That a crisis (and hence also overproduction) be general it is enough that it seize hold of the leading articles of commerce'.[145]

In this case the disproportionality between the different industries is the *cause* of the decline of the rate of profit and the decline of the consumption of the masses, and these three factors together bring about the crisis.

It may also happen, however, that the disproportionality between the different industries is the result of the decline of the rate of profit or the underconsumption of the masses even though it in turn influences them. Where on the basis of a certain rate of profit there exists a certain tempo or rate of accumulation, it is here the rate of profit that determines the demand for means of production and thus makes for a certain relation between the demand for the products of the department of means of production and the demand for the products of the department of means of consumption. A decline in the rate of profit, by causing a decline in the rate of accumulation, immediately changes the pattern of demand; and so the proportional relations that previously existed between the production of means of production and the production of means of consumption is turned into a disproportional relation. A similar relation exists between the underconsumption of the masses and the proportionality or disproportionality between the different industries. As Lenin said:

> The 'small consuming power of society', and 'the proportionality of the various branches of production'—these are absolutely not individual, independent, unconnected conditions. On the contrary, a certain state of consumption is one of the elements of proportionality.[146]

One of the expressions of the disproportional development of different industries is the changes in the output of raw materials in comparison with the demand for them. This expresses itself in changes in the prices of raw materials compared with the prices of finished goods. In most cases at the beginning of the revival the supply of raw material exceeds the demand, and their price is therefore low. With the upswing of economic activity, the price of raw materials rises, thus increasing the cost of production, which adversely affects the rate of profit.[147] The fact that in most cases the price of raw materials rises more than the price of finished goods during a boom and falls much more steeply during a crisis, is due to the supply of raw materials being far less elastic than the supply of finished goods.

An additional factor expressing the disproportionality between the different industries, which is more the result than a cause of the economic cycle, but which has nevertheless an important reflex influence, is the rate of interest. The active capitalist—the entrepreneur—does not receive the whole surplus value, but only what remains after the deduction of rent, taxes and interest. In general, at the beginning of the revival, there is an excess of credit over the demand for it, so that the rate of interest is low, in turn encouraging the revival. During the boom the rate of interest continues low, until a short time before the end of the boom when it rises sharply, reaching its maximum with the crisis. After this it falls very sharply.[148] Thus, while the curve of the general rate of profit and the curve of the economic cycle as a whole roughly correspond, the rate of interest makes much more convulsive zig-zags, cutting across the curve of the economic cycle: it is very low at the revival and at the depression—it is very high at the height of the boom and at the crisis. It serves on the one hand to spur the revival on to a wild gallop and on the other to deepen the crisis.

One aspect of the relation between the rate of interest and the profit of enterprise is the plethora and dearth of credit. Credit has made it possible for capitalism to advance at an unprecedented tempo, but at the same time it increases the instability of the system. It blinds the industrialists to the real situation of the market, so that they continue to expand production beyond the point at which they would have stopped if all payment were done in cash. This postpones the actual outbreak of the crisis, but it deepens it when it comes.

One further contributory factor in bringing about the crisis is the chain of middlemen that usually exists between the industrial capitalist and the consumers. Owing to their activity production can within certain limits increase without the sale of products to the consumers correspondingly increasing. The unsold products remain as stocks in the hands of the merchants.[149]

(4) State capitalism and the crisis: the posing of the problem

Even a superficial glance shows that some of the causes which bring about a crisis of overproduction in traditional capitalism would not exist under conditions of state capitalism. For instance, the last factor mentioned above, the chain of middlemen between producers and consumers, which blinds the producers to the true situation of the market, not only would not exist under state capitalism, but even under individual capitalism is theoretically capable of elimination, by the industrialist selling his product directly to the consumer through a trading network of his own. Credit too, as a factor encouraging production beyond the point it would go to if all payments were in cash, as well as the influence of the rate of interest as a factor accentuating the boom and deepening the crisis, would not act under state capitalism as a contributory cause of the oscillatory movement of production: here, as the state is the owner of all capital, credit acts in fundamentally the same way as if each capitalist used only his capital; in other words, as if credit does not exist at all. The factor of disproportionality as the initial cause of the crisis (not as an accompanying phenomenon of the decline of the rate of profit or underconsumption of the masses) will also not exist under state capitalism. Although mistakes in investment are not excluded, and it is possible that the supply of a certain product may exceed the demand, the fact that the state plans production and demand excludes wide disproportionalities. Moreover, as the state is the owner of all the industries, in place of the cumulative process of decline in prices and a decline of the rate of profit which spreads from one industry to another, the whole economy will *directly* bear the difficulties which are the result of a partial overproduction. Then, when the next production turnover takes place, the production of this product will be decreased and equilibrium restored. That these factors do not exist is conditioned on a consideration of the internal relations of the state capitalist economy alone. If the state capitalist economy produces for the world market, receives credit from other countries, etc, these factors will have a certain influence on it. (This will be dealt with more extensively below.)

But what about the fundamental dilemma which traditional capitalism is always faced with: how can a high rate of profit be achieved while at the same time the surplus value is realised; how can a quick accumulation be undertaken without undermining the market which is necessary for it? We know that in a certain phase of the cycle—the boom—traditional capitalism temporarily solves the problem: a high rate of profit brings about a quick accumulation, that is a big rise in the production of means of production relatively to the means of consumption, so that the market for the realisation of a big part of the surplus value is in the department of means of production, which is the system of production itself. (*This alone* is sufficient to explain why the underconsumption of the masses does not cause a permanent crisis and prevent the expansion of production under capitalism altogether.) If capitalism could transform the phase of the boom from a temporary to a permanent one, overproduction would never exist. Can state capitalism do this? Can it ensure a high rate of profit, a high rate of accumulation, a high level of production, while yet preserving the antagonistic way of distribution, 'the poverty and restricted consumption of the masses'?

Before answering these fundamental questions, we shall diverge a little from our subject, but only to take a short cut to the answer.

Two important economists tried to prove that, however restricted the consumption of the masses, a crisis of overproduction is not inevitable. The one is Mikhail Tugan-Baranowsky, the most original theoretician of revisionism, the other Dr F A von Hayek, the outstanding bourgeois economist. Their analyses may serve a useful purpose as an introduction to the solution of the problem posed.

(5) Hayek

Dr Hayek, in his book *Prices and Production* (London, 1931), describes the structure of production as a triangle made up of different layers of production. The base is the means of consumption end, and the apex is the producers' goods end. During recovery and boom, as he correctly states, the production of means of production increases as against the production of means of consumption; during a crisis the production of means of production drops sharply, the drop being larger than that of the production of means of consumption. Recovery and boom produce the sides of the triangle, lengthening the structure, while the crisis shortens it. Again he correctly concludes from this that in order to make the boom a permanent phenomenon it is necessary to keep on raising the apex. Concretely this means that there should be a continuously high rate of profit and high rate of accumulation, so that the production of means of production is always big compared with the production of means of consumption. How can this be achieved? With the technical change, workers and capital must be transferred from the production of means of consumption to the production of means of production: more people will be employed in the production of machinery in order to produce machinery in order to produce machinery and so on, so that the total quantity of means of consumption produced will increase very slowly notwithstanding the tremendous rise in productive capacity. John Strachey, who deals fully with and competently criticises Hayek's ideas in his book *The Nature of Capitalist Crisis*, sums up the Hayekian 'solution' in these words:

> The structure of production must get longer and longer. The sides of the Hayekian triangle must be produced and produced. This, then, is the Hayek-Robbins solution of the dilemma. It is possible, they imply, for all the conditions which are necessarily to the existence of capitalism to be fulfilled simultaneously. It is possible for wages to be kept down to 'economic levels', and yet for there to be no glut of consumers' commodities. For if the demand for consumers' commodities is thus minimised, no excess of consumers' commodities will be produced. The entire increase of society's productive power will be devoted to increasing the production of production's goods. And if this is done, then there will be no need to increase

the ultimate market. The entire increase in the supply of commodities will be an increase in producers' commodities, which can be absorbed *within* the structure of production. For that structure will be getting longer and longer. Hence there will be no need for any increased supply of actual consumers' commodities ever to emerge from the productive process. Industry can take in its own washing on an ever more gigantic scale and forever. The overwhelming majority of mankind can continue to live on a subsistence level in perpetuity and our ever growing powers of production can be permanently absorbed by the task of producing new means of production. Thus there need be no crisis. Capitalism need never feel the lack of a larger market for consumers' goods, for it will never increase the production of consumers' goods. *The market for which capitalism will produce will be within itself. It will be within its own ever lengthening structure of production.*[150]

(6) Tugan-Baranowsky

Similar conclusions were reached by Tugan-Baranowsky about 50 years ago. However low the rate of profit, he says, and however low the purchasing power of the masses, no crisis need break out if a certain relation be kept between the two departments of industry so that means of consumption decline more and more relatively to means of production. Taking his conclusion to its end he writes:

> If all workers except one disappear and are replaced by machines, then this one single worker will place the whole enormous mass of machinery in motion and with its assistance produce new machines—and the consumption goods of the capitalists. The working class will disappear, which will not in the least disturb the self-expansion process (*Verwertungsprozess*) of capital. The capitalists will receive no smaller mass of consumption goods; the entire product of one year will be realised and utilised by the production and consumption of the capitalist in the following year. Even if the capitalists desire to limit their own consumption, no difficulty is presented; in this case the production of capitalists' consumption goods partially ceases, and an even larger part of the social product consists of means of production, which serve the purpose of further expanding production. For example, iron and coal are produced which serve always to expand the production of iron and coal. The expanded production of iron and coal of each succeeding year uses up the increased mass of products turned out in the preceding year, until the supply of necessary minerals is exhausted.[151]

Clearly, as Tugan-Baranowsky himself remarks, the main point of his analysis is not:

> ...the wholly arbitrary and unreal assumption that the replacement of manual labour by machinery leads to an absolute diminution in the number of workers...but rather the thesis that, given a proportional distribution of social production, no decline in social consumption is capable of producing a surplus product.[152]

(7) Why the Hayek-Tugan 'solution' is impossible under individual capitalism

Tugan-Baranowsky's and Hayek's 'solution' is impossible of realisation under individual capitalism because of the mutual dependence of the two departments of production, and the blind method of exchange between them.

Capitalist production is on the one hand a production of use values. On the other it is a production of values. Insofar as it is a production of use values, its aim is independent of the social form of production, the aim being the satisfaction of human needs. Insofar as it is a production of values, its aim is accumulation—'to conquer the world of social wealth, to increase the mass of human beings exploited by him [the capitalist]'.[153] Though the capitalist consider use value but the bearer of value, though he consider consumption but a means and not an end, nevertheless the means is vital, as without it the end cannot be achieved. Accumulation is the objective end of capitalism, but consumption is the objective end of human beings. The former cannot exist without the latter:

> Consumption produces production by creating the necessity for new production…
> No wants, no production. But consumption reproduces the want.[154]

The dependence of accumulation on consumption necessarily means the dependence of the department of means of production on the department of means of consumption. Under individual capitalism this dependence works out blindly. If the ratio of the supply and demand of means of production increases relatively to that of means of consumption, the price of means of production will decrease relatively to the price of means of consumption; as a result the rate of profit will decrease in Department I (means of production) and will increase in Department II (means of consumption); the outcome of this will be: (1) a slackening of accumulation in Department I and an acceleration of it in Department II; (2) a stream of capital flowing from Department I to Department II. This will continue till proportionality between the two departments is restored.

A necessary element in this process is the free movement of the price of commodities, and the free movement of capital from one department to another. An additional element is the rise in the wage rate following on the extensive employment in Department I which causes an increase in the demand for the products of Department II.

These factors make the application of the Hayek-Tugan 'solution' impossible under individual capitalism.

(8) The Hayek-Tugan 'solution' can be realised for a certain time under state capitalism

The Hayek-Tugan 'solution', despite its absurdity from a capitalist standpoint, objectively has a sound basis. The 'solution' is in reality merely the extension of the phase of revival and boom, a phase in which accumulation increases more than personal consumption, and the production of means of production increases more quickly than the production of means of consumption. For a certain number of years accumulation can far exceed consumption without disturbing the equilibrium. This and the fact that the material basis which unites the cycle of the rate of profit, accumulation and employment is the life and death of fixed capital (the machinery, buildings, etc), suggest that if it were possible to prevent increased production in Department II, and at the same time continuously and steadily to increase production in Department I, the length of the boom would be longer than in the decennial cycle. This can be done by state capitalism. The state, by its ownership of the total capital, can, while greatly increasing the production of Department I relatively to Department II, prevent the stream of capital from Department I to Department II.

State capitalism eliminates another cause of the turn from boom to crisis under individual capitalism, and gives a basis for the realisation of the Hayek-Tugan 'solution' for a time. Under individual capitalism a high rate of profit causes quick accumulation, extensive employment and high wages. This process proceeds to a point where the wages reach such a level that the rate of profit is adversely affected and drops catastrophically, dragging down with it accumulation, employment and wages. When the workers under capitalism are relatively free to bargain over the sale of their labour power, the 'relative surplus population is...the pivot upon which the law of demand and supply of labour works. It confines the field of action of this law within the limits absolutely convenient to the activity of exploitation and to the domination of capital'.[155]

Under a totalitarian state capitalist regime, even if there is relatively no surplus population, and full employment prevails, wages can for a long time remain 'within the limits absolutely convenient to the activity of exploitation and to the domination of capital'.

The Tugan-Hayek 'solution' is therefore possible of realisation in a state capitalism which lags behind world capitalism, in which means of production are scarce and where therefore the production of machinery in order to produce machinery in order to produce machinery and so on reflects the necessities of the national capitalist economy.

But what will happen when the production of machinery to produce machinery to produce machinery and so on raises the state capitalist country out of its backwardness? Will the crisis of overproduction break out in highly developed state capitalist economies?

The only Marxist theoretician to pose and deal with this question was Bukharin.

(9) Bukharin on the crisis in state capitalism

In his polemical book on Rosa Luxemburg's theory of accumulation, *Der Imperialismus und die Akkumulation des Kapitals*, Bukharin poses, among other problems, the question of the process of reproduction on an enlarged scale in state capitalism, and discusses whether a crisis of overproduction would take place in it. He defines state capitalism in these words: 'The capitalist class united in one united trust, an organised economy, but one which is at the same time, from the standpoint of the *classes*, antagonistic'.[156]

He continues:

> Is accumulation possible here? Naturally. *The constant capital grows, since the consumption of the capitalists grows* [my emphasis]. New branches of production corresponding to new needs are always established. The consumption of the workers, although definite limits are placed upon it, grows. Despite this 'underconsumption' of the masses no crisis arises, *as the demand of the various branches of production for each other's products as well as the demand of the consumers*, capitalists as well as workers, is fixed in advance. (Instead of 'anarchy' of production—what is from the standpoint of capital a rational plan.) *The consumption of the capitalists is the motive power for production and for the production plan* [my emphasis]. Consequently there is in this case not a *specially* rapid development of production (there is a small number of capitalists).[157]

The words 'in this case not a *specially* rapid development of production' are liable to mislead. Production not only will be 'not especially rapid', but will be very slow compared with the production capacity of capitalist economy: there will be stagnation.[158]

At first glance it might seem that Bukharin's description of the relation between state capitalism and the crisis of overproduction is the absolute opposite of the Tugan-Hayek 'solution'. Whereas Tugan and Hayek speak about capitalism in which there is a very rapid rise of production and accumulation, Bukharin speaks about capitalism in which production and accumulation are very slow. While Tugan and Hayek speak about accumulation increasing entirely independently of consumption, Bukharin speaks about accumulation as a dependant, an accompaniment of consumption. But notwithstanding the antagonism between Tugan-Hayek and Bukharin, they are connected with each other in both pointing to the fundamental contradiction which exists in capitalism between accumulation and consumption. The former points to the possibility of overcoming this contradiction by fully liberating accumulation (and production) from consumption; the latter points to the possibility of overcoming it by slowing down accumulation (and production) in accordance with consumption. The former says production for accumulation's sake alone; the latter that quick accumulation is impossible and production will therefore slow down. The former reflects the boom phase of the capitalist cycle in which accumulation far surpasses consumption; the latter the phase of crisis in which accumulation falls far below consumption. In both the worker remains oppressed by capital.

The Tugan-Hayek 'solution' is possible for state capitalism in a backward country. Bukharin's description fits state capitalism which reaches the saturation point of means of production.[159] This latter is a capitalism apparently free of crisis, but in reality in permanent crisis. A crisis which expresses itself in production's not rising above the demand is fundamentally the same as stagnation in which production is *restricted* to the demand. Both express the conflict between the productive forces and the capitalist relations of production and distribution.

When the Tugan-Hayek process ends and the Bukharinist period begins, will unemployment appear?

It will not. Under individual capitalism, the change in the relative size of the reserve army regulates the level of wages: with the decline of the rate of profit, the economy reacts automatically by throwing workers out of industry and increasing the reserve army, which, after a shorter or longer period, brings about a decline in wages and the restoration of the rate of profit, encouraging capitalist production from anew. Under state capitalism this automatism is replaced by the administrative action of the employer-state, which achieves the same objective result of cutting costs of production (necessary in the state capitalist country to encourage production in the interests of its competition on an international scale) in a different way. In a crisis under individual capitalism, let us say 20 percent of the workers are thrown out of employment and the standard of living of the masses (those who receive wages as well as the unemployed who receive relief) falls by 50 percent; state capitalism can achieve exactly the same results in the level of production and costs of production by keeping full employment, but cutting wages by 50 percent and cutting the time every worker works by 20 percent. (In addition to what the workers suffer through their wages being cut, this would mean further hardships for them as they would be shifted from one industry to another, would have to migrate from one place to another, etc.)

(10) Will the development of production in a state capitalist economy receive a cyclical form?

We have explained that the material basis for the oscillatory movement of economy is the life and death of fixed capital. As in Russia the renewal of the fixed capital does not take the form of a one-time expansion and then stoppage, the anarchy in the renewal of fixed capital (that is the anarchy in accumulation) is not a factor making for an oscillatory movement.

We have seen that the decline of the rate of profit has two aspects: the one, the continuous slow decline of the rate of profit as a result of the rise of the organic composition of capital; the other, the swift decline of the rate of profit as a result of changes in the wage level. The latter alone constitutes a cause of the oscillatory movement. Because of the total suppression of the workers by the state in Russia, this factor does not affect it. The only factor which does affect it is the general decline of the rate of profit consequent upon the continuous rise in the organic composition of capital. This does not drive Russian economy towards an oscillatory movement, but towards eventual stagnation (which in the present Tugan-Hayek stage is overcome, as we have explained, by the production of machinery in order to produce machinery in order to produce machinery and so on).

As credit does not push production in Russia beyond the point where it would have stopped had all payments been made in cash, the money market is not a cause of the cyclical movement of the economy. Strachey describes the movement of the economy under creditless capitalism:

If we can imagine a creditless capitalism in which every transaction was mediated by hard cash, then it is true that the oscillatory form of the crisis, but not the crisis itself, might be abolished. We should get a slow, steady decline of the rate of profit which would act upon the system like a creeping paralysis.[160]

(11) How will state capitalism try to overcome the stagnation?

Before approaching this question, let us see how capitalism has hitherto overcome crises. On this *The Communist Manifesto* says:

> And how does the bourgeoisie get over these crises? On the one hand by enforced destruction of a mass of productive forces; on the other by the conquest of new markets, and by the more thorough exploitation of the old ones. That is to say, by paving the way for more extensive and more destructive crises, and by diminishing the means whereby crises are prevented.

The same idea Marx expressed in *Wage Labour and Capital* thus:

> In the measure that the capitalists are compelled...to exploit the already existing gigantic means of production on a larger scale and to set in motion all the mainsprings of credit to the end, to the same measure do the industrial earthquakes increase, in which the trading world can only maintain itself by sacrificing a part of wealth, products and even of productive forces, to the gods of the underworld—in a word, crises increase. They become more frequent and more violent, if only because in the same measure in which the mass of production, and consequently, the need for extended markets, grows, the world market becomes more and more contracted, fewer and fewer new markets remain available for exploitation, since every preceding crisis has subjected to world trade a market hitherto unconquered or only superficially exploited.

Thus the bourgeoisie overcomes crises not only by the destruction—including the important factor of devaluation—of many of the productive forces, but also by the conquest of new markets. The importance of these conquests for the overcoming of crises was expressed most lucidly by Marx in the chapter on crises in *Capital*:

> This is a law of capitalist production imposed by incessant revolutions in the methods of production themselves, the resulting depreciation of existing capital, the general competitive struggle and the necessity of improving the product and expanding the scale of production, for the sake of self-preservation and on penalty of failure. The market must, therefore, be continually extended, so that its interrelations and the conditions regulating them assume more and more the form of a natural law independent of the producers and become ever more uncontrollable. This internal contradiction seeks to balance itself by an expansion of the outlying fields of production. But to the extent that the productive power develops, it finds itself at variance with the narrow basis on which the conditions of consumption rest.[161]

State capitalism, on coming to the crisis of overproduction, will be faced with much deeper contradictions than individual capitalism, and at the same time the means of overcoming them *inside the country itself* will be much smaller. That the surplus of products will be immense is clear from the fact that state capitalism brings to its peak the antagonistic character of distribution, the accumulation of capital, while it depresses to the extreme the standard of living of the masses. With the abolition of individual peasant economy, with the transformation of the masses of peasants into wage earners, with the transformation of Russia as a whole into one state capitalist economy, the possibilities of overcoming the crisis with the help of internal forces alone cease to exist. To emerge from the crisis demands: cutting wages, cutting the price of raw materials, devaluating fixed capital, and finding new markets.

(1) As regards the cutting of wages: even if we assume that the wages in Russia are not the physical minimum, to cut them will not overcome the crisis, but will only increase the rate of exploitation; in order, however, that the surplus value be realised, it is necessary to enlarge the markets. In the conditions of individual capitalism, where, besides workers and capitalists, there are millions of peasants, urban petty bourgeoisie, etc, the cutting of the wages of the industrial workers does not eliminate the possibility of finding new markets inside the country (at least as long as the capitalist economy is not developed, as long as the internal contradictions are not too deep for the pre-capitalist elements in the country to carry). In the conditions of state capitalism the increase in the rate of exploitation in itself will not pull the economy out of the crisis. Expansion to other countries will be imperative.

(2) As regards the lowering of the prices of raw materials: during a crisis, under conditions of individual capitalism, the price of raw materials usually drops, and through this the rate of profit in industry rises. In this way industry puts the burden of its difficulties on the shoulders of the producers of raw materials—first and foremost the agriculturists in the colonies. Not only, however, does agriculture suffer, but monopolist industry increases its rate of profit at the expense of other industries also. Under conditions of state capitalism all the branches of the economy comprise different elements of one and the same economic enterprise, and the rate of profit cannot rise through one branch raising its prices against another.

(3) As regards the devaluation of capital, in a crisis in the countries of individual capitalism a large part of the fictitious capital is annihilated. Financial manipulations connected with this process bring about a redivision of the surplus value among a smaller number of capitalists, so that the rate of profit increases. Connected with this process, and one of its expressions, is the selling of industrial enterprises to new buyers for low prices—such low prices as make the enterprises profitable concerns even in a crisis. Self-evidently a precondition for this process is the existence of individual ownership over the means of production—state capitalism excludes it. The only means of capital devaluation possible during a crisis under state capitalism is the wear and tear of the machines which lie idle, including their 'moral' wear and tear, ie obsolescence.

(4) As regards the finding of new markets: as we have said, state capitalism which has reached the stage of overproduction cannot, during a crisis when the building of new industries stops, find new markets of any considerable size inside the country itself. It must expand to foreign markets.

In the Tugan-Hayek stage, while Russia's monopoly of foreign trade preserves it from foreign commodities, Russia itself directs its efforts not to production for foreign markets, but to production for its own industries. We have already seen how restricted is Russia's foreign trade, which is directed mainly towards selling products in order to buy new means of production. In 1937, for instance, means of production made up 90.9 percent of all the imports, while means of consumption made up only 9.1 percent.[162]

If the end of the Tugan-Hayek phase were to approach, Stalinist Russia, faced with the creeping paralysis Bukharin describes—which cannot be overcome internally—would be thrown onto the world market.

The rise of Russia's productive capacity itself will produce certain bottlenecks as a result of the uneven tempo of development of certain industries. (Even today there is a serious bottleneck in the lag of oil output behind that of the other basic industries.) In order to overcome these, to take advantage of certain superior natural conditions and to decrease the disadvantages of other natural conditions, Russia will tend to increase international exchange relations.

The need to accumulate—the result of industrial and military competition—will also at this stage drive Russia to compete on the world market.

There is no Chinese wall between the Tugan-Hayek and the Bukharinist stage. Between the tendency towards national economic autarky and the expansion to the world market, there is also no Chinese wall. Insofar as both transitions take place simultaneously, the picture of developed state capitalism given by Bukharin will need correction. On the background of the general stagnation of state capitalist economy, a cyclical movement will arise as a result of the cycles on the world market. Not one of the waves, however, will bring a boom which to any considerable extent ameliorates the conditions of the masses.

(12) Production and consumption of means of destruction

As we have said, so long as a state capitalist country is backward, production can, in spite of antagonistic distribution, of the 'restricted consumption of the masses', rise continuously, as means of production produce means of production to produce means of production and so on. When the production of means of production reaches saturation point (which is a relative concept compared with other countries) then 'the consumption of the capitalists is the motive of production'. But as 'the capitalist process of production is essentially a process of accumulation',[163] production whose motive is consumption is clearly the negation of capitalism. This negation reveals itself in traditional capitalism in the recurring crises of overproduction at which time accumulation ceases altogether and there is even disaccumulation, which bears witness to the fact that

the capitalist relations of production and distribution have become an impediment to the accumulation of capital. It reveals itself in state capitalism when
the economy reaches the 'Bukharinist' stage of stagnation: the accumulation of
the past becomes an impediment to additional accumulation, the relations of
production and distribution become an impediment to accumulation, capital
becomes the limit for the accumulation of capital.

From the standpoint of the economy as a whole, what is specific about the
consumption of the capitalists is the fact that it *does not* constitute part of the
process of reproduction. The consumption of means of production reveals itself
in new means of production or consumption, the means of consumption consumed by the workers reveal themselves in the reproduction of labour power
which is a necessary element of the process of reproduction as a whole, but the
products consumed by the bourgeoisie do not appear as an element in any form
in the new production cycle. It is only a negative element, a subtraction from
the process of reproduction.

There is, however, one kind of consumption which, while it is a subtraction
from the process of reproduction just as much as the personal consumption of
the bourgeoisie, nevertheless constitutes a *means* in the hands of the bourgeoisie to get new capital, new possibilities of accumulation, to 'accumulate…to
conquer the world of social wealth, to increase the mass of human beings exploited'. This is war production. If we called the one kind the 'personal consumption of the capitalist', we should have to call the armaments, equipment
and stores of the soldiers the 'collective consumption of the capitalist class'.
Although both the 'personal consumption of the capitalist' and the 'collective
consumption of the capitalist class' are a subtraction from the process of reproduction, there is a fundamental difference between them from the standpoint
of the capitalist class, and from the standpoint of humanity as a whole.

Let us begin by analysing the difference from the standpoint of the capitalist class.

The employment of a certain number of workers to cater for the 'personal consumption of the capitalist' will have the same direct results as the employment
of the same number of workers to serve the 'collective consumption of the capitalist class'; but *indirectly* the latter has invaluable advantages from the standpoint of the capitalist class: for in the event of a military victory the wealth of
the victorious capitalist state will increase at the expense of the vanquished.

The production of guns, let us say in Germany, did not influence the accumulation or the rate of profit in any way other than if palaces for the bourgeoisie had been built, or even if uncompetitive products (ie uncompetitive
with existing enterprises such as public palaces, parks, etc) had been produced
which had been distributed gratis to the people. But the necessities of capitalist competition drove the German bourgeoisie to employ part of the population,
not in the construction of palaces for the people, nor even for the bourgeoisie
itself, but in war economy and war.[164]

The common factor of a war economy and a crisis of overproduction is that real
accumulation is very small. If we add to this small accumulation the personal

consumption of the capitalists, then subtract the wear and tear of capital, the destruction, etc from this sum, the rate of profit will be seen to be very low or even many times negative. (At the same time one industrial enterprise increases its capital at the expense of another.) Seeing that in respect of accumulation crisis and war have fundamentally the same results, it can be assumed theoretically that in place of the boom-crisis-boom cycle will come the boom-war-boom cycle. And seeing that the tendency of declining capitalism is the lengthening and deepening of the crisis, and the shortening of the boom which also becomes ever more superficial, we may theoretically assume that capitalism will enter a period whose characteristic feature is a cycle of wars and booms in which the former become ever longer and more destructive, and the latter ever shorter and more superficial. The *only impediment* to the complete transformation of the capitalist cycle from boom-crisis-boom to boom-war-boom is the social opposition of the masses. This alone can prevent the US, for instance, from making even vaster preparations for a third world war, or beginning the war itself when the post-war boom and the Marshall Plan exhaust themselves. Whereas in respect of capital accumulation, the direct result of a war economy is in essence the same as that of a crisis, in respect of the level of production, the use of productive capacity, a war economy is like a capitalist boom: in both the economy works at full blast. The boom-war-boom cycle would thus appear as the abolition of the economic cycle, as all the time there would be full employment, and the economy would be working at full blast.

The crisis of overproduction is at one and the same time an affirmation and negation of the capitalist mode of production. It is an affirmation because it is specific to it, and a negation because it throws into relief the impediments to this mode of production embodied in itself. This is equally true as regards the war economy. But here we must go further. A capitalist war does not lead only to a stoppage of accumulation and a destruction of capital to a point where accumulation becomes possible from anew. It can lead to destruction of such dimensions as signify a tendency towards the *absolute* negation of capitalism (on condition, of course, that the proletarian revolution does not negate capitalism) by barbarism. The war, like the crisis, is a partial negation of capitalism, but may lead to its absolute negation.

Once again we see that when the bourgeoisie comes into the most extreme conflict with the needs of humanity, as it does when entering the war cycle out of the crisis cycle, it uses elements of a socialist society. The state, intervening ever more in the direction of the economy, uses the socialist element of planning in the interests of stabilising its oppressive regime. In a war economy, as in a socialist economy, production goes on at full blast. But production at full blast where the relations of distribution are antagonistic, where the large-scale accumulation of the past impedes new accumulation, is possible only if a large part of the products is not exchanged, is not produced as values, but as use values. In a socialist economy the aim of production is use values; in a capitalist war economy a major part of production too is the production of use values. But use values in a socialist society are those needed by the masses, while in a capitalist war economy they comprise guns, equipment and stores for soldiers, etc—use values determined in the interests of an exploiting minority. In a socialist society use values are the aim of production; in a capitalist war economy use values are means to 'conquer the world of social wealth, to increase the mass of human beings exploited'. What is common to a capitalist war economy and a socialist economy make them extreme opposites.

If Stalinist Russia is not overthrown by the proletarian revolution or smashed in an imperialist war, and it completes the Tugan-Hayek stage, the bureaucracy will then have three methods open to it of circumventing overproduction and stagnation: (1) raising the standard of living of the masses; (2) increasing the personal consumption of the bureaucracy; (3) increasing the 'collective consumption' of the bureaucracy (war production). In the light of the masses' lack of control over the means of production, and the sharpening antagonisms among the different powers, we may incontrovertibly say that the tendency overshadowing everything will be the third.

It is childish to ask whether Russia's development in the Tugan-Hayek direction, or at a later stage towards the stagnation of production or towards a war economy, is the outcome of *internal* forces alone. It is as childish as to ask the same question regarding *one* individual capitalist in another country. If accumulation is necessary, it is only because of a competition between one capitalist and other capitalists. If accumulation at a certain stage comes to a standstill, but the capitalists do not build pyramids or palaces for the people, it is not because the individual capitalist gets less profit from this than by producing guns, but because the production of guns holds on its horizon the promise of control over wealth and people—and this is a necessity of competition.

It has been a necessary abstraction at a certain stage of our analysis to assume that only with the completion of the Tugan-Hayek stage would Russia be driven to a production whose motive is the consumption of the bureaucracy, and primarily their 'collective consumption'. Now it is necessary to approach nearer to reality.

The Stalinist regime, as we have said, came into being as the result of two factors: the maturity of the world for socialism, and the backwardness of the Russian economy. The backwardness of Russia explains the possibility of the Tugan-Hayek stage; the maturity of the world in the face of the belatedness of the proletarian revolution brings the imperialist war to the foreground, which poses the necessity for Russia to undertake war production. Russia, therefore, produces machinery to produce machinery and so on, and at the same time must undertake war production. The war economy itself postpones the completion of the Tugan-Hayek stage.

(13) The perspectives of Russian economy and the social character of the regime

As we know, every ruling class develops the productive forces up to a certain stage. We could hence define the class character of the regime in Russia according to the stage to which this regime can develop the productive forces.

If we find that the existing regime in Russia can (if it is not overthrown) develop the productive forces to a higher stage than capitalism did and could, it is sure proof that the ruling class in Russia is not fulfilling only the historical mission of the capitalist class. We should then have a new class to define.

The unparalleled tempo of development of the economy in Russia does not in itself prove the non-capitalist character of its system. We know, for instance, that United States capitalism developed incomparably more quickly than British capitalism. What we need to know in order to characterise the regime is the limits to which the productive forces in it can develop.

According to Marx, the only limit to the development of the productive forces under capitalism, the only limit to the accumulation of capital, is capital itself. Capitalist relations of production engender the conflict between production and consumption, the tendency towards the decline of the rate of profit, etc. Now, as we have shown, these same limits will restrict the development of the productive forces in Russia. After the point of saturation of the economy with means of production (which depends on the prevailing productive forces in the world) the productive forces in Russia will meet the same impediments as those in other countries. Thus, if we assume that Russia will not be conquered and destroyed by another power, it will succeed in developing its productive forces only to the same stage as world capitalism did, even though it may be the strongest power in the world. The Tugan-Hayek 'solution' and the Bukharinist stage are expressions of the incapacity of the regime to use production in the interests of the masses, and the regime is therefore driven either to the production of machinery to produce machinery and so on, or to stagnation, or to a war economy as a means 'to conquer the world of social wealth, to increase the mass of human being exploited'.

One may say that all this is true only if one assumes that the antagonistic mode of distribution does not cease to exist. But to assume that the privileged rulers of Russia, who find themselves in opposition to the toilers on the one hand and to other capitalist powers on the other, will abolish this is as logical as to assume that the American capitalists will do it. The fact that the existing regime in Russia thus limits the development of the productive forces proves the capitalist character of this regime.

This throws new light also on another question that has already been dealt with—the relations of production and distribution in Russia. According to Trotsky the relations of distribution prevailing in Russia are capitalist relations, while the relations of production are not. As we have remarked, the abstraction of relations of distribution from relations of production is foreign to Marxism. The analysis of this chapter has furnished a new proof of this: on the basis of the existing productive forces, an antagonistic capitalist method of distribution must have the same effect on the *general* development of the productive forces. We see again that the relations of distribution make up one of the important elements in the law of movement of the productive forces—they are part and parcel of the relations of production.

The above analysis of the limits of the development of the productive forces in Russia also takes the ground from beneath all those who try to define the ruling class in Russia as non-capitalist and non-proletarian, those who say that it is bureaucratic collectivist, managerial, etc.

One must not understand the words 'limit to the development of the productive forces' mechanistically and take them to mean that there are absolute, inflexible limits. Under feudalism the limits to the development of the productive forces were the feudal relations of production: the productive forces could not develop beyond the limits of individual production. The socialisation of labour brought with it the destruction of feudalism. But although the limits of production under feudalism were the same in the different countries, the level of technique, productivity of labour and so forth reached were not exactly the same. The same applies to the limits of development on manorial or church property.

And we may say that just as the feudal character of church property is proved by the identity of the limits of development on this and on manorial property so the capitalist character of Russia is proved by the identity of the limits of its productive forces and those of world capitalism.

Chapter 9: The imperialist expansion of Russia

Empires existed before the monopolist stage of capitalism, and even before capitalism itself. The Persian Empire rose at an almost unparalleled tempo between 555 and 525 BC, and comprised an area eight times larger than that of Germany; subsequently the Greek Empire rose, then the Roman Empire. The decline of feudalism and the rise of commercial capital saw the rise of the big Spanish, Portuguese and Dutch empires. With the advent of the industrial revolution, England in two generations—from the beginning of the Seven Years War (1756) to the end of the Napoleonic Wars (1814)—built its empire by conquering Canada, the decisive section of India, South Africa and Australia.

The imperialism of every period, however, is different in its motives and results, and the use of the one word, imperialism, to describe the different phenomena is therefore liable to bring about more confusion than clarity. Lenin used the term for the highest stage of capitalism, when it is in decline, and the proletarian revolution is on the order of the day. But the empires of even this one period have very different characters. Zinoviev says in his article 'What is Imperialism?'

> In doing this [defining what modern imperialism actually is] we must not forget that there are various types of imperialism. British imperialism differs from German imperialism, etc. There is a European imperialism, an Asiatic imperialism and an American imperialism; there is a white imperialism and a yellow imperialism. Japanese imperialism doesn't resemble the French type; Russian imperialism is of quite a unique type, because it is a backward (it is not even possible any longer to say an Asiatic) imperialism, developing on the basis of an extraordinary backwardness.[165]

If, as Lenin explains, the *typical feature* of imperialism is the search for fields of capital export, while for young capitalism the typical feature was the search for markets, it seems wrong to have called Tsarist Russia imperialist. But all the Marxists, including Lenin and Trotsky, did call it imperialist. And they were correct. For in the context of world economy, and the relations prevailing between Tsarist Russia and the highly developed countries, which is the criterion for its definition, Tsarist Russia was imperialist in the Leninist sense.

Lenin's definition of imperialism gives:

...the following five essential features:
(1) The concentration of production and capital developed to such a stage that it creates monopolies which play a decisive role in economic life.
(2) The merging of bank capital with industrial capital, and the creation, on the basis of 'finance capital', of a financial oligarchy.
(3) The export of capital, which has become extremely important, as distinguished from the export of commodities.
(4) The formation of internal capitalist monopolies which share the world among themselves.
(5) The territorial division of the whole world among the greatest capitalist powers is completed.[166]

Of the first feature state capitalism is certainly a species, as it consists of one general state monopoly. As regards the second feature, the merging of bank and industrial capital reaches the highest stage when the state is the industrial and banking capitalist together. As regards the fourth feature, the increasing competition between the imperialist powers drives the state—especially emphasised in Germany and Japan—to cut across the international capitalist monopolies. It is clear that the economic invasion of an international capitalist monopoly is nearly excluded in a state capitalist economy. (Some foreign concessions, of course, are not excluded.) The third and fifth features—the relation of Russian state capitalism to the export of capital, and to the territorial division of the world—need further elaboration.

(1) The example of Japanese imperialism

Of all the countries in the world excluding Stalinist Russia, that which reached the highest centralisation of capital was Japan. It was estimated that the 'Big Four' zaibatsu (family monopoly organisations) controlled 60 percent of the capital invested in all Japanese joint stock companies (the parallel figure for 1929 was 45 percent).[167] At the same time as the centralisation of capital in Japan is much higher than in any other capitalist country, excluding Stalinist Russia, the productive forces of Japan lag far behind those of the countries of the West. This combination of highly centralised capital and the great backwardness of the country as a whole explains the specific character of Japanese imperialism, which distinguishes it from other imperialisms, and makes it *very similar* in many respects to Stalinist imperialism. An outline of the specific features of Japanese imperialism will therefore help us to clarify some of the aspects of Stalinist imperialism.

The industrial output of Japan advanced very rapidly during the present century. In the years 1913 to 1928, the tempo of this advance was about three times that of Britain in the years 1860 to 1913, that is, every year they produced on average 6 percent more than the year before. Between 1927 and 1936 the industrial output of Japan increased by approximately 100 percent, and E B Schumpeter could justifiably write:

It is no longer possible to state, as one careful and well informed writer did in 1930, that Japan can never become a manufacturing nation of major importance because of the lack of fuel and iron, which are essential in peace as well as in war. Japan has become a major manufacturing nation. The rise of the heavy industries has been the striking development of recent years. Before the Depression it was the textile industries, food preparation, pottery and paper manufacturing which predominated. In 1935 just under half, in 1937 about 55 percent and in 1938 about 61 percent of the total value of industrial production was accounted for by metals, chemicals, machinery and engineering products. This meant that Japan produced her own ships and many of her own airplanes, but imported automobiles and parts; she was no longer dependent on the outside world for a large part of her steel, fertiliser, arms, ammunition and machinery, although she still had to import a substantial part of the raw materials from which they were manufactured. Since 1937, Japan has made a great effort to develop the raw material resources of the Yen Bloc and of adjacent regions in the Pacific area.[168]

From 1920 to 1936 the output of pig iron increased four times, that of steel eight times, and the kilowatt capacity of electric power stations five and a half times. The main increase in industrial output took place in the department of means of production. Thus the value of the output of chemical, metal and machine industries rose from about 2,000 million yen in 1926 to more than 9,000 million in 1937, ie four and a half times. The output of all the other industries increased only from about 5,150 million yen to 7,420 million, ie an increase of 44 percent. In the same years prices rose by 40 percent, so that we may conclude that the output of means of production rose about three times, while the output of means of consumption remained unchanged. That the increase in the output of heavy industry cannot be explained only, or even mainly, as a result of armament production will be clear from the following fact:

Between 1933 and 1936, the value of metals, chemicals, machinery and tools produced in establishments employing five or more people increased from 3 to 6 billion yen whereas the total expenditure on the army and navy, only a fraction of which was spent on armaments, rose from 0.5 billion yen in 1931-32 to 1.1 billion yen in 1936-37.[169]

Between 1931-32 and 1936-37 'the total annual expenditure of the army and navy increased by 600 million yen…while the annual national income increased by 7,000 million yen or nearly 12 times as much'.[170]

In this situation of the rapid rise of industrial output in Japan, which was the result of its general backwardness on the one hand and the high concentration of capital on the other, 'superfluous' capital did not appear and the rate of profit remained high. Extremely low wages were another important factor allowing this high rate of profit: 'Average corporate earnings in 1936 and 1937 were from 16 to 20 percent of paid-up capital and dividends averaged 8 to 9 percent'.[171]

In the light of this, it would be wrong to say that Japanese imperialism sought fields of capital investment because it was faced with a 'superfluity' of capital and a low rate of profit in Japan itself. That the rate of profit was high, and that it did not suffer from an abundance of capital but from a lack of it is, however, but the other side of the coin of its backwardness. This causes a very interesting dialectical development: the backwardness of Japan drove it to export on an extremely large scale, and to conquer a tremendous empire. In the words of F Sternberg:

> When Great Britain and France founded their empires they were both leading industrial countries. Their empires were never intended to strengthen their own industrial position. Japan was in a very different situation. Her aim was to achieve a rate of development which would reduce the industrial gap between her and the other capitalist countries, and to become at least as strong and if possible still stronger than they were.[172]

After the First World War the foreign investments of the highly developed countries which suffered from an enormous 'superfluity' of capital, except for the US, did not increase, but on the contrary decreased. Even with the US the foreign investments of these countries did not rise beyond the level of 1914, as the following table shows:[173]

CAPITAL INVESTED ABROAD (BILLION FRANCS OF PRE-1914 PARITY)

Year	By Great Britain	By France	By Germany	By US	Together
1862	3.6	–	–	–	3.6
1872	15	10 (1869)	–	–	25
1882	22	15 (1880)	?	–	37
1893	42	20 (1890)	?	–	62
1902	62	27–37	12.5	2.6 (1900)	104–114
1914	75–100	60	44	9.9 (1912)	189–214
1930	94	31–40	4.9–6.1	81	211–220
1935	58	*	*	41.9	130–140*

Thus, while in the years 1860 to 1914 the quantity of capital invested abroad by the advanced capitalist countries grew almost uninterruptedly, from 1914, by when imperialism had reached maturity, the quantity of capital invested abroad never rose above the level of 1914, and even declined below it.

As against this, Japan undertook an immense export of capital, especially to Manchuria, the only important colony it had until the Sino-Japanese war:[174]

JAPANESE INVESTMENTS IN MANCHURIA (MILLION YEN)

1932	97.2
1933	151.2
1934	271.7
1935	378.6
1936	263
1937	348.3
1938	439.5
1939	1,103.7
1940-43	2,340.0

The Manchurian Five-Year Plan (1937-41) planned an investment of 2,800 million yen, which was subsequently raised to 4,800 million in the revised plan, and then, in September 1938, to 6,000 million yen. This figure was impossible of achievement owing to the lack of equipment in Japan, and the scarcity of labour in general and skilled labour in particular. Investments reached only about 3,000 million yen in the period laid down by the plan. But even this expressed a very big rise in production, as the following table shows:[175]

OUTPUT OF SOME PRODUCTS OF MANCHURIA

Year	Coal (million tons)	Iron ore (million tons)	Pig iron (thousand tons)	Electricity (million kWh)
1932	7.1	0.7	368.2	593
1936	13.6	1.3	633.4	1,351
1940	21.0	–	1,061.2	3,250
1944	30.0	5.3 (1943)	1,174.9	

The steel industry, established in 1935, was after a few years producing more than a million tons per annum. Machinery factories were established, which supplied the majority of equipment for Machurian industry. In 1939 a car industry was established which planned to employ 100,000 workers. A large aeroplane factory was also established. The construction of ships up to 5,000 tons was begun. The railway system of Manchuria increased from 5,570 kilometres in 1932 to 15,000 kilometres in 1943—more than the whole railway system of China proper.

In the light of this development it is clear why one writer could say, 'Manchuria...was to be developed as an extension of the homeland'.[176] Sternberg remarked:

> The given historical conditions in which Japanese imperialism developed caused it to encourage and force the development of industrialisation in its empire, while different historical conditions caused the European imperialists to prevent or retard industrial development in their empires.[177]

> In the ten years between Japan's invasion of Manchuria and her entry into the Second World War (1931-41) she so accelerated the industrialisation of Manchuria that although Manchuria's population is only about 10 percent of British India's, as much, if not more, industry was created there in one decade as was created in India in a century of imperialist rule.[178]

The industrialisation of Manchuria was not left to the blind, unorganised activity of the different Japanese companies, but was carried out by mixed companies of the state and the monopoly companies according to a plan. Such organisation was necessary for rapid industrialisation.

(2) The motives for the expansion of the Stalinist bureaucracy

Just as the privileges of the bourgeoisie are conditioned by an unceasing advance of accumulation, so are the privileges of the Russian bureaucracy conditioned. But, unlike the bourgeoisie of the West, Russian state capitalism in its Tugan-Hayek stage suffers neither from a 'superfluity' of capital, from a restriction of the possibilities of accumulation which the antagonistic mode of distribution causes in traditional capitalist countries, nor from a rise of wages which would threaten the rate of profit. In these respects Russian state capitalism is more similar to Japanese imperialism before its defeat in the Second World War than to the Western imperialist countries. There is, however, one important difference: seeing that nearly all the means of production in Russia belong to the state, the industrial development of its colonial regions, ie the areas of the nations oppressed by the Russian bureaucracy, is *directly* a part of the general industrial development of Russia itself. The Japanese state saw in Manchuria 'an extension of the homeland'. The Stalinist state looks upon the Ukraine, the Caucasus, Romania, Bulgaria, etc in the same way, and, because of its monopolistic economic position, its development of these regions is and will be more efficient than that of Japanese imperialism in Manchuria. Just as Japanese imperialism looked upon the development of Manchuria as a necessary step to bridge the distance between it and the advanced powers of the West, so the Stalinist bureaucracy is driven to an imperialist policy for the same reason.

The same relative backwardness drives Russia not only towards the establishment of industries in the countries of the oppressed nations, but, as the second side of the same coin, to loot capital wherever Russia can lay hold of it.

Japanese imperialism carried out large-scale plunder in China. As regards Germany, 'In the conquered territories, German firms have taken over the assets of resident concerns by right of conquest, not through "business as usual".'[179]

Stalinist Russia looted all the countries of Eastern Europe and Manchuria. It did so not only by transferring factories to Russia, but also, as Nazi Germany did, by concluding barter agreements with its own vassals, which were ruinous to them. The concentrated monopoly capitalism of Japan and Germany and the state capitalism of Russia thus reveal another feature characteristic of the period of the primitive accumulation of capitalism—that trade and plunder were indistinguishable. If Alfred Marshall could say of that time that 'silver and sugar seldom came to Europe without a stain of blood', today the looted property is much bloodier; and it is not silver or sugar that is plundered, but means of production.

An additional motive for the imperialist expansion of Russia is the lack of certain raw materials. Middle East oil, for example—that of northern Iran in particular—plays a big role in the plans of the Stalinist bureaucracy. This is the result primarily of the tardiness in the execution of the oil extraction plans in Russia. Thus, for instance, the Second Five-Year Plan set the increase in production from 23.3 million tons in 1932 to 47.5 million tons in 1937. In fact, it increased only to 30.5 million tons. In 1940 production did not reach more than 35 million tons, although the plan laid down a level of more than 50 million tons. With these miscalculations, the Fourth Five-Year Plan sets a more moderate aim for 1950—35.4 million tons. On examining the general plan for increase of production, it is clear that oil will be one of the most important bottlenecks in Russia. The Stalinist bureaucracy tries to overcome this bottleneck by taking over Romania and northern Iran (it did not succeed in the latter).

Another factor motivating the expansion of Russia is the need for new labour power. In the highly developed countries the export of capital is a reaction to the rise of wages which cuts into the rate of profit; it is directed to areas where labour power is cheap, and thus increases the amount of labour exploited by the same quantity of capital. The same result was achieved in a different way when Nazi Germany brought millions of workers from the conquered countries, particularly of the East, into Germany. A cheaper labour power than that of the Russian worker, especially of the slave labourer, is not to be found in Europe, so that the annexation of new areas to Russia cannot be motivated by the need to find cheaper labour power. But this does not mean that it is not motivated by the necessity to find an additional *quantity* of labour power. Even though the quantity of capital relative to the population in Russia is very small, it still suffers from a lack of labour power. This is to be explained by the wasteful use of labour power caused by the lack of capital, so that side by side with the lack of capital appears the lack of labour power: hence slave labour and the low productivity of labour in agriculture. Every factor that impedes the productivity of labour—the bureaucracy itself included—will increase the wastage of labour power. This explains why, in spite of the gigantic population of Russia, the government finds it necessary to take special measures to increase the population, such as the prohibition of abortion, fines for bachelors, and prizes for families with many children. This process goes round in a vicious circle: lack of capital causes a wastage of labour power which causes a lack of labour power which makes it difficult to accumulate sufficient quantities of capital, and so on. The addition to Russian of 100 million people from the countries of Eastern Europe is therefore an important motive for the expansion of Russian imperialism, paralleling the export of capital in the countries of advanced capitalism.

One further motive for the expansion of Stalinist Russia is strategical considerations.

The factors mentioned till now are not specific to Stalinist Russia alone. One factor, however, about which we have very incomplete information is specific. That is a slowing down of the rise in the productivity of labour.

According to our previous calculation the productivity of labour (which official Russian statisticians claim rose by 172 percent) in reality rose probably by 96.6 percent between 1928 and 1937. Whichever figure we accept, the rise is very rapid. And yet in 1937 the productivity of labour in Russian industry was still only 30 to 40 percent of that in American industry, even though the mechanisation of Russian factories is the last word in technique, and the portion of their equipment installed very recently much larger than in the US. It is not excluded theoretically that the productivity of labour rises much more quickly when the new machinery is installed than years later. For, seeing that the bureaucracy is not under workers' control as it is in a workers' state on the one hand, and on the other that the income of every bureaucrat is not directly connected with the quality of his management, a miscalculation at one stage of production may be introduced into the basis of planning and calculation at other stages, and so on in a cumulative process. Bureaucratic state capitalism thus may not be able to achieve the same productivity of labour using the same machinery as monopoly capitalism, not to speak of a workers' state.

From 1941 the Russian authorities stopped systematically publishing figures showing the absolute quantity of different products produced. They publish practically only relative figures. When they say, for instance, that the output of coal in, for example, 1940 was such and such a percentage higher than in 1945, we are still in the dark, as we do not know the output for 1945. According to official Russian statistics the productivity of labour rose very much during the war years. It was, in industry as a whole, 17 percent higher in 1941 than in 1940; in 1942 it rose in the armament industry by 15 percent above 1941, in aircraft by 30 percent, in tanks by 38 percent, in light industry by 46 percent. In 1943 the productivity of labour in the armament industry was nearly 20 percent higher than in 1942, in aircraft 15.1 percent higher, in the electrical industry 19.1 percent higher, in the chemical industry 12.7 percent higher, in light industry 15.1 percent higher. Thus the productivity of labour in the armament industry in 1943 was about 70 percent higher than in

1940.[180] The rise in the productivity of labour, as well as the saving in raw materials, according to official statistics, brought about a decline in the costs of production of war materials of 30 to 40 percent.[181] Of course such figures cannot be checked, and always in the past it has been found that the rise in percentage of uncheckable figures has been incomparably higher than in those that can be checked. It has been found, for example, that the rise in the production of coal, iron, steel, electricity, cement, textiles, etc, products whose quantity is measured in volume, has been much less than the rise in production of those products whose quantity is given only in prices, such as machinery, chemicals, etc. In addition it is difficult to know to what extent the Russian statisticians took into account the lengthening of the labour day during the war from eight to 11 or 12 hours.

The last absolute figures as regards output were given systematically for the years 1937-40. These figures show a general extreme slowing down of the rise in production.

ANNUAL INCREASE IN PRODUCTION[182]

Year	Steel	Rolled steel	Pig iron	Oil and gas	Coal	Electricity
1928–29	0.6	0.5	0.7	2.0	4.5	1.5
1929–30	0.9	0.6	1.3	5.1	7.8	1.9
1930–31	-0.2	-0.3	-0.4	4.3	9.0	2.3
1931–32	0.3	0.1	1.3	-0.8	7.6	2.8
1932–33	0.9	0.6	0.9	0.2	11.6	2.9
1933–34	2.8	1.8	3.3	3.0	17.5	4.1
1934–35	2.9	2.7	2.0	1.2	15.3	5.8
1935–36	3.8	3.0	2.0	2.5	17.2	6.7
1936–37	1.4	0.6	0.1	-0.8	10.2	3.3
1937–38	0.3	0.3	0.1	1.7	5.0	3.2
1938–39*	0.2	0.15	0.15	1.0	13.0	0.6
1939–40*	0.2	0.15	0.15	1.0	18.7	0.6

The tempo of the rise of the annual output will become even clearer if we compare the rise in the output of one product with its output in the previous year.

ANNUAL INCREASE IN PERCENTAGES

Year	Steel	Rolled steel	Pig iron	Oil and gas	Coal	Electricity
1928-29	14.0	14.7	21.2	17.1	12.7	24.0
1929-30	18.4	15.4	32.5	37.0	19.4	35.5
1930-31	-3.4	-6.7	-7.5	22.7	18.8	27.4
1931-32	5.4	2.4	26.5	-3.4	13.6	26.2
1932-33	15.3	13.9	14.5	0.9	17.9	21.5
1933-34	40.6	35.3	46.5	13.3	23.0	25.0
1934-35	29.9	39.1	28.2	4.0	16.4	28.3
1935-36	30.2	31.2	19.2	9.3	15.8	23.2
1936-37	8.5	4.8	0.7	-2.8	8.1	10.3
1937-38	1.7	2.3	0.7	5.6	3.9	8.7
1938-39	1.1	0.9	1.0	3.1	9.8	1.5
1939-40	1.1	0.9	1.0	3.0	12.8	1.5

Except for coal, the years 1936-40 show a sharp drop in the rate of increase of output. The table as a whole shows to what extent bureaucratic management leads to a jerky development of production. The drastic decline in the rate of increase in the last years before the war may have been the result of the mass 'purges' carried out at that time, but it is possible, on the other hand, that the drop was a main cause of the panic of the government which drove it to employ the weapon of 'purges' in an attempt to break the bottlenecks in production. The data are too paltry to decide this question conclusively. In a few years time we shall know without doubt whether the bureaucracy has become a factor which, while it does not absolutely prevent a rise in the quantity produced and the productivity of labour, has become a factor slowing down the rate of this rise. If this is the case, to the extent that it is so it constitutes an additional motive for Stalinist Russia's imperialist expansion, which is specific to state capitalism run by a bureaucracy.

The looting of the occupied countries, the use of their labour reserves to increase the surplus value and capital dominated over by the Russian bureaucracy, the creation of an industrial proletariat among the oppressed nations—all this creates a volcano of social and national antagonisms. The congruency of the social and national antagonisms of the local proletariat with the Russian bureaucracy must develop in the long run into a tremendous movement of national and social liberation.[183]

Chapter 10: The class struggle in Russia
(1) It is wrong to speak of a Stalinist epoch

The rise of the bureaucracy to become a ruling class expresses the fact that the historical mission of the Stalinist bureaucracy, which is to establish capitalism in Russia, is already exhausted on an international plane, but not yet exhausted on a national plane. At the same time the bureaucracy, by relying on planning—an element of the 'invading socialist society'—which it nevertheless applies to its capitalist mission of the accumulation of capital, in a few decades oversteps the traditional historical course which the bourgeoisie of the West took about 200 years to accomplish. Relying on elements of the future society in order to fortify relations of the past, the bureaucracy undermines these relations of the past themselves very quickly, and in so doing prepares a new, glorious edition of the proletarian revolution on a much stronger material base than in 1917.

The fact that the bureaucracy in its youth as a ruling class has the totalitarian characteristics of decaying, ageing capitalism proves that it was born as an historical anomaly with no future. This is corroborated by the fact that the bureaucracy is compelled to carry on a vast propaganda campaign against bureaucratism, to pose as the defender of the workers against the bureaucracy. This shows not only that the bureaucracy has a guilty conscience, but more especially that it is a usurper lacking historical legitimacy.

Capitalist state ownership raises the ire of the masses. From the beginning of the bureaucracy's constitution as a class, therefore, the sword of Damocles hangs ominously above its head. While the capitalist of the 16th to 19th centuries could visualise a glorious future with himself as the representative of humanity as a whole, the Stalinist bureaucracy today fulfilling the historical function of this capitalist cannot but feel that its roots are in a temporary and passing concatenation of national and international circumstances. Hence the totalitarianism.

The terror of the bureaucracy against the bureaucrats themselves indicates the anomalous position of this hybrid. In traditional capitalism the competition between the capitalists ensures that each will be as efficient as possible. In socialist economy the social consciousness, the care for the interests of society, the harmonious relations between people, is the basis of efficiency (which is higher quantitatively and different qualitatively from that prevailing in capitalist economy). The Stalinist bureaucracy is a result and a cause of the lack of harmoniousness in the relations between people, of class and personal antagonisms, of the unlimited egotism prevailing. Therefore on the one hand the motive at the basis of planned socialist economy—the control of producers in the interests of the producers themselves—does not exist in Russia and cannot ensure the efficiency of production; on the other hand the direct connection between the efficiency of the individual enterprise and the income of its directors that exists under individual capitalism also does not exist. The only means of ensuring efficiency remaining to the bureaucratic state is a terror directed against the individual bureaucrats.

The terror has an additional function besides this. As Ciliga writes:

> This original method of calming the anger of the people [the terroristic purges] reminded me of Marco Polo's report of the Mongol emperor who reigned in Peking at that time. It was customary once every ten or 15 years to deliver over to the crowd the minister most abhorred by it, which allowed the emperor quietly to oppress his people for the next ten or 15 years. What I saw in Russia was to bring this Mongol emperor repeatedly to my mind.[184]

As a much deeper abyss exists between the Stalinist bureaucracy and the masses than ever existed in history between rulers and ruled, it is of the utmost importance to the bureaucracy that scapegoats be found.

Although the bureaucracy was born with all the marks of age of a declining class, it would be too great a simplification to say that every step forward of the productive forces, every addition to the working class, will directly and immediately undermine the position of the bureaucracy. No, reality is much more complicated than that.

(2) The initial direct influence of industrialisation and 'collectivisation' on the relation of forces between the proletariat and the bureaucracy

In the First Five-Year Plan the number of workers in Russia increased very rapidly. While in 1928 the number of people occupied in manufacturing industries and the extraction of minerals was 3 million, in 1932 it reached 8 million, an increase of 160 percent. The overwhelming majority of the working class were thus raw elements just come from the villages, as yet not educated and organised by the process of social production.

At the same time the quick industrial development, with the acute shortage of technicians, skilled workers, officials, etc, opened the gates of the bureaucracy to many workers of long standing. And of course the more experienced and intelligent the worker, the more possibility he had of rising in the hierarchy.

These two factors of the dilution of the working class by raw elements and the exodus of militant elements from it were in different historical circumstances in the US a grave impediment to the rise of an independent workers' movement some decades ago. But in Russia the difficulties on the path of the workers' movement during the Five-Year Plans are much greater than American difficulties, not only because of the terrible pressure of the secret police, because of the weariness of the masses after many years of superhuman effort, because of the ideological disorientation which appears both as a result and cause of the weakness of the Russian workers' movement at that time, but also for another reason. This is the creation by the bureaucracy of a layer of elite among the oppressed. This is one of the most efficient weapons the oppressor can wield in its oppression of the masses.

When Napoleon said that even the heaviest cannons could not stand up against empty stomachs, he was not entirely correct. Empty stomachs under certain circumstances lead not to revolt but to submission. Such was the case in the first years of the industrialisation by the Stalinist bureaucracy. As Victor Serge said:

> A vast misery will spring from its [the bureaucracy's] policy, but in this misery the tiniest material benefits become precious. It will now suffice to offer a worker a plate of soup the least bit nourishing and a shelter the least bit habitable in the winter for him to attach himself to the privileged amid the general destitution... In that way a stratum of subordinate bureaucrats will be formed in the enterprises, in the party cells, and in the villages where the collectivisation is to result in a new differentiation between leaders and led. Around the former will gravitate a clientele eager to serve. The misery will consolidate those who conjured it up.[185]

(3) The pressure of the totalitarian police machine

One cannot overestimate the difficulties which the police machine makes for the independent organisation of the workers in Russia. The working class is atomised and any attempt at building up any independent organisation whatsoever or at giving expression to the desires of the masses is brutally suppressed. The workers are compelled to belong to organisations led and controlled by the state and teeming with its spies. The combination of propaganda and a terror designed to ensure the bureaucracy's monopoly of propaganda puts no limit to the lies it spreads, to the terror against the soul of the masses. The state's organisation even of the leisure time of the masses, driving them to mass demonstrations and public meetings, compelling them to debase themselves and sing the praises of their oppressors—all these weapons of the bureaucracy make the molecular process of the organisation and education of the workers very difficult. There is every indication that even the experienced, cultured German proletariat would have needed many years, perhaps some decades, till it could have succeeded in smashing the oppressive Nazi machine with its own strength. It is significant that even in the hours of Nazi Germany's greatest military defeat no mass revolts of workers broke out on the home front. (In connection with this, one must not overlook the important effect Ilya Ehrenburg's chauvinistic propaganda had in helping the Nazis to cement the cracks in the wall of German 'national unity'.) The raw Russian proletariat, the overwhelming majority of whom have but a few years ago come from the villages, of whom less, probably, than 10 percent knew the conditions under Tsarism when trade unions were legal, when the different workers' parties had a legal press, will find the utmost difficulty in learning the ABC of organisation and socialist ideology under the rule of Stalin.

(4) The military victories of Russia

An additional factor which strengthened the rule of the bureaucracy was the military victories. They were the result of various factors. Firstly, the absolute suppression of the masses allows Stalin to devote a larger portion of the national income than the countries of the West to war aims. He could, for instance, achieve the 'miracle of the evacuation of Russian industry' by transferring millions of workers to the east, housing them in holes in the ground. Secondly, the police oppression ensures quiet on the home front, which is another 'advantage' Russia has over the democratic capitalist countries. The same two factors caused the absolute supremacy of Germany over France and Britain, which was put an end to only by the cooperation of the American industrial machine (producing four times as much as Germany) and the Russian. While the Russian military victories were to a large extent the result of the 'quiet' on the home front, of the depression and despair of the toiling masses, they in their turn become an important factor in the stabilisation of the Russian regime. To make an analogy, one cannot underestimate Nazi Germany's victories in the Saar, Austria, Sudetenland, Czechoslovakia, Poland and France as a factor in influencing the psychology of the German masses.

(5) The bureaucracy creates its gravedigger

The initial result of the industrialisation and 'collectivisation' in Russia was to strengthen the position of the bureaucracy. After a few years an opposite process began: now every step forward of the productive forces undermines the position of the bureaucracy.

In the First Five-Year Plan the number occupied in manufacture and mining rose from 3 million to 8 million, a rise of 160 percent. In the Second Five-Year Plan it rose only from 8 million to 10.1 million, a rise of 25 percent. The Third Five-Year Plan planned an increase to 11.9 million in 1942, a rise of 16.7 percent. Thus, despite the liquidation of many of the workers in the 'purges', the number of workers with many years of participation in the process of production behind them is steadily growing.

At the same time the gates of the bureaucracy draw together, decreasing the recruitment of the best elements among the workers into the bureaucracy. This can be shown by a few facts. It can be shown that from the middle of the 1930s the direct promotion of workers from the bench to administrative positions almost ceases. Higher education is then placed beyond the grasp of the workers. In 1938 the total number of students in higher institutes was 533,000; of this number 181,000 were manual workers and the children of manual workers (33.9 percent), 115,000 were peasants and the children of peasants (21.6 percent) and 225,000 were salaried employees and specialists and the children thereof (42.2 percent). As the total number of the higher layer of the bureaucracy is about two and a half to three million, it is highly improbable that of the 225,000 'salaried employees and specialists and the children thereof' there were many from the ranks of the lower bureaucracy. An important step towards the closing of the gates of the bureaucracy was the decree of 2 and 12 October 1940, which fixed fees for education in secondary schools (8th, 9th and 10th grades of elementary schools) and technicums and colleges. Fees range from 150-200 roubles a year for secondary schools to 300-500 roubles a year for colleges. To indicate the largeness of this sum, we need but remember that in 1940 the average wage and salary (of everyone from charwoman to director) was 335 roubles a month. The great majority of the workers did not earn more than 150 roubles per month. Hence the fees for the 8th, 9th and 10th grades of elementary schools amounts to about a month's wage of a worker, of the colleges and technicums two to three months.[186]

Bertrand D Wolfe justifiably wrote about this decree:

> This decree does not 'go back to the bourgeois world' but to the last monarch of 19th century Russia, Alexander III, and his minister of education Delyanov, who issued the celebrated ukase which read, 'The children of coachmen, servants, cooks, laundresses, small shopkeepers, and suchlike persons, should not be encouraged to rise above the sphere in which they were born.'

The crystallisation of the proletariat due to the dwindling stream of raw elements coming into it and the dwindling stream of experienced elements going out of it is a process of great importance.

The historical task of the bureaucracy is to raise the productivity of labour. In doing this the bureaucracy enters into deep contradictions. In order to raise the productivity of labour above a certain point, the standard of living of the masses must rise, as workers who are undernourished, badly housed and uneducated are not capable of good production. The bureaucracy approaches the problem of the standard of living of the masses much in the same way as a peasant approaches the feeding of his horses: 'How much shall I give in order to get more work done?' But workers, besides having hands, have heads. The raising of the standard of living and culture of the masses means to raise their self-confidence, increase their appetite, their impatience at the lack of democratic rights and personal security, and their impatience at the bureaucracy which preserves these burdens. On the other hand, not to raise the standard of living of the masses means to endanger the productivity of labour which is fatal for the bureaucracy in the present international relations, and also to drive the masses sooner or later to revolts of despair.

The bureaucracy increases the working class on the basis of the highest concentration history has known. And try as it may to bridge the abyss between concentrated wage labour and concentrated capital, try as it may to veil it under the slogan of 'socialist property', the bureaucracy is bringing into being a force which will sooner or later clash violently with it.

The fact that only a few years after the industrialisation and 'collectivisation', when the working class was yet young and relatively raw, Stalin was compelled to be entirely totalitarian and to make such mass frame-ups as have no precedent in history, indicates the quick tempo at which the class struggle in Russia develops.

In the countries of capitalist democracy, and to a large extent even in Tsarist Russia and the colonial countries, the class struggle of the proletariat initially takes the form of partial, 'peaceful', organised and 'planned' economic struggles. In Stalinist Russia, because of the brutal police oppression, such struggles are excluded. Here, as in the armies of the capitalist countries where the soldiers are continuously under the whip of martial law, the molecular process of the crystallisation of mass opposition to the rulers does not receive clear immediate external expression. Only when conditions have become unendurable *and* it becomes clear to the masses that a *decisive* victory is possible, are they able to join battle. For the Russian masses today to join battle is even more difficult than it was for the soldiers in Tsarist Russia. The Tsarist soldiers rebelled only *after* they saw that the mass of people was in revolt. The barricades built by the workers gave the soldiers confidence in the people's strength and inspired them to revolt against their officers. In Russia today there is no group of people which is not under closer surveillance than ever the Tsarist army was. Only, therefore, when the anger and resentment embedded in the hearts of the masses cumulates till it is ready to burst will the masses break out in revolt. (A proletarian revolution in the West can obviously accelerate this process to an incalculable extent.) The class struggle in Stalinist Russia *must inevitably* express itself in gigantic spontaneous outbursts of millions. Till then it will seem on the surface that the volcano is extinct. Till then the omnipotent sway of the secret police will make it impossible for a revolutionary party to penetrate the masses or organise any systematic action whatsoever. The spontaneous revolution, in smashing the iron heel of the Stalinist bureaucracy, will open the field for the free activity of all the parties, tendencies and groups in the working class. It will be the first chapter in the victorious proletarian revolution. The final chapter can be written only by the masses—self mobilised, conscious of socialist aims and the methods of their achievement, and led by a revolutionary Marxist party.

Notes

1 L Trotsky, *Problems of the Development of the USSR: A Draft of the Thesis of the International Left Opposition on the Russian Question* (New York, 1931), p36.

2 *New International*, April 1943.

3 L Trotsky, *The Revolution Betrayed* (London, 1937), p235

4 Editor's note: the NKVD (People's Commissariat of Internal Affairs) was the security service, including the secret service, and a forerunner of the KGB.

5 K Marx, *The Poverty of Philosophy* (London, no date), pp129-130.

6 Ibid, p166.

7 Sources used on feudalism in the Arab East: A N Poliak, *Feudalism in Egypt, Syria, Palestine and Lebanon* (London, 1939); A N Poliak, 'Les Révoltes Populaires en Egypte a l'Epoque des Mamelukes et leurs Causes Economiques', *Revue des Etudes Islamiques* (Paris, 1934); A N Poliak, various articles in Hebrew in *Hameshek Hashitufi* (Tel Aviv); A Kremer, *Geschichte der Herrschenden Ideen des Islams* (Leipzig, 1868); A Kremer, *Kulturgeschichte des Islams unter der Chalifen* (Vienna, 1875-77); C H Becker, *Beiträge zur Geschichte Aegyptens* (Strasbourg, 1903).

8 L Trotsky, *The Revolution Betrayed*, op cit, p110.

9 Ibid.

10 K Marx, 'Introduction', *A Contribution to the Critique of Political Economy* (Chicago, 1918), pp285-286.

11 L Trotsky, *In Defence of Marxism* (New York, 1942), pp63, 70.

12 L Trotsky, *Stalin* (London, 1947), p408.

13 L Trotksy, *The Living Thoughts of Karl Marx* (London, 1940), p9.

14 L Trotsky, *The Revolution Betrayed*, op cit, p238.

15 L Trotsky, *War and the Fourth International* (New York, 1934), p22.

16 Bruno R, *La Bureaucratisation du Monde* (Paris, 1939).

17 IS Draft Thesis, 'The Fourth International and Stalinism', November 1947.

18 This theory leads to the most absurd contradictions. We know when the workers of Petrograd took power. It was on 7 November 1917. When did they take power in Prague? If one says the last week of February 1948 it means that the workers came to power three years after 70 percent of the industry was nationalised and working according to a plan, ie three years after Czechoslovakia was already a workers' state. If, on the other hand, one says that the workers took power at the same time as the major industries were nationalised, it means that the revolution was carried out by a coalition government with a 'communist' minority, without any semblance of soviets or action committees, in the presence of the American army of occupation, and at the same time as about 3 million Germans were expelled. And it is surely strange that three years after a proletarian revolution the Marxists both inside and outside Czechoslovakia did not know it had taken place. The fact that even the date of the revolution cannot be fixed by those who declare Czechoslovakia to be a workers' state shows how unfounded is their assertion. The mass demonstrations of February 1948 certainly prove that the overwhelming majority of the working class in Czechoslovakia has confidence in the Stalinist government, but by itself it does not prove anything about the class character of Czechoslovakia. The action committees, for the short time they existed, were auxiliary to the standing army and police, controlled by the Stalinists. They did not smash the old capitalist state machine and replace it. The replacement of ministers and generals while the structure of the army and the state bureaucracy remains the same not only diverges from what Marx and Engels visualised as the first step in a proletarian revolution—the smashing of the state machine—but is its very opposite.

19 F Engels, *Anti-Dühring* (London, 1943), p312.

20 Quoted in L Laurat, *Marxism and Democracy* (London, 1940), p69.

21 IS Draft Thesis, op cit.

22 K Marx, *The Poverty of Philosophy*, op cit, p148.

23 F Engels, *Anti-Dühring*, op cit, p320.

24 K Marx, *Capital* (New York, 1932), vol I, pp396-397.

25 Because of the double role of the technicians in their relation to the workers in the process of production, the founders of Marxism pointed out that the subordination of the technicians to the interests of society as a whole will be one of the greatest difficulties experienced by a new society. Thus Engels wrote, 'If...a war brings us to power prematurely, the technicians will be our chief enemies; they will deceive and betray us wherever they can and we shall have to use terror against them but shall get cheated all the same'—K Marx and F Engels, *Selected Correspondence* (London, 1942), p493.

26 K Marx, *Selected Works* (London, 1942), vol 1, p221.

27 K Marx, *Capital*, op cit, vol I, p652.

28 K Marx, *Selected Works*, op cit, vol I, pp563-566.

29 K Marx, 'Die Moralisierende Kritik und die Kritische Moral. Beitrag zur Deutschen Kulturgeschichte', in K Heinzen, *Aus dem Literarischen Nachlass von Marx, Engels und Lassale* (Stuttgart, 1902), 2nd edn, p456.

30 C Clark, *The Conditions of Economic Progress* (London, 1940).

31 There is a close connection between the high percentage of agriculturists in the Russian population and the smallness of the national income per occupied person. This is primarily because Russian agriculture lags behind the agriculture of the developed countries, even more than its industry. Thus the income produced per occupied person in Russian agriculture

lags behind that produced in the agriculture of the developed countries much more than the income produced in Russian industry per person occupied in it lags behind that produced in the industry of the developed countries. The smallness of the income produced in Russian agriculture per occupied person will be clear from the following figures:

NET AGRICULTURAL PRODUCTION PER PERSON OCCUPIED IN AGRICULTURE (1925-34 ANNUAL AVERAGE)

New Zealand	2,444
Australia	1,524
Argentina	1,233
Uruguay	1,000
United States	661
Denmark	642
Canada	618
Holland	579
Germany	490
Great Britain	475
Switzerland	433
France	415
Belgium	394
Sweden	352
Czechoslovakia	287
Estonia	268
Poland	195
Japan	120
USSR	88

32 K Marx, 'Die Moralisierende Kritik und die Kritische Moral', op cit (my emphasis).
33 F Engels, 'Socialism: Utopian and Scientific', in K Marx and F Engels, *Selected Works*, vol 1, p183 (my emphasis).
34 * = *Socialist Structure of USSR, 1936*, p3; ** = Calculated according to *Summary Production—Financial Plan for Industry for 1927-8*; *** = According to S N Prokopovich, *Russlands Volkswirtschaft unter den Sowjets* (Zurich, 1944), p302.
35 * = This average wage includes every earner from charwoman to chief director; ** = Calculated according to official data by S N Prokopovich, op cit, p306.
36 According to this calculation, which is based on official data, the productivity of labour rose by 96.6 percent between 1928 and 1937. The official Russian statisticians claim a much bigger rise—172 percent. They axaggerate, however. Of course, to accept their calculation strengthens our point considerably.
37 *Soviet Weekly Supplement*, 18 December 1947.
38 *Ministry of Labour Survey for British Workers*, April 1947.
39 Quoted in N Bukharin and E Preobrazhensky, *The ABC of Communism* (London, 1927), pp401-402.

40   A Baykov, *The Development of the Soviet Economic System* (London, 1946), p115.
41   *Pravda*, 7 September 1929.
42   *Pravda*, 11 March 1937.
43   Economic Institute of the Academy of Sciences, *Economics of Socialist Industry* (Moscow, 1940).
44   Programme of the Russian Communist Party, 1919.
45   Quoted in L Lawton, *Economic History of Soviet Russia* (London, 1932), vol II, pp359-361.
46   In addition we must remember that the specialists, bureaucrats, etc could not bequeath more than 10,000 roubles to their heirs, ie the income of a skilled worker over four years.
47   Orders of the Commissariat for Fuel, 20 June 1939. For ferrous mettalurge, Orders of the Commissariat for Fuel, 16 July 1939; *Industriya*, 21 June 1939 and 21 July 1939 respectively.
48   G Poliak, 'On the Director's Funds in Industrial Enterprises', *Planned Economy* 4 (1938), p61.
49   M Yvon, *L'URSS telle qu'ele est* (Paris, 1938), p111.
50   L E Hubbard, *Soviet Labour and Industry* (London, 1942), p221.
51   The official scale of income tax indicates the same differentiation. It covers incomes from below 150 roubles per month to above 25,000 roubles per month. The tax on high incomes, incidentally, is much less than in Britain.
52   Quoted in D J Dallin and B I Nicolaovsky, *Forced Labour in Soviet Russia* (London, 1948), p193.
53   V Serge, *Russia Twenty Years After* (New York, 1937), p66.
54   Ibid, p68.
55   Labour Law, Item 13, Article 58.
56   Quoted in D J Dallin and B I Nicolaovsky, op cit.
57   A Ciliga, *The Russian Enigma* (London, 1940), p249.
58   *Sotsialisticheskii Vestnik*, 'A Few Statistics'.
59   *Pravda*, 14 March 1946.
60   D J Dallin and B I Nicolaovsky, op cit, p88.
61   Ibid, p86.
62   After deduction of seeds from gross yield.
63   V I Lenin, *Selected Works*, vol I, p179.
64   The fact that the quantity of agricultural products per capita retained by the peasants after making obligatory deliveries rose does not mean that the conditions of the mass of agriculturists improved, because first of all the differentiation in distribution among the agrculturists at the same time rose very sharply, to the disadvantage of the masses. We cannot deal with this here. But any analysis of the statistics of Russian agriculture will inevitably lead us to the conclusion that Victor Serge reached from his direct contact with Russian toilers: 'The vast majority of the peasants live more poorly than before the collectivisation, that is, on the whole, at a level lower than pre-war' (V Serge, op cit, p37).
65   A technical term denoting a period not exactly equal to the physical labour day: in skilled work it is higher than it, in unskilled lower.
66   In one fundamental point the process connected with collectivisation is dissimilar to the process which took place in Britain. In Britain the eviction of the peasants brought into existence a surplus of agricultural products which was *sold* in the towns. In Russia the overwhelming majority of the surplus of agricultural products is appropriated by the government as taxes without anything being given in exhange.
67   K Marx, *Capital*, op cit, vol I, p786.
68   K Marx and F Engels, *Selected Correspondence*, op cit, pp509-510.
69   'Are Government Bonds the Harbingers of a Transformation of the Form of Property?', p70.
70   The interest paid in Russia on a million roubles is as much as the wages of ten workers. In England a capitalist who wants to receive interest equal to the wages of ten British workers must put an amount of about £250,000 in the bank. But while the British capitalist must pay income tax, in Russia the income received from state bonds is free of tax!
71   In reality there is an extremely small turnover tax on means of production (the income from the turnover tax on producers' goods makes up less than 10 percent of the total turnover tax, although means of production make up two thirds of total production). At the

same time the most elementary daily necessities are burdened with a high turnover tax. Thus in 1934 the rate of tax on wheat and rye was 75 to 76 percent of the gross selling price, ie about 300 percent of the net price. (In 1931 it was only 8 percent on wheat and rye, but in February 1933 it was raised to 30 percent, and in August of the same year to 76 percent.) On meat it is 63 to 69 percent of the gross selling price; butter and eggs 70 to 75 percent; dairy products 50 to 62 percent; sugar 84 to 87 percent; tea 86 percent; coffee 86 percent; soap 62.3 percent; kerosene 67 percent; alcohol 90 percent; tobacco 80 percent; textile knit goods 74.2 percent; boots and shoes 70 to 86 percent of the gross selling price.

72   L Trotsky, *The Revolution Betrayed*, op cit, p211.

73   Quoted in D F White, *The Growth of the Red Army* (Princeton, 1944), p189.

74   Ibid, pp63-64.

75   Ibid, p121.

76   Ibid, p223.

77   E Wollenberg, *The Red Army* (London, 1940), pp182-183.

78   Ibid, pp185-188.

79   D F White, op cit, p303.

80   Ibid, p304.

81   Voroshilov's speech at the Eighteenth Congress of the Party, 1939.

82   D F White, op cit, pp379-380. This turnover throws some light on the extent of the officers' privileges. The number of officers in 1937 was 80,000 (we have not got the figure for 1935, but it was definitely lower). The turnover of the Voentorg per officers' family was thus about 20,000 roubles a year. The prices in the Voentorg shops are much lower than in other shops, thus adding to the value of this sum. This sum does not include all the goods and services the officers' family consumes: travelling, education, entertainment, etc not being included—200,000 roubles, however, is a large enough sum on its own. The average of annual wages and salaries in 1935 was 2,265 roubles (and, as we have noted, the majority of workers earn much less than this average).

83   *Red Star*, 22 October 1940, quoted in *Word*, September 1941.

84   To ensure the esprit de corps of the officers, officers' schools have been established, starting at kindergarten age. Dancing lessons are obligatory at the War Colleges, and 'noble' sports such as polo and tennis have been introduced.

85   L Trotsky, *The Revolution Betrayed*, op cit, pp232-233.

86   J Burnham, *The Managerial Revolution* (London, 1945), pp103-104.

87   For a fuller elaboration of this see the chapter 'The Russian Economy and the Law of Value', p80.

88   V I Lenin, *Collected Works*, vol XX, book II, p236.

89   K Marx, *Capital*, op cit, vol III, p712.

90   Ibid, p517.

91   V I Lenin, *Imperialism: The Highest Stage of Capitalism* (London, 1939), p20.

92   V I Lenin, *Collected Works*, vol XXI, book I, pp210-211.

93   N Bukharin, *Oekonomie des Transformationsperiode* (Hamburg, 1922), pp131-133.

94   F Engels, *Anti-Dühring*, op cit, pp306-307.

95   V I Lenin, *Selected Works*, vol IX, pp432-433.

96   N Bukharin, *Historical Materialism* (London, 1926), p276.

97   F Engels, *The Origin of the Family, Private Property and the State* (London, 1943), p201.

98   K Marx, *Capital*, op cit, vol I, pp648-652.

99   In a letter to Schmidt, Engels dealt broadly with the question of the relation between concept and reality. He cites this example of the divergence between them: 'Did feudalism ever correspond to its concept? Founded in the kingdom of the West Franks, further developed in Normandy by the Norwegian conquerors, its formation continued by the French Norsemen in England and Southern Italy, it came nearest to its concept—in Jerusalem, in the kingdom of a day, which in the Assizes de Jerusalem [the statute book of Godefroi de Bouillon for the kingdom of Jerusalem in the 11th century] left behind it the most classic expression of the feudal order. Was this order therefore a fiction because it only achieved a shortlived existence in full classical form in Palestine, and even then mostly—

on paper?' (1 March 1895, K Marx and F Engels, *Selected Correspondence*, op cit, p530).

100 K Marx, *Capital*, op cit, vol III, p449.

101 Ibid, p450.

102 Ibid, p455. Another factor strengthening the illusion that profit of enterprise is a reward for labour performed is that part of what the capitalist earns and thinks to be a profit is *in reality* wages for the work of management, which is socially necessary in the same way as any other kind of labour in the process of production, and must be renumerated accordingly even under socialism.

103 See K Marx, *Capital*, op cit, vol III, p428.

104 Quoted by B Souvarine, *Stalin* (London, 1939).

105 G Plekhanov, *The Materialist Conception of History* (London, 1940), p32.

106 F Engels, *Anti-Dühring*, op cit, p309.

107 R Luxemburg, *Sozialreform oder Revolution?* (Leipzig, 1908).

108 V I Lenin, *State and Revolution* (London, 1942).

109 'Fourth International and the Soviet Union', thesis adopted by the First International Conference for the Fourth International, July 1936.

110 V I Lenin, *Imperialism: The Highest Stage of Capitalism*, op cit, p109.

111 J Kuczynski, *Weltproduktion und Welthandel in den letzten 100 Jahren* (Libau, 1935), pp20-21.

112 K Marx, *Capital*, op cit, vol I, p188.

113 Ibid, p49; or 'groups of individuals', ibid, p84.

114 Ibid, p84.

115 Ibid, p114.

116 Ibid, pp390-391.

117 K Marx and F Engels, *Selected Correspondence*, op cit, p246. Thus the only difference between the division of labour time into necessary labour and surplus labour in different societies is in the *form* in which this division is carried out. Marx said, 'The essential difference between the various economic forms of society, between, for instance, a society based on slave labour and one based on wage labour, lies only in the way in which this surplus labour is extracted from the actual producer, the labourer' (K Marx, *Capital*, op cit, vol I, p286).

118 R Hilferding, *Das Finanzkapital* (Vienna, 1910), p286.

119 K Marx, *Capital*, op cit, vol I, p105.

120 V I Lenin, *Collected Works*, vol XX, book II, p236.

121 The word 'almost' is used to remind us that there are some border cases in which the control of the state is not complete. The labour time of the kolkhoznik on his private plot is an example of this, likewise the labour of the artisan. But even if these are not consciously planned by the state, they are not absolutely free from a certain control. Through the lever of prices, taxes and especially the state's planning of the *main* field of production, these peripheral activities are also consciously drawn into certain channels.

122 K Marx, *Capital*, op cit, vol I, p126.

123 Ibid.

124 Ibid, p633.

125 Ibid, pp186-187.

126 In the Nazi economy, as we have said, the quantity of means of consumption produced was regulated by the state; the freedom of selling labour power abregated; the division of the total labour time of society between different branches of industry determined not by the automatism of the market but by the state's allocation of orders and the raw materials required, by its prohibition of the investment of capital in certain branches and its diversion of the stream of capital into other branches. Nevertheless not all *autonomic* relations between different enterprises in Germany was abolished.

Seeing that state orders as a factor in determining (a) the exchange of relation between commoditiessb) the relative quantity produced, and (c) the distribution of the total labour time of capitalist society is different only in degree from the Nazi economy or even from a capitalist state which is the repository of the means of production, Bukharin was quite right when he denoted by the term 'state capitalism' both a capitalist war economy and the stage in which the capitalist state becomes the repository of all the means of production. We, on our side, in order to avoid any confusion, use the term ' state capitalism' only to denote the latter.

127 There is one imprtant result of this: while the relations in traditional capitalism are befogged by what Marx calls the fetishism of commodities, which makes all commodity owners appear equal, the class antagonisms in Russia are crystal clear. Hence the bureaucracy is compelled from the beginning to use the most btutal terroristic measures of suppression.

128 R Hilferding, 'State Capitalism and Totalitarian Economy' (1940), published in *Left*, September 1947.

129 Ibid.

130 Ibid.

131 The following are the figures for import and export (in million pre World War One gold roubles).

Year	Export	Import
1913	1,520.1	1,375
1924/25	577.8	723.4
1927/28	791.6	945.5
1932	574.9	704
1937	377.2	294.2
1938	287.8	300.4

Thus during the period of the Five-Year Plans, when industrial production multiplied many times, imports and exports declined very much.

132 N Bukharin, *Imperialism and World Economy* (London, 1929), p157. I find it necessary to remark here that Shachtman in his article in the *New International* of February 1948, 'The Nightfall of Capitalism', cites the same extract from Bukharin, but gives it an opposite meaning to that intended by Bukharin. He deletes the words 'the organisation of all world economy as one gigantic state trust'. He excludes the entire sentence about the world market and he only quotes the end of the passage, so that the impression is gained that Bukharin tried to prove the theoretical impossibility of state capitalism, which is exactly the opposite of what Bukharin intended to prove. We hope this is an accidental error. If not, it reminds one strongly of the blurb writer who 'quoted' a critic. The critic said, 'This cannot be called a really good book.' The blurb read: '...a really good book'.

133 F Engels, *Anti-Dühring*, op cit, p341.

134 We shall deal with the concepts of these tendencies extensively in a later document, in which we shall analyse in particular detail the position of R H Johnson and F Forrest.

135 Some of these factors also explain the extraordinarily rapid development of Japanese industry.

136 K Marx, *Capital*, op cit, vol III, p286.

137 Ibid, pp312-313.

138 Ibid, p568.

139 See, for instance, ibid, p199.

140 Ibid, p283.

141 Ibid, p303.

142 K Marx, *Capital*, op cit, vol II, pp475-476.

143 K Marx, *Capital*, op cit, vol I, pp694-695.

144 K Marx, *Capital*, op cit, vol II, p211.

145 K Marx, *Theorien über den Mehrwert*, vol II/2, p293, quoted in P M Sweezy, *The Theory of Capitalist Development* (London, 1946), p157.

146 *Das Kapital*, Marx-Engels-Lenin edition, vol II, p562, quoted in P M Sweezy, op cit, p186.

147   See K Marx, *Capital*, op cit, vol III, pp140-141.

148   See particularly ibid, pp569-576.

149   See K Marx, *Capital*, op cit, vol II, pp86-87.

150   J Strachey, *The Nature of Capitalist Crisis* (London, 1935), pp290-291.

151   M Tugan-Baranowsky, *Theoretische Grundlagen de Marxismus*, p230, quoted in P M Sweezy, op cit, p168.

152   M Tugan-Baranowsky, op cit, pp230-231, quoted in P M Sweezy, op cit, p169.

153   K Marx, *Capital*, op cit, vol I, p649.

154   K Marx, *Critique of Political Economy*, op cit, pp278-279.

155   K Marx, *Capital*, op cit, vol I, p701.

156   N Bukharin, *Der Imperialismus und die Akkumulation des Kapitals* (Berlin, 1926), p80.

157   Ibid, pp80-81.

158   It is interesting to note that Marx already connected stagnation or dormancy with a decrease in the number of capitalists to a mere handful in the whole world.. He writes, 'The rate of profit, that is the relative increment of capital, is above all important for all new offshoots of capitalism seeking an independent location. And as soon as the formation of capital were to fall into the hands of a few established great capitals, which are compensated by the mass of profits for the loss through a fall in the rate of profits, the vital fire of production would be extinguished. It would fall into a dormant state' (K Marx, *Capital*, op cit, vol III, p304).

159   Of course, in all probability, long before Stalinist Russia could reach this stage the proletarian revolution would have been victorious in Russia and the world.

160   J Strachey, op cit, pp304-305. The difference between a crisis which expresses itself cyclically or in a creeping paralysis continuing for decades is not fundamental from the standpoint of the Marxian theory of crisis. Let us remember how Bernstein was refuted when he sought in 1898 to prove that Germany's freedom from crises for the past 25 years proved the bankruptcy of the Marxist theory of crisis. Rosa Luxemburg in *Sozialreform oder Revolution?* shows that the law of periodicity of the crisis—whether the period be ten or 20 years (or even 40 or 50 years)—is not essential to the Marxist theory of crises, but is 'their *internal mechanism* and deep general causes'.

161   K Marx, *Capital*, op cit, vol III, pp286-287.

162   The analysis in this chapter should clearly show why Trotsky's prognosis, which he repeated from 1925 onwards, that trade connections between Russia and the world would increase, was wrong.

163   K Marx, *Capital*, op cit, vol III, p255.

164   The source of financing the palaces would have been the same as the source of financing the guns. Hitler did not reach financial bankruptcy as bourgeois and reformist financiers had mistakenly prophesied since 1933. When Hitler camw to power the national debt was 40 percent of the annual national income, and the pre-Hitler government found it extremely difficult to bear such a debt burden. After a few years of Hitler's rule the national debt was many times higher, but Hitler found no difficulty in paying the interest on it. The reason is that with the working of previously unused factors of production the source of finance—the national income—increases correspondingly with war production. When the unused factors of production are brought into use by the economy's going onto a war footing the employment of people in the production of guns does not always cause a decline in the consmption of the masses or in the accumulation of the capitalists, but may be accompanied by a rise. Thus, for instance, if 3 million of 6 million unemployed are put into the production of guns, the purchasing power distributed among them will cause the employment of, let us say, an additional 2 million in the production of means of consumption and 1 million in the production of new means of production. The employment of 3 million in the production of guns thus does not cause a decline in the *volume* of the capital accumulated or in the consumption of the masses, but a certain increase due to the fact that instead of 6 million unemployed producing nothing there are now only 3 million who add nothing to the process of reproduction. This internal contradiction in capitalism causes a subtraction to appear as an addition. It was such conditions that caused the national income in Germany till 1943 and in the US during the whole war to grow more than the war expenditure.

This of course does not abolish the fundamental antagonism between the production of guns and butter, which is clearly revealed in the destruction of factors of production in the enemy countries brought about in the process of consuming the guns.

165 *New International*, February 1942.

166 V I Lenin, 'Imperialism: The Highest Stage of Capitalism', in V I Lenin, *Selected Works*, vol V (London, 1936), p81.

167 This is an indication why it is not excluded theoretically, although in practice there is no ground to assume that it will happen, that all the national capital will be concentrated in the hands of one trust.

168 G C Allen, M S Gordon, E F Penrose and E B Schumpeter, *The Industrialization of Japan and Manchukuo, 1939-1940* (New York, 1940), p10.

169 Ibid, p15.

170 Ibid, p33.

171 Ibid, pp26-27.

172 F Sternberg, *The Coming Crisis* (London, 1947), p73.

173 New data for E Varga and L Mendelsohn (eds), V I Lenin, *Imperialism: The Highest Stage of Capitalism* (London, 1939), p141. * = We have estimated the investments of France and Germany for 1935 to be 30 to 40 billion francs. This is, if anything, an overestimation.

174 For 1932-39, G C Allen, M S Gordon, E F Penrose and E B Schumpeter, op cit, p399; for 1940-43, A J Grajdanzev, 'Manchuria: An Industrial Survey', *Pacific Affairs*, December 1945.

175 Sources: K L Mitchell, *Industrialisation of the Western Pacific* (New York, 1942), pp75-78; Allan Rodgers, 'The Manchurian Iron and Steel Industry and its Resource Base', *Geographical Review* (New York), January 1948; A J Grajdanzev, op cit.

176 A Rodgers, op cit, p40.

177 F Sternberg, op cit, p74.

178 Ibid, p73.

179 R A Brady, *Business as a System of Power* (New York, 1943), p3.

180 P Kharomov, *Propagandist* no 7-8, 1944.

181 S Turetzky, *Bolshevik* no 3-4, 1945.

182 * = For all products except coal we have the rise for the two years 1938-40. We have divided the rise equally for 1938-39 and 1939-40.

183 This chapter is of necessity incomplete, as an analysis of Stalinist imperialism is impossible without taking into account the nature of the Stalinist parties, the relation between them and the masses, and the relation between them and the bourgeoisie in the newly occupied countries of Eastern Europe. We shall deal with this in the following document which discusses the Stalinist parties and the perspectives and tasks of the Fourth International.

184 A Ciliga, op cit, p97.

185 V Serge, op cit, p166.

186 In Britain the 8th and 9th grades were compulsory and free even before the Labour government came to power. The Labour government added the 10th.

All that glitters is not gold
A reply to Germain's 'From the ABC to Current Reading: Boom, Revival or Crisis?'

RCP internal document, September 1947

Comrade E Germain's article 'From the ABC to Current Reading: Boom, Revival or Crisis?' has as its objective, according to the writer, to break 'through the curtain of fractional smoke that has been lowered over the debate' in the discussion on Britain. The article, according to its author, is written for educational purposes. But all that glitters is not gold. It abounds with the most elementary mistakes which are put forward as great truths. It reveals a gross lack of knowledge of the Marxist theory of crises and a mechanistic, superficial conception of capitalist decline. To prove this, let us follow Comrade Germain's arguments.[1]

Germain misquotes Marx

Germain quotes these sentences from Marx: 'The enormous power, inherent in the factory system, of expanding by jumps, and the dependence of that system on the markets of the world, necessarily beget feverish production, followed by overfilling of the markets, whereupon contraction of the markets brings on crippling of production. *The life of modern industry becomes a series of periods of moderate activity, prosperity, upswing ('essor'), overproduction, crisis and stagnation*'.[2]

The most important part of this quotation for Germain's analysis is the sentence he emphasises. He concludes from it that Marx's synonym for the word 'boom', which is not to be found in *Capital*, is 'upswing' (*essor*). Seeing that this is the key point of his analysis, one would naturally expect Germain at least to quote with meticulous care. In the sentence from Marx's *Capital* under discussion, not six, but only five stages are mentioned: '...moderate activity, prosperity, overproduction, crisis and stagnation'. *The word upswing (*essor*) is added to Marx's sentence by Germain*.

I do not wish to imply that this is a conscious falsification. It is probably the result of carelessness and a lack of seriousness in dealing with theoretical problems. He copied too hastily from Kautsky's edition of *Das Kapital*, in which, to popularise the work, Kautsky added popular German words to the anglicisms or difficult words used by Marx. These he put in square brackets after the original word. In the sentence quoted by Germain, after the word '*Prosperität*' two words are added by Kautsky in a square bracket: '*Gedeihen*' and '*Aufschwung*'. Germain overlooked the square bracket, arbitrarily deleted one of the two words, and out of the second made a special phase of the economic cycle.

This, to say the least, does not speak well for his scientific conscientiousness.[3]

Germain states that one must identify the boom with only one phase in the ascendance of the cycle, otherwise it 'would lead to this schematism: reduce the whole cycle of capitalist production to two stages—the crisis and the boom'. This argument, which sets out to attack the RCP document, in truth attacks the whole concept of Marx, Engels, Lenin and Trotsky. Sufficient to remind Comrade Germain of the following quotation from Trotsky: 'Capitalism does live by crises and booms, just as a human being lives by inhaling and exhaling. First there is a boom in industry, then a stoppage, next a crisis, followed by a stoppage in the crisis, then an improvement, another boom, another stoppage and so on'.[4]

Of course, these two basic aspects of the cycle—the ascendance and the decline—can be divided into two or three subsections: the resumption, moderate activity, the peak of the activity, the beginning of the decline, moderate decline, the end of the decline, etc. For this purpose, we could divide inhalation and exhalation into different subsections also. We know that Marx divided the cycle sometimes into two, sometimes into four and sometimes into five parts. But if only one subsection of the ascending curve is to be termed 'boom', as Germain seeks to do, then Trotsky too must be accused of 'distorting even the ABC' and vulgarising Marxism.

But there are none so confusing as those who forget what they say from day to day. Comrade Germain comes into conflict with what he had to say on another occasion. Thus, according to Comrade O'Daniel, in his document 'A Note on Discussion Methods', Comrade Germain, at the IEC, said, 'The RCP majority leadership make a fifth distortion… The PB…certainly could not have helped observing that it [the report of Jerome to the October Plenum of the IEC] described the revival of British economy as an "*essor*"—a soaring one.'

To make the position perfectly clear, it must be mentioned that the third member of the IS who wrote about British economic perspectives, Pablo, mentions with approval, in one and the same document, the analysis of both Germain and O'Daniel. Yet he himself, on another occasion, described the word '*essor*' as 'boom'.[5] It is time the Majority IS members found agreement among themselves on this question, which, according to Germain, is the ABC!

Now let us read further and analyse the main traits which Germain considers characteristic of a boom. The first one is that production expands '*in relation to the preceding boom*' [Germain's emphasis].

Does a boom require that production expand beyond the peak of the former boom?

Germain's answer is in the affirmative. While he admits there is lively economic activity in Britain today (which affirms the perspectives of the British majority and contradicts those of the IS of a year and a half ago) he seeks to find a bridge whereby he can attack the RCP and defend the IS. All this amounts to nothing less than a mere sleight of hand trick. *Production in Britain today, he asserts, is lower than the peak of the last boom. Ergo, there is no boom.*

But if his assertion is correct, and a boom requires that production expand beyond the peak of the former boom, then the years 1924-29 in Britain were not years of boom at all, since production was below the level of 1913. In which case, Trotsky made a gross blunder in defining these years as a period of boom. Is this so, Comrade Germain?

More than this. By basing himself on this formulation he does not prove that there is not a boom in England. Unwittingly he proves quite the contrary. British industrial production in 1937 was higher by 23.6 percent than in 1929. Thus 1937, according to Germain's theory, was a year of boom! Now, is British production today higher or lower than 1937? According to Germain it is lower, proof of which, apparently, is merely the fact that Germain asserts it. Factual evidence he does not find it necessary to adduce. Possibly he relies on the same sources as Pablo did when he wrote, 'The year 1946 ended with a total production which has been estimated at about 80 percent of 1938.'

By whom was it estimated? And on what basis? Comrade Pablo lets the cat out of the bag by writing in reference 4 at the conclusion of his article, 'The *New York Herald Tribune* of 30 March 1947, basing its calculation on the indices of imports of raw materials in 1946, on which all industrial activity in Britain depends, evaluated total production at only 72 percent.'

Pablo forgot a few not unimportant factors—the shift from textiles to engineering, which relatively decreases the dependence on foreign sources of raw material; the change in exports from steel to engineering; the big expansion of the chemical industry—all factors which make it fallacious to estimate Britain's production on the basis of her imports of raw materials. But for Comrade Pablo, as it appears for Comrade Germain, it is enough that the imports of raw materials to Britain is about 75 percent of pre-war for them to conclude that British production today relative to pre-war, must also be about this figure!

A document of the RCP Minority states this even more bluntly. It says: 'A revival of economic activity is taking place in Britain today. It has now reached 72 percent of the 1938 level of production (*Herald Tribune*, 30 March 1947)'.[6]

Pablo and the British Minority at least explain how they arrived at the idea that production in Britain is lower than pre-war. Germain does not find this necessary. His pontifical declarations, it would appear, are infallible.

What are the facts? According to the *Economist*, the *Financial Times* and other reliable economic journals, employment is higher in Britain than ever before, and furthermore, productivity of labour on the average has risen by at least 10 percent. It is therefore impossible that production is lower than pre-war. The *Economist* of 2 August 1947 says, 'There is really very little room for doubt that the aggregate output of the British community today is from 10 to 20 percent higher in volume than it was in 1938.' An earlier issue of the *Economist* comes to the conclusion that the gross national income is up by 17 percent in real terms, in comparison with pre-war, or net national income up by 13-14 percent (19 April 1947). *Labour Research* of May 1947 comes to the same conclusions. We could cite similar conclusions from all the serious economic journals.

If we accept Germain's definition of a boom we will arrive, to say the least, at some very odd conclusions: in 1913 there was a boom; in 1929 there was not a boom; in 1937 there was a boom; yet in 1947, when production is higher than the IS's 'boom' of 1937, Germain says there is not a boom! Also, between two periods of boom, there are sometimes two cycles, and sometimes one cycle! But no matter how he contradicts himself, even if we accept his definition and base ourselves not on his and Pablo's 'facts' but on real facts, the British Majority are right. There is a boom in Britain.

Is abundance of raw materials and their cheapness a condition for boom?

Germain writes:

> Throughout the period of stagnation and resumption, sufficient stocks of raw material have been built up to create abundance in this field. *The prices of the raw materials*—the principal constituent of the total price of the production of a capitalist commodity—*stand at a level relatively lower than the prices of finished commodities*, allowing in this way a very accentuated rise in the average rate of profit, which constitutes the basis of this extraordinary impetus received by industry during the period of boom [Germain's emphasis].

There are at least four errors in this one paragraph.

Error 1: It is false to say that 'the prices of the raw materials' are 'the principal constituent of the total price of the production of a capitalist commodity'. In order not to waste too much space, I shall quote only one figure which answers Germain with the facts. In the United States in 1929, raw materials constituted 32.8 percent of the price of production of total industry.[7]

Error 2: It is false to say that it is a condition for a boom that at the beginning of the revival the prices of raw materials should 'stand at a level relatively lower than the prices of finished commodities', or that at the end they are relatively dearer. Sometimes it is the case; as often it is not. Sufficient to state that in the years 1866, 1873, 1890 and 1900, which were all years of maximum employment, were peak years of boom, the prices of raw materials were the *lowest* in the whole cycle as against the prices of finished goods. On the other hand, in the years 1825, 1839, 1847, 1857, 1882, 1929 and 1937, also years of the highest peak of production, the prices of raw materials were the *highest* in the whole cycle as against the prices of finished goods.[8]

To make it absolutely clear that this second allegedly necessary condition for boom, which for Germain is a condition *sine qua non*, is absurd, we add a diagram which makes the position perfectly clear.[9]

United States group prices (wholesale)

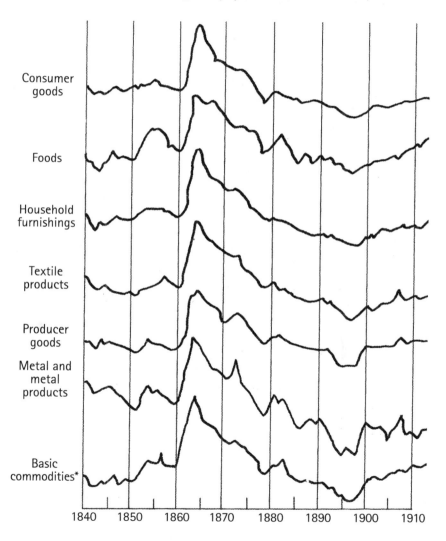

Consumer goods

Foods

Household furnishings

Textile products

Producer goods

Metal and metal products

Basic commodities*

1840 1850 1860 1870 1880 1890 1900 1910

A little knowledge of the history of capitalism, a little seriousness in relation to it, and more care than to make statements that have no foundation, would have restrained Germain from making the question of price one of prime importance. Fluctuations in price can deepen the fundamental disproportionalities that arise in capitalism, but they are always a secondary factor. We can thus find the interesting fact that there were upswings connected with constant prices (1873, 1893), by rising prices (1907, 1920), and again by constant prices (1929).[10]

Error 3: It is false to say that necessarily at the beginning of the economic ascendancy of a cycle there are abundant stocks of raw materials. Again, a little knowledge of the history of capitalism will demonstrate the incorrectness of this assertion. Marx dealt with the situation of the weaving industry in England which, despite its acute shortage of cotton yarn due to the backwardness of the spinning industry, experienced a tremendous boom. The American Civil War, which caused a 'cotton crisis'—an acute shortage of cotton—did not prevent Britain experiencing, at the same time, a tremendous boom even in the spinning industry.[11]

Error 4: It is not true that the relative cheapness of raw materials as against the price of finished goods is a necessary condition for a high rate of profit. The increasing rate of exploitation, the full use of the productive capacity, the low rate of interest, the quick circulation of capital, the cutting of capital values—by these and many other means does the crisis prepare the ground for the rise of the rate of profit and the boom. The relative cheapness of raw materials as against finished goods was an important factor in many cycles. But it is not the only factor, nor the main one, and certainly not the *sine qua non* of a high rate of profit. If it were, many economic cycles of the 19th century would have passed by without experiencing any boom, and such a conclusion is too fantastic, even for Germain.

Germain writes, 'Far from being a result of the boom the coal shortage is a factor limiting the revival and making its development towards a boom impossible.'

This conclusion could have some foundation if not for the fact that already today the consumption of coal in British industry is higher than ever it has been. So the coal crisis of underproduction is another proof of the correctness of the characterisation of the existing period in Britain as one of boom.[12]

The boom and the reserves of labour power

The third characteristic of a boom that Germain lays down arises also from a misunderstanding of Marx: 'Sufficient reserves of man power,' he writes, 'must be present in order to allow a serious expansion of industry. According to Marx, *the essential basis of the boom is proletarian overpopulation*' [Germain's emphasis].

True, Marx says that the process of capitalist accumulation finds 'a check in the natural limits of the exploitable labouring population'.[13] But this does not mean that if there are not big reserves of unemployed there cannot be a boom. Nor, conversely (even if one accepts Germain's first characteristic of a boom that production is higher than in the previous boom), that development towards a boom is impossible because of the lack of labour power. It is very easy to prove this. Let us take the percentage of unemployed among industrial workers in Germany[14] for the years 1887-1913. It was as follows:[15]

PERCENTAGE OF UNEMPLOYED AMONG INDUSTRIAL WORKERS IN GERMANY 1887–1913

Year	Percentage	Year	Percentage
1887	0.2	1901	6.7
1888	3.8	1902	2.9
1889	0.2	1903	2.7
1890	2.3	1904	2.1
1891	3.9	1905	1.6
1892	6.3	1906	1.2
1893	2.8	1907	1.6
1894	3.1	1908	2.9
1895	2.8	1909	2.8
1896	0.6	1910	1.9
1897	1.2	1911	1.9
1898	0.4	1912	2.0
1899	1.2	1913	2.9
1900	2.0		

Even Germain could not say that during these 27 years, because the percentage of unemployed was higher than 3 percent in only four cases, the economy could not reach the level of a boom. His argument becomes clearly ridiculous when we notice that the year 1887, which was the beginning of the ascendancy of the economic cycle, showed an unemployment of only 0.2 percent, and that other years similarly placed in the cycle showed: 1893, 2.8 percent unemployment, 1902, 2.9 percent, 1908, 2.9 percent. How on earth did the cycle of production reach a boom if, from the beginning, there was almost full employment?

Has Germain heard of the process of rationalisation, the raising of the productivity of labour, etc? There is in Britain today about 2 percent unemployment. *This has not prevented a rise of production.*

Germain writes that 'the number of active *men* has *declined* by 211,000 in relation to 1939'. And he adds, 'Really this is a funny kind of boom in manpower' [Germain's emphasis].

What is funny is that Germain does not mention at the same time that the number of active *women* rose by 671,000. More than this, it can happen that during a boom the number of employed men and women not only does not rise, but even declines. This takes place if the volume of production rises less rapidly than the productivity of labour. Thus, for instance, in the years 1920-29 the number of workers in American manufactures, railroads and coal mining decreased by 1,003,000.[16]

To say that the lack of labour power proves either that there is not a boom in Britain, or that there cannot be a big rise in production to higher levels even than exists today, is ridiculous.

At the beginning of the existing boom in Britain there were about 5.2 million people in the armed forces. Today the number is only 1.2 million, besides which about a million women left employment after the end of the war. This means that about 4 million served as a reserve of labour power. Germain forgets this. But even if this reserve did not exist, the boom in Britain would not have been impossible.

The rate of profit and the boom

Germain writes:

> We have limited ourselves to these four points, but it is obvious that the boom has still other characteristics that one only needs to take the trouble to look up in the works of Marx. Let us note this essential point: *It is the movement of the average rate of profit…which determines the unfolding of the cycle of capitalist production* [Germain's emphasis].

Of the four characteristics given by Germain as the *sine qua non* of the boom at least three, we have seen, were wrong. It is the point which he adds here about the rate of profit which is really the factor which characterises the boom. Since the profit motive is the driving force of capitalism, there cannot be a boom without a high rate of profit. The extraction of surplus value and its transformation into capital are thus necessary attributes of a capitalist boom. They are, in fact, its basis. If, therefore, it could have been proved either that the rate of profit in Britain is low, or that the rate of accumulation is low, then we may have said with certainty that there is no boom in Britain. As usual, Germain finds it sufficient to *assert* whatever comes into his head, without adducing any facts. He writes:

> The average rate of profit [in Britain] is kept to such a low level and the new investments bring such little hope of immediate and abundant profit that an enormous mass of capital *refuses* to converge towards industry—exactly the opposite phenomenon to that which is produced during a period of boom [Germain's emphasis].

What abysmal ignorance! That the rate of profit is very high, and the rate of investment extraordinarily high, will become only too clear from a few cold facts. Of the total national income in 1947, according to the government white paper *Economic Survey of 1947*, 20 percent will be devoted to capital equipment and maintenance, or 13 percent to capital equipment alone. This will be the highest investment *in volume* to be made in the last 100 years.[17] This represents the tremendous sum of £1,700 million against which about £600 million must be set off for depreciation and maintenance, leaving a new net capital formation of £1,100 million. As against this, the annual investments in Britain in 1860-69 were on the average £150 million; in 1907, £248 million; in 1924, £327 million; in 1929, £314 million; in 1932, £29 million; in 1935, £325 million; in 1937, £354 million (including £60 million in armament production).

Taking into account the price changes that have occurred, there is no doubt that British investments today are the highest in volume for the past 100 years.[18]

A few more weeds from Germain's garden

Germain poses the question, 'Is there a "feverish push of production in all the branches of industry" (Marx) in Britain?'

He answers simply: in Britain today 'there is nothing which resembles' this. It is difficult to comprehend what Germain understands in this reference from Marx. Is almost full employment a sign of such a 'feverish push of production in all the branches of industry'? Are tremendous investments a sign of it? Is a rapid increase in the productivity of labour a proof of it? One is driven to reiterate once again, Comrade Germain, that pontifical declarations do not suffice.

The lack of gold and hard foreign currency also is not, as Germain thinks, proof that there is not a boom in England. We need only mention the boom in Germany in the years 1924-29 in which equilibrium could not have been achieved in her balance of payments if not for the American loans.

The difficulties Britain is experiencing in attaining her balance of payments are neither proof nor refutation of a boom. Let us recollect that at the beginning of the crisis of 1929-33 Britain's balance of payments turned against her, being a reflection of the tremendous rise in imports due to the readiness of the foreign producers to flood the British market with goods at the cheapest prices. After a while, however, and especially after leaving the gold standard, the conditions of slump reflected themselves in a change in the terms of trade to Britain's benefit and a greater ease in gaining equilibrium in her balance of payments. From Britain's difficulties in attaining equilibrium today, therefore, nobody with any knowledge of economics would assert that this is proof that there is not a boom.

One could go on pulling the weeds out of Germain's garden. But I am afraid that were this to be done, nothing would remain at all.

Germain's analysis of the cycle of production under conditions of decadent capitalism

After showing such a lamentable lack of understanding of the theory of cycles, Germain tries to apply it to the conditions of declining capitalism. He gives four characteristics. The first is almost entirely a quotation from Trotsky, and is, therefore, correct. All the rest are based on a mechanical interpretation of the ABC of Marxism, and on a complete misunderstanding of the realities of capitalism in decline.

He writes:

> The world market ceases to expand *globally. There is no more boom on a world scale*. The splitting up of the world market or the violent destruction of a competitor alone allows for the development of feverish booms *in certain capitalist countries* [Germain's emphasis].

It is difficult to imagine the concentration of more mistakes in so few words. Instead of explaining that the decline of capitalism means that historically the productive forces expand more rapidly than the market; that, while not standing still, they lag far behind the potential productive possibilities; that more and more productive capacity is left unused; that production is ever further diverted from the production of means of production and means of consumption to the production of means of destruction—instead Germain puts forward the above-quoted vulgarisation of Marxism. A few simple facts will prove how careless he was in writing.

Let us begin by comparing industrial production on a world scale from the peak of one cycle to the peak of the next.[19]

WORLD INDUSTRIAL PRODUCTION (1913 = 100)	
1891	33
1900	51
1906	73
1913	100
1920	102
1928	148

While immediately after the First World War and certainly after the Second World War European production was lower than before the war, there is no question but that on a world scale production today, as against the situation after the First World War, is considerably higher than before the war. In 1929 all the countries of Europe except Britain overreached the level of production of the peak year, 1913. It would be wrong even to say that the world market shrinks *absolutely* during the whole period of the decline of capitalism. As the accumulation of capital determines the market, builds it, limits it, and undermines it, to speak about an absolute decline of the world market as a permanent phenomenon, and not as a stage in a cycle, is tantamount to declaring that the accumulation of capital ceases to take place in the period of the decline of capitalism. Such a theory can take its place not among revolutionary Marxists, but among IKDers, with their 'theory of retrogression'.

Let us bring a few facts about the development of world trade from the time of the transition of rising industrial capitalism to decadent monopoly capitalism until today.[20]

VOLUME OF WORLD TRADE (IN BILLION SWISS FRANCS, 1913 PRICES)

1870	45.5
1880	68.8
1890	94.2
1900	118.7
1913	197.8
1920	193.3
1929	261.7

During the cycle of 1929-37 world trade declined tremendously at the beginning but then rose—not, however, reaching the 1929 volume even at its peak: it was 4 percent lower. There are no statistics as regards world trade today.

Germain writes:

> There is no more all-round development of productive forces on a national scale. Even during the period of 'prosperity' certain branches develop only at the expense of other branches. Advances in technology are no longer or are only very partially incorporated in production.

If we understand this to be relative, and not as Germain considers it, to be absolute, it is correct. It simply repeats in other words what Lenin wrote in *Imperialism*: 'It would be a mistake to believe that this tendency to decay precludes the possibility of the rapid growth of capitalism. It does not. In the epoch of imperialism, certain branches of industry, certain strata of the bourgeoisie and certain countries betray, to a more or less degree, one or another of these tendencies. On the whole, capitalism is growing far more rapidly than before. But this growth is not only becoming more and more uneven in general; its unevenness also manifests itself, in particular, in the decay of the countries which are richest in capital (such as England)'.[21]

From this no one, except perhaps Germain, would conclude that technological developments are only partially, or not at all, incorporated in industry today. That this is not so will be clear from a comparison of the changes in the productivity of labour in England in the 50 years before the Second World War, when this country showed traits of decadence to a much greater extent than any other capitalist country. These are the facts:[22]

PRODUCTIVITY PER WORKER PER HOUR (1913 = 100)

Trade cycle	Productivity
1880–86	71
1887–95	75
1895–1903	80
1904–08	87
1909–14	93
1924–32	105
1933–39	119

A summing up of Germain's conception of the rise and decline of capitalism, can best be illustrated by drawing the following graphs:

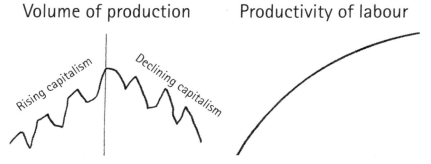

In reality the graphs should look something like this:

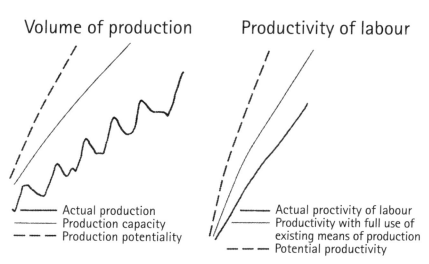

The standard of living of the masses in the period of the decline of capitalism

Germain writes, 'There is no more all-round amelioration of the standard of living of the industrial workers from one revival to another.'

Ascendant capitalism did not yield a general improvement in the living standards of the workers from one boom to another. Proof of this is to be found in the pages of the first volume of *Capital*, which describes the labour conditions in this period and points not only to the relative impoverishment of the working class, but also to its absolute impoverishment, not only to the decline of the workers' portion of the total product, but also to the absolute decline of real wages. Excellent proof of this is also to be found in Engels' *The Condition of the Working Class in England in 1844*, written in a year of boom. The connection between the general economic situation and the standards of living of the working class is determined by many different factors: by the tempo of accumulation of capital; by the relationship between the increase of production and the rise of the productivity of labour which influences employment; by the extent of the proletarianisation of petty bourgeois strata (peasants, artisans and others) following upon industrialisation, which influences the supply of labour; by the general price structure influenced by national and international factors, etc, etc; and, most important of all, the relation of class forces.

Whereas until about the 60s and 70s of the 19th century the living standards of the working class declined, there is no doubt that in all the developed countries during the last few decades of the 19th century the absolute standards of living of the workers rose. Now, with capitalism in decline, the general and continuous rise that took place for these few decades not only stopped but was even reversed for a certain period in some countries. To proceed from this to the oversimplified conclusion of Germain would be no less mistaken than to infer that throughout the rise of capitalism there was a general and continuous improvement in the living standards of the workers. It is most important to guard against underestimating the influence of the class relationship of forces in determining the value and price of labour power. To demonstrate that the decline of British capitalism has not yet been accompanied by a decline in the standard of living of the workers between the peaks of the cycles, let us look at some figures:[23]

REAL WAGES IN BRITAIN (1914 = 100)

1880	69
1890	93
1900	103
1914	100
1924	111
1929	118

This rise in real wages, of course, does not preclude a decline in wages relative to total production, ie an increase in the rate of exploitation. Thus relative wages in Britain were:[24]

RELATIVE WAGES IN BRITAIN (1900 = 100)

Cycle	Wages
1859–68	124
1869–79	111
1880–86	96
1887–95	95
1895–1903	94
1904–08	91
1909–14	88
1924–32	76

Germain writes that although 'there is no more all-round amelioration of the standard of living of the industrial workers from one revival to another', this 'does not exclude either a relative "amelioration" between the crisis and the revival, or a relative amelioration of the position of unemployed or peasants, etc, transformed during the "revival" into industrial workers'.

We have already explained that an amelioration of the standard of living of the workers between two revivals, even in the period of the decline of capitalism, is not excluded. It is even not excluded that the position of the unemployed *during the depression* will not be worse than the position of the unemployed in a previous depression, or indeed even than the position of the employed workers in a previous boom.

Colin Clark, who made excellent statistical investigations into the British national income and its distribution, points out, 'During recent years of low food prices, it has been about true to say that an unemployed man with a wife and two children drawing benefits has been better off than an unskilled labourer in full work in 1913'.[25]

These few facts are a warning to us not to interpret mechanically and in the spirit of the 'Third Period' the words of Trotsky when he said that in the 'epoch of decaying capitalism…in general, there can be no discussion of systematic social reforms and the raising of the masses' living standards…every serious demand of the proletariat and even every serious demand of the petty bourgeoisie inevitably reaches beyond the limits of capitalist property relations and of the bourgeois state'.[26]

Although the 19th century was the century of reforms, this did not prevent the short-lived Paris Commune from coming into existence. In the same way, the fact that the 20th century is the century of socialist revolution, does not exclude the possibility of certain reforms or semi-reforms being introduced.

But these reforms cannot be of a general and lasting nature; necessarily, they must be very meagre as against the vast potentialities of production.[27]

A few remarks in conclusion

It is outside the scope of this article to make an exhaustive analysis and elaboration of the Marxist theory of crises. Nor does it attempt to show how the theory of crises applies to world capitalism in general, and Britain in particular, or attempt to analyse the influence of the war on the economic cycle. Nevertheless, if it succeeds in throwing some light on these questions it will have accomplished what it set out to do.

In view of the fact that Comrade Germain writes extensively and prolifically on many theoretical and political subjects requiring considerable study, it is very necessary for the wellbeing of the Fourth International that he prepares his writings with scientific conscientiousness. The analysis of his article under review proves that sweeping confidence and pontifical declarations regarding facts and theoretical generalisations are no substitute for really scientific work. And this holds good not only for current reading, but also for the ABC.

Notes

1 Editor's note: in this chapter, IS stands for the International Secretariat and IEC for International Executive Committee (of the Fourth International)—and the standpoint defended by Germain/Mandel. RCP stands for the Revolutionary Communist Party, whose majority position Cliff was defending, and PB for its political bureau. The IKD was a group of German Trotskyists.

2 K Marx, *Capital*, vol I, translated S Moore and E Aveling (Modern Library, 1936), p495; K Marx, *Capital*, vol I, translated S Moore and E Aveling (Swan Sonnenschein, Lowrey & Co, 1887), p455; K Marx, *Capital*, vol I, translated Eden and Cedar Paul (Everyman's Library, 1946), p486.

3 Germain's juggling with words makes up such an important part of his article that, although we do not intend to weed out every error he makes, this particular one deserves mention, even if only in the form of a note.

He says that there are 'two terms by which Marx characterises the period that we call "boom": the term "upswing" (*essor*) and the term "production at high pressure".' He arrives at this conclusion after citing two quotations from Marx describing the cycle. Even if the passage from Marx was not wrongly quoted, the way Germain derives his definitions from them is absolutely arbitrary.

In the first passage (wrongly quoted) the cycle is divided into six subsections: moderate activity, prosperity, upswing, overproduction, crisis and stagnation. In the second, it is divided into four subsections: moderate activity, production at high pressure, crisis and stagnation.

Now, by eliminating the common terms in these two formulations, we would be left in the first formulation with: *prosperity, upswing and overproduction*. In the second we are left with *production at high pressure*. If production at high pressure is, for Germain, identical with boom, why does he exclude Marx's terms of prosperity and overproduction from being part of the boom?

4 L Trotsky, *The First Five Years of the Communist International*, p200.

5 *Quatrième Internationale*, December 1946.

6 CC Minority, 'Some Comments on the PE Reply to the IS Letter'.

7 L Corey, *The Decline of American Capitalism* (New York, 1934), p114.

8   C Clark, *The Conditions of Economic Progress* (London, 1940), p454.

9   J Schumpeter, *Business Cycles*, vol II (New York, 1939), p478. *Includes the prices of 30 basic commodities, farm products, minerals, textiles, and the like.

10 L Corey, op cit, p186.

11 K Marx, *Capital*, vol I, translated S Moore and E Aveling (Modern Library, 1936), p457.

12 The implication that the comrades of the RCP Majority consider the coal shortage to be 'a result of the boom' is readily shattered by an analysis of their resolutions for several years and especially by the article to which Germain pens his reply.

13 K Marx, *Capital*, vol I, translated S Moore and E Aveling (Modern Library, 1936), p694.

14 It would be possible to establish the same facts as regards other industrial countries also, but let this one example suffice.

15 J Kuczynski, *A Short History of Labour Conditions in Germany, 1800 to the Present Day* (London, 1945), p163.

16 L Corey, op cit, p227.

17 C Clark, op cit, p396.

18 Ibid.

19 J Kuczynski, *Weltproduktion und Welthandel in den letzten 100 Jahren* (Libau, 1935), pp20-21.

20 Ibid.

21 V I Lenin, *Imperialism: The Highest Stage of Capitalism* (London, 1939), p109.

22 J Kuczynski, *A Short History of Labour Conditions in Great Britain and the Empire to the Present Day* (London, 1942), p96.

23 A Bowley, *Wages and Income in the United Kingdom Since 1860* (London, 1937), p30.

24 J Kuczynski, *A Short History of Labour Conditions in Great Britain and the Empire to the Present Day*, op cit, pp64, 301.

25 C Clark, *National Income and Outlay* (London, 1937), p270. In the light of the above-quoted figures of real wages, and of a comparison of the existing conditions in Britain today, with those described by people living before the First World War, it is clear that the writers of the editorial in the Fourth International of March 1947 were not very well informed when they wrote, 'The prospects in England are dimmer and dimmer for a return to the living levels of 1939, let alone the levels achieved before 1914.' According to this the standard of the British worker today is lower than in 1939, and in 1939 it was lower than in 1913!

26 L Trotsky, 'The Death Agony of Capitalism and the Tasks of the Fourth International' (1938).

27 In order to prevent any misunderstanding, it is necessary to point out: while Germain is wrong when he speaks of the inevitability of the standard of life decreasing from one peak of a cycle to another in the period of decadent capitalism, it does not follow that every boom must bring a standard of life to the masses higher than in the preceding boom. No, definitely not. Marxist economic laws are not of this schematical character. If the RCP Majority perspectives speak about reforms and semi-reforms at the present time, they could not derive this prognosis from the fact that Britain is in a period of economic boom alone. There were many booms not accompanied by a rise in the standard of life of the masses. The RCP perspectives were conditioned, and must be conditioned by three factors: one, the existence of a boom; two, the prevailing relation of forces in Britain; three, an American loan which will bridge the big deficit in the balance of foreign trade. As Trotsky formulated it: 'Every historical prognosis is always conditional, and the more concrete the prognosis, the more conditional it is.'

The theory of bureaucratic collectivism: a critique

Duplicated document, 1948.
Reprinted in *International Socialism* (first series) 32, Spring 1968

Introduction

For obvious reasons, discussion of the nature of Soviet society was central to the thinking of most socialists of the last generation.

The conception of Russia under Stalin and his heirs as socialism, or a deformed kind of socialism ('degenerated workers' state' in the language of dogmatic 'orthodox' Trotskyists), has met two kinds of critique by Marxists. The first, to which the present writer subscribes, defines the Stalinist regime as state capitalist. The second sees it as neither socialism of any sort nor capitalism. This last school of thought coined a special term for the Stalinist regime—bureaucratic collectivism. The first writer to coin this term was the Italian Marxist Bruno R, in his book *La Bureaucratisation du Monde* (Paris, 1939). The same term was adopted and the idea developed (without acknowledgement of the work of Bruno R) by the American socialist Max Shachtman.

The subject of the present article is an evaluation and criticism of this thesis.

It is difficult to make a critique of bureaucratic collectivism because the authors never actually published a developed account of the theory. It is true that Shachtman wrote hundreds of pages of criticism of the theory that Stalinist Russia was a socialist country or a workers' state of any sort (he dismissed the theory of state capitalism in a sentence or two). But he wrote scarcely a paragraph on the laws of motion of the 'bureaucratic collectivist' economy, and made no analysis at all of the *specific* character of the class struggle within it. The place of bureaucratic collectivist society in the chain of historical development is not clearly stated and, in any case, Shachtman's account is often inconsistent.

A central thesis of the present article is that the theoretical poverty of the theory of bureaucratic collectivism is not accidental. We will try to show that the theory of bureaucratic collectivism is only *negative*. It is thus empty, abstract, and therefore arbitrary.

Criticism of the theory will suggest a number of characteristics that are common, implicitly at least, to other conceptions of Stalinism—from that of the apologists to that of George Orwell's *Nineteen Eighty-Four*. In criticising the theory, the strength or weakness of the alternative theory of Stalinist Russia as state capitalist will emerge.

The place of bureaucratic collectivism in history

At first glance what is more plausible than describing Stalinist Russia as neither a capitalist nor a workers' state? But this simplification is of little value, for it tells us little about the regime; feudalism too was neither capitalism nor socialism, similarly slave society, and any other regime that has not existed but is created by our imagination. Spinoza was right when he said that 'definition is negation', but not all negations are definitions. The statement that the Stalinist regime was neither capitalist nor socialist left the latter's historical identity undetermined. Hence Shachtman could say on one occasion that bureaucratic collectivism was more progressive than capitalism (however unprogressive it was, compared with socialism), and a few years later that it was more reactionary than capitalism.

Shachtman first called Russia a bureaucratic collectivist state in 1941. A resolution on the Russian question passed at the 1941 Convention of his organisation, the now defunct Workers' Party, stated, 'From the standpoint of socialism, the bureaucratic collectivist state is a reactionary social order; in relation to the capitalist world, it is on an historically more progressive plane.'

On the basis of this, a policy of 'conditional defencism' was adopted. The resolution states:

> The revolutionary proletariat can consider a revolutionary (that is, a critical, entirely independent, class) defencist position with regard to the Stalinist regime only under conditions where the decisive issue in the war is the attempt by a hostile force to restore capitalism in Russia, where this issue is not subordinated to other, more dominant, issues. Thus, in case of a civil war in which one section of the bureaucracy seeks to restore capitalist private property, it is possible for the revolutionary vanguard to fight with the army of the Stalinist regime against the army of capitalist restoration. Thus, in case of a war by which world imperialism seeks to subdue the Soviet Union and acquire a new lease of life by reducing Russia to an imperialist colony, it is possible for the proletariat to take a revolutionary defencist position in Russia. Thus, in case of civil war organised against the existing regime by an army basing itself on 'popular discontent' but actually on the capitalist and semi-capitalist elements still existing in the country, and aspiring to the restoration of capitalism, it is again possible that the proletariat would fight in the army of Stalin against the army of capitalist reaction. In all those or similar cases, the critical support of the proletariat is possible only if the proletariat is not yet prepared itself to overthrow the Stalinist regime.

In logic, when, a few months after this convention, Hitler's Germany attacked Russia, Shachtman and his followers should have come to the defence of Russia, as it was 'on an historically more progressive plane'.

The argument Shachtman put now was that, even though Russia was more progressive than capitalist Germany, its war was nevertheless only a subordinate part of the total war, the basic character of which was a struggle between two capitalist imperialist camps. He wrote:

> The character of the war, the conduct of the war and (for the present) the outcome of the war, are determined by the two couples of imperialist titans which dominate each camp respectively, the United States and Great Britain, and Germany and Japan. (Within each of the two, in turn, there is a senior and a junior partner!) *All* the other countries in the two great coalitions are reduced to vassalage to the giants which differs in each case only in degree. This vassalage is determined by the economic (industrial-technical), and therefore the financial, and therefore the political, and therefore the military, domination of the war by the two great 'power-couples'. Italy is less dependent upon the masters of its coalition than Hungary, and Hungary less than Slovakia. But these facts do not alter the state of the vassalage—they only determine its degree. Stalinist Russia is less dependent upon the masters of its coalition than China (it would lead us too far afield to show in what sense, however, it is even more dependent upon US-England than China), and China less than the Philippines. But again, these facts only determine the degree of their vassalage. Except, therefore, for inconsequential cranks and special pleaders in the bourgeois world, everyone in it understands the total nature of the war as a whole; the total nature of each coalition; the relative position and weight of each sector of the coalition; the mutual interdependence of all fronts.[1]

Thus, although bureaucratic collectivism is more progressive than capitalism, a defeatist position was adopted because of Russia's vassalage to Anglo-American imperialism. The *New International* of September 1941 emphasised the point: 'Stalin has lost the last vestige of independence... Soviet diplomacy is already dictated in London.'

We shall not dwell on the factual mistakes. These are less serious than the method by which Shachtman arrives at his conclusions. Marxism demands that from sociological definitions we draw political conclusions. When the course of the war contradicted his judgement of Russia as a vassal state, Shachtman should have rejected his previous defeatist position, for bureaucratic collectivism, he said, is more progressive than capitalism. Instead he held to the political conclusion of defeatism and altered the sociological basis. Bureaucratic collectivism now came to be called the new barbarism, the decline of civilisation, etc. Yet in no document did he give any new analysis of the Russian economy after the resolution of the 1941 convention.

The only two constant elements in the theory have been: first, the conclusion that in any concrete conditions Stalinist Russia must not be defended (no matter that the concrete conditions change all the time); second, that the name of the Stalinist regime is bureaucratic collectivism.

With regard to the first element, serious Marxists, while seeking to hold consistently to the same principles, often change their tactics, as tactics must change with changing circumstances. Marxists should not decide on one tactic and hold to it when the justification for it is proved incorrect. This is eclecticism, impressionism. But exactly this approach was adopted by Shachtman. He draws the same conclusion from two opposite and mutually exclusive assumptions, the one that bureaucratic collectivism is more progressive than capitalism, the other that it is the image of barbarism—more reactionary. Defeatism is the tactic. Why? Once because Russia was not the main power, but only a vassal of Anglo-American imperialism, now because Russia is a major imperialist power which threatens to conquer the world.

As for the name, we might well repeat Marx's apt criticism of Proudhon, who used to invent lofty words, thinking in this way to advance science. Marx quoted the following: 'Wo Begriffe felhen, da stellt zur rechten Zeit ein Wort sich ein.' ('Where there is a lack of ideas, an empty phrase will do.')

In Marx and Engels' analysis of capitalism, the fundamentals—the place of capitalism in history, its internal contradictions, etc—remained constant from their first approach to the problem until the end of their lives. Their later years brought only elaborations of and additions to the basic theme. The theory of bureaucratic collectivism in its short history has had a much less happy fate. Shachtman first considered bureaucratic collectivism more progressive than capitalism, and then as 'totalitarian barbarism'. Another proponent of the theory, Bruno R, *at one and the same time* considers it both a slave society and the threshold of a peaceful transition to communism.

Bruno R on bureaucratic collectivism

Bruno R differs from Shachtman in many fundamentals. His analysis of the genesis of bureaucratic collectivism, for instance, is basically different from Shachtman's. They agree on the genesis of the system in Russia. But when they step beyond its borders, they are at variance. While the resolution of the Workers' Party convention of 1941 maintained that 'bureaucratic collectivism is a nationally-limited phenomenon, appearing in history in the course of a single conjuncture of circumstances', Bruno R saw it as a society which would replace capitalism on a world scale through the expropriation of the bourgeoisie by the Stalinist bureaucracy and the fascist bureaucracy. However, on the characterisation, description and analysis of bureaucratic collectivism as such—as a social order—they are in entire agreement.

In his book *La Bureaucratisation du Monde*, Bruno R writes:

> In our opinion, the USSR represents a new type of society led by a new social class: that is our conclusion. Collectivised property actually belongs to this class which has introduced a new—and superior—system of production. Exploitation is transferred from the individual to the class.[2]

In our opinion, the Stalinist regime is an intermediary regime; it eliminates out-dated capitalism, but does not rule out socialism for the future. It is a new social form based on class property and class exploitation.[3]

In our opinion, in the USSR, the property owners are the bureaucrats, for it is they who hold force in their hands. It is they who direct the economy as was usual among the bourgeoisie; it is they who appropriate the profits to themselves, as was usual among all exploiting classes, and it is they who fix wages and the prices of goods: once again, it is the bureaucrats.[4]

What is the character of the ruled class? Does there exist a Russian proletariat, or, just as the bourgeoisie was substituted by a new exploiting class, is the proletariat substituted by a new exploited class? Bruno R answers thus:

Exploitation occurs exactly as in a society based on slavery: the subject of the state works for the one master who has bought him, he becomes a part of his master's capital, he represents the livestock which must be cared for and housed and whose reproduction is a matter of great importance for the master. The payment of a so-called wage, consisting partly of state services and goods, should not induce us into error and lead us to suppose the existence of a socialist form of remuneration: for indeed, it only means the upkeep of a slave! The sole fundamental difference is that in ancient times the slaves did not have the honour or carrying arms, whilst the modern slaves are skilfully trained in the art of war... The Russian working class are no longer proletarians; they are merely slaves. It is a class of slaves in its economic substance and in its social manifestations. It kneels as the 'Little Father' passes by and deifies him, it assumes all the characteristics of servility and allows itself to be tossed about from one end of the immense empire to the other. It digs canals, builds roads and railways, just as in ancient times this same class erected the Pyramids or the Coliseum.

A small part of this class have not yet lost themselves in complete agnosticism; retaining their faith, they meet in caves for purposes of discussion, as of old, the Christians praying in the catacombs. From time to time the Pretorians organise a raid and round everybody up. 'Monster' trials are staged, in the style of Nero, and the accused, instead of defending themselves, say 'mea culpa'. The Russian workers differ completely from the proletarians in every respect, they have become state subjects and have acquired all the characteristics of slaves.

They no longer have anything in common with free workers except the sweat on their brow. The Marxists will truly need Diogenes' lamp if they intend to find any proletarians in the Soviet towns.[5]

Even though Bruno R describes Stalinist Russia as the renewal of slavery (with all the historical retrogression connected with it), he nevertheless says that this regime is more progressive than capitalism, and, further, that it leads directly, without leaps or struggles, to communist society. He says:

We believe that the new society will lead directly to socialism, because of the enormous volume attained by production.

The leaders (so will now be called those whom we have contemptuously labelled bureaucrats and the new class will be called leading class), having satisfied their material, intellectual and moral needs, may of course find a pleasurable occupation in the constant material, intellectual and moral elevation of the working class.[6]

The totalitarian state should not impress the Marxists. For the time being, it is totalitarian rather in the political than in the economic sense. These factors will be reversed in the course of the forthcoming and normal social developments. The totalitarian state will more and more lose its political characteristics and retain only its administrative characteristics. At the end of this process we will have a classless society and socialism.[7]

A new 'withering away'—of 'collective slavery', of 'totalitarian bureaucratic collectivism', in communism! And this development Bruno R proudly proclaims '*the triumph of historical materialism*'! (See particularly the chapter in his book under this name.)

Bruno R's bureaucratic collectivism leads directly, automatically, to communism. It is undoubtedly a materialist conception, but it is not dialectical. It is a mechanical, fatalist approach to history which denies the class struggle of the oppressed as the necessary motive force.

The Stalinist regime—barbarism?

Shachtman writes about the Stalinist regime:

> It is the cruel realisation of the prediction made by all the great socialist scientists, from Marx and Engels onward, that capitalism must collapse out of an inability to solve its own contradictions and that the alternatives facing mankind are not so much capitalism or socialism as they are: socialism or barbarism. Stalinism is that new barbarism.[8]

If the Stalinist regime denotes the decline of civilisation, the reactionary negation of capitalism, then, of course, it is more reactionary than the latter. Capitalism has to be defended from Stalinist barbarism.

But Shachtman ties himself in knots.

When Marx spoke of the 'common ruin of the contending classes'—as in Rome after slave society disintegrated—it was associated with a general decline of the productive forces. The Stalinist regime, with its dynamic development of the productive forces, certainly does not fit this description.

Barbarism in Marx's concept meant the death of the embryo of the future in the womb of the old society. The embryo of socialism in the body of capitalism is social, collective, large-scale production and, associated with it, the working class. The Stalinist regime not only did not weaken these elements, but spurred them on.

The motive for exploitation in bureaucratic collectivist society

Shachtman explains the motive for exploitation in bureaucratic collectivist society thus: 'In the Stalinist state, production is carried on and extended for the satisfaction of the needs of the bureaucracy, for the increasing of its wealth, its privileges, its power.' Now if the motive for exploitation under bureaucratic collectivism was simply the needs of the rulers, how does this relate to the general historical roots of exploitation in different social systems?

Engels explains why, in the past, society was divided into exploiters and exploited:

> The division of society into an exploiting and an exploited class, a ruling and an oppressed class, was the necessary outcome of the low development of production hitherto. So long as the sum of social labour yielded a product which only slightly exceeded what was necessary for the bare existence of all; so long, therefore, *as all or almost all the time of the great majority of the members of society was absorbed in labour, so long was society necessarily divided into classes.* Alongside of this great majority exclusively absorbed in labour, there developed a class, freed from direct productive labour, which managed the general business of society: the direction of labour, affairs of state, justice, science, art and so forth.[9]

In an economy in which the motive for production is the production of use values for the rulers, there are certain limits to the extent of exploitation. Thus for instance in feudal society, village and town alike were subjugated to the feudal lords' need for consumption goods, and so long as the produce which the serfs gave to their lord was not widely marketed, 'the walls of his stomach set the limits to his exploitation of the peasant' (Marx). This does not explain the existence of exploitation under capitalism. The walls of the capitalist's stomach are undoubtedly much wider than those of the feudal lord of the Middle Ages, but, at the same time, the productive capacity of capitalism is incomparably greater than that of feudalism. We should therefore be quite mistaken if we explained the increase in the exploitation of the mass of workers as the result of the widening of the walls of the bourgeoisie's stomach.

The need for capital accumulation, dictated by the anarchic competition between capitals, is the motivation for exploitation under capitalism.

Actually, if the bureaucratic collectivist economy is geared to the 'needs of the bureaucracy'—is not subordinated to capital accumulation—there is no reason why the rate of exploitation should not decrease in time, and as the productive forces in the modern world are dynamic, this will lead willy-nilly to the 'withering away of exploitation'.

With the dynamism of highly developed productive forces, an economy based on gratifying the needs of the rulers can be arbitrarily described as leading to the millennium or to 1984. Bruno R's dream and George Orwell's nightmare—and anything in between—are possible under such a system. The bureaucratic collectivist theory is thus entirely capricious and arbitrary in defining the limitation and direction of exploitation under the regime it presumes to define.

Class relations under bureaucratic collectivism

The essence of Shachtman's position is summed up in the statement that the rulers of Russia under Stalin were neither workers nor private owners of capital. What is decisive, according to the Marxist method, in defining the class nature of any society? As the history of all class society is the history of the class struggle, it is clear that what determine the place of any regime in the chain of historical development are these factors which determine the character of the class struggle in it. Now, the character, the methods and the aims of the class struggle of the oppressed class are dependent on the nature of the oppressed class itself: the position it has in the process of production, the relation between its members in this process, and its relation to the owners of the means of production. These are *not* determined by the mode of appropriation or mode of recruitment of the *ruling* class. A few examples will explain this.

We know that in the Middle Ages the feudal lord had the right to bequeath his feudal rights to his heirs; on the other hand the bishop did not have this right, nor even that of raising a family. The feudal lord was the son of a feudal lord, a nobleman. The bishops were recruited from different classes and layers of society, often from the peasantry. (Engels pointed to the plebeian origin of the upper hierarchy of the church—and even of a number of popes—as one of the causes for the stability of the church in the Middle Ages.) Thus the mode of recruitment of the bishops was *different* from that of the private feudal lords. As regards the form of appropriation, the difference was equally great: the feudal lord, as an owner, was entitled to all the rent he could collect from his serfs, while the bishop was legally propertyless and, as such, entitled only to a 'salary'. But did these differences between the mode of appropriation and the mode of recruitment of the feudal lords and the upper hierarchy of the church make any *basic* difference to the class struggle of the serfs on church land, or on the lord's land? Of course not. The peasant with his primitive means of production, with the individualistic mode of production, had the same relation to other peasants, the same relation to the means of production (primarily the land), and the same relation to his exploiter, whether he was a feudal lord or a collective exploiter—the upper clergy (or as Kautsky calls them in a book highly recommended by Engels, the 'Papacy Class').

Similarly, in slave society there was, besides the private ownership of slaves, collective state ownership, as in Sparta.[10]

From the standpoint of the exploiters the question of their mode of appropriation and recruitment is of prime importance. Thus, for instance, Kautsky, in *Thomas More and His Utopia*, says:

> It looked as if the church aspired to become the sole landed proprietor in Christendom. But the mightiest were to be curbed. The nobles were always hostile to the church; when the latter acquired too much land, the king turned to the nobles for assistance in setting limits to the pretensions of the church. Moreover,

the church was weakened by the invasion of heathen tribes and the Mohammedans.[11]

The church acquired, not without a struggle (in which one of the weapons it used was the forging of deeds of gift), about a third of all the land in Europe as a whole, in some countries the majority share of the land (eg Hungary, Bohemia). Perhaps, therefore, the nobles considered the differences between themselves and the upper clergy—in their origin and mode of appropriation—of importance.

But from the standpoint of the class struggle of the serfs or the rising bourgeoisie against feudalism, these differences were of quite *secondary* importance. It would not be correct to say that they were of no importance, as the differences in the composition of the ruling class to some extent conditioned the struggle of the serfs or the rising bourgeoisie. Thus, for instance, the concentration of the means of production in the hands of the church made the struggle of the serfs against the church much more difficult than their struggle against individual landlords. The ideological justification of feudal ownership was different in form when blue blood and coats of arms were presented than when religious phrases were quoted in Latin. And the fact that while church property was officially called 'patrimonium pauperum' (the inheritance of the poor) private feudal property was not endowed with this exalted title helps to show that these judicial differences were not unimportant. But from the standpoint of the historical process as a whole, ie from the standpoint of the class struggle, all the differences in the mode of appropriation and method of recruitment of the different groups are only secondary.

Shachtman and Bruno R (as well as 'orthodox' Trotskyists) forget Marx's statement of a century ago: that the form of property considered independently of the laws of motion of the economy, from the relations of production, is a metaphysical abstraction.

Thus the big differences between the mode of appropriation and recruitment of the Russian bureaucrats and that of the bourgeoisie, in itself, does not at all prove that Russia represents a non-capitalist society, a new class society of bureaucratic collectivism. To prove this, it is necessary to show that the *nature* of the ruled class—its conditions of life and struggle—is fundamentally different in Russia from what exists, even for Shachtman, in capitalism. And this is exactly what Bruno R, and later Shachtman, tried to do.

The nature of the working class in Russia

On the question of whether the workers in Russia are proletarians, the proponents of the theory of bureaucratic collectivism answer, and must answer, that they are not. They compare the Russian with the classical worker who was 'free' of the means of production and also free of any legal impediments to selling his labour power. It is true that there often were legal impediments to the movement of Russian workers from one enterprise to another. But is this a sufficient reason to say that the Russian worker was not a proletarian? If so, there is no doubt that the German worker under Hitler was also not a proletarian. Or, at the other extreme, workers in power are also not proletarians inasmuch as they are not 'free' as a collective from the means of production. No doubt an American worker is very different from an indentured girl in a Japanese factory who is under contract for a number of years and must live in the company's barracks for that time. But basically they are members of one and the same class. They were born together with the most dynamic form of production history has ever known; they are united by the process of social production; they are in actuality the antithesis of capital, and in potentiality socialism itself (because of the dynamics of a modern economy, no legal impediments in fact put an end *altogether* to the movement of workers from one enterprise to another under Stalin's regime).

Hilferding, Bruno R and Dwight MacDonald were consistent and maintained that, just as they did not consider a Russian worker to be a proletarian, so they did not consider a worker in Hitler's Germany to be a proletarian. The Shachtmanites tried to avoid this conclusion. In so doing they were led to falsify facts. For instance, they claimed that the German workers under Hitler were freer to move than the Russian, that they were freer to bargain with their employers, and that slave labour was never as widespread in Germany as in Russia. Thus Irving Howe, one of Shachtman's followers at the time, wrote:

> The Nazis did not use slave labour to the extent that Stalinist Russia has; under the Hitler regime, slave labour never became as indispensable a part of Germany's national economy as it has become for Russia under Stalin…industry under Hitler was still largely based on 'free labour' (in the Marxist sense; that is, free from ownership of the means of production and thereby forced to sell labour power, but also possessing the freedom to decide whether or not to sell this labour power). For all of the Hitlerite restrictions, there was considerable bargaining between the capitalist and proletarian, as well as between capitalists for workers during labour shortages.[12]

In reality the Russian worker, notwithstanding all restrictions, moves from one factory to another much more than the German worker, or, for that matter, than any other worker in the whole world. As early as September 1930 workers were prohibited from changing their place of work without special permission, and year after year brought new prohibitions. Despite this the rate of turnover was tremendous. In 1928, as against 100 workers employed in industry, 92.4 leavings were registered; in 1929, 115.2; 1930, 152.4; 1931, 136.8; 1932, 135.3; 1933, 122.4; 1934, 96.7; 1935, 86.1. In later years figures were not published, but it is clear that the large turnover continued, to which the frequent declamations in the press bear witness. Even the war did not put an end to it. The German administration was incomparably more efficient in combating the free movement of labour under Hitler. This, in addition to other factors (especially the relatively much greater dynamism of the Russian economy), made the labour turnover in Germany much lower than in Russia.

What about the slave camps in Stalin's Russia? Shachtman tried to suggest that slave labour was the basic factor of production in Russia. But this is absolutely wrong. The labour of prisoners is suitable only for manual work where modern technique is not used. It is therefore employed in the construction of factories, roads, etc. Despite its cheapness, it is necessarily only of secondary importance to the labour of workers, as 'unfree' labour is always relatively unproductive. If not for the fact that slave labour were an impediment to the rise of the productivity of labour, the decline of Roman society would not have taken place. Likewise, although in different circumstances, slavery would not have been abolished in the United States. In the face of special circumstances—the lack of means of production and the abundance of labour power—it is explicable that the Stalinist bureaucracy should introduce and use slave labour on a large scale. But it is clear that the main historical tendency is in an opposite direction. All the factories in Russia producing tanks and aeroplanes, machinery, etc were run on wage labour. During the war Hitler's Germany found it expedient to use 12 million foreign workers, most of whom had been recruited as prisoners and forced labourers.

Marx maintained that the historical tendency towards the degradation of the proletariat, its increased oppression by capital, is fundamental to capitalism, whereas the substitution of the proletariat by a new, or rather, ancient, class of slaves is quite contrary to the general tendency of history. As we have said, only a lack of means of production and an abundance of labour power can explain the widespread use of prison labour in Stalin's Russia. Hence its almost complete disappearance since the death of Stalin, since Russia reached industrial maturity.

Shachtman's theory of bureaucratic collectivism must lead to its logical conclusion. If the Russian worker is not a proletarian, the German worker under Hitler was not a proletarian, and in Hitler's Germany there was not a wage labour system, but a system of 'collective slavery'. Accordingly, the ruling class in Hitler's Germany could not be called a capitalist class, as capitalists are exploiters of proletarians. Bruno R, Dwight MacDonald and Hilferding, at least, have the merit of consistency. They drew these conclusions and were therefore justified in calling Hitler's Germany bureaucratic collectivist (Bruno R and Dwight MacDonald) or a 'totalitarian state economy' (Hilferding).

If we accepted that workers employed by the Stalinist state are not proletarians, we should have to come to the absurd conclusion that in the Western powers' zones of Berlin the workers are proletarians, but in the Russian zone those employed in the nationalised German enterprises are not proletarians, while those employed in the Russian zone by private industry are proletarians!

Again we should have to come to the absurd conclusion that non-workers under Stalin have been gradually transformed after his death into proletarians.

Above all, if Shachtman is right and there is no proletariat in the Stalinist regime, Marxism as a method, as a guide for the proletariat as the subject of historical change, becomes superfluous, meaningless. To speak about Marxism in a society without a proletariat is to make of Marxism a suprahistorical theory.

Historical limitations of bureaucratic collectivism

If one accepts the state capitalist nature of the Stalinist regime, one not only accepts its laws of motion—the accumulation of capital as dictated by the pressure of world capitalism—but also the historical limitations of its role. Once capital is amassed and the working class is massive, the ground is undermined beneath the feet of the bureaucracy.

For a Marxist who thinks Russia is state capitalist, the historical mission of the bourgeoisie is the socialisation of labour and the concentration of the means of production. On a world scale this task had already been fulfilled. In Russia the revolution removed the impediments to the development of the productive forces, put an end to the remnants of feudalism, built up a monopoly of foreign trade which defends the development of the productive forces of the country from the devastating pressure of world capitalism, and also gave a tremendous lever to the development of the productive forces in the form of state ownership of the means of production. Under such conditions all the impediments to the historical mission of capitalism—the socialisation of labour and the concentration of the means of production which are necessary prerequisites for the establishment of socialism, and which the bourgeoisie was not able to fulfil—are abolished. *Post-October Russia stood before the fulfilment of the historical mission of the bourgeoisie*, which Lenin summed up in two postulates: 'Increase in the productive forces of social labour and the socialisation of labour.'

Once the Stalinist bureaucracy created a massive working class and massive concentrated capital, the objective prerequisites for the overthrow of the bureaucracy had been laid. The Stalinist bureaucracy thus created its own gravedigger (hence the post-Stalin convulsions in Russia and Eastern Europe).

The theory of bureaucratic collectivism is inherently incapable of saying anything about the historical role and limitations of the Stalinist bureaucracy. Hence socialism also appears simply as a utopian dream, not a necessary solution to contradictions inherent in the Stalinist regime itself. Abstracted from the contradictions of capitalism, the urge towards socialism becomes merely an idealistic chimera.

Attitude to the Stalinist parties

From the assumption that bureaucratic collectivism is more reactionary than capitalism, Shachtman draws the conclusion that if a choice has to be made between social democratic parties which support capitalism and Communist parties—agents of bureaucratic collectivism—a socialist should side with the former against the latter.

Thus Shachtman wrote in September 1948:

> *Stalinism is a reactionary, totalitarian, anti-bourgeois and anti-proletarian current* **in** *the labour movement but not* **of** *the labour movement...where, as is the general rule*

nowadays, the militants are not yet strong enough to fight for leadership directly; where the fight for control of the labour movement is, in effect, between the reformists and the Stalinists, it would be absurd for the militants to proclaim their 'neutrality' and fatal for them to support the Stalinists. Without any hesitation, they should follow the general line, inside the labour movement, of supporting the reformist officialdom against the Stalinist officialdom. In other words, where it is not yet possible to win the unions for the leadership of revolutionary militants, we forthrightly prefer the leadership of reformists who aim in their own way to maintain a labour movement, to the leadership of the Stalinist totalitarians who aim to exterminate it...while the revolutionists are not the equal of the reformists and the reformists are not the equal of the revolutionists, the two are now necessary and proper allies against Stalinism. The scores that have to be settled with reformism—those will be settled on a working class basis and in a working class way, and not under the leadership or in alliance with totalitarian reaction.[13]

Again there is a lack of historical perspective, of real analysis of social forces, an oversimplification. The dual role of the Communist parties in the West—as agents of Moscow and as a collection of fighting individual militants, strangled by the same bureaucracy—is completely overlooked. Shachtman's attitude to the Communist parties, if adopted by any socialists in the West, would firstly, strengthen the right wing social democratic parties, and secondly strengthen the hold of the Communist Party leadership on their rank and file. It is a sure way to liquidate any independent working class tendency.

In conclusion

The theory of bureaucratic collectivism is suprahistorical, negative and abstract. It does not define the economic laws of motion of the system, or explain its inherent contradictions and the motivation of the class struggle. It is completely arbitrary. Hence it does not give a perspective, nor can it serve as a basis for a strategy for socialists.

Notes

1 M Shachtman, 'China in the World War', *New International*, June 1942.
2 Bruno R, *La Bureaucratisation du Monde* (Paris, 1939), p31.
3 Ibid, p95.
4 Ibid, p56.
5 Ibid, pp72-74.
6 Ibid, p283.
7 Ibid, p284.
8 M Shachtman, *The Bureaucratic Revolution* (New York, 1962), p32.
9 F Engels, 'Socialism: Utopian and Scientific', in K Marx and F Engels, *Selected Works*, vol I, p183. My emphasis.
10 Kautsky describes this regime: 'The Spartans made up the minority, perhaps a tenth of the population. Their state was based on real War Communism, the barrack communism of the ruling class. Plato drew his ideal of the state from it. The ideal differed from real Sparta only in that it was not the military chiefs but the 'philosophers', that is, the intellectuals,

who directed the war communism'— K Kautsky, *Die Materialistische Geschichtauffassung* (Berlin, 1927), pp132-133.

11 K Kautsky, *Thomas More and His Utopias* (London, 1927), p38.

12 *New International*, December 1947.

13 M Shachtman, op cit, pp306, 308-309. A by-product of this hysterical anti-Stalinism is softness, even idealisation, of social democracy: 'In most of the countries of Europe west of the barbed-wire frontiers, the socialist parties not only represent the sole serious alternative to the futile and futureless parties of the status quo but are the political instrument of the democratic working class.'

Perspectives for the permanent war economy

Socialist Review, March 1957

The economic level of society, the level its productive forces have reached, is the decisive factor in the organisation of its armies. As Marx said, 'Our theory that the organisation of labour is conditioned by the means of production is, it seems, nowhere as brilliantly corroborated as in the "human slaughter industry".'

In the early period of capitalism the backwardness of the economy made it impossible to feed and arm large armies. Compared with the mass armies mobilised during the First and Second World Wars, the armies of early, rising capitalism were very small.

Even during the Napoleonic Wars, France, ruler of practically the whole of Europe, did not at any time have more than half a million troops. The British armed forces at the time were less than a tenth of those of France.

All this changed with the First World War. Then France, whose population was only some 10 million more people than during Napoleonic times (40 million against 30), mobilised as many as 5 million soldiers. The other belligerent countries showed similar increases.

Together with the tremendous increase in the size of the armies during the last half century, there came a change in the role of the military sector in the national economy.

Frederick the Great declared of the wars of the 18th century, 'The peaceful citizen should not even notice that his country is at war.' Even during the wars of the 19th century—the Napoleonic Wars, the Opium Wars, the Crimean War, etc—the life of the belligerent nations was on the whole hardly affected.

1914: the turning point

However, during the First World War, with a significant proportion of the population mobilised and a major portion of the economy harnessed to the service of war, not only the soldiers engaged in battle, but also millions of industrial workers, peasants, etc—in fact, the whole civilian population—felt the impact.

Before the First World War, although the imperialist powers were to some extent prepared for the struggle, it was usual for the economy to be hardly geared to armament production at all. It was only *after* the outbreak of the war that it was accommodated to the situation it was now squarely faced with—guns or butter.

Up to the First World War, therefore, it was possible to analyse the development of capitalism without paying much attention to wars or preparations for them, as they played a minor role in economic development.

Immediately after the First World War the military sector of the economy again dwindled: the large armies were to a major extent demobilised and armament production was drastically cut.

However, in the wake of the great slump of the 1930s and Hitler's rise to power, a powerful peacetime military sector appeared for the first time in history. The Western capitalist powers—Britain, France and the US—were slow to enter the armaments race. And although the industries of these countries did get some benefit from war orders, even at the outbreak of the war the war sector of the economy was not decisive: thus there were 11 million unemployed in the US and one and a half million in Britain; the index of industrial output in the US in 1939 had not yet reached the level of 1929. It was not until a few years later that the Western powers harnessed their countries fully to the waging of the war.

Between 1939 and 1944 the production of munitions multiplied in Germany five times, in Japan ten times, in Britain 25 times, and in the US 50 times.[1]

THE WAR ECONOMY

	Germany (milliard marks)		Britain (million pounds)		United States (million dollars)	
	1939	1943	1938	1943	1939-40	1944-45
(1) National income	88*	125*	5.2	9.5	88.6*	186.6*
(2) Government expenditure (mainly arms)	60*	100*	1	5.8	16	95.3
(2) as percentage of (1)	68	80	19.2	61.1	18	51

Whereas after the First World War there was a period of about a decade and a half in which no advanced country had a relatively large war sector, after the Second World War there was no such break. Soon after its end the armaments race was once again on.

It is clear that even with the present level of labour productivity no economy can allow half or more of its gross output to be devoted to war over a long period. The war sector had, as a matter of fact, eaten into the national capital of all the belligerent countries; factories and their equipment had worn out and not been maintained or replaced; housing had been neglected; cars, furniture, clothing, etc, had hardly been replaced .

On the whole, even during prosperous periods of capitalism, some 80 percent of the national income has been consumed by the civilian population, and at most 20 percent or so devoted to capital accumulation. The following figures show the rate of accumulation in the national income in the past: Britain: 1860-69, 16.6 percent; 1900-10, 12.2 percent; 1919-24, 8.1 percent; 1925-30, 7.6 percent; 1934-37, 7 percent. US: 1900-10, 14.3 percent; 1919-24, 12.2 percent; 1925-30, 10.9 percent; 1934-37, 5 percent. France: 1870-79, 6 percent; 1900-10, 9 percent; 1913, 12.5 percent; 1925-30, 11.2 percent. Germany: 1900-10, 19.1 percent; 1925-30, 7.7 percent; 1934-37, 11.8 percent. Japan: 1919-24, 21.9 percent; 1925-30, 19.8 percent; 1934-37, 21.9 percent.[2]

If, even with the present level of technique, 20 percent of the national income were spent on armaments for any length of time, there would be scarcely any resources left for capital accumulation—in other words, the economy would stagnate.

Even if the military sector makes up, let us say, 10 percent of the national economy of the capitalist countries, its effect on the economy in general is *fundamental*. Let us see how this comes about.

Arms, boom and slump

For more than a century capitalism has gone through a rhythmical cycle of prosperity and slump. Slumps occurred more or less regularly every ten years. But since the advent of a permanent war economy the cycle has somehow been broken. Twenty four years have passed since the low point in the slump of the 1930s—1933. Even since mass unemployment has gone from the major Western capitalist countries, some 18 years have passed.

To understand how this has come about, how a military sector of some 10 percent or less of the national economy could prevent a general slump, we should first shortly sum up the cause of slumps under capitalism.

Cause of crises

The basic cause of capitalist crises of overproduction is the relatively low purchasing power of the masses compared with the production capacity of industry. As Marx said, 'The last cause of all real crises always remains the poverty and restricted consumption of the masses as compared to the tendency of capitalist production to develop the productive forces in such a way that only the absolute power of consumption of the entire society would be their limit'.[3]

In the *final* analysis, the cause of the capitalist crisis is that a greater and greater part of the income of society falls into the hands of the capitalist class and a greater and greater part of this is directed not towards buying means of consumption but instead means of production, that is, it is directed towards the accumulation of capital. But, as all means of production are *potentially* means of consumption—that is, after a certain lapse of time, the value of the means of production becomes incorporated in means of consumption—the relative increase in the part of the national income directed to accumulation compared with the part directed towards consumption must lead to overproduction. And this is a cumulative process. The increase in accumulation is accompanied by rationalisation, resulting in an increased rate of exploitation. The greater the rate of exploitation, the greater is the fund from which accumulation is drawn as compared with the wages of the workers and the revenue of the capitalist. Accumulation breeds accumulation.

Effect of arms budget

Now the armament economy has very great influence on the level of popular purchasing power, the level of real capital accumulation, and the amount of goods seeking a market.

Let us assume that there are a million people seeking employment in a certain country; further, that 10 percent of them are employed by the government in producing arms—some 100,000 people. Their purchasing power would bring about the employment of more people elsewhere. The numerical relation between the size of the first group and the second is called by the great bourgeois economist Keynes the multiplier. For brevity this term can usefully be borrowed. If the multiplier is 2 the employment of 100,000 workers by the state will increase general employment by 200,000. If the multiplier is 3, the increase will be 300,000, and so on.

Hence there is no doubt that the cumulative effect of an arms budget of 10 percent of the national income can be quite out of proportion to its size in increasing the purchasing power of the masses.

Guns and butter

Again, when 10 percent of the national income goes to arms, the capital resources seeking investment are drastically cut: in our example, from 20 percent of the national income to 10 percent. And the increasing purchasing power of the people, together with the new state demands for arms, army clothing, barracks, etc, gives greater openings for capital investment.

In addition, the war economy naturally has a big effect on the rate of increase of the supply of non-military goods seeking civilian purchasers.

With the possibilities of employment increasing, wages may well rise. But this, paradoxically, does not deny the possibility of increasing profits: capital is working more fully than otherwise; there is much less capital working at a loss; its turnover is greater. Thus, for instance, in the years 1937-42 total wages in US industry rose by 70 percent, profits by 400!

With the stupendous productive forces available to society at present, the increase in the armaments burden does not necessarily and always lead to a cut in civilian consumption. This was shown most clearly in the richest capitalist country in the world—the US—during the Second World War. Although in

1943 the US spent the huge sum of $83.7 milliard on the war, civilian consumption did not fall, but was actually higher than before the war, rising from $61.7 milliard in 1939 to $70.8 milliard in 1943 (expressed in 1939 prices), ie an increase of 14.7 percent. The consumption of food rose by $70 per head of the population, expenditure on housing and repairs by $12 and purchases of clothing by $25. Spending on other goods, with the exception of cars, also rose. So long as armaments do not consume beyond a certain limit, the increased production of guns does not exclude an increased production of butter.

Why arms alone

Let us see what are the basic characteristics which distinguish the armaments economy as a great stabilising factor for capitalist prosperity.

To succeed as a stabiliser, the 'public works' undertaken by the state must have the following basic characteristics:

(1) That they do not compete with private interests which produce in the same field. Thus a state factory producing, let us say, shoes, and competing with private shoe producers, would not decrease the danger of overproduction of shoes, but increase it. But in the field of, say, barrack building the state stands alone.

(2) That they employ the industries which are generally most affected by slumps—capital goods industries, heavy industry, industries whose weight in the economy is increasing and whose chiefs are predominant in the ruling class.

Seeing that whatever 'public works' are undertaken some sections of the capitalist class will benefit, such as, for instance, the producers of building materials, these sections will be quite ready to support such a programme. Other sections which benefit less, but have to foot the bill through taxation, may well oppose or try to curtail it. Only if the main sections of the ruling class—those in heavy industry, the monopolists and the bankers—have a direct interest in the 'public works' proposed, can these be carried out on a scale wide enough to prevent a slump.

(3) That they do not add much—in preference should subtract from—the productive capacity of capitalism and should, as far as possible, slow down the growth of social capital.

(4) That they do not add much, if at all, to the output of mass consumer goods and thus are not dependent on higher wages for an increasing market.

(5) That, while not adding to the national productive capital, the capitalist class should consider them an important factor in defence of its wealth and even a weapon for enlarging its prospective markets, in which case the capitalists would be quite happy to accept them.

Thus, for instance, the American capitalists who had been very angry with Roosevelt for incurring an annual budget deficit of $2 milliard to $4 milliard (1934 $3.6 milliard, 1935 $3.0 milliard, 1936 $4.3 milliard, 1937 $2.7 milliard) did not mind a deficit of $59 milliard in 1941-42.

(6) That all major countries indulge in these 'public works' to an extent corresponding to their level of national output and wealth. If only one or a few countries were to do so, they would have less resources for capital accumulation,

would suffer more than others from inflation and would be defeated in competition on the world market. Only if *all* major countries indulge in them will each dare to do so.

Only armaments fit these necessary six characteristics of prosperity—stabilising 'public works'.

Arms breed difficulties

There are three kinds of basic contradictions into which the permanent war economy may fall.

First, although on the whole there is conformity between the productive forces of society and the technique of the 'slaughter machine', the conformity is far from absolute. The burden of armaments may grow much quicker than the national output. Armaments can so cut into workers' standards of living as to cause great social upheavals, and even a socialist revolution. Thus they could lead not to the prosperity of capitalism, but to its overthrow.

Secondly, although armaments may eat up a large portion of the national surplus value seeking investment, and thus weaken the forces leading to overproduction and slump, they may encourage a big advance in general technique and with it increasing pressure towards a slump. (Thus automation was, in part, the child of war industry.) Under such conditions, to keep capitalist prosperity going, instead of 10 percent of the national income devoted to military ends, 20, 40 percent or more will have to be devoted. This may create strong opposition among workers and lower middle class people, and perhaps mild opposition even among sectors of the capitalist class who would not benefit directly from the armaments drive.

Competitive disarmament

Thirdly, the powers might compete so fiercely on the world market that each, in order to strengthen its position, would start to cut arms expenditure. We are at present witnessing Britain's being pushed to cut its 'defence budget' through competition with Germany, and deterioration of its international balance of payments. Up to now no country has been able to match the US, force it to abandon the arms race and start competing on 'who cuts the arms budget quickest'. The US can afford the greatest military budget in the world and the greatest absolute investment in industry. But with the huge strides of Russian industry, it is possible that in another ten or 20 years Russia may, even if it does not reach the absolute level of US industry, at least challenge the US on the world market in certain branches—those of heavy industry. Then the US may learn from Sandys and Macmillan how to cut the defence budget in order to circumvent defeat on the world market. The war economy may thus less and less serve as a cure for overproduction, a stabiliser of capitalist prosperity. When the war economy becomes expendable, the knell of the capitalist boom will surely toll.[4]

Notes

1 F Sternberg, *Capitalism and Socialism on Trial* (London, 1951), p438. * = approximate figures.
2 C Clark, *The Conditions of Economic Progress* (London, 1940), p406.
3 K Marx, *Capital*, (New York, 1932), vol III, p568.
4 Of course, certain capitalist countries may face great economic upheavals and hardships even during the era of American prosperity. Thus capitalist Britain and France suffer from balance of payments crises caused by the general, military-induced, world prosperity. They are also affected gravely by the national uprisings of the colonial peoples. But in all probability, so long as the US (with some half of the world industrial output) continues to prosper, the lifebelt will be thrown to the European junior partners of US imperialism. Britain, France and Germany may well become more and more dependent on the US. But as long as Uncle Sam is prosperous, he will not stop dishing out the dole.

Economic roots of reformism

Socialist Review, June 1957

We live in a critical period for civilisation. During the last half century humanity has suffered two terrible wars and is now living in the shadow of total annihilation. The present generation has witnessed mass unemployment and hunger, fascism and the gas chamber, barbarous murders of colonial peoples in Kenya and Malaya, Algeria and Korea.

However, in the midst of these terrible convulsions the working class in a number of countries in the West—the United States, Britain, Canada, Norway, Sweden, Holland, Denmark, Germany and others—shows a stubborn adherence to reformism, a belief in the possibility of major improvement in conditions under capitalism, and a rejection of the revolutionary overthrow of capitalism. Why is this so? Why the general political apathy and rejection of revolutionary changes in society, when humanity as a whole is in the grip of life and death struggles?

Only if we find the correct answer to this question can we answer a further one: for how long can reformism push aside revolutionary aspirations in the working class? There can scarcely be a question more vital for socialists in the West and hence for the world socialist movement. The present article is an attempt to contribute something towards the clarification of these problems.

Lenin's theory

The most important Marxist to define the roots of reformism was Lenin.

In 1915, in an article entitled 'The Collapse of the International', Lenin explained reformism or, to use the term he coined, opportunism, thus: 'The period of imperialism is the period in which the distribution of the world amongst the "great" and privileged nations, by whom all other nations are oppressed, is completed. Scraps of the booty enjoyed by the privileged as a result of this oppression undoubtedly fall to the lot of certain sections of the petty bourgeoisie and the aristocracy and bureaucracy of the working class.'

How big was the section of the working class which received these 'scraps of booty'? Lenin says: 'These sections...represent an infinitesimal minority of the proletariat and the working masses.'

And in line with this analysis Lenin defines reformism as 'the adherence of a section of the working class with the bourgeoisie against the mass of the proletariat'.

The economic foundation of the small 'aristocracy of labour' is to be found, according to Lenin, in imperialism and its super-profits. He writes in a preface, dated 6 July 1920, to his book *Imperialism, the Highest Stage of Capitalism*:

> Obviously, out of such enormous *super-profits* (since they are obtained over and above the profits which capitalists squeeze out of the workers of their 'own' country) *it is possible to bribe* their labour leaders and an upper stratum of the labour aristocracy. And the capitalists of the 'advanced' countries do bribe them: they bribe them in a thousand different ways, direct and indirect, overt and covert.
>
> This stratum of bourgeoisified workers or 'labour aristocracy', who have become completely petty bourgeois in their mode of life, in the amount of their earnings, and in their point of view, serves as the main support of the Second International and, in our day, the principal social (not military) *support of the bourgeoisie*. They are the real *agents of the bourgeoisie in the labour movement*, the labour lieutenants of the capitalist class, the real carriers of reformism and chauvinism.

Conclusion versus facts

An inevitable conclusion following upon Lenin's analysis of reformism is that a small, thin crust of conservatism hides the revolutionary urges of the mass of the workers. Any break through this crust would reveal a surging revolutionary lava. The role of the revolutionary party is simply to show the mass of the workers that their interests are betrayed by the 'infinitesimal minority' of 'aristocracy of labour'.

This conclusion, however, is not confirmed by the history of reformism in Britain, the United States and elsewhere over the past half century: its solidity, its spread *throughout* the working class, frustrating and largely isolating all revolutionary minorities, makes it abundantly clear that the economic and social roots of reformism are not in 'an infinitesimal minority of the proletariat and the working masses' as Lenin argued.

Showing where Lenin's analysis went wrong will help us to see more clearly the real economic, social and historical foundations of reformism.

How to throw crumbs

The first question one has to ask in tackling Lenin's analysis is this: how did the super-profits of, say, British companies in the colonies lead to the 'throwing of crumbs' to the 'aristocracy of labour' in Britain? The answer to this question invalidates the whole of Lenin's analysis of reformism.

To take an example, the Anglo-Iranian Oil Company has been drawing magnificent super-profits over decades. How does this lead to crumbs being thrown to the aristocracy of labour? First of all, this company employs only a small number of workers in Britain. And even these are certainly not given higher wages simply because its rate of profit is high. No capitalist says to the workers,

'I have made high profits this year, so I am ready to give you higher wages.'

Imperialism, and the export of capital, can of course greatly affect the wages level in the industrial country by giving employment to many workers who produce the machines, rails, locomotives, etc, which make up the real content of the capital exported. This influence on the level of employment obviously affects the wages level generally. But why should it affect only the real wages of an 'infinitesimal minority'? Does the increase of employment possibilities, and decline in unemployment, lead to the rise of a small 'aristocracy of labour' while the conditions of the mass of the working class are hardly affected at all? Are conditions of more or less full employment conducive to increasing differentials between skilled and unskilled workers? They are certainly not.

One may argue that the high super-profits of the capitalists on their investments in the colonies led to a rise of wages in another way: the capitalists do not oppose labour laws defending workers' conditions as strongly as they would do if profits were low. This is so. But these laws cannot be said to lead to an increasing differentiation of living standards between the different layers of the working class.

We go up together

Look at simple examples like the prohibition of child labour or limitations on female labour in certain industries. This does not affect the supply, and hence wages, in the skilled labour market more than in the unskilled. The limitation of the workday also does not affect the skilled labour market more than the unskilled. Indeed, everything that raises the standard of living of the mass of the workers, unskilled and semi-skilled, *diminishes* the difference between their standards and those of the skilled workers. The higher the general standard of living, including the educational level, the easier is it for unskilled workers to become semi-skilled or skilled. The financial burden of apprenticeship is more easily borne by better-off workers. And the easier it is for workers to learn a skill, the smaller is the wage differential between skilled and unskilled workers.

Again one can argue that imperialism throws 'crumbs' to workers through the fact that it gets foodstuffs (and raw materials) extremely cheaply from the backward colonial countries. But this factor, again, affects the standard of living not only of a minority of 'aristocracy of labour' but of the whole of the working class of the industrial countries. To this extent, by raising general living standards, it *diminishes* differences between sections of this same working class.

The effect of trade unions and the political activity of the labour movement on the whole is similar. The better the general conditions of the workers, the less is the income differentiation between its sections. (This was only partly counteracted when the trade unions consisted only of skilled workers.)

In fact, all historical experience testifies that the fewer the workers' rights and the more downtrodden they are, the greater are the differentials, especially between skilled and unskilled workers. This is clearly illustrated by the following table comparing the wages of skilled and unskilled workers between the two world wars in an economically advanced country like Britain and a backward one like Romania:[1]

SKILLED WAGES AS PERCENTAGE OF UNSKILLED

	Britain	Romania
Pattern makers	131	200
Fitters and turners	127	210
Iron moulders	130	252
Plumbers	147	300
Electricians	152	182
Carpenters	147	223
Painters	146	275

Or, to take another example: 'a locomotive engineer of ordinary length of service and rating receives 3.3 times the wages of an unskilled man of ordinary length of service in Spain, while in New Zealand the ratio is only 1:2'.[2]

It can be shown statistically that in the last century the differentiation in the working class of Britain (as well as in many other industrial countries) has become smaller, and that not only an 'infinitesimal minority', but the whole of the working class, benefited from increasing living standards. To prove this one last point, one need but compare present conditions in Britain with the conditions of the workers described in 1845 by Engels in *The Condition of the Working Class in England*.

Where we came from

This is his description of typical housing conditions:

> In the parishes of St John and St Margaret there lived in 1840, according to the *Journal of the Statistical Society*, 5,366 working-men's families in 5,294 'dwellings' (if they deserve the name!), men, women, and children thrown together without distinction of age or sex, 26,830 persons all told; and of these families three quarters possessed but one room.
>
> They who have some kind of shelter are fortunate, fortunate in comparison with the utterly homeless. In London 50,000 human beings get up every morning, not knowing where they are to lay their heads at night. The luckiest of this multitude, those who succeed in keeping a penny or two until evening, enter a lodging-house, such as abound in every great city, where they find a bed. But what a bed! These houses are filled with beds from cellar to garret, four, five, six beds in a room: as many as can be crowded in. Into every bed four, five, or six human beings are piled, as many as can be packed in, sick and well, young and old, drunk and sober, men and women, just as they come, indiscriminately. Then come strife, blows, wounds, or if these bedfellows agree, so much the worse; thefts are arranged and things done which our language, grown more humane than our deeds, refuses to record. And those who cannot pay for such a refuge? They sleep where they find a place, in passages, arcades, in corners where the police and the owners leave them undisturbed.

Health, clothing, sanitation, education were all of the same standard. One scarcely needs further proof that the conditions of the working class *as a whole*, and not only of a small minority, have improved radically under capitalism this last century.

Imperialism and reformism

As we have seen, there has been a close connection between the imperialist expansion of capitalism and the rise of reformism. Risking some repetition, we think it is worthwhile summing up the connection between the two.

■The markets of the backward colonial countries, by increasing demand for goods from the industrial countries, weaken the tendency for overproduction there, decrease the reserve army of unemployed, and so bring about an improvement in the wages of workers in the industrial countries.

■The increase in wages brought about in this way has a cumulative effect. By increasing the internal market in the industrial countries, the tendency for overproduction is weakened, unemployment decreases and wages rise.

■The export of capital adds to the prosperity of the industrial countries as it creates a market for their goods—at least temporarily. The export of cotton goods from Britain to India presupposes that India is able to pay for it straight away, by exporting cotton, for instance. On the other hand, the export of capital for the building of a railway presupposes an export of goods—rails, locomotives, etc—beyond the immediate purchasing power, or exporting power, of India. In other words, *for a time*, the export of capital is an important factor in enlarging markets for the industries of the advanced countries.

Boomerang effect

However, in time this factor turns into its opposite: capital once exported puts the brake on the export of goods from the 'mother' country after the colonial countries start to pay profit or interest on it. In order to pay a profit of £10 million to Britain (on British capital invested in India), India has to import less than it exports, and thus save the money needed to the tune of £10 million. In other words, the act of exporting capital from Britain to India expands the market for British goods: the payment of interest and profit on existing British capital in India restricts the markets for British goods.

Hence the existence of great British capital investments abroad does not at all exclude overproduction and mass unemployment in Britain. Contrary to Lenin's view, the high profit from capital invested abroad may well be not a concomitant of capitalist prosperity and stabilisation in the imperialist country, but a factor of mass unemployment and depression.

■The export of capital to the colonies affects the whole capital market in the imperialist country. Even if the surplus of capital looking vainly for investment were very small, its cumulative influence could be tremendous, as it would create pressure in the capital markets, and strengthen the downward trend of the rate of profit. This in turn would have a cumulative effect of its own of the activity of capital, on the entire economic activity, on employment, and so on the purchasing power of the masses, and so again in a vicious circle, on the markets.

The export of surplus capital can obviate these difficulties and can thus be of great importance to the whole capitalist prosperity, and thus to reformism.

■By thus relieving pressure in capital markets the export of capital diminishes competition between different enterprises, and so diminishes the need of each to rationalise and modernise its equipment. (This to some extent explains the technical backwardness of British industry, the pioneer of the industrial revolution, as compared with that of Germany today, for example.) This weakens the tendencies to overproduction and unemployment, wage cuts, etc. (Of course, in changed circumstances, in which Britain has ceased to have a virtual monopoly in the industrial world, this factor may well cause the defeat of British industry in the world market, unemployment and cuts in wages.)

Buying cheap raw materials and foodstuffs in the colonies allows real wages in the industrial countries to be increased without cutting into the rate of profit. This increase of wages means widened domestic markets without a decrease in the rate and amount of profit, ie without weakening the motive power of capitalist production.

The period during which the agrarian colonial countries serve to broaden markets for the industrial countries will be longer in proportion to (a) the size of the colonial world compared with the productive power of the advanced industrial countries, and (b) the extent that the industrialisation of the former is postponed.

Vested interest in nationalism

All the beneficial effects of imperialism on capitalist prosperity would disappear if there were no national boundaries between the industrial imperialist countries and their colonies.

Britain exported goods and capital to India and imported cheap raw materials and foodstuffs, but it did not let the unemployed of India—increased by the invasion of British capitalism—enter Britain's labour market. If not for the barrier (a financial one) to mass Indian immigration into Britain, wages in Britain would not have risen throughout the last century. The crisis of capitalism would have got deeper and deeper. Reformism would not have been able to replace revolutionary Chartism.

Here again the weakness of Lenin's theory of the aristocracy of labour is shown clearly. According to Lenin, reformism is a creature of the period of what he called 'the highest stage of capitalism'—the period of the export of capital which earns a high rate of profit and allows for crumbs from this profit to fall into the hands of the 'aristocracy of labour'. This period of big export of capital began in Britain in the last decade or so of the 19th century.

Wages rise before empire

As a matter of fact, a tremendous rise in workers' wages took place long before: in 1890 real wages of industrial workers in Britain were some 66 percent higher than in 1850.[3] The reason was quite obvious: the most important factor in improving real wages in Britain was the expansion of work opportunities—the expansion of production—based on an enlargement of the market for the industrial goods. And this took place long before the period of export of capital.

To put it roughly, between 1750 and 1850, when the expanding output of British industry was accompanied by the ruin of many British artisans and Irish peasants, these went into the British labour market and so kept wages very low. But since the middle of the 19th century British artisans and, after the 'Hungry Forties', the surplus agricultural population of Ireland were either absorbed into British industry or emigrated. From then on it was the Indian artisan and peasant who were ruined by the competition of British industry—but they did not enter the British labour market to depress wages.

That the turning point in the British wages trend took place long before the end of the 19th century, and actually at the time when indigenous unemployed artisans and peasants were already absorbed into industry while the colonial unemployed were prevented from entering the British labour market, ie during the 30s and 50s of the 19th century, is clear from the following interesting table:[4]

REAL WAGES 1759 TO 1903 (1900 = 100)

Decades and trade cycles	Index	Decades and trade cycles	Index
1759–68	62	1833–42	51
1769–78	60	1843–49	53
1779–88	60	1849–58	57
1789–98	58	1859–68	63
1799–1808	50	1869–79	74
1809–18	43	1880–86	80
1819–28	47	1887–95	91
1820–26	47	1895–1903	99
1827–32	48		

■The effects of imperialism on capitalist prosperity, and thus on reformism, do not limit themselves to the imperialist powers proper, but spread to a greater or lesser degree into all developed capitalist countries. Thus a prosperous Britain, for instance, can offer a wide market to Danish butter, and so spread the benefits derived by British capitalism from the exploitation of the empire to Danish capitalism.

Economic basis of the right

■The expansion of capitalism through imperialism made it possible for the trade unions and Labour Parties to wrest concessions for the workers from capitalism without overthrowing it. This gives rise to a large reformist bureaucracy which in its turn becomes a brake on the revolutionary development of the working class. The major function of this bureaucracy is to serve as a go-between between the workers and the bosses, to mediate, negotiate agreements between them, and 'keep the peace' between the classes.

This bureaucracy aims at prosperous capitalism, not its overthrow. It wants the workers' organisations to be not a revolutionary force, but reformist pressure groups. This bureaucracy is a major disciplinary officer of the working class in the interests of capitalism. It is a major conservative force in modern capitalism.

But the trade union and Labour Party bureaucracies are effective in disciplining the working class in the long run only to the extent that the economic conditions of the workers themselves are tolerable. In the final analysis the base of reformism is in capitalist prosperity.

Labour imperialism

■If reformism is rooted in imperialism, it becomes also an important shield for it, supporting its 'own' national imperialism against its imperialist competitors and against the rising colonial movements.

Reformism reflects the immediate, day to day, narrow national interests of the whole of the working class in Western capitalist countries under conditions of general economic prosperity. These immediate interests are in contradiction with the historical and international interests of the working class, of socialism.

As capitalist prosperity, together with relatively favourable conditions in the labour market, can be helped by imperialist expansion, by the exploitation of the colonies, reformism has been to a large extent the expression of the imperialist domination over backward countries.

As, however, prosperity with more or less full employment and relatively tolerable wages may be induced at least for a time by the conditions of the permanent war economy,[5] reformism has economic roots also where the imperialist war economy takes the place of imperialist expansion.

The war economy

During the 1930s, in the face of the deep world slump, unemployment and fascism, it looked as if the foundations of reformism were undermined for good. Writing in that period and prognosticating the future, Trotsky wrote, 'In [the] epoch of decaying capitalism, in general, there can be no discussion of systematic social reforms and the raising of the masses' living standards, when every serious demand of the proletariat and even every serious demand of the petty bourgeoisie inevitably reaches beyond the limits of capitalist property relations and of the bourgeois state'.[6]

If serious reforms are no longer possible under capitalism, then the knell of bourgeois parliamentary democracy is sounded and the end of reformism is at hand.

The war, as a sharpener of contradictions in capitalism, would lead to the acceleration of these processes, according to Trotsky.

However, Trotsky's prognosis was belied by life. The war, and the permanent war economy gave a new lease of life to capitalism and hence to reformism in many of the Western capitalist countries.

In itself the increasing dependence of reformism on the permanent war economy shows its bankruptcy and the need for a revolutionary overthrow of capitalism with its twins—the permanent war economy and reformism. However, this bankruptcy of reformism is not yet apparent to every worker through his daily experience. As I tried to show in my article in the May issue of *Socialist Review*, it will be a matter of some years till the permanent war economy leads to a big deterioration of workers' conditions, and thus to a withering away of the roots of reformism.

For this to happen it is not necessary, of course, that the standard of living of workers should be cut to the bone. An American worker would react very strongly to a threat to his car and television set, even if workers elsewhere look at these things as undreamt-of luxuries. To the extent that past reforms are accepted as necessities, a series of new reforms becomes the expected course of events. With the eating comes the appetite. When capitalism, however, decays to the extent that any serious demands of the working class reach beyond its limits, the bell will toll for reformism.

A realistic understanding of the foundations of reformism, its strength and depth, as well as the factors undermining it, is necessary to an understanding of the future of the socialist movement. As Engels put it more than 100 years ago, 'The condition of the working class is the real basis and point of departure of all social movements at present... A knowledge of proletarian conditions is absolutely necessary to be able to provide solid ground for socialist theories'.[7]

Of course, even when the economic roots of reformism wither away, reformism will not die by itself. Many an idea lingers on long after the disappearance of the material conditions which brought it forth. The overthrow of reformism will be brought about by conscious revolutionary action, by the propaganda and agitation of consistent socialists. Their job will be facilitated by a future sharpening of the contradictions in capitalism.

Every struggle of the working class, however limited it may be, by increasing its self confidence and education, undermines reformism: 'In every strike one sees the hydra head of the revolution.' The main task of real, consistent socialists is to unite and generalise the lessons drawn from the day to day struggles. Thus can it fight reformism.

Notes

1   C Clark, *Conditions of Economic Progress* (London, 1950), p460.

2   Ibid, p461.

3   W Layton and G Crowther, *An Introduction to the Study of Prices* (London, 1935).

4   J Kuczynski, *A Short History of Labour Conditions in Great Britain 1750 to the Present Day* (London, 1947), p54.

5   See T Cliff, 'Perspectives for the Permanent War Economy', *Socialist Review*, May 1957.

6   L Trotsky, 'The Death Agony of Capitalism and the Tasks of the Fourth International' (1938).

7   F Engels, 'Preface', *The Condition of the Working Class in England*.

Permanent revolution

International Socialism (first series) 12, Spring 1963

Trotsky's greatest and most original contribution to Marxism was his theory of permanent revolution.

In this study the theory will first be restated. It will then be considered in the light of the colonial revolution experienced over the last decade or so, developed and expanded. We shall be compelled to reject a large part of it. But if the result proves to be a set of ideas which differs quite considerably from Trotsky's, it nevertheless leans heavily on his.

Trotsky developed his theory with the 1905 revolution in the background. Practically *all* Marxists of the day, from Kautsky to Plekhanov to Lenin, believed that only advanced industrial countries were ready for socialist revolution. To put it crudely, they argued that countries would achieve workers' power in strict conformity with the stage to which they had advanced technologically. Backward countries could see their future image mirrored in the advanced countries. Only after a long process of industrial development and a transition through a parliamentary bourgeois regime could the working class mature enough to pose the question of socialist revolution.

All the Russian democrats—Mensheviks as well as Bolsheviks—postulated that Russia was approaching a *bourgeois* revolution, resulting from a conflict between the productive forces of capitalism on the one hand, and the autocracy, landlordism and other survivals of feudalism on the other. The Mensheviks concluded that the bourgeoisie would necessarily lead the revolution, and would take political power into their own hands. They thought that the Social Democrats should support the liberal bourgeoisie in the revolution, at the same time defending the special interests of the workers within the framework of capitalism by struggling for the eight-hour working day and other social reforms.[1]

Lenin and the Bolsheviks agreed that the revolution would be bourgeois in character and that its aim would not overstep the limits of a bourgeois revolution. 'The democratic revolution will not extend beyond the scope of bourgeois social-economic relationships,' wrote Lenin.[2] Again, 'This democratic revolution in Russia will not weaken, but will strengthen, the domination of the bourgeoisie'.[3] He returned to the theme again and again.

It was not until after the revolution of February 1917 that Lenin discarded this view. In September 1914, for example, he was still writing that the Russian revolution must limit itself to three fundamental tasks: 'the establishment of a democratic republic (in which equality of rights and full freedom of self-determination would be granted to all nationalities), confiscation of the estates of the big landowners, and application of the eight-hour day'.[4]

Where Lenin differed fundamentally from the Mensheviks was in his insistence on the independence of the labour movement from the liberal bourgeoisie, on the need to carry the bourgeois revolution through to victory against their resistance. Instead of the Menshevik-sponsored alliance between the working class and the liberal bourgeoisie, Lenin called for an alliance of the working class with the peasantry. Where the Mensheviks expected a government composed of liberal bourgeois ministers after the revolution, Lenin envisaged a coalition comprised of the workers' party and a peasant party, a 'democratic dictatorship of the workers and peasantry', in which the peasant party would have the majority. The 'democratic dictatorship' would establish a republic, expropriate the large landowners and enforce the eight-hour day. Thereafter the peasantry would cease to be revolutionary, would become upholders of property and of the social status quo, and would unite with the bourgeoisie. The industrial proletariat, in alliance with the proletarian and semi-proletarian village population, would then become the revolutionary opposition, and the temporary phase of 'democratic dictatorship' would give way to a conservative bourgeois government within the framework of a bourgeois republic.

Trotsky was as convinced as Lenin that the liberal bourgeoisie could not carry out any revolutionary task consistently, and that the agrarian revolution, a fundamental element in the bourgeois revolution, could only be carried out by an alliance of the working class and peasantry. But he disagreed with him about the possibility of an independent peasant party, arguing that the peasants were too sharply divided among themselves between rich and poor to be able to form a united and independent party of their own.

'All the experience of history', he wrote, 'shows that the peasantry is completely incapable of playing an independent role'.[5] If in all revolutions since the German Reformation the peasants had supported one faction or another of the bourgeoisie, in Russia the strength of the working class and the conservatism of the bourgeoisie would force the peasantry to support the revolutionary proletariat. The revolution itself would not be confined to the carrying out of bourgeois democratic tasks, but would proceed immediately to carry out proletarian socialist measures:

> The proletariat grows and strengthens together with the growth of capitalism. In this sense, the development of capitalism signifies the development of the proletariat towards the dictatorship. But the day and hour when the power passes into the hands of the proletariat depend directly not upon the state of the productive forces, but upon the conditions of the class struggle, upon the international situation, finally, upon a series of subjective factors: tradition, initiative, readiness for struggle...

In an economically backward country the proletariat can come to power sooner than in the economically advanced countries. In 1871 it had consciously taken into its hands the management of social affairs in petty bourgeois Paris—in truth only for two months—but it did not for one hour take power in the robust capitalist centres of England and the United States. The conception of some sort of automatic dependence of the proletarian dictatorship upon the technical forces and resources of the country is a prejudice derived from an extremely oversimplified 'economic' materialism. This view has nothing in common with Marxism.

The Russian revolution, in our opinion, creates such conditions under which the power can pass over to the proletariat (and with a victorious revolution it must) even before the policy of bourgeois liberalism acquires the possibility to bring its state genius to a full unfolding.[6]

Another important element in the theory was the international character of the coming Russian revolution. It would begin on a national scale, but could only be completed by the victory of the revolution in the more developed countries:

How far, however, can the socialist policy of the working class go in the economic conditions of Russia? Only one thing we can say with certainty: it will run into political obstacles long before it will be checked by the technical backwardness of the country. Without direct state support from the European proletariat the working class of Russia cannot remain in power and cannot convert its temporary rule into a prolonged socialist dictatorship.[7]

The basic elements of Trotsky's theory can be summed up in six points:
(1) A bourgeoisie which arrives late on the scene is fundamentally different from its ancestors of a century or two earlier. It is incapable of providing a consistent, democratic, revolutionary solution to the problem posed by feudalism and imperialist oppression. It is incapable of carrying out the thoroughgoing destruction of feudalism, the achievement of real national independence and political democracy. It has ceased to be revolutionary, whether in the advanced or backward countries. It is an absolutely conservative force.
(2) The decisive revolutionary role falls to the proletariat, even though it may be very young and small in number.
(3) Incapable of independent action, the peasantry will follow the towns and, in view of the first five points, must follow the leadership of the industrial proletariat.
(4) A consistent solution of the agrarian question, of the national question, a break-up of the social and imperial fetters preventing speedy economic advance, will necessitate moving beyond the bounds of bourgeois private property. 'The democratic revolution grows over immediately into the socialist, and thereby becomes a *permanent* revolution'.[8]
(5) The completion of the socialist revolution 'within national limits is unthinkable... Thus the socialist revolution becomes a permanent revolution in a newer and broader sense of the word; it attains completion only in the final victory of the new society on our entire planet'.[9] It is a reactionary, narrow dream to try and achieve 'socialism in one country'.

(6) As a result, revolution in backward countries would lead to convulsions in the advanced countries.

The 1917 revolution in Russia proved *all* of Trotsky's assumptions to be right. The bourgeoisie was counter-revolutionary; the industrial proletariat was the revolutionary class *par excellence*; the peasantry followed the working class; the anti-feudal, democratic revolution grew over immediately into the socialist; the Russian Revolution did lead to revolutionary convulsions elsewhere (in Germany, Austria, Hungary, etc). And finally, alas, the isolation of the socialist revolution in Russia led to its degeneration and downfall.

Another classic confirmation of Trotsky's theory was the Chinese Revolution of 1925-27. Unfortunately, the confirmation was, to an even larger extent than in the Russian Revolution, a negative demonstration. Although points one to four were confirmed, Stalinist betrayal ensured that the revolution ended not in the victory of the proletariat, but in its defeat. As a result the peasants were also defeated, and not only was the socialist revolution not consummated, but the democratic neither; nor were the agrarian revolution, the unity of the country and its independence from imperialism achieved. Points five and six thus did not have the chance of being tested empirically. Since then, however, two events of world importance, Mao's rise to power in China, and Castro's in Cuba, seem to challenge practically all the assumptions of the theory.

The industrial working class played no role whatsoever in the victory of Mao. Even the social composition of the Chinese Communist Party was completely non working class. Mao's rise in the party coincided with its transformation from a working class party. Towards the end of 1926 at least 66 percent of the membership were workers, another 22 percent intellectuals and only 5 percent peasants.[10] By November 1928 the percentage of workers had fallen by more than four fifths, and an official report admitted that the party 'did not have a single healthy party nucleus among the industrial workers'.[11] The party admitted that workers comprised only 10 percent of the membership in 1928, 3 percent in 1929, 2.5 percent in March 1930, 1.6 percent in September of the same year, and virtually nothing at the end of it.[12] From then and until Mao's final victory the party had no industrial workers to speak of.

For a number of years the party was confined to insurgent peasant movements deep in the provinces of central China, where it established a Chinese Soviet Republic; later, after a military defeat in the central provinces (1934), it moved to northern Shensi, in the north west. In both these areas there was no industrial working class to speak of. A Comintern organ was not exaggerating when it wrote that 'the Border Region is socially and economically one of the most backward regions of China'.[13] Chu Teh repeated, 'The regions under the direction of the Communists are the most backward economically in the whole country'.[14] Not one real town came under the control of the Communists until a couple of years before the establishment of the Chinese People's Republic.

So unimportant were workers in Communist Party strategy during the period of Mao's rise to power that the party did not find it necessary to convene a National Congress of Trade Unions for 19 years after the one held in 1929. Nor did it bother to seek workers' support, as witnessed in its declaration that it did not intend to maintain any party organisation in the Kuomintang-controlled areas during the crucial years 1937-45.[15] When, in December 1937, the Kuomintang government decreed the death penalty for workers who went on strike or even agitated for a strike while the war was in progress, a Communist Party spokesman told an interviewer that the party was 'fully satisfied' with that government's conduct of the war.[16] Even after the outbreak of civil war between the Communist Party and the Kuomintang, hardly any Communist Party organisations existed in the latter's areas, which included all the industrial centres in the country.

Mao's conquest of the towns revealed more than anything else the Communist Party's complete divorce from the industrial working class. Communist leaders did their best to prevent any workers' uprisings in the towns on the eve of their being taken. Before the fall of Tientsin and Peking, for example, General Lin Piao, commander of the front, issued a proclamation calling on people:

> ...to maintain order and continue in their present occupations. Kuomintang officials or police personnel of provincial, city, country or other level of government institution; district, town, village, or *pao chia* personnel...are enjoined to remain at their posts.[17]

At the time of the crossing of the Yangtze River, before the great cities of central and south China (Shanghai, Hankow, Canton) fell to them, Mao and Chu Teh again issued a special proclamation stating among other things:

> It is hoped that workers and employees in all trades will continue to work and that business will operate as usual...officials of the Kuomintang Central, Provincial, Municipal or County Governments of various levels, or delegates of the 'National Assembly', members of the Legislative and Control Yuans or People's Political Council members, police personnel and heads of *pao chia* organisations...are to stay at their posts, obey the orders of the People's Liberation Army and People's Government.[18]

The working class obliged and remained inert. A report from Nanking on 22 April 1949, two days before the People's Liberation Army occupied it, described the situation in this way:

> Nanking's populace is showing no signs of excitement. Curious crowds were seen this morning to gather at the river wall to watch the gun duel on the opposite side of the river. Business is going on as usual. Some shops are closed, but it is due to lack of business... Movie houses are still showing to packed houses.[19]

A month later a *New York Times* correspondent wrote from Shanghai, 'The Red troops began putting up posters in Chinese instructing the populace to be calm and assuring them they had nothing to fear'.[20]

In Canton, 'after their entry the Communists made contact with the police station and instructed the officers and men to remain at their posts to keep order'.[21]

A case in which neither the working class nor the peasantry played a serious role, but where middle class intellectuals filled the whole arena of struggle, is Fidel Castro's rise to power. C Wright Mills's book, *Listen Yankee*, which is a more or less authentic monologue spoken by the Cuban leaders, deals first of all with what the revolution was *not*:

> The revolution itself was not a fight…between wage workers and capitalists… Our revolution is not a revolution made by labour unions or wage workers in the city or by labour parties, or by anything like that.[22]

> The wage workers in the city were not conscious in any revolutionary way; their unions were merely like your North American unions: out for more money and better conditions. That was all that really moved them. And some were even more corrupt than some of yours.[23]

Paul Baran, an uncritical supporter of Castro, wrote, after discussions with Cuban leaders, regarding the negligible role of the industrial proletariat in the revolution:

> It would seem that the employed segment of the industrial working class re-mained on the whole passive throughout the revolutionary period. Forming the 'aristocratic' layer of the Cuban proletariat, these workers partook of the profits of monopolistic business—foreign and domestic—were well paid by Latin American standards, and enjoyed a standard of living considerably higher than that of the masses of the Cuban people. The fairly strong trade union movement was dominated by 'business unionism', United States style, and was thoroughly permeated by racketeering and gangsterism.[24]

The indifference of the industrial proletariat accounted for the complete failure of Castro's call for a general strike on 9 April 1958, that is, some 16 months after the beginning of the uprising and eight months before the fall of Batista. The workers were apathetic, and the Communists sabotaged. (It was some time later that they jumped on Castro's bandwagon.)[25]

The role of the peasantry in Castro's rise to power has been commented on more positively. Wright Mills reports that during the insurrection:

> …the peasants played the big role. Together with the young intellectuals, they became the rebel army that won the insurrection. They were the decisive ones, the intellectuals and the campesinos… Rebel soldiers [were] formed of peasants and led by young intellectuals.[26]

Who were these peasants? 'Really a sort of agricultural wage worker, who, most of the year, were unemployed'.[27] In similar vein Baran reports, 'The class that made the revolution is the rural campesinos'.[28] And these were agricultural wage earners, not petty owners. 'Not being inhabited by a petty bourgeois stratum of small peasant proprietors, the Cuban countryside…never became a "breeding ground of bourgeois ideology".'[29]

This description, however, is belied by two things: the peasantry was involved very little in Castro's army. As late as April 1958 the total number of armed men under Castro numbered only about 180 and at the time of Batista's fall had only grown to 803.[30] The cadres of Castro's bands were intellectuals. And peasants that did participate were not agricultural wage earners, collectivist in inspiration, as Mills and Baran state. Witness 'Che' Guevara on the peasants who joined Castro in the Sierra Maestra:

> The soldiers that made up our first guerrilla army of country people came from the part of this social class which shows its love for the possession of land most aggressively, which expresses most perfectly the spirit catalogued as petty bourgeois.[31]

The Castro movement was middle class. The 82 men under Castro who invaded Cuba from Mexico in December 1956 and the 12 who survived to fight in the Sierra Maestra all came from this class. 'The heaviest losses were suffered by the largely middle class urban resistance movement, which created the political and psychological acids that ate into Batista's fighting force'.[32]

Quite characteristically 'Che' Guevara raises the weakness and impotence of the industrial working class as a central element in all future socialist revolutions:

> The campesinos, with an army made up of their own kind fighting for their own great objectives, primarily for a just distribution of land, will come from the country to take the cities... This army, created in the countryside, where subjective conditions ripen for the seizure of power, proceeds to conquer the cities from the outside.[33]

Industrial advance is described as an impediment to the socialist revolution:

> It is more difficult to prepare guerrilla bands in these countries that have undergone a concentration of population in great centres and have a more developed light and medium industry, even though not anything like effective industrialisation. The ideological influence of the cities inhibits the guerrilla struggle.[34]

> Even in countries where the predominance of the cities is great, the central political focus of the struggle can develop in the countryside.[35]

Paying lip service to the role of the industrial proletariat, Che says that the peasant guerrillas will have to accept 'the ideological base of the working class—Marxism', forgetting that the very heart of Marxism is the fact that the socialist revolution is the act of the working class itself, the result of the proletariat becoming the subject and not the object of history.

From the outset Castro's programme did not go beyond the horizon of broad liberal reforms acceptable to the middle classes. In an article to the magazine *Coronet* of February 1958, Castro declared that he had no plans for expropriating or nationalising foreign investments:

> I personally have come to feel that nationalisation is, at best, a cumbersome instrument. It does not seem to make the state any stronger, yet it enfeebles private enterprise. Even more importantly, any attempt at wholesale nationalisation would obviously hamper the principal point of our economic platform—industrialisation at the fastest possible rate. For this purpose, foreign investments will always be welcome and secure here.

In May 1958, he assured his biographer, Dubois:

Never has the 26th of July Movement talked about socialising or nationalising the industries. This is simply stupid fear of our revolution. We have proclaimed from the first day that we fight for the full enforcement of the Constitution of 1940, whose norms establish guarantees, rights and obligations for all the elements that have a part in production. Comprised therein is free enterprise and invested capital as well as many other economic, civic, and political rights.[36]

As late as 2 May 1959 Castro declared to the Economic Council of the Organisation of American States in Buenos Aires, 'We are not opposed to private investment... We believe in the usefulness, in the experience and in the enthusiasm of private investors... Companies with international investments will have the same guarantees and the same rights as the national firms'.[37]

The impotence of the contending social classes, workers and capitalists, peasants and landlords, the inherent historical weakness of the middle class, and the omnipotence of the new Castro elite, who were not bound by any set of coherent, organised interests, explains the ease with which Castro's moderate programme of the years 1953-58, based on private enterprise, was cast aside and replaced by a radical programme of state ownership and planning. It was not before 16 April 1961 that Castro announced that the revolution had been socialist. In the words of the President of the Republic, Dr Osvaldo Dorticós Torrado, the people 'one fine day...discovered or confirmed, that what they have been applauding, which was good for the people, was a Socialist Revolution'.[38] An excellent formulation of Bonapartist manipulation of the people as the object of history, not its conscious subject!

While the conservative, cowardly nature of a late-developing bourgeoisie (Trotsky's first point) is an *absolute law*, the revolutionary character of the young working class (point two) is neither absolute nor inevitable. The reasons are not difficult to appreciate. The prevailing ideology in the society of which the working class forms a part is that of the ruling class; in many cases the existence of a floating, amorphous majority of new workers with one foot in the countryside creates difficulties for autonomous proletarian organisations; lack of experience and illiteracy add to their weakness. This leads to yet another weakness: dependence on non-workers for leadership. Trade unions in the backward countries are almost always led by 'outsiders'. Thus it is reported from India:

Practically all Indian unions are led by persons who have no background in industry, ie 'outsiders'... Many of the outsiders are associated with more than one union. A national leader of considerable stature remarked that he was president of about 30 unions, but added that obviously there was nothing he could contribute to the work of any of these![39]

Weakness and dependence on outsiders leads to a personality cult:

Many unions are still in the habit of revolving around personalities. A strong personality dominates the union. He determines all its policies and actions. The union becomes known as his union. Workers look up to him to solve all their difficulties and to secure for them all their demands. They rely upon him as their defender and champion and are prepared to follow him wherever he may lead them. There is a large element of hero worship in this attitude. There is a good number of such heroes in the movement. They are of help in getting for workers some of their demands, but not of much help in developing self-reliant democratic organisations. The latter will not grow unless workers learn to stand on their own legs and not pathetically rely on eminent personalities to solve for them all their problems.[40]

Another weakness of the labour movement in many backward countries is its dependence on the state. It was reported from India:

The state has already taken upon itself many of the functions which, in a free society, normally belong to trade unions. As things stand at present the state, and not collective bargaining between employers and employees, plays the major part in the determination of wages and other conditions of work. That was inevitable to some extent owing to the background condition of the economy and the weakness of workers and their trade unions.[41]

And from French West Africa:

Direct union efforts against employers have rarely brought real wage increases to African labour... It is rather social legislation and the labour movement's political influence which have been responsible for most of the real wage gains of recent years.[42]

And from Latin America: 'Union representatives seek to achieve their gains through government interference and dictation'.[43]

The penalty for dependence on the state is subordination to government policies, avoidance of policies antagonistic to the political rulers, and a limitation of trade union activity to narrow 'economist' demands or, to use Lenin's term, 'trade unionist' policies.

This, in turn, leads to alienation of the trade unions from the agricultural toilers' struggle. The difference between town and country living standards is generally very big in backward countries, much more so than in the advanced countries. Under such conditions, and with the mass rural unemployment and underemployment, the achievement of standards of wages and working conditions in industry depends largely on maintaining the closed shop, that is, hiring of workers for an industry through the union. This could hardly be done without state support—the close alliance of the trade unions with the government—to the neglect of rural toilers. This was the set-up in Peron's Argentina, Vargas's Brazil, Batista's Cuba. The result was a labour movement that was conservative, narrow, bereft of idealism.

The last, but by no means least, factor determining whether the working class in the backward countries is *actually* revolutionary or not is a subjective one, namely the activities of the parties, particularly the Communist parties, that influence it. The counter-revolutionary role of Stalinism in backward countries has been dealt with too often to need repetition here.

To sum up, up to now experience has shown both the strength of revolutionary urges among industrial workers in the emergent nations and their fatal
weaknesses. An automatic correlation between economic backwardness and
revolutionary political militancy does not exist.

Once the constantly revolutionary nature of the working class, the central
pillar of Trotsky's theory, becomes suspect, the whole structure falls to pieces. His
third point is not realised, as the peasantry cannot follow a non-revolutionary
working class, and all the other elements follow suit. But this does not mean that
nothing happens. A concatenation of national and international circumstances
makes it imperative for the productive forces to break the fetters of feudalism and
imperialism. Peasant rebellions take on a deeper, broader sweep than ever before.
In them is rooted also national rebellion against the economic ruin brought by imperialism and for the higher living standards which it as surely demonstrated.

The needs of the productive forces plus the rebelliousness of the peasantry
would not by themselves have been sufficient to break the yoke of landlordism
and imperialism. Three other factors helped:

(1) The weakening of world imperialism as a result of increasing contradictions
between the powers, and the paralysis affecting their mutual intervention brought
about by the existence of the H-bomb.

(2) The growing importance of the state in backward countries. It is one of
the tricks of history that when an historical task faces society, and the class
that traditionally carries it out is absent, some other group of people, quite often
a state power, implements it. State power, under such conditions, plays a very
important role. It reflects not only, or even mainly, the national economic base
on which it rises, but the supranational character of the world economy today.

(3) The growing importance of the intelligentsia as the leader and unifier of
the nation, and above all as manipulator of the masses. This last point will need
special elaboration.

The importance of the intelligentsia in a revolutionary movement is in direct
proportion to the general backwardness—economic, social and cultural—of the
masses from whose midst it arises. It is characteristic that the Russian Populist
movement, which more than any other emphasised the need to revolutionise the
most backward elements of society, the peasants, was also the group to put the
greatest premium on the intelligentsia, masters of 'critical thinking'.

Although all revolutionary movements in Russia were composed largely of
intellectuals, Populist intellectuals championing the cause of the peasants, and
Marxist intellectuals championing that of the industrial workers, there was a
basic difference in the way they saw the relations between 'leaders' and
'masses'. The workers' movement, at least during the height of the struggle,
was organised; hence the intellectuals were *accountable* to the workers' collective, and notwithstanding their inherent tendency to divorce themselves
from, and rise above, the masses, they were checked by this collective. The
Populist intellectuals' milieu was less restrictive, hence they showed clearer
and much more extreme tendencies towards elitism, arbitrariness, as towards
vacillations and splits. As Lenin said at the time, 'No one will undertake to

deny that it is precisely its individualism and incapacity for discipline and organisation which in general distinguished the intelligentsia as a separate stratum of modern capitalist society'.[44]

The revolutionary intelligentsia has proved itself a much more cohesive factor in the emergent nations of today than in Tsarist Russia. Quite understandably bourgeois private property is bankrupt, imperialism is intolerable; state capitalism—through the weakening of imperialism, the growing importance of state planning, plus the example of Russia, and the organised, disciplined work of the Communist Parties—gives them a new sense of cohesion. As the only non-specialised section of society, it is the obvious source of a 'professional revolutionary elite' which appears to represent the interests of the 'nation' as against conflicting sectional and class interests. In addition, it is the section of society most imbued with the national culture, the peasants and workers having neither the leisure nor education for it.

The intelligentsia is also sensitive to its countries' technical lag. Participating as it does in the scientific and technical world of the 20th century, it is stifled by the backwardness of its own nation. This feeling is accentuated by the 'intellectual unemployment' endemic in these countries. Given the general economic backwardness, the only hope for most students is a government job, but there are not nearly enough of these to go round.[45]

The spiritual life of the intellectuals is also in a crisis. In a crumbling order where the traditional pattern is disintegrating, they feel insecure, rootless, lacking in firm values. Dissolving cultures give rise to a powerful urge for a new integration that must be total and dynamic if it is to fill the social and spiritual vacuum, that must combine religious fervour with militant nationalism.

Before their country gains political freedom, the intellectuals find themselves under dual pressure—privileged beyond the majority of their people, yet subordinated to the European rulers. This explains the hesitations and vacillations so characteristic of their role in the national movement. But the big changes since have introduced new elements in their attitude—a feeling of guilt, of 'debt' towards the 'dark' masses, and at the same time a feeling of divorcement from, and superiority to, them. They are anxious to belong without being assimilated, without ceasing to remain apart and above. They are in search of a dynamic movement which will unify the nation, and open up broad new vistas for it, but at the same time will give themselves power.

They are great believers in efficiency, including efficiency in social engineering. They hope for reform from above and would dearly love to hand the new world over to a grateful people, rather than see the liberating struggle of a self-conscious and freely associated people result in a new world for themselves. They care a lot for measures to drag their nation out of stagnation, but very little for democracy. They embody the drive for industrialisation, for capital accumulation, for national resurgence. Their power is in direct relation to the feebleness of other classes, and their political nullity.

All this makes totalitarian state capitalism a very attractive goal for intellectuals. And indeed they are the main banner bearers of Communism in the emergent nations. 'Communism has found acceptance in Latin America among students and the middle class,' writes a Latin American specialist.[46] In India, at the Congress of the Communist Party in Amritsar (March-April 1958), 'approximately 67 percent of the delegates were from classes other than the proletariat and peasantry (middle class, landowning class, and 'small traders'); 72 percent had some college education'.[47] (In 1943 it was found that 16 percent of all party members were full time functionaries.)[48]

Those forces which should lead to a socialist, workers' revolution according to Trotsky's theory can lead, in the absence of the revolutionary subject, the proletariat, to its opposite, state capitalism. Using what is of universal validity in the theory and what is contingent (upon the subjective activity of the proletariat), one can come to a variant that, for lack of a better name, might be called the 'deflected, state capitalist, permanent revolution' .

In the same way as the 1905 and 1917 revolutions in Russia and that of 1925-27 in China were classic demonstrations of Trotsky's theory, Mao's and Castro's rises to power are classic, the purest, and most extreme, demonstrations of 'deflected permanent revolution'. Other colonial revolutions—Ghana, India, Egypt, Indonesia, Algeria, etc—are deviations from the norm. In these countries the political and military retreat of imperialism, plus the financial backing of the local ruling classes—quite often including basic sections of the bourgeoisie—plus the hamstringing of the local Communist parties by Moscow, have prevented a Simon-pure state capitalism dominated single-handedly by a new Stalinist bureaucracy. But, although Nehru's India, Nkrumah's Ghana or Ben Bella's Algeria deviate more or less from the norm of 'deflected permanent revolution', they can best be understood when approached from the standpoint of, and compared with, the norm.

Some strategic conclusions follow for the international labour movement from the working out of the 'deflected permanent revolution' whether in its pure or its bastard form. First, for the workers in the emergent nations: having failed to carry out the permanent revolution, to lead the democratic revolution on to socialist rails, to combine the national and social struggles, they will now have to fight against their 'own' ruling class (and Nehru proved no less harsh when incarcerating striking workers than the British Raj). The industrial workers will nevertheless become more and more ready for the socialist revolution. Under the new national regimes they experience an increase in numbers and hence, in the long run, in cohesion and specific social weight.

For revolutionary socialists in the advanced countries, the shift in strategy means that, while they will have to continue to oppose any national oppression of the colonial people unconditionally, they must cease to argue over the national identity of the future ruling classes of Asia, Africa and Latin America, and instead investigate the class conflicts and future social structures of these continents. The slogan of 'class against class' will become more and more a reality. The central theme of Trotsky's theory remains as valid as ever: the proletariat must continue its revolutionary struggle until it is triumphant the world over. Short of this target it cannot achieve freedom.[49]

Notes

1 The Menshevik spokesman Martynov wrote on the eve of the 1905 revolution, 'The coming revolution will be a revolution of the bourgeoisie; and that means that...it will only, to a greater or lesser extent, secure the rule of all or some of the bourgeois classes... If this is so, it is clear that the coming revolution can on no account assume political forms *against the will of the whole* of the bourgeoisie, as the latter will be the master of tomorrow. If so, then to follow the path of simply *frightening* the majority of the bourgeois elements would mean that the revolutionary struggle of the proletariat could lead to only one result—the restoration of absolutism in its original form.' Martynov's implied conclusion is that the working class should impose self-restraint on itself so as not to 'frighten' the bourgeoisie; but at the same time he states that it should persistently press the bourgeoisie to lead the revolution: 'The struggle to influence the course and outcome of the bourgeois revolution can be expressed simply in *the proletariat's exerting revolutionary pressure on the will of the liberal and radical bourgeoisie*, the more democratic "lower" section of society compelling the "higher" section to *agree* to lead the bourgeois revolution to its logical conclusion'—A Martynov, *Dve Diktatury* (Geneva, 1905) pp57-58.

Similarly the Menshevik paper *Iskra* wrote at the time, 'When looking at the arena of struggle in Russia, what do we see? Only two powers: Tsarist autocracy and the liberal bourgeoisie, the latter organised and of tremendous specific weight. The working masses are split and can do nothing; as an independent force we do not exist, and therefore our task consists in the support of the second force—the liberal bourgeoisie; we must encourage it, and on no account frighten it by putting forward the independent demands of the proletariat. Quoted by G Zinoviev, *Istoriia Rossiiskoi Kommunisticheskoii Partii (Bolshevikov)* (Moscow-Leningrad, 1923), p158.

2 V I Lenin, 'Two Tactics of Social Democracy in the Democratic Revolution' (1905), in *Sochineniia* (4th edn), vol IX, p40.

3 Ibid, p9.

4 Ibid, vol XXI, p17.

5 L Trotsky, *Perspektivy Russkoi Revoliutsii* (selection from his book *Nasha Revoliutsiia*) (Berlin, 1917), p46.

6 Ibid, p36.

7 Ibid, p48. Trotsky's theory was a development, application and expansion of Marx's analysis of the 1848 revolution. Even before that revolution *The Communist Manifesto* had predicted that because of the 'advanced conditions' and 'developed proletariat' of Germany 'the bourgeois revolution in Germany' would be 'but the prelude to an immediately following proletarian revolution'—K Marx, *Selected Works*, vol I (London, 1942), p241. And after the defeat of 1848 Marx stated that, faced with the incapacity of the bourgeoisie to carry out the anti-feudal revolution, the working class had to struggle for the growth of the bourgeois revolution into the proletarian, and of the national revolution into the international revolution. In an address to the Central Council of the Communist League (March 1850) Marx said, 'While the democratic petty bourgeois wish to bring the revolution to a conclusion as quickly as possible and with the achievement at most of the above demands, it is our interest and our task to make the revolution permanent, until all more or less possessing classes have been displaced from domination, until the proletariat has conquered state power, and the association of the proletarians, not only in one country but in all the dominant countries of the world, has advanced so far that competition among the proletarians of these countries has ceased and that at least the decisive productive forces are concentrated in the hands of the proletarians.' And Marx ended his address with the phrase, 'Their [the workers'] battle-cry must be: the permanent revolution!'—K Marx, *Selected Works*, vol III (London, 1942), pp161-168.

8 L Trotsky, *Permanent Revolution* (Calcutta, 1947), p168.

9 Ibid, p169.

10 R C North, *Kuomintang and Chinese Communist Elites* (Stanford, 1962), p32.

11 H R Isaacs, *The Tragedy of the Chinese Revolution* (London, 1938), p333.

12   Ibid, p394.
13   *World News and Views*, 22 April 1939.
14   S Gelder, *The Chinese Communists* (London, 1946), p167.
15   See Communist manifesto published in Chungking on 23 November 1938, *New York Times*, 24 November 1938.
16   H R Isaacs, op cit, p456.
17   *New China News Agency*, 11 January 1949.
18   Ibid, 3 May 1949.
19   *North China Daily News*, 23 April 1949.
20   *New York Times*, 25 May 1949.
21   *South China Morning Post*, 17 October 1949.
22   C Wright Mills, *Listen Yankee* (New York, 1960), p46.
23   Ibid, p47.
24   P A Baran, *Reflections on the Cuban Revolution* (New York, 1961), p17.
25   The Communist Party of Cuba, the People's Socialist Party, had a lot to live down. It supported Batista's rule between 1939 and 1946. It participated in Batista's first ministry with two ministers, Juan Marinello and Carlos Rafael Rodriguez. In 1944 the Communist paper *Hoy* addressed Batista as the 'idol of a people, the great man of our national policy, the man who incarnates the sacred ideals of a new Cuba'. Castro was declared a petty bourgeois adventurer. As stated above, the Communists did not cooperate in the April 1958 strike. As late as 28 June 1958 they were timidly advocating 'clean democratic elections' to get rid of Batista.
26   C Wright Mills, op cit, pp 46-48.
27   Ibid, p44.
28   P A Baran, op cit, p11.
29   Ibid, p12.
30   Speech by Castro of 1 December 1961, *El Mundo La Habana*, 22 December 1961.
31   E Guevara, 'Cuba: Exceptional Case?', *Monthly Review* (New York), July-August 1961, p59.
32   T Draper, 'Castro's Cuba. A Revolution Betrayed?', *Encounter* (London), March 1961.
33   E Guevara, op cit, p63.
34   Ibid, pp65-66.
35   Ibid, p68.
36   Quoted in T Draper, op cit.
37   *Plan for the Advancement of Latin America* (Havana, 1959), p32.
38   O D Torrado, 'The Institutional and Political Changes made by the Cuban Revolution', *Cuba* (Havana), November 1961.
39   C A Mayers, 'India', in W Galenson (ed), *Labor and Economic Development* (New York, 1959), pp41-42.
40   V B Karnik, *Indian Trade Unionism: A Survey* (Bombay, 1960), pp227-228.
41   Ibid, p236.
42   E Berg, 'French West Africa', in W Galenson (ed), op cit, p227.
43   United States Senate, 86th Congress, Second Session, *United States-Latin American Relations* (Washington, 1960), p645.
44   V I Lenin, *Selected Works*, vol 7 (Moscow, 1946), p248.
45   Thus, for instance, a survey made in India showed that about 25 percent of the students who received their master's degree from Lucknow University in Arts, Science, Commerce and Law between 1949 and 1953 were still unemployed in 1957. The survey also reported that about 47 percent of the liberal arts students, 51.4 percent of the science students, 7 percent of the commerce students, and 85.7 percent of the education students said they went to the university to get the necessary qualifications for government service. About 51 percent of the degree holders concluded that university education was a 'waste of time'. M Weiner, *Party Politics in India* (Princeton, 1957), pp8-10.
46   V Alba, 'The Middle Class Revolution', *New Politics* (New York), Winter 1962, p71.
47   G D Overstreet and M Windmiller, *Communism in India* (Berkeley and Los Angeles, 1959), p540.

48   Ibid, p358.

49   For lack of space the present article has concentrated on the relevance of the theory of
permanent revolution to the backward countries, and not dealt with its implications in the
advanced countries. This second element—that the victory of the colonial revolution must
lead to the socialist revolution in the advanced metropolitan countries—was not originally
(in 1906) part and parcel of Trotsky's theory, but has since become grafted upon it. For some
of the relevant considerations, see M Kidron, 'Imperialism, Highest Stage But One',
International Socialism (first series) 9 (Summer 1962), reprinted in *International Socialism*
(first series) 61 (June 1973).

Mao Tse-Tung and Stalin

Socialist Review, April 1957

During recent events in Hungary the Chinese press came out firmly in support of Moscow's oppressive policy. Thus, for instance, the editorial for 5 November in Peking's *People's Daily*, entitled 'Celebrate The Great Victory Of The Hungarian People', stated, 'The joyful news has arrived that the Hungarian people...with the support of the Soviet armed forces have overthrown the reactionary Nagy government which betrayed the Hungarian people and the Hungarian nation.' Every victory of Russian arms in Hungary was applauded in ever more glowing terms.

On 29 December 1956 the *People's Daily* published a major pronouncement entitled 'More On The Historical Experience Of The Dictatorship Of The Proletariat'. This approved the general course of Moscow's policy, in the main justified Stalin's career, supported Russia's policy in Hungary and reproved Tito. It emphasised the 'leading role of the Soviet Union in the socialist camp'. Chou En-lai again and again harped on the same theme throughout his tour of Moscow, Warsaw and Budapest in January this year. It was indicative that Chou applauded the loudest after Khruschev had said, 'All of us Communists...consider it a matter of pride for us to be as true to Marxism-Leninism as was Stalin himself'.[1]

Not unexpected

To many a sincere Communist, suffering under the profound illusion that Mao and his regime are not Stalinist, this must have come as a great shock. However, to anyone using the Marxist method of analysis, which looks at the economic foundation of politics, Mao's extreme Stalinism is not unexpected.

To understand Mao's policies one must bear in mind the main historical task facing the Chinese bureaucracy: the task of industrialising the country. The Chinese bourgeoisie proved incapable of accomplishing this. The Chinese working class, after the defeat of the 1925-27 Revolution, the world slump and the Japanese invasion, being pulverised and leaderless, has not played an active, decisive role for the last three decades. The task of industrialising an extremely backward country when it cannot rely on the aid of industrially advanced socialist centres is extremely difficult. It demands that the people tighten their belts in order to make quick capital accumulation possible. A considerable tightening of the belt cannot be done democratically for any length of time. Hence the more backward the country and the greater the drive towards quick industrialisation, the more harsh and totalitarian the regime has to be. The rulers of such a regime, while being the guardians of capital accumulation, will not, of course, forget themselves; they accordingly derive increasing privileges from their position of absolute control over the economy, society and state.

China's poverty

China is extremely backward economically. Thus, for instance, steel consumption per head of the population in 1950 was 2 lbs, as against 11 in India, 111 in Japan, 278 in Russia, 556 in Britain and 1,130 in the United States.[2] The output of electricity in 1950 was 3,500 million kWh in China, as against 5,063 million in India and Pakistan (whose population is about two thirds of China's), 38,840 million in Japan and 91,200 million in Russia.[3] The number of spindles in China was 4 million as against 10.8 million in India.[4] Chinese transport is also extremely backward. It was estimated that prior to the Second World War there was 1km of railways per 25,300 people in China, as against 1km per 6,878 in India.[5] In motor transport China was even more backward relative to India.

As a result of economic backwardness, China's national income is extremely low. Colin Clark estimates that the net income produced per head of population in China (1933-35) was 138 International Units (he defines the unit as the amount of goods and services which $1 would produce in the US over the average of the period 1925-34); in India (1944-45) 246: USSR (1937) 379; Hungary (1938-39) 408; Poland (1938) 508; Japan (1940) 600; Britain (1947) 1,383; US (1947) 2,566.[6]

The plans

The rate of industrial growth aimed at by Mao in his First Five-Year Plan is quite ambitious, although it falls short of Russia's aims in her First Five-Year Plan (see Table 1).

So meagre are China's initial resources that even after her First Five-Year Plan she will be far behind Russia's level of production not only after its First Five-Year Plan, but even before it was started. This can be seen clearly from Table 2. China will need a number of Five-Year Plans to reach the level Russia reached even prior to her Plan era.

China's First Five-Year Plan shows an even greater emphasis on heavy industry than Russia's First Five-Year Plan. According to the plan, of all gross capital investment in industry, 88.8 percent will be devoted to means of production industries, and only 11.2 percent to light industries.[7] In Russia the corresponding figures were 85.9 and 14.1.

TABLE 1[8]

	China		Russia	
	Index for 1957 (1952 = 100)	Yearly rate of increase	Index for 1932 (1928 = 100)	Yearly rate of increase
Value of gross industrial output	198.3	14.7	202	19.3
Output of large-scale industry	207	15.7	230	23.2

TABLE 2: PER CAPITA OUTPUT OF DIFFERENT GOODS IN CHINA AND RUSSIA[9]

	Unit	China		Russia	
		1952	1957 (target)	1928	1932
Power supply	kWh	12.71	25.2	32.5	81.7
Cotton cloth	kh	2.36	6.54	27.6	35.8
Steel	metres	6.7	8.85	18	16.3
Grain	kg	286.95	305.74	475.2	421.5

Consumption bows to investment

The subordination of consumer goods industries to the needs of capital goods is shown in the fact that while the amount of profits of light industries in the years 1952-55 was some 10.8 billion yuan larger than the amounts invested in these same industries, this sum went mainly to capitalise heavy industry.[10]

With the national income very low, capital investment takes up a big portion of the national income. It has been stated that gross capital investment in 1952 made up 15.7 percent of the national income; in 1953 it was 18.3 percent; in 1954, 21.6 percent; in 1955, 20.5 percent; in 1956, 22.8 percent.[11] This rate is only a little lower than in Russia during her First Five-Year Plan, but seeing that in absolute terms the level of income in China is some three times lower than in Russia at the time, a rate of 20 percent accumulation is a much greater burden than a rate of even 30 percent would have been in Russia.

In absolute terms, however, the capital accumulation in China is quite small. Thus the average annual investment rate during the five years 1953-57 was planned to be 8,548 million People's Dollars, or, at the official rate of exchange, some 3,650 million US dollars.

In Canada, with a population one fortieth of China's population in 1956, capital investment reached US$7,900 million. (Even if we consider possible differences in price levels between the two countries, the picture would not alter radically.)

The burden of arms

The military budget of China made up 18.1 percent of the national income in 1952; in 1953, 15.9 percent; in 1954, 15.2 percent; and in 1955, 16.2 percent.[12] These figures compare with the military budget of Russia in 1928, which made up only 2 percent of the gross national product of the country.

With a high rate of capital accumulation, and with the great burden of the military budget, workers' wages naturally lag far behind their output, that is, the rate of exploitation is high—and is rising.

This was underlined by a *People's Daily* editorial which stated, 'In 1952, the workers of state-operated enterprises produced a yearly average rate of 100 million People's Dollars per worker. Of this, except for $500,000 as the average monthly wage for each worker, 94 percent directly represented capital created for the state'.[13] The above figures probably exaggerate the rate of exploitation of the workers, but there is no doubt that it is extreme.

Growing exploitation

As time goes by, the rate of exploitation is increasing, as can be seen clearly from the lag of wages behind labour productivity. This was the situation according to the *People's Daily*:[14]

	Labour productivity increase (percent)	Wage increase (percent)
1953	13	5
1954	15	2.6
1955	10	0.6

(For reasons that cannot be dealt with in the present article, it can be proved that it is doubtful if real wages showed even the rise mentioned in this table.)

The exploitation of the peasantry is even more extreme than that of the industrial workers. For lack of space we shall mention only a few facts to show this.

Vice-Premier Chen Yun stated that in the year July 1954 to June 1955, the state acquired, in the form of grain tax and compulsory deliveries of produce, a total of 52 million tons of grain, or some 30 percent of the total grain output of the country.[15] This figure is not far behind that taken by the Russian state as taxation in compulsory deliveries: in 1938 it was some 33 percent.[16]

The figure for China exceeds what the peasantry used to pay as rent under the Kuomintang regime—some '30 million tons of grain'.[17]

Forced labour

Capital being so very scarce and human labour so very plentiful and cheap, the natural result is the widespread use of forced labour—including prisoners, or slave labourers.

Unlike Moscow, Peking is not shy about giving information on forced labour. Thus, for instance, in a 'Report on the Work of the Kwangtung Provincial Government during the Past Ten Months', given by Ku Tats'un, its vice-chairman, on 15 September 1951, it was stated that in the province of Kwangtung alone during ten months, a total of 89,701 counter-revolutionaries were arrested, 28,332 were executed, while 'those whose crimes were punishable by death, but who did not incur the intense hatred of the public, were sentenced to death but had their execution delayed for two years, during which time they were made to undertake forced labour to give them a chance to reform themselves'.[18] If some 60,000 people were condemned to slave labour in only one of China's 27 provinces in a matter of ten months, the size of the slave labour force in the country as a whole must be huge. Po I-po, at the time Minister of Finance, claimed that in three years 'more than two million bandits' were liquidated,[19] the majority presumably not being killed but put to work.

A milder form of forced labour is the compulsory conscription of peasants to public works. Thus, Fu Tsoyi, Minister of Water Conservancy, stated on 28 October 1951, 'During the two years (October 1949-October 1951) a total labour force of 10,370,000 workers was mobilised for various conservancy projects'.[20] The average pay for this kind of work was some 2-3 catties of rice for a 12-hour workday.[21] Under the Kuomintang in the years 1929-33, the average daily wage of agricultural workers was equal to 14 catties of rice.[22]

The low level of the productive forces at the disposal of the Chinese bureaucracy makes for an even harsher political regime than in Russia. Space allows for only a few points to be dealt with in this connection.

Police dictatorship

As in Russia so in China, there is also a system of internal passports, the obligation to register with the police any change of address, etc.[23]

To control the population three sets of regulations were issued. First, Organic Regulations of Urban Inhabitants' Committees; secondly, Organic Regulations of Urban Street Offices; and thirdly, Organic Regulations of Public Security Sub stations. All three were adopted by the Standing Committee of the National People's Congress on 31 December 1954.

To strengthen these organisations, special Denunciation Rooms and Denunciation Postboxes were set up all over the country.

Sons against fathers

Nothing shows the extreme of totalitarianism reached in China more than the demand that children should denounce their own 'counter-revolutionary' parents. To give one example: The *China Youth Journal* published an open letter by a student called Lu Ch'eng-hsu, accusing her father of being an agent of Chiang Kai-shek. The letter opens with these words:

> Lu Hsu,
>   When I write out this stinking name of yours, I feel ashamed and intolerably insulted. In the past I looked upon you as my father, but now I have seen your true face: you are a cannibal with your teeth bared in madness and your paws whipping about in the air.

It ends with these words:

> Now, I am a member of the New Democratic Youth League, and you are the people's enemy, forever unpardonable. Between us there is nothing in common now. I would rather be a daughter of the people than the slave of a special agent. It is our sworn principle that we will never coexist with our enemy. So no matter where you hide yourself, we will get you in the end. You just wait and see. [24]

Such a level of depravity imposed by the totalitarian state was not surpassed, indeed not even reached, by Stalinist Russia.

Cult of the individual

The cult of Mao is, in a way, even more extreme and nauseating than the former cult of Stalin. Portraits of Mao hang everywhere. Five storeys high, they adorn Shanghai and other cities. Trains carry portraits of Mao over the boiler. In many peasant houses his picture replaces the former kitchen god, and a kind of grace is said before meals by the household: 'Thank Chairman Mao for our good food.' His pictures occupy the tiny household shrines where formerly clay images were kept. A report of the Peking Municipal People's Government quotes a peasant approvingly: 'Formerly we worshipped Kuan Kung, who was said to be omnipotent. Where is his omnipotence? Who shall we worship? To my mind, we should worship Chairman Mao'.[25]

Special obeisance is made to Mao at all public meetings. A description of a mass trial ran: 'The meeting opened with the singing of the national anthem. Then everybody took off their hats and bowed to the national flag and to the portrait of Chairman Mao',[26] just as they had formerly done to the landlord as he was borne past them.

Not to be outdone, Wa-ch-mu-chi, Governor of the Yi Nationality Autonomous *chou* in Lianshen (Sikang) sang the following hymn of praise at the National People's Congress: 'The sun shines only in the day, the moon shines only at night. Only Chairman Mao is the sun that never sets'.[27] Practically the same words were used about Stalin: 'I would have compared him to the shining moon, but the moon shines at midnight, not at noon. I would have com-pared him to the brilliant sun, but the sun radiates at noon, not at midnight'.[28]

China's Stalinism

The basic facts of the Stalinist regime are the subordination of consumption to the needs of quick capital accumulation, the bureaucratic management of in-dustry, the limitation of workers' legal rights, the enforced 'collectivisation' of agriculture, the differentiation of society into privileged and pariahs and the to-talitarian police dictatorship. All these traits are to be found in Mao's China. Being a relatively late comer and rising on extremely backward productive forces, the oppressive facets of the system are even more accentuated in Mao's China than they were in Stalin's Russia. The historical function of the bu-reaucracy is the accumulation of capital on the one hand and the creating of a working class on the other (a function fulfilled by the bourgeoisie in the West). The less capital a country is endowed with and the smaller its working class, the deeper are the roots of bureaucratic state capitalism and the longer its span of life, if taken in isolation.

To put it differently, as the backwardness of China is so much greater than that of Russia, not to speak of the European satellites, the working class so small in size and so lacking in cohesion and culture, the forces compelling the bureaucracy to give concessions and even threatening to explode the regime in revolution are much weaker in China than in Russia, not to speak of Eastern Europe. In all probabil-ity, if not for the influence of revolutionary events elsewhere, China will have to go through a whole generation, or perhaps two, until its working class becomes a strong enough power to challenge the rule of the bureaucracy. In isolation the present regime in China will probably surpass in harshness as well as in length of life its Russian Stalinist precursor. In this we find one reason why Peking did not take kindly to the 'reformers' in Eastern Europe and why it applauded the defeat of 're-actionary Nagy'.

There is another reason, connected with the above, for Mao's support for 'Stalinist' policies, and—if there is a split in the Kremlin—for the 'Stalinist' fac-tion. Being interested in China's rapid rise to be a giant industrial and military world power, Mao cannot but oppose any weakening or softening of the austere regimen in Russia and Eastern Europe, a regimen that makes for emphasis on heavy industry at the expense of popular consumption. Mao prefers to get steel, machine tools, turbines, etc, rather than that the Russian or Hungarian people should get better housing, food and clothing.

Mao's China is a tremendous rock on which probably many revolutionary anti-Stalinist waves will break. However, in the long run, probably after a few decades, this rock will begin to crumble not only, or perhaps even mainly, through the effect of anti-Stalinist revolutions in Europe, but through revolu-tionary events in China itself.

Notes

1 *Manchester Guardian*, 18 January 1957.
2 W S Woytinsky and E S Woytinsky, *World Population and Production* (New York, 1953), p1124.
3 Ibid, p967.
4 Ibid, p1067.
5 United Nations, *Economic Survey of Asia and the Far East 1947* (Shanghai, 1948), p113.
6 C Clark, *Conditions of Economic Progress*, 1st edn (London, 1940) and 2nd edn (London, 1951).
7 Li Fu-chun, *Report on the First Five-Year Plan* (Peking, 1955), p34.
8 Yang Chien-pai, 'A Comparative Analysis of China's First Five-Year Plan and the Soviet Union's First Five-Year Plan', *Statistical Work Bulletin* (Peking), August 1955.
9 Ibid.
10 *Statistical Bulletin* (Peking), 14 November 1956.
11 *Jen Min Jih Pao* (*People's Daily*), 20 September 1956.
12 Calculated from Wang Tzu-ying, 'On Public Finance', *Ta Kung Pao* (Tientsin), 29 January 1955.
13 *People's Daily*, 13 December 1953.
14 *People's Daily*, 19 June 1956.
15 *New China News Agency*, 30 April 1955.
16 A Arina, 'Kolkhozes in 1938', *Sotsialisticheskoe Selskokhozyaistvo* (Moscow), December 1939.
17 Chen Han-seng, 'Industrialisation Begins', *China Reconstructs* (Peking), January-February 1953.
18 *Nan Fang Jih Pao* (Canton), 18 September 1951.
19 *New China's Economic Achievements, 1949-52* (Peking, 1952), p152.
20 *People's Daily*, 30 October, 1951
21 Calculated from the book of the Stalinist, W G Burchett, *China's Feet Unbound* (London, 1952), p157.
22 J L Buck, *Land Utilisation in China* (Shanghai, 1937), pp305-306.
23 See the decree of the Ministry of State Security, 'Provisional Regulations Governing Urban Population', *New China News Agency*, 16 July 1951; Ministry of State Security, 'Provisional Rules for Control of Hotels and Lodging Houses', *New China News Agency*, 4 August 1951; State Council, 'Directive Concerning the Establishment of a Permanent System for Registration of Persons', *New China News Agency*, 2 July 1955.
24 *China Youth Journal* (Peking), 8 May 1951.
25 'General Report of Peking Municipal People's Government on Agrarian Reform in Peking Suburban Areas', approved by Government Administrative Council on 21 November 1950.
26 Hsiao Ch'ien, *How the Tillers Win Back their Land* (Peking, 1954), p72.
27 *New China News Agency*, 26 July 1953.
28 *Znamya* (Soviet Authors' Union Monthly), October 1946.

Crisis in China

International Socialism (first series) 29, Summer 1967

(1) In Stalin's footsteps: everything subordinated to heavy industry

To understand the forces behind the Cultural Revolution, one must start by analysing the socioeconomic problems with which China is wrestling.

Up to 1957, the end of the First Five-Year Plan (FYP), China followed Stalin's model of economic advance: the emphasis was on heavy industry to the detriment of light industry and agriculture. Thus, for instance, during the First FYP, agriculture received only 6.2 percent of state investment, while industry's share was 61.8 percent. Of the amount invested in industry, only 11.2 percent was scheduled for light industry (even lower than in Russia during her First FYP when the corresponding figure was 14.1 percent).[1] As the figures refer to gross investment, that is, without taking into account depreciation of existing capital, it is doubtful if the plan envisaged any net investment at all in light industry.

There can be no doubt that one of the main factors behind the very high rate of industrial growth in the USSR was the fact that a very large portion of the capital invested in industry went into capital-goods rather than consumer-goods industries. A machine to produce machines plays a greater role in capital formation than a machine producing, say, shoes for the people to wear.

There is an intimate connection between the neglect of light industry and the neglect of agriculture in both Russia's and China's First Five-Year Plans. If the light industry which supplies the needs of the peasants is neglected, the peasants have little incentive to increase agricultural output. In Russia the springboards for the fantastic achievements of industry under Stalin were forced collectivisation and the enforced siphoning off of grain to the towns to feed the newly recruited industrial working class that was engaged primarily in heavy industry.

Alas, as early as towards the end of the First FYP, it became clear that Mao simply could not follow in Stalin's footsteps, that the Soviet model of development could not be transferred effectively to China. First of all, the industrial base from which Mao started was much narrower than that from which Stalin launched his industrialisation drive. Even in absolute terms, China's industrial output in almost every sector lagged well behind that of Russia in 1913. Per head of population China was still worse off, her population being four times as big as Russia's at that time. Second, however swiftly China developed industrially (and during the First FYP her advance was very impressive—a 14 percent annual rate of growth!), the growth of employment possibilities lagged far behind the growth of population. Thus, non-agricultural employment rose from 36.5 million in 1953 to 40.9 million in 1957, or by 4.4 million. The average annual increase in employment outside agriculture was, therefore, 880,000. The population of working age increased during the same period by an annual average of 4 million (a figure that probably rose to 5 million in the years 1958-62 and to 7 million in the years 1963-67). The result was that the agricultural labour force did not decline—as happened in Russia under Stalin—but rose by 75 million from 222 million in 1952 to 297 million in 1957.[2] A third cause for anxiety at the time was the way that agriculture threatened to lag behind the multiplying population. One must remember that China, prior to Mao's coming to power and for more than two generations, had been a net importer of grain (unlike Russia which, prior to the revolution, was a granary for western Europe). Any deterioration in her precarious grain balance—either a decline in the productivity of agriculture, or even a failure to keep pace with the increase in population—would wreak havoc, given the infinitesimal margin of output above the absolute minimum needed to avoid famine.

With the lagging of agricultural output behind population growth, and especially with the rise in the size of the agricultural population, Mao found it more and more difficult to get hold of agricultural surpluses to feed the towns and for exporting abroad to get the wherewithal to import machinery and the like. State procurements and taxation in kind, which in the agricultural year 1953-54 together amounted to 29.12 percent of all grain produced, declined to 25.15 precent in the year 1956-57.[3]

But above all, there were, and are, other fundamental reasons why the methods of forced siphoning off of agricultural output from the countryside could not work as effectively in China as in Russia. The failure of forced deliveries in China was forecast in 1957:

> In Russia, state control over the machine tractor stations guarantees that a big portion of whatever the peasants produce will go into the state treasury to provide capital for industrialisation. In China the role of the machine tractor stations—even in the few places where they do exist—could not be as commanding, as intensive agriculture, especially garden cultivation, is not, and could not be, as dependent upon mechanisation. The converse of this greater importance of human labour is that the will to work, care and zeal in production play a much greater role in China's agriculture than in Russia's. Forced deliveries, together with the emphasis on heavy industry, inevitably pour cold water on the peasant's desire to increase production: not only is he prevented from eating more, but no consumer goods are offered to induce him to sell his surplus output. And without inducement, increased

output from intensive agriculture is most unlikely.

The conclusion that the pattern of Russian collectivisation is likely to prove a false guide to China gains support from the economic history of the two countries... Ever since Chinese agriculture became dependent on irrigation, serfdom gave place to a peasant economy based on private property. However exploited and oppressed the peasant may have been, it was not the whip which urged him to work. As against this, serfdom and the feudal whip were the salient features of rural society in Russia, with its extensive agriculture, for a thousand years.[4]

In 1958 Mao tried to break out of the above contradictions by a new forced march.

(2) 'Walking on both feet'

The People's Communes and the Great Leap Forward had as their slogan 'Walking on both feet'—agriculture to keep pace with industry. The aims of the Great Leap Forward can be summarised thus:
(1) To increase agricultural output and radically redistribute it in order to siphon off large surpluses;
(2) To widen employment opportunities, not only in large-scale industry, but also in agriculture, in construction work in the countryside, and in small industry and handicrafts;
(3) To siphon off agricultural products for the 'surplus' population—who were to be in visible proximity to the peasants, engaged on work that was obviously contributing to their income—by having the peasants feed them directly. This was intended to help overcome the difficulty of getting the food to follow those who migrated from the countryside into the towns.

In a gallant and heroic effort to accomplish these great tasks the unique experiment of the People's Commune was launched. Millions were mobilised in the countryside to work on water conservancy. In the three years 1949-52, 'about 20 million people took part in water conservancy work',[5] but for 1957 and 1958 it was reported by Vice-Premier Po I-po (in February 1958): 'At present nearly 100 million men and women are going out every day in China to work on irrigation work,' each working for an average of 100 days.[6] Millions were mobilised to build steel ovens, and 60 million were engaged in iron smelting and steel-refining furnaces.[7]

However, the Great Leap Forward ended in disarray.[8]

(3) Third Turn: priority to agriculture

Once again Peking had to change course. That the Great Leap Forward ended in a shambles is clear from the Chinese authorities' complete silence since 1959 on the subject of actual output or even planned output expressed in physical terms. When one compares this statistical blackout with Peking's eagerness to publish a multitude of statistics beforehand—even on the number of flies eliminated—one may be sure that the production figures were not favourable.

The first clear hint of the coming Third Turn was given in the Report of Li Fu-ch'un to the National People's Congress in March 1960. He put forward the idea that agriculture should be regarded as the foundation, with industry taking the lead in economic development.[9] But no indication was given yet that the basic policy of giving priority to the development of heavy industry had been changed. It was in the autumn of 1960, when the harvest turned out to be much worse than expected, that a new policy turn became apparent. In late September a movement of 'all people to agriculture and food grains' was brought to a peak by cadres all over the country.[10] This represented a complete turnabout from the nationwide movement of 'all people to iron and steel' that had taken place in the late summer of 1958.

In January 1961 Li Fu-ch'un, in his report to the Eighth Plenum of the Central Committee, admitted that the planned agricultural output for 1960 had not been attained because of 'severe natural calamities in 1959', and 'natural calamities in 1960 that were unprecedented in 100 years'. This led the plenum to reaffirm the movement of 'all the party and all people to agriculture and food grains'. The plenum decided further that 'since there had been tremendous development in heavy industry in the last three years—its output of major products already far in excess of the planned level for 1961 and 1962—the scale of basic construction should therefore be appropriately reduced'. The general industrial policy was to be that of 'readjustment, consolidation, reinforcement and improvement'.[11]

Chou En-lai's report to the National People's Congress on 27 March 1962, entitled 'The Work of Readjusting the National Economy and Our Immediate Tasks', put forward ten immediate tasks, three of which were of direct concern to industry:

Task 3. Contract further the basic construction front, and redirect the materials, equipment and manpower to the most urgent areas.

Task 4. Properly reduce urban population and workers and functionaries, the first move being to send those workers and functionaries who came from the rural districts back to take part in agricultural production, so as to strengthen the agricultural front...

Task 10. Improve further the work in planning and try to attain a comprehensive balance among different sectors in the national economy in accordance with the (declining priority) order of agriculture, light industry and heavy industry.[12]

That a great shift from industry to agriculture in the balance of the economy probably did take place after the retreat from the Great Leap Forward is clear from the following estimate of the gross national product of China and its composition:[13]

	Gross national product of China (1952 prices)		
	1957	**1959**	**1962**
Aggregate in million yuan	95.2	110.5	82.7
	Percentages		
(1) Agriculture	39.2	32.2	47.1
(2) Modern industry	20.3	29.5	14.5
(3) Handicrafts	5.7	5.3	6.4
(4) Others	34.8	33.0	32.0

(4) Relaxation in agriculture

After the end of the Great Leap Forward there was a marked relaxation of state control in agriculture. The People's Communes have in many places become empty shells, while the small production teams and peasants' private plot are the important factors of production.

In 1958, all the Chinese peasants were organised in 24,000 Communes with an average of over 20,000 people per Commune. All land and other means of production, such as livestock and ploughs, were declared the common property of the Commune, which, besides managing agriculture, was to own and manage industrial undertakings and educational and other social institutions such as schools, nurseries and hospitals. All members of the Commune were to be fed in a number of common mess-halls. The Commune was also declared to be a political-military unit of the state and party.

The Commune ownership of practically all means of production was only a transition stage to state ownership, 'the completion of which may take less time—three or four years—in some places, and longer—five or six years or even longer—elsewhere'.[14] The transition to complete communism in China as a whole was on the horizon:

> The People's Communes are the best form of organisation for the attainment of socialism and gradual transition to communism. They will develop into the basic social units in communist society… It seems that the attainment of communism in China is no longer a remote future event. We should actively use the form of the People's Communes to explore the practical road of transition to communism.[15]

In tightening the control over peasants, an end was put to the elements of private property that still existed in the agricultural producer co-operatives.

To realise the Great Leap, a big effort was made to raise the rate of capital accumulation in the Communes. Thus, the *People's Daily* recommended that 30 to 40 percent of the net income of Communes should be put to reserves 'over the following several years'.[16] However, the high tide of Commune building lasted only a few short months; then came the ebb. A turning point was reached in August 1959 at a plenum of the Central Committee, which criticised the Commune movement for 'tendencies to overcentralisation, to egalitarianism and extravagance'.[17] The production team of some 10 to 20 families was now to become the basic accounting and production unit.

There was no more talk of the imminent transfer of Commune property to full state ownership. In the high fever of Commune building, all garden plots, livestock and other property had been expropriated on the promise that all needs would be satisfied by the Commune. In the about-face, individual initiative and work were to play a significant role. Small plots of land were returned to individual householders for private cultivation. In addition, 'the Commune members should be enabled to utilise their spare time to grow some food grains, melons, vegetables, and fruit trees, and raise some small domestic animals and domestic poultry on vacant plots and land, and waste land'.[18]

As a result, *individual* farming was now going to play quite a considerable role in the life of the peasantry. It was found, for example, in P'enghsing Commune, Hupeh province, that the share of individual farming in the general income of production brigade members was: one brigade, 36.38 percent; a second brigade, 28 percent; a third brigade, 19.76 percent.[19] In Hsiaokang People's Commune, Hupeh, peasants individually raised 65 percent of all pigs sold and 95 percent of all chickens and eggs sold.[20] One paper noted, in 1965, that 70 percent of subsidiary production in agriculture was on private plots.[21] As the income from subsidiary production makes up over 60 percent of the total income from agriculture,[22] it is to be concluded that income from private plots constitutes as much as 40 percent of the total income from agricultural production.

Peasants were now no longer obliged to work on Commune enterprises. Thus, for instance, the Kwangtung Provincial Committee of the Communist Party decided that 'the enterprises of the Communes (including those in the categories of industry, communications, forestry, animal husbandry, subsidiary production and fishery) are as a rule not allowed to draft more that 8 percent of the labour power of the production brigades'.[23]

Production brigades were now allowed to deduct only up to 3 percent of their income for accumulation.[24] The hullabaloo about Commune-run industry subsided completely. Now we are informed:

> To initiate Commune industry, rural People's Communes should depend mainly on the profits of Commune enterprises and Commune reserve funds, and may not expect funds either from above (the state) or from below (brigades). Under present conditions, Commune industry should generally not take up more than 2 percent of the total number of labourers in production brigades.[25]

At the time of the Great Leap Forward, we were informed that the building of the People's Communes helped the party to keep the countryside under its control. 'Why do we say that with the setting up of People's Communes the party leadership will be strengthened?... A large-scale, highly-centralised organisation is naturally easier to lead than a small-scale, scattered organisation'.[26]

Now, with the great retreat, a relaxation of party control over the country-side took place.

(5) Relaxation of control over industrial management

During the Great Leap Forward, the authority of party committees at the local and enterprise levels was enhanced. A system of 'close coordination among management, workers, technical personnel and administrative staff under the leadership of the enterprise's party committee' was inaugurated.[27] The secretary of the party committee became, to all intents and purposes, the chief executive of the enterprise. The emphasis was, as the press put it at the time, on 'redness' not 'expertness'.

However, when the Great Leap Forward met with reverses, the policy had to change. In April 1959, the weather-cock, Chou En-lai, put it thus: 'Every industrial enterprise must carry through the system of the manager taking full responsibility under the party committee's leadership'.[28] However, some time later, at the end of 1960, the manager re-emerged as the recognised 'head of enterprise'.[29] Thus the balance tilted in favour of the 'professionals' at the expense of the party.

Later, on 10 August 1961, Marshal Ch'en Yi, the foreign minister, made the emphasis on 'expertness', not 'redness', even plainer:

> At present we should stress specialised studies because failure to do so will keep our country perpetually backward in science and culture. In the early years of the liberation, it was completely necessary for the party and the government to stress political study... There is a need for us...to train a large number of specialists...
>
> To make efforts in the study of his special field is the political task of the student... The students...should devote most of their time and efforts to specialised studies. Of course these students should also study politics to equip themselves with a certain degree of political consciousness.[30]

After 1961, all aspects of 'independent managerial authority' were stressed, and it was made clear that it was up to the enterprise manager to make the correct economic decisions with the capital granted him and the task the state assigned him.[31] The party sphere of influence shrank radically and the morale of the party cadres suffered correspondingly.

(6) Intellectual relaxation and Mao's withdrawal

Not only did the intellectuals take advantage of the limited liberalisation of 1960-62 to criticise the party and its policies of the Great Leap Forward, but they resisted subsequent efforts to reform them. Mao himself was moved to comment on their obstinacy. In 1963, it is now revealed, he said that in the cultural field 'very little had been achieved so far in socialist transformation... Wasn't it absurd that many communists showed enthusiasm in advancing feudal and capitalist art, but no zeal in promoting socialist art.' In 1964 Mao complained that most of the associations of literary and art workers and their publications 'had not carried out the policies of the party and had acted as high and mighty bureaucrats, had not gone to the workers, peasants and soldiers and had not reflected the socialist revolution and construction. In recent years they had even slid to the verge of revisionism. If serious steps were not taken to remould them, they were bound at some future date to become groups like the Hungarian Petofi Club'.[32]

One significant expression of the general relaxation of party control over agriculture, industry and the intellectuals was Mao's relinquishing of the chairmanship of the People's Republic of China. He kept his other job, as chairman of the Central Committee of the party, the first job going to Liu Shao-ch'i. The extent of the party's retreat, the loss of self-confidence and nerve, can be seen also in the fact that for a number of years the Central Committee had held no plenary session: the Tenth Plenary Session of the Eighth Central Committee was held in September 1962, while the 11th Session took place in August 1966, some four years later. (Article 33 of the 1945 party constitution provides that regular sessions of the Central Committee should take place every six months!)

(7) Bukharinism raises its head

In many ways the period after the Great Leap Forward was similar to the NEP period in Soviet history. In the years 1924-28 a remarkable debate on economic policies took place in Russia. (An excellent account of this can be found in Erlich's book.[33]) One of the main protagonists was Nikolai Bukharin, by far the best-educated economist of the party. His arguments have been repeated, practically word for word, by Chinese economists since 1961 (though it is very doubtful if there has been any direct influence of the former over the latter).

Bukharin argued that the key problem facing the Soviet economy of the mid-1920s revolved around the relation between agriculture and industry, and that the development of the latter was dependent on that of the former. Agricultural production should be encouraged by incentives: by lowering the prices of industrial goods supplied to the peasants, and relatively improving the prices paid for the farm produce. He vehemently opposed turning the terms of trade against the farm as a means of siphoning off resources from agriculture into industry. This method was suggested by Preobrazhensky, Bukharin's most consistent opponent. Preobrazhensky called this 'the primitive accumulation of capital', which he defined as:

> ...the accumulation in the hands of the state of material resources obtained chiefly from sources lying outside the state economic system. This accumulation will, necessarily, in a backward agrarian country, play a colossal role... Primitive accumulation will predominate during the period of industrialisation... We must, therefore, term this whole stage as the period of primitive or preparatory socialist accumulation.[34]

Bukharin argued that if the terms of trade turned against agriculture, there was a danger that the peasantry would turn away from the market, cut supplies to the towns, and indulge in self-sufficiency. It was in this context that Bukharin disinterred Guizot's famous '*enrichissez-vous*' which was later to haunt him for years: 'We have to tell the whole peasantry, all its strata: get rich, accumulate, develop your economy'.[35]

To the extent that industry developed, the emphasis, Bukharin argued, should be on light industry, not heavy industry:

> We believe that the formula which calls for a maximum of investments in heavy industry is not quite correct, or rather, quite incorrect. If we have to put the main emphasis on the development of the means of production, we must combine this development with a corresponding expansion of light industry which has a quicker turnover and repays within a shorter time the amounts spent on it. We must attempt to get the optimal combination of both.[36]

After all, 'Our economy,' Bukharin declared, 'exists for the consumer, and not the consumer for the economy'.[37]

If the speed of industrialisation is dictated by its subordination to the pace of advance of agriculture, while heavy industry is subordinated to light industry, it is just too bad if industry crawls forward. This is unavoidable: 'We have come to the conclusion that we can build socialism even on this wretched technological level...that we shall move at a snail's pace, but that we shall be building socialism and that we shall build it'.[38]

It is really uncanny how Bukharin's arguments have been resurrected in China after 1962 in practically every detail. First of all a number of Chinese economists made it clear that industrial development should be dictated by the development of agriculture:

> As the foundation of the national economy, agriculture demands that all production departments including those of industry, all construction units and all cultural and educational undertakings develop themselves with the actual conditions of agricultural production as the starting point and give due consideration to the quantities of commodity grain and industrial raw materials and to the sizes of the market and the labour force which agriculture can supply. In other words, all social undertakings cannot separate themselves from these conditions which agriculture provides... Agriculture plays a decisive role in influencing and restraining the national economy and the whole social life... It is only after agricultural production has been rehabilitated and expanded and after agriculture, the foundation of the national economy, has been consolidated that industry, communications and transport, and cultural and educational undertakings can be better developed... National economic plans should be formulated in the order of agriculture, light industry and heavy industry.[39]

The Chinese economists went much further than Bukharin did in subordinating industrial advance to agriculture. Some of them argued that for a long time *industrial advance should help release labour power from the towns to the countryside*, instead of leading to the more common, opposite direction of population movement:

> Productivity of labour in industrial and mining enterprises must be raised, labour must be saved, *the number of workers and employees must be reduced and the population of the cities must be decreased. In this way, more people will go back to the countryside to increase the labour force there and greatly strengthen the agricultural front and hasten the development of agriculture.*[40]

The terms of trade, which have historically been against farming, have to be radically changed in its favour.

While Preobrazhensky recommended the siphoning off of capital surpluses from agriculture to industry, and Bukharin aimed at industry and agriculture travelling on parallel rails, Chinese economists went further and argued for *capital transfer from industry to agriculture*:

> Under the present conditions in our country, so far as the source of accumulation is concerned, the accumulation from industry will increase at a faster rate than that from agriculture, because the rate of growth of industry and the rise of its labour productivity are faster than those of agriculture. So far as the allocation of accumulation is concerned, *the accumulation used for agriculture will increase at a faster rate than that used for industry*, because the production level of our agriculture is still very low at present and so is its labour productivity, and the state must place the emphasis of its economic work on agriculture and invest heavily in agriculture and give it massive material support, so as to change the backward aspect of agriculture as soon as possible and enable it to meet the needs of the development of all branches of the national economy.[41]

Practically repeating Bukharin's words that 'the economy exists for the consumer and not the consumer for the economy' and the need to subordinate heavy to light industry, one Chinese economist wrote:

> Under ordinary conditions, should arrangements be made first for the necessary consumption of the people throughout the country and then, if circumstances permit, for accumulation? Or, should arrangements be made after accumulation has been guaranteed? According to the basic aim of socialist production, it should be the former and not the latter.[42]

(8) Mao does not like Bukharinism

The Chinese neo-NEP widened the gap between rich and poor, advanced and backward areas and villages, and increased the earnings of factory managers, technicians and better-off peasants.

Yet it is fraught with the greatest dangers to a large section of the bureaucracy. It weakens party control and could in the long run undermine its monolithism, threatening to fracture the party under the pressure of sectional interests. Its continuation would also put an end to any grand nationalist ambitions for the quick transformation of China into a country of heavy industry and a mighty military-industrial establishment.

The alternative to Bukharinism, ie the continuation of NEP, has been supplied by the history of Russia—when Stalin broke with Bukharin and carried out forced industrialisation and collectivisation, enforcing the severe regimentation of workers and peasants. But in trying to follow the same path, Mao is hampered by much greater obstacles than Stalin was (and one should not forget how tough the going was in Russia). First, there are the objective factors mentioned above (the much narrower industrial base, from which Mao has to launch his industrialisation, than Stalin had; the lower agricultural output; the greater population pressure; the difficulty of state control of intensive rice farming, etc). Further obstacles accrue from the fact that the administrative set-up in China is not conducive to easy victory of the centre over centrifugal tendencies.

Because the Communists came to power in the different provinces at the head of marching armies, there has not been the wide, even if not complete, separation of the personnel of the party, army, police and state administration that existed in Russia.

Prior to 1949 it was difficult to distinguish between party and military leaders, because of the widespread practice whereby the same people held military, party and state offices at the same time. After 1949 this practice continued in the military and administrative committees. Practically all party leaders have a military rank: General Mao Tse-tung, General Chou En-lai, General Teng Hsiaop'ing (general secretary of the party), Marshal Ch'en Yi (foreign minister), etc. The regional military commanders show an impressive continuity if one examines their military careers after liberation and before the establishment of the regions in 1954:

> Ten out of the 13 commanders in the period 1954-58 (of whom eight are still in office either as commander or political commissar) had held leading military positions within the region after liberation. Thus Huang Yung-sheng, commander of Canton until 1958 and again after 1962, had been deputy commander and then commander of Kwangsi military district until 1954, Ch'en Tsai-tao, commander of Wuhan since 1954, had commanded the Honan military district from 1950 onwards. Two more, Teng Hua (Shenyang) and Hsieh Fu-chih (Kunming) were appointed to their military regions after service in Korea. Only one of the 13 original commanders, Wang Hsint'ing (Tsinan), was moved directly from one part of China to another (from Szechwan to Shantung)... Information on political commissars is less revealing. It seems that in many cases until 1958 the posts of commander and commissar were held concurrently, and that their functions were separated and the deputy commissar promoted to full commissar at the time of the Great Leap Forward. (In Inner Mongolia and Sinkiang the posts are still concurrent.) In general, most leading military officers in the field have remained almost stationary within their particular region since the early fifties.[43]

There is a large overlap in the jobs of Political Commissar of the Army and

First Secretary of the Provincial Party Committees.

Out of 15 commissarships identified in or around 1960, nine were held by the first secretary of the province. The commissars of Peking and Shanghai garrisons were also ranking party secretaries. All these appointments appear to date from the Great Leap Forward and the increasing attempts at that time to establish more effective party control over the army. On a much smaller scale, this trend can also be noted in the military regions, where the most recent appointment to the post of political commissar (Tsinan region, 1964) was given to the first party secretary of Shantung, T'an Chi-lung. Earlier, T'ao Chu, the first secretary of Kwantung province, became political commissar of Canton region, relinquishing the post again in 1962. In the key defence areas of Inner Mongolia, Sinkiang and Foochow, the commander and/or commissar since 1954 has also been the party secretary (Wu Lan-fu, Wang En-mao and Yeh Fei).[44]

The tie-in between the security service and the party machine is probably also quite close, although for obvious reasons this cannot be documented.

Stalin used one arm of the bureaucracy against another; if need be, he used the secret police against the party; and when he wanted to purge the secret police itself (as when he got rid of its chief Yagoda in 1936 and, subsequently, his successor, Yezhov, in 1938) he used his own private security organisation, headed by the sinister General Alexander Poskrebyshev. Mao cannot use the same weapons in the same swift and effective way.

A further obstacle to smooth centralised control is the fantastic size of China: in area it is larger than the whole of Europe, but it has a minute railway system, only two thirds the length of Britain's, or a third of India's!

Central sway is also hampered by the fact that a very large proportion of industry is under local administrative control. During the Great Leap Forward the control of industry was decentralised, and this has not been reversed. The changes during those years show clearly in the following figures (percentages):[45]

	1957	1958	1959
Central control	46	27	26
Local control	54	73	74

The increasing dispersal of industry must also strengthen the centrifugal tendencies.

Another factor strengthening the centrifugal tendencies is the impact of neo-NEP conditions—trade and speculation—on farming.[46] There is a great divide between the southern provinces (above all Szechwan province) which have a grain surplus and the northern provinces which are always grain deficient.

(9) On whom can Mao rely?

One of the most striking aspects of the 'Cultural Revolution' is that Mao *did not* mobilise the party with its more than 20 million members, nor the Young Communist League (YCL) and the Pioneers with their 150 million members. Instead he created a new body, the Red Guards. The movement started its own paper, *Red Guard*, on 1 September 1966 soon after the disappearance of *China Youth* on 16 August and *China Youth News*, the daily paper of the Central Committee of the YCL, on 20 August. Since then little has been heard of the YCL, but posters in Peking attacked Hu Yao-pang, First Secretary of the YCL, and other former YCL leaders, who were accused of seeking to 'convert the YCL into a low, popular Komsomol of the Soviet type'.

Why does Mao look to the students for his main support? First, the students are fairly privileged compared with the overwhelming majority of the people. As one professor put it, 'The state provides very favourable conditions for university students to study—annual expenditure for one university student is equivalent to the fruit of labour of six to seven peasants toiling through the entire year'.[47]

Second, the students are not yet integrated into the ruling bureaucracy, and hence are less affected by the moods of those bureaucrats who mellowed under the neo-NEP.

Third, on the whole, students see themselves as a non-specialised section of society, and in a manner of speaking they represent the interests of the 'nation' as against conflicting sectional interests. Students are also most sensitive to the technical lag of their country behind the advanced countries. Participating in the scientific and technical world of the 20th century, they are stifled by the backwardness of their own country. They aspire to industrialisation and modernisation so as to leap from medievalism to the nuclear age.

Fourth, having passed through a radical, revolutionary change in knowledge through their own lifetime—especially if they come from peasant or workers' families—the sky is the limit for them, and Mao's voluntarism strikes a willing chord.[48]

There is also a purely technical reason why Mao finds it so convenient to use the students in his 'Cultural Revolution'. Students' demonstrations are quite easy to organise centrally: by simply closing the schools, or part of them as need be, by fiat. As one English teacher who worked in China for a year described the 'spontaneous' demonstrations:

> If it is a 250,000-man demonstration…then a third of every class will go. If it is a 500,000-man demonstration…then two thirds will go, but if it is a million-man demonstration, the whole college will be out for the whole day.[49]

Closing schools for some nine months is one thing; to close factories—for any length of time—is a totally different business.

Besides the student body, another instrument Mao used is the army. As early as 1960 Lin Piao, the Minister of Defence, had begun to move into the 'cultural struggle'. He founded an Arts Institute in the People's Liberation Army which graduated its first class in 1965. Writers were in 1964 one of the first groups directed to display the revolutionary tradition of the PLA in their work. A novel by a member of a PLA drama troupe, *The Song of Ouyang Hai*, the story of a PLA squad leader, was the most important literary event of the first half of the 1960s. Members of the PLA became authoritative critics of the arts, film, theatre, and literature. When the 'Cultural Revolution' unfolded, key army people grasped complete control over propaganda and agitation: T'ao Chu, former head of the Army Political Department of the Fourth Army, became the new head of propaganda, and Lieutenant-General Hsiao Wang-tung became acting Minister of Culture. Actually, *Liberation Army Daily* made the running in the 'Cultural Revolution' from its inception. It played an incomparably greater role than the party paper, the *People's Daily*. Again and again the PLA has been set up as a revolutionary model for the whole country. There was a frequent coupling of Lin Piao's name with that of Mao, attributing to him, as to no other leader, the distinction of 'creatively' applying Mao's ideas.

At the first mass rally of the 'Cultural Revolution'—18 August—Mao, as well as his wife, Chiang Ch'ing, appeared wearing army uniforms. (Next day the *Liberation Army Daily* published an editorial stressing the great significance of Mao's wearing his military uniform.) Speaking to the rally, Chou En-lai called on the Red Guards to observe the PLA's 'three main rules of discipline and eight points of attention', adding, 'The Red Guards must be built into a highly organised and disciplined militant army with a high level of political consciousness and become the reliable reserve force of the Liberation Army.' Many of those present at the rally wore army-style uniforms and were transported in army lorries.

Since then at every stage of the 'Cultural Revolution'—which for lack of space cannot be described here—and especially its latest stage, that of establishing new authorities (the so-called 'Three-Way Alliance'), the PLA played a central role. There are a number of reasons why the PLA on the whole—notwithstanding provincial and regional centrifugal tendencies—sides with Mao. First of all, the army rises above society. It is identified with national grandeur and above all with the development of a heavy industry/military establishment.

One notion quite widespread in the West, about the egalitarian nature of the PLA, is completely unfounded. The PLA officers are a privileged group. It is true that originally and for many years, the prevailing system provided both officers and men with food and small allowances in lieu of salaries. However in 1955 the system was replaced by cash payments. 'The present scale of pay—which ranges from US$2.50 per month for a private to $192-236 for a full general' is indicative of the differentials.[50] The stratification in the PLA is reflected in privates' cotton uniforms, officers' gabardine; in privates' fourth-class travel in trains, officers'—from captain upwards—first-class fares.

Above all, Mao must know that if political loyalties cannot be imposed on the army, with its advantages of military discipline and total control of personnel, there is no hope at all of regimenting civilian life.

(10) Voluntarism gone mad

The greater the objective impediments—including popular resistance—to the dictates of a centralised state capitalist bureaucracy, the greater the emphasis on voluntarism, on the omnipotence of the will of the righteous people, ie of those who blindly follow the Leader. Maoist voluntarism by far surpasses its Stalinist precursor. Stalin tried to pull Russia up by her bootstraps industrially-militarily; Mao tries to do the same to a country without boots and without straps. Stalin repeated again and again that 'there is nothing that Bolsheviks cannot do'—but he always made it clear that this was by using German techniques or, in later years, American techniques. Mao's whole ideology is the omnipotence of sheer will.

It is this that explains why Mao found it necessary in the midst of the 'Cultural Revolution' to swim nearly 15 kilometres in the Yangtse in just over one hour![51]

This extreme voluntarism of Mao bestows superhuman qualities on him. The cult of Mao far surpasses that of Stalin. To quote a few examples, selected at random: an article entitled 'Chairman Mao, You are the Red Sun in our Hearts', in the theoretical organ of the Central Committee, *Hung Ch'i (Red Flag)*[52] ends like this:

> The seas may dry up, the mountains may rot. The red hearts of us hundreds of militia men who are loyal to you will never change. Whoever opposes you is also removing our hearts and taking our lives. To defend you we are willing to go up mountains of knives, descend into seas of fire. Let our hearts roll and let our hot blood flow.
>
> O, most beloved Chairman Mao, you are the Red Sun in our hearts. We cheer every day and sing every day. There are many intimate words we want to say to you. There are many songs we want to sing to you from the bottoms of our hearts. All words of praise in the world may be exhausted, but they cannot do full justice to your wisdom and greatness. All hymns in the world may be exhausted, but they cannot do full justice to your abundant merits and great achievements. I can't help jumping and shouting at the top of my voice a thousand times, ten thousand times: Long live, long live, long live the great teacher, great leader, great commander, great commander and great helmsman, Chairman Mao!

A paper called *New Sports*, of 19 May 1966, had an article entitled 'A Talk on the Philosophical Problem of Selling Watermelons in a Large City'. The conclusion of the article was that Mao's teachings are the main inspirer for selling watermelons. The *People's Daily* shows a picture of a mother and son reading Mao Tse-tung's book. The title is 'Parents are not so dear as Chairman Mao. Nothing is so good as Chairman Mao's writings'.[53]

New China News Agency quotes a Chinese seaman saying, 'If the water in all seas were ink, it would not suffice for us to write about our warm love for Chairman Mao, nor are thousands of songs adequate to express our gratitude to Chairman Mao'.[54]

One mass meeting of commanders and privates of the PLA sent a message to Mao stating:

Respected and beloved Chairman Mao, if all the trees in the world were pens and all its waters ink we still could not say enough about your love and concern for our upbringing. You are our greatest teacher, leader, supreme commander and helmsman.

(11) Extreme Zhdanovism

To assume that the 'Thoughts of Mao Tse-tung' are omnipotent, one must accept that not only the Leader but also his cultural *aides-de-camp*—the writers, poets, artists, etc—are 'human engineers', 'engineers of the soul'. It demands a rejection of the validity of any artistic creation or tradition taken from the past, as these reflect the limitations of the individual. In 'socialist realism' there are no Hamlets or Othellos—in the real world they are all too common. Zhdanovism is the necessary price of bureaucratic omnipotence. In China, recently, during the 'Cultural Revolution', Zhdanovism reached depths even lower than did its Russian archetype. To quote only a few examples of cultural nihilism:

Yang Hen-sheng, former vice-chairman of the All-China Federation of Literary and Art Circles, was denounced for extolling such bourgeois literary men as Shakespeare, Molière, and Ibsen.[55]

Chou Yang, who translated Chernyshevsky and Tolstoy into Chinese, was accused in *Red Flag* of the crime of praising the 'foreigners' (this word is actually used in the accusation) Belinksy, Chernyshevsky and Dobrolubov.[56] Chou Yang 'stubbornly announced' that 'in aesthetics he was a faithful follower of Chernyshevsky'.[57]

Chao Feng, formerly secretary of the Secretariat of the Association of Chinese Musicians and Vice President of the Central Conservatory of Music, was accused of having 'produced Beethoven's Ninth Symphony which proclaimed "love of mankind" [ie Khrushchevite Revisionist ideology]'.[58] He also 'extolled *Swan Lake*'.[59]

For some 30 years Mao, and his mouthpiece on literary affairs, Chou Yang, had accepted, if critically, the Chinese literary tradition. Yet in the summer of 1966 all the culture of the past—even such classics as *The Dean of the Red Chamber*—was labelled feudal and rejected. All this nihilism in the name of culture!

(12) A new stage in the 'Cultural Revolution'

At the time of writing, the 'Cultural Revolution' has reached a new stage: with the bureaucracy split from top to bottom, the industrial working class has stepped into the arena. For the first time since the Revolution of 1925-27, mass strikes took place in China, in December 1966 and January 1967.

The only source of information regarding the strikes has been the official declarations from the Maoist authorities who opposed them. Hence we cannot be sure of the actual breadth of the strike movement. But that the strikes have been very widespread is clear from the statements of the authorities themselves, who certainly would have liked to conceal them.

A preliminary remark is necessary. The Maoist press explains the strikes as the work of a 'handful of persons in authority within the party who were taking the capitalist road'. This is repeated hundreds of times. It is very doubtful if there is any more truth in this kind of explanation than there is in the usual explanation in the Western capitalist press of strikes in the West as the handiwork of a 'handful of troublemakers'.

A strike of stevedores and dockers in Shanghai port went on for nearly a fortnight.[60] Strikes paralysed railway traffic between Shanghai and Hangchow and between Shanghai and Nanking for 12 days, from 30 December to 10 January 1967.[61] Workers also stopped work at the Yangshupu Power Plant.[62] In Nanking, in the Urban Transport Company, supporters of Mao 'set out to gain control over the company's finances and stopped paying a bonus which had originally been issued to sap the fighting will of the revolutionary workers'.[63] In the Taching Oil Field, the 'handful' used 'material incentives to lure large numbers of workers to leave their production posts'. They were 'using state money to sabotage production'.[64]

Similar stories come from a number of factories: 'A large number of workers at the Shanghai No 17 Textile Mill were taken in and deserted their posts'.[65] In the Shanghai Glassmaking Machinery Factory, the 'handful' deceived a number of workers, including heads of work teams, technical personnel and other cadres in the basic production units, and incited them to desert their production posts. Some of them 'hid blueprints and other technical data, left their posts and of course affected production'.[66] In Shanghai No 2 Camera Plant, as a result of a strike 'only 9.2 percent of the [production] target was completed in the first 14 days of January'.[67] Peking's No 2 Machine-Tool Plant fulfilled 'in the first 18 days of January…only one third of the month's production target'.[68] Seven hundred and fifty workers of the National Cotton Mill No 31 of Shanghai, incited by 'bad elements', left the factory.[69] Similarly, 'a large number of workers at the Shanghai No 17 Textile Mill were taken in and deserted their posts'.[70]

One of the most interesting phenomena is that throughout the 'Cultural Revolution' the trade unions and their daily paper *Kung Jen Jih Pao* was *not once* quoted as playing any role at all.

(13) A missing link

The similarities and differences between the problems facing contemporary China and Russia at the time of her industrialisation drive have been the central themes of the present article. One factor that played a key role in Russia on the eve of her industrialisation and collectivisation drive was the Marxist-Leninist Opposition—the Trotskyist Left Opposition. This, or a tendency similar to it, is completely missing in China.

On the face of it, there is a formal similarity between the Trotskyist programme of the years 1923-28 and the policy of Stalin after 1928. Trotsky, in opposition to the Stalin-Bukharin bloc, advocated economic planning, accelerated industrialisation and the collectivisation of agriculture. Stalin opposed this policy, saying in his usual crude way that the peasant needed a cow; 'he needs Dnieproskroy like he needs a gramophone.'

With Stalin's launching of the FYP in 1928, and subsequently, it seemed as if Stalin simply stole Trotsky's clothes. Many of Trotsky's followers (Preobrazhensky, Radek, Smilga, Smirnov, and so on) believed this to be the case, and decided to join Stalin's bandwagon. With hindsight it is easy to see that there was only a purely formal similarity between Trotskyism and Stalinism.

For Stalin, the workers were the object of industrialisation and planning. They were to be planned, regimented by industrialisation. Collectivisation was to do the same to the peasantry. The workers had to be completely disenfranchised, politically and economically.

For Trotsky, the working class was the *subject* of history, whose self-emancipation—improvement in material and cultural conditions, extended democratic control over all levers of power—were the rungs on the ladder to socialism and communism. To cite at random a few extracts from Trotsky: in November 1928, Trotsky stated that the 'criterion of socialist upswing is constant improvement of labour standards', and wages 'must become the main criterion for measuring the success of socialist revolution'. The 1927 Platform of the Left Opposition called for 'a consistent development of workers' democracy in the party, the trade unions and the Soviets'.[71]

> Workers' democracy means freedom to judge openly all party life, free discussion on it, and also election of the responsible governing personnel and the collegiums from top to bottom.[72]

> The work of the trade unions should be judged primarily by the degree to which it defends the economic and cultural interests of the workers.[73]

> The absolute independence of the shop committee and local committees from the organs of management must be guaranteed.[74]

Trotsky in 1931 said, 'The standard of living of the workers and their role in the state is the highest criterion of socialist success.[75]

If it was axiomatic for Trotsky that the active creator of socialism was the working class, it was also axiomatic that the arena for the establishment of socialism must be international. 'Socialism in one country' is nothing but prostration before the pressures of world capitalism. As long as world capitalism is stronger than the workers' state in one country, and especially in a backward country, its pressures must lead to distortions in the workers' state and finally to its degeneration and collapse.[76]

While there is without doubt a 'Bukharinist' wing in the Chinese Communist Party, and a Stalinist (Maoist) wing even though there are differences between them and their precursors, in their different national and international environments—there is not a Trotskyist or Left Oppositionist wing.

The Left Opposition in Russia represented the continuation of the traditions of the working class which came to power in 1917. The Chinese urban
working class played no role at all in the rise to power of Mao. Hence there is
no Left Opposition inheritance. The workers' strikes in China, therefore, do not
yet find political expression.

However, without indulging in crystal gazing, one may be quite optimistic
about the future development of a revolutionary working class movement in
China. First, the Chinese working class, in absolute terms, is much bigger than
was the Russian in the 1920s—four or five times bigger. Second, while working class activity was quite low in Russia during the years of struggle of the Left
Opposition,[77] in China the movement is rising very stormily. Third, while the
1920s, and even more so the 1930s, were years of working class defeat in one
country after another, today the international scene is much more favourable.
Last, and most important, the crisis in the Russian economic development of
the 1920s could be overcome by sheer Stalinist brute force. In China the impediments to development are much greater, and hence the crisis is much deeper
and more prolonged, and it is bound to effect deep cleavages in the bureaucratic
structure. The crisis from above may also spur on a new, revolutionary working
class political movement below.

Notes

1   Li Fu-chun, *Report on the First Five Year Plan for Development of the National Economy of the
    People's Republic of China in 1953-57* (Peking, 1955), p47.
2   Shigeru Ishikawa, *Long-Term Projections of Mainland China's Economy, 1957-1982* (Tokyo,
    1965), p32.
3   Ibid, p36.
4   Y Gluckstein, *Mao's China* (London, 1957), pp171-172.
5   *New China's Economic Achievements, 1949-52* (Peking, 1952), p196.
6   *New China News Agency* (NCNA), 13 February 1958.
7   Ibid, 19 November 1958.
8   One important sidelight: it has been estimated that the value added in the iron-smelting and
    steel-making Communes sector was actually negative—the product was of lesser value than
    the materials used in the manufacture. See Wu Yuan-li, *The Steel Industry in Communist
    China* (New York, 1965), ch IV.
9   *Jen-min Jih-pao* (JMJP, *People's Daily*), 31 March 1960.
10 Ibid, 27 September 1960.
11 Kung Hsiang-cheng, 'Produce More and Better Light Industrial Products for Daily Use',
    Hung-ch'i (*Red Flag*), 10 February 1962.
12 *JMJP*, 17 April 1962.
13 Y L Wu, F P Hoeber and M M Rockwell, 'The Economic Potential of Communist China'
    (1963), quoted in Choh-ming, 'China's Industrial Development, 1958-63', *China Quarterly*
    no 17, p18.
14 *People's Communes in China* (Peking, 1958), p7.
15 Ibid, p8.
16 *JMJP*, 31 October 1958; *Survey of the Chinese Mainland Press* (SCMP) 1961.
17 NCNA, 26 August 1958.
18 *Chung-kuo Ch'ing-nien Pao* (*China Youth News*), 8 July 1959; SCMP 2086.
19 *JMJP*, 24 August 1959; SCMP 2092.
20 Ibid.

21 *Ta-kung Pao*, 2 June 1965; SCMP 3490.

22 *JMJP*, 19 July 1965; SCMP 3520.

23 *JMJP*, 11 July 1960; SCMP 2301.

24 *Kung Jen Jih Pao* (Peking), 21 July 1961; *Current Background* (CB) (Hong Kong) 669.

25 *Kung Jen Jih Pao*, 28 July 1961; CB 669.

26 *Che Hsueh Yen Chiu* (*Philosophical Study*) no 5, 10 September 1958; *Extracts from China Mainland Magazines* (ECMM) 149.

27 Liu Shao-ch'i, 'The Triumph of Marxism-Leninism in China', *JMJP*, 1 October 1959.

28 *JMJP*, 19 April 1959.

29 Hsu Hsin hsueh, 'Strengthen Further the System of Responsibility in Industrial Enterprises', *Hung-ch'i*, 16 October 1961.

30 *Chung-kuo Ch'ing-nien Pao*, 1 September 1961.

31 Chin Li, 'Discussions in the Very Recent Period by our Country's Economists on Problems of Socialist Economic Accounting', *Ching-chi Yen-chiu* (*Economic Research*), 11 November 1962, pp66-67.

32 'Raise High the Great Red Banner of Mao Tse-Tung's Thought and Carry the Great Proletarian Cultural Revolution to the End', pp18, 17.

33 A Erlich, *The Soviet Industrialisation Debate, 1924-1928* (Cambridge, Mass, 1960).

34 E A Preobrazhensky, 'The Law of Primitive Socialist Accumulation', published in 1924 and then included as a chapter in E A Preobrazhensky, *New Economics* (Moscow, 1926), vol 1, part 1, pp57-58, published in English as *The New Economics* (Oxford, 1965).

35 A Erlich, op cit, p16.

36 Ibid, pp81-82.

37 Ibid, p79.

38 Ibid, p78.

39 Lu Hsu'n and Li Yün, 'On the Practice of Economy', *JMJP*, 21 August 1962; SCMP 2817.

40 Sun Meng-ming, 'On the Proportional Relationship between Industry and Agriculture', *Ta-kung Pao*, 15 June 1962; SCMP 2882 (my emphasis).

41 Ouyang Ch'eng, 'Concerning the Question of Harmony or Disharmony in the Proportional Relationship between Industry and Agriculture', *Ta-kung Pao*, 22 October 1962; SCMP 2863 (my emphasis). Once the concept that industry will not get resources from agriculture is accepted, more care must be given to cost-accounting, as the profit of the industrial plant is the source of capital accumulation. (During forced industrialisation, with the emphasis on heavy industry and the exploitation of farming, the *gross volume* of industrial output was accepted as the criterion of success.) On 19 July 1962, the *People's Daily* published an article by two economists who are generally identified with the less liberal wing, in which the following statement occurs: 'Cost accounting is the foundation of economic accounting of enterprises... We believe that we should principally use the cost target and the profit target for the evaluation of the economic results of the enterprises, the two being equally important... In spite of the fact that there are defects to the profit target, it is, after all, the quality target for the whole work of enterprises. It includes results that cannot be reflected by the cost target, and it is also the principal basis for the calculation of accumulation for the state because the realisation of the financial budget of the state is represented by the profits that have been paid to the government' (Yang Jun-jui and Li Hsün, 'A Tentative Discussion on Economic Accounting of Industrial Enterprises,' *JMJP*, 19 July 1962; SCMP 2817).

42 Yang Ch'i-hsien, 'On the Need to Arrange National Economic Plans in the Order of Agriculture, Light Industry and Heavy Industry', *Ta-kung Pao*, 11 December 1961; SCMP 2649.

43 J Gittings, 'Military Control and Leadership, 1949-1964', *China Quarterly*, no 26, p95.

44 Ibid, pp99-100.

45 Choh-ming Li, 'China's Industrial Development, 1958-63', *China Quarterly*, no 17, p16.

46 For some time in 1961 the official retail price of rice in Nanking was 0.13 yuan per shih catty (1.1lb) while the free market price was 3 yuan. The official price of cooking oil in Shanghai was 0.61 yuan per catty while the free market price was 30 yuan (*JMJP*, 14 March

1961; Yuan-li Wu, *The Economy of Communist China* (London, 1965), p96). The scarcity conditions with the lag of agricultural output behind population growth explain these huge differences.

47 *Chung-kuo Ch'ing-nien Pao*, 21 July 1962; SCMP 2795.

48 These generalisations are very schematic. It must be borne in mind that students are not an island separated from the rest of society, hence they do not constitute a homogeneous body which supports Mao completely in the 'Cultural Revolution'.

49 D Lowry, 'Teaching English in China', *China Quarterly*, no 24, p7.

50 E Snow, *The Other Side of the River: Red China Today* (New York, 1962), p289.

51 Incidentally, this achievement was so staggering that the president of the World Professional Marathon Swimming Federation, Senor Carlos Larriera, invited Mao to enter two ten-mile swimming races in Canada since his reported time was almost four times as fast as the world record for 10 miles.

52 1 October 1966.

53 *JMJP*, 22 September 1966.

54 NCNA, 10 January 1967.

55 *Kuang-ming Jih-pao*, 27 December 1966; SCMP 3681.

56 *Hung-ch'i*, 1 January 1967.

57 Ibid.

58 The Maoists, it seems, have not noticed that Karl Marx had a lifelong admiration for Shakespeare, that Lenin loved Beethoven and that Chernyshevsky had a decisive formative influence on Lenin!

59 *Kuang-ming Jih-pao*, 22 January 1967; SCMP 3872.

60 *Hung-ch'i*, 1 February 1967; SCMM 564.

61 NCNA, 9 February 1967.

62 Ibid, 16 January 1967.

63 Ibid, 14 January 1967.

64 Ibid, 15 January 1967.

65 Ibid, 9 January 1967.

66 Ibid, 15 January 1967.

67 Ibid, 17 February 1967.

68 *JMJP*, 2 February 1967; SCMP 3881.

69 NCNA, 28 January 1967.

70 Ibid, 9 January 1967.

71 L Trotsky, *The Real Situation in Russia* (London, 1928), p100.

72 Ibid, p 129.

73 Ibid, p56.

74 Ibid, p57.

75 L Trotsky, *Problems of the Development of the USSR* (New York, 1931), p40.

76 Bukharin was *formally* further away from Trotsky than Stalin—both Stalin and Trotsky suggested planning, accelerated industrialisation and collectivisation, while Bukharin did not. But in content Bukharin was much nearer to Trotsky. He still represented a wing of Bolshevism. He reflected the pressure of factory managers and trade-union bureaucrats on Bolshevism, but did not, like Stalin, repudiate all the aspirations of Bolshevism, did not aim at the total expropriation of the political and economic rights of the workers. The fact, too, that the supporters of both Trotsky and Bukharin were massacred by Stalin suggests the degree of basic agreement between both and Bolshevism.

77 The number of workers involved in strikes in state-owned enterprises in Russia, was: 1922, 192,000; 1923, 165,000; 1924, 43,000; 1925, 34,000; 1926, 32,900; 1927, 20,000.

Marxism and the collectivisation of agriculture

International Socialism (first series) 19, Winter 1964-65

One of the most important problems for world socialism is the interrelation of the peasantry and the reorganisation of agriculture in cooperative, or collective, farms. This is especially so as two thirds of humanity are peasants and as the chain of world capitalism again and again breaks at its weakest links—the agrarian countries.

In this article I shall deal with Marx's approach to the subject and that of his followers, particularly Kautsky and Lenin. But before embarking on it a few preliminary remarks need to be made. First, for lack of space, the present article does not deal with latifundia agriculture (as in Cuba prior to Castro). Second, it uses little historical demonstration, except what is absolutely necessary to illustrate the argument. Third, it is a revisionist article.

This last point needs some comment. It is very common for Marxists to speak about Marxism as a science and not a dogma, needing, as all sciences, persistent criticism and revision in face of empirical data. But while the principle is accepted by many who claim to be Marxists, a real critical evaluation of Marx's dicta is frequently lacking. Marxism is transformed into a suprahistorical theory, a religious dogma. But religion, after all, is 'the opium of the people'. So if the reader of the present article finds that the author deviates *radically* from Marx's statements regarding agriculture and its cooperative reorganisation, he must remember that he was warned.

Introduction

For Marx the socialist revolution depended on the predominance of large-scale enterprise in industry, commerce and banking, which would make possible the expropriation of the capitalists by workers organised into collectivities in the actual process of capitalist production. He envisaged the embryo of socialism—the large socialised enterprise—growing inside capitalism itself, ready to emerge complete into life. Marx, as we shall see later, presumed that under capitalism, in agriculture no less than in industry, the victory of large-scale social production was assured, alive though he was to the fact that the impediments in the path of large-scale farming are relatively far greater than those in the path of large-scale industry, and hence that the speed of capital concentration in agriculture is slower than in industry proper.

If, however, history shows that small-scale production continues to be predominant in agriculture, scarcely evincing any tendency to wither away and be replaced by large-scale enterprise, our idea of post-revolutionary agriculture naturally has to undergo radical modification.

This is especially so, as socialism—involving planning and the abolition of the exploitation of man by man—cannot by its very nature be envisaged in industry, banking and commerce as long as individual production and competition—and hence planlessness and inequality—prevail in the countryside. The two systems could be visualised existing side by side for a time, both cooperating and clashing with each other. But after a certain lapse, unless the collectivist system were to attain a predominant position, progressively invading and finally undermining the individualist sector of production, the march towards socialism and its eventual victory would be wholly thwarted.

Associated with Marx's assumption of the victory of large over small farming is a second assumption, that the rural population will become differentiated into ever more clearly defined social classes: a small minority of rich farmers and a growing majority of agricultural workers, the latter progressively freeing itself from the influence and authority of the village nabobs. Marx's policy was based on an alliance of the industrial with the agricultural working class against the capitalists of town and country.

Now, if the victory of the large over the small farm were not as sharply defined as Marx assumed, the process of class differentiation in the rural population would necessarily remain less distinct. It follows that it would be difficult for the Marxist party to find for the industrial working class allies in the rural areas who are not attached to private property and individual farming, and are bent on collectivisation. Having to bid for the support not only of the rural wage earners, but also for the support of all *peasants*, would necessitate a basic change in the Marxist concept of the struggle for socialism in the countryside.

Again Marx foresaw the socialist revolution breaking out in the most advanced industrial countries. Had this occurred, had revolution swept through countries like Britain or the United States, then however incorrect Marx's prognosis might have been regarding the future of small farming under capitalism, and however unclear the differentiation of agricultural workers—natural allies in the struggle for the collectivisation of agriculture—from the rest of the rural population, the modifications necessary in the policies of the Marxist parties would have been marginal. For agriculture is indeed only marginal to the national economies of Britain or the United States. But when the revolution broke out in a predominantly backward agricultural country, as Russia was in 1917, these difficulties loomed more ominously. One and the same problem, posed in different historical contexts, can have entirely different implications.

Finally, Marx also believed that immediately after the socialist revolution the highly developed industry of the advanced countries would provide the material resources to help agriculture along the road to complete cooperative organisation. Industry would assist agriculture to develop, to transform itself. Marx never posed the question, what path would agricultural collectivisation follow where it was *not* enriched by a bountiful industry, but where instead it had to build industry up, where agriculture was exploited to carry out the uncompleted industrial revolution?

The above short, schematic counterposing of Marx's ideas on collectivisation of agriculture with the actual historical circumstances in which the problem has time and again been posed rather runs ahead of the story. Let us turn back, then, to Marx's views on the future of agriculture.

Marx: the peasantry doomed under capitalism

When dealing with Marx's attitude to the peasantry, it must be remembered that the core of his research and analysis was the transition from capitalism to socialism. He looked upon the peasantry as a class as a social form characteristic of the feudal order, an untypical survival inside capitalism of an obsolete social order, which capitalism would drive out of existence. In the *Communist Manifesto* Marx and Engels forecast the doom of the peasantry as of other petty bourgeois groups. Replying to a question on the attitude of Communists to the property of these groups, they said:

> Are you speaking of the petty bourgeois, of the small peasant property which was before the bourgeois property? We do not need to do away with it. The evolution of industry has done, and is daily doing away with it.

The International Workingmen's Association reiterated the same ideas in its Manifesto of 1869, stating that capitalism and science 'condemn small-scale peasant farming to gradual extinction, without appeal and without mercy'.

So long as the peasantry and other petty bourgeois groups hold on to their property, they try to 'roll back the wheel of history'. The peasantry, Marx wrote, is 'the class that represents barbarism without civilisation'.[1] Together with other petty bourgeois groups, they are not only conservative, but reactionary.

> If by chance they are revolutionary, they are so only in view of their impending transfer into the proletariat; they thus defend not their present, but their future, interests; they desert their own standpoint to place themselves at that of the proletariat.[2]

Again in his life's work, *Capital*—where in analysing the capitalist order Marx used, it is true, an abstract model and not a picture of existing society (but a model nevertheless that sought to demonstrate the *lines* along which capitalism was developing)—he found no place for the peasants or for other small producers. They were destined, it seems, to disappear with the advance of capitalism.

However, in further work on the problem, and especially in volume III of

Capital, Marx made some reservations regarding the future of the peasantry under capitalism. When he explained his theory of rent (part IV of volume III) he restricted his analysis to the English type of landownership and rent. Here there were only three social groups in the countryside: landowners, capitalists and wage workers, a scheme of things which left no place for the peasantry. But he makes it very clear that this is only *one* model. He ends this section with a short analysis of an alternative model, with small peasant farmers in the role of sellers and debtors subordinated to trade and money capital, and a resulting degeneration of agriculture. He makes it clear that the latter model is a less pure form of capitalist development in agriculture, and he does not state whether under the continued development of capitalism peasant farming would be swept away by the victory of large-scale production. Thus it is true to say that Marx, in further elaborating his great work, intended to move the English type of landownership away from the centre of the stage. Indeed Engels stated in his preface to the third volume of *Capital* that Marx intended to rewrite the part on rent, with Russia, rich in a 'variety of forms of real estate and the exploitation of the agricultural producer', playing an equal role to that of England in the first volume, which deals with industry and industrial wage labour.[3] It need scarcely be remarked that the 'variety of forms' did not include the English model of large farms.

It would be erroneous to conclude from this, however, that Marx ever abandoned the central theme that small farming is doomed under capitalism: Russia, after all, did not represent a capitalist, but a pre-capitalist, semi-feudal society. On the contrary, till the end of his life Marx took it for granted that small-scale agricultural production was doomed: 'Large industry and large agriculture on an industrial scale work together'.[4]

Marx's conception of the prospects of the peasantry under capitalism must undoubtedly have been influenced by the fact that since 1850 he had lived in the only country in the world where the peasantry had practically disappeared and large-scale farming was predominant.

Marx on the role of the peasantry in the socialist revolution

Marx argued that inside capitalism, that is, after the bourgeoisie's rise to power, the peasantry is a reactionary force to the extent that it is still attached to property. Thus he says that it was 'the relentless property fanaticism of the peasant' which in 1848 isolated the Parisian working class and led to the defeat of the revolution.[5]

Only insofar as the peasant becomes conscious of the hopelessness of individual farming can he play a progressive, even revolutionary, role. When:

> ...the French peasant parts with his belief in his smallholding...the proletarian revolution obtains that chorus without which its solo song in all peasant nations becomes a swan song.[6]

History was to show time and again that when individual farming was threatened by capitalist development, as for instance in Germany during the great depression of the 1930s, the peasant did not join the proletarian revolution as a 'chorus' but sided with its enemies.[7]

Marx and Engels on land distribution among the peasants

Because Marx saw in small farming a remnant of feudalism being crushed and swept away under the advance of capitalism, his attitude to private peasant land ownership when it faced capitalist ownership differed from his attitude when it faced large feudal ownership.

It is clear that Marx supported the small peasants' struggle for the distribution of large feudal properties, while he always rejected the support of small property in opposition to large capitalist property and gave priority to collective production, wherever he believed that it could be established in place of individual production. Collective ownership was to be supported against small private ownership.

The Communist League of Germany's programme of 1848 stated:

> The royal and other feudal estates, all mines, pits, etc, shall be transformed into state property. On these estates agriculture is to be conducted on a large scale and with the most modem scientific means for the benefit of all society.[8]

The Address of the Central Council to the Communist League of Germany, written by Marx in 1850, warned the German comrades against allowing the landed estates to be handed over to the peasants as had been done in the French Revolution:

> The first point on which the bourgeois democrats will come into conflict with the workers will be the abolition of feudalism. As in the first French Revolution, the petty bourgeois will give the feudal lands to the peasants as free property. That is to say, try to leave the rural proletariat in existence and form a petty bourgeois peasant class which will go through the same cycle of impoverishment and indebtedness which the French peasant is now going through.
>
> The workers must oppose this plan in the interests of the rural proletariat and in their own interests. They must demand that the confiscated feudal property remains state property and be converted into labour colonies cultivated by the associated rural proletariat with all the advantages of large-scale agriculture through which the principle of common property immediately obtains a firm basis in the midst of the tottering bourgeois property relations.[9]

The same idea reappeared in 1869 in the resolution of the Basle Congress of the International Workingmen's Association on agrarian policy. It called upon the agricultural workers to form a 'labourers' union' which would take possession of state, church and large-estate lands.[10]

Again Engels, in a letter to Bebel on 11 December 1884, wrote:

> The demand should be made that *the great demesnes which are not yet broken up should*

be let out to cooperative societies of agricultural labourers for joint farming.[11]

Thus, while Marx and Engels supported bourgeois peasant property in the struggle against feudalism, they argued that in the socialist revolution distribution of the large estates among private owners should be opposed, and instead these estates should be transformed into cooperatively run large farms.

Despite certain shifts in Marx's views on farming, certain assumptions remain constant:

(1) Large farming under capitalism is bound to crush small farming out of existence, whether at a quicker or slower pace, entirely or not quite completely;

(2) The defence of small-scale farming is reactionary;

(3) The ally of the industrial working class in the struggle for socialism is the agricultural working class;

(4) The socialist revolution denotes the immediate transformation of large estates into state or cooperative property.

We shall find that Marx's followers—Karl Kautsky, Rosa Luxemburg, Lenin, Trotsky—in the main followed Marx's position on the basic question of the historical role of the peasantry in bourgeois and socialist revolutions, on the attitude of socialists to land distribution, and on the means for making agricultural production cooperative. However, on the prospects of small farming versus large farming as the process of industrialism proceeded—a question of prime importance for the whole problem—Kautsky and Lenin, the two main exponents of a Marxist analysis of agricultural economics, held a position which was more ambivalent than Marx's; they were much less definite about the victory of large over small farming consequent upon capitalist development.

Kautsky

Soon after the appearance of the Third Volume of *Capital* in 1894 Marx's theory of the concentration of capital in agriculture and the victory of large over small farming came under attack from the German 'Revisionists' Eduard Bernstein and Eduard David. To support their argument they used the German population census of 1895 which showed that since the previous census of 1882 small and medium farms had lost no ground at all.

The foremost Marxist theoretician of the time, Karl Kautsky, dealt with the problem in *Die Agrarfrage* (*The Agrarian Question*), 1889, which is the most important and elaborate work ever published on the subject. While vehemently attacking Bernstein and David, Kautsky in practice shifted *radically* from Marx's concept regarding the withering away of the small farm under capitalism.

Kautsky began with an acceptance of the existence of basic differences between the paths of capitalist development in agriculture and in industry:

There is not the slightest doubt—we are prepared to accept this *a priori*—that agriculture does not develop according to the pattern in industry: it is subject to special laws.[12]

There are branches of agriculture, he argued, in which small production can

compete successfully with large production—for example, vegetable garden-
ing, vine growing, etc.[13] But these branches occupy a position subordinate to the
principal branches of agriculture—grain and livestock. And in the latter sectors 'large-scale production is decidedly superior to small production'.[14]

He went on to enumerate factors which made large-scale farming superior to
small-scale. The large farm saves on animals, implements, houses, etc, per unit
of land. The smaller the agricultural area, the larger the relative portion of land
lost on boundary demarcations. The large farm uses *absolutely* more equipment,
and can therefore turn a more advanced division of labour to better advantage.
It derives far greater benefit from the specialisation of machinery and other
equipment than the small farm, and there is certain machinery that it alone can
use. The same applies to livestock. The small farmer uses a cow in numerous ways:
milking, draft work and breeding. Specialisation of livestock is possible only in
large farms. As regards specialisation and cooperation of labour, the large farm
again has decisive advantages over the small. It can employ specialists.[15] It keeps
workshops beyond the means of the small farm for the repair of machinery and
the making of simple implements.[16] It can arrange buildings and organise irrigation
to better advantage than the small farm.[17] Above all, 'the more capitalistic agriculture becomes, the more it develops the qualitative difference between the technique of small production and that of large-scale production'.[18]

Added to the advantages of the large farm in the sphere of production are
many more in the field of trade and credit: 'There is no field in which the advantages of the large farm over the small one are greater than in that of trade'.[19]

The position of the small farmer among the sellers and buyers in the market
is very weak. His knowledge of the market situation is poor. His ability to take
advantage of favourable, or safeguard himself in advance against unfavourable,
circumstances is minimal. To make matters more difficult, his dealings in the
market, unlike those of the small artisan, are very varied. While a shoemaker
needs to buy, besides implements, only leather, nails and cord, and sells only
shoes, a farmer, in addition to equipment, has to buy livestock, seeds, fodder,
fertilisers, insecticides, etc, and to sell livestock, grain, milk, butter, eggs, etc.
'There is no other art as dependent on trade as his.' This dependence is most
binding when the trader is also the usurer and when the farmer is compelled,
in order to pay his debts, to sell his goods at any price.[20]

But Kautsky argues that there are some important factors which prevent the
complete victory of large farming over small. First, the use of machinery en-
counters greater difficulties in agriculture than in industry, partly for technical
reasons connected with the layout of the land, etc, partly because of the sea-
sonal nature of agriculture, which makes it relatively more expensive to keep
machinery, and partly because low wages in agriculture make the use of machinery less profitable than it would be if wages were higher.[21]

Second, the cost of internal transport, and the wastage it too involves, tends
to limit the optimal size of the farm more than in the case of industrial plant.[22]

Third, the more intensive the farm, the more important is the transport
factor in restricting the optimal size of the farm, owing to the greater amount

of fertilisers, seeds, etc, which have to be transported per unit of land.[23]

Fourth, the larger the farm, the higher the cost of supervising labour. Under capitalism, for which strict labour supervision is necessary, this factor is important in limiting the size of the farm.[24]

Fifth, as the main source of labour for the large farm is the offspring of the small farmers, if the number of small farms goes down, the supply of labour power to the large farms dwindles.[25] A shortage of workers due to emigration of the rural population compels the big landowners to allot land to the agricultural workers in order to create a small peasantry which will then provide labour power for the landlords. (Marx actually mentioned this factor in an article in the *Neue Rheinische Zeitung* as early as 1850, as a limitation on the growth of large farming.)

A sixth factor helping to preserve the small farm is the policy of capitalist governments, which, increasingly threatened by socialism, try to bolster up the small farms as a factor of social conservatism and stability.[26]

And seventh, a feature distinguishing agriculture from industry is the natural limit to the supply of land, the most important agricultural means of production. In industry there is no such natural limit to an increase in the quantity of means of production. There the accumulation of capital, that is, the use of part of the profit to increase the means of production, can be carried out independently of the concentration of capital, that is, the concentration of many capitals into a small number of agglomerated masses. And this accumulation usually precedes concentration. The large capital becomes larger and larger until it undermines the independence of the small capitals. This undermining is generally the *result* and *not the prerequisite* of the creation of large capital—in order to build a shoe factory one does not have to *start* with the expropriation of the small shoemakers. The situation in agriculture is just the opposite: entirely dependent on land as it is, the expropriation of the small farms, moreover in a continuous area, is a precondition for the building up of a large farm. Thus the private ownership of the land hampers the concentration and accumulation of capital in agriculture.[27]

All these factors, however, could only retard the victory of large over small farming for a time. But there is one paramount factor, according to Kautsky, which prevents the disappearance of the small farm, and which overshadows all the others. After arguing the case for the overall technical superiority of large-scale production in agriculture, he asks, 'What can small production set off against the advantage of large-scale production?' And he replies, 'The greater diligence and greater care of the worker who, unlike the hired labourer, works for himself, and the low level of requirements of the small independent farmer which is even lower than that of the agricultural labourer'.[28]

Not only the small farmer himself, but his children too, are made to toil to the limit.[29] Their willingness to work day and night, a willingness not characteristic of the agricultural labourer, is of particular importance in the busy seasons.[30] Kautsky goes on to quote a large number of facts from France, England and Germany to support the argument that overwork and undernourishment are the main bulwark of small farming.

Lenin

Lenin accepted Kautsky's *Die Agrarfrage* without reservation, and his theoretical writings on the subject of large versus small farms were largely repetitions and elaborations of Kautsky's arguments aided by new statistical data. Any deviations from Kautsky were in the direction of greater emphasis on the ruination of small farming under capitalism. Thus he wrote:

> The fundamental and main trend of capitalism is the elimination of small production by large-scale production both in industry and in agriculture. But this process must not be taken only in the sense of immediate expropriation. This elimination process also includes a process of ruination, of deterioration of the conditions of farming of the small farmers which may extend over years and decades. This deterioration manifests itself in overwork or underfeeding of the small farmer; in an increased burden of debt; in the deterioration of cattle fodder and the condition of the cattle in general; in the deterioration of the methods of cultivating and manuring the land; in the stagnation of technical progress, etc.[31]

And again:

> Small production in agriculture is doomed to extinction and to an incredibly crushed, oppressed position under capitalism... Being dependent on big capital, and being backward compared with large-scale production in agriculture, small production can hold on only because of the desperately reduced consumption and laborious, arduous toil. The dispersion and waste of human labour, the worst forms of dependence of the producer, exhaustion of the strength of the peasant family, of peasant cattle and peasant land—this is what capitalism brings to the peasant everywhere.[32]

The stubborn facts

Whatever the factors working for or against the survival of small farms, the march of two centuries of capitalism has shown in incontrovertible form that agriculture *did not* follow industry in concentrating the major portion of production in a small number of farm units. Even accepting all Kautsky's and Lenin's arguments, the decisive fact remains: the production unit in agriculture is extremely small, large-scale production is not predominant, and agriculture as a whole is atomised into millions of relatively tiny units of production. And as years pass into generations, the small farms show no inclination to disappear.

In Britain, for instance, the country of large-scale farming *par excellence*, which served as a model for Marx's study of capitalist agriculture, the concentration in farming is very far behind that in manufacturing industry. It is estimated that in 1957 some 77 percent of regular full time workers in England and Wales were on farms employing fewer than 11 people, and 53 percent were in units with fewer than five. The following table compares the concentration in a branch of industry and in agriculture:[33]

Size of unit	Percentage of total workers employed	
Number of workers	Mechanical engineering industry	Agriculture
1–4	}3	53
5–10		24
11–25	2	14
25–49	4	6
50–99	}3 7	2
100–1,000	44	1
1,000 and above	40	0

In fact, since Marx wrote *Capital* the number of wage earners in British agriculture has not increased either absolutely or relatively compared with the number of farms, but on the contrary has considerably declined. The total number of farms in Britain recorded in 1851 was 303,000, while in 1951 it was practically the same, 302,000. Meanwhile the number of agricultural contract workers declined from 1,473,000 to 544,000.[34] The distribution of farm staffs in England and Wales in 1851 and 1951 was as follows:

Number of regular workers per farm	Percentage of workers	
	1851	1941
1	5.0	13.2
2	8.4	17.1
3	7.8	12.9
4	8.5	9.6
5–6	11.6	12.1
7–9	11.9	10.0
10–19	24.7	13.1
20 and over	22.1	12.0

In 1851, 18.6 percent of the farms had regular staffs of five or more workers and there were 16,500 farms with ten or more workers. In 1941 only 8.3 percent of the farms employed five or more workers, while the number of farms employing ten or more workers was reduced to 6,800. At the other end of the scale the number of farms staffed entirely by the occupier and his wife with one regular worker in addition increased from 117,700 in 1851 to 192,800 in 1941.[35]

In other capitalist countries too there are few wage workers in agriculture. Thus, for instance, in Austria 79 percent of the total farm labour force, according to the 1951 census, was accounted for by owners of holdings and members of their families, and only 21 percent consisted of hired labourers. The corresponding figures for Ireland were 85 and 15 percent.[36] In Germany the corresponding figures (in 1933) were 76 and 24 percent.[37] In France the 1954 census revealed that, out of 5.1 million people engaged in agriculture, only 1.2 million, or some 23.5 percent, were farm labourers.[38]

It is true there are vast corporations and other farms in the United States, which control the major part of the sale of farm products. But even here the small unit is *incomparably* more stubborn than in industry. Thus in 1950, out of a total labour force of 10.4 million in agriculture in the US, only 2.3 million, or 17.4 percent, were hired workers. It was estimated that there were an average of 1.5 million male wage and salary workers in agriculture, compared with 4.1 million male farmers, and 0.7 million male members of farmers' families working in agriculture. Thus only 24 percent of all males engaged in agriculture were wage or salary workers.[39]

Moreover, the number of wage workers in US agriculture has declined more quickly than the number of farmers. Thus between 1929 and 1948 the number of people employed in US agriculture declined from 11.3 million to 10.7 million, or by 5.3 percent, while the number of hired workers declined from 2.98 million to 2.31 million, or by 22.5 percent.[40]

If one accepts Lenin's contention, in his discussion of US agriculture, that the volume of hired labour is the most direct indication of the development of capitalist operations in agriculture, then it must be argued that, while capitalism in general has advanced, capitalism in agriculture has hardly advanced at all, in fact has even retreated in the most advanced industrial countries.

Now, as we have seen, one of the basic assumptions underlying Marx's policy for the socialist transformation of agriculture was the great superiority of large farming over small, a superiority which would lead to the existence of a considerable sector of farms under capitalism that would serve as a point of support for the general process of making farm production cooperative after the socialist revolution. The above facts undermine this assumption.

Social stratification in the countryside

Rooted in the idea of the assumed victory of large farming under capitalism was the related notion that there would be increasingly clear demarcation of the agricultural wage earners into a class separate and distinct from the property owners. On this Marx and Engels, Kautsky and Lenin based their strategy: they relied on the rural wage earners to carry out the socialist revolution and the cooperative organisation of farming against the rich peasants.

Unhappily for this assumption, class divisions in the countryside are much more obscure than in the towns. In town one can easily distinguish between a manufacturer, large or small, and a wage earner, and the passage from one class to another is infrequent and difficult. In the countryside, owing to the fact that large farming has not the same superiority over small as large manufacturing over artisanry, mobility between the classes is great, and there is a frequent changeover from wage earner to poor peasant, poor peasant to middle peasant, but much more often in the opposite direction. Since the land is divisible, and since division does not noticeably alter its productivity, it can be split up among the farmer's heirs, each of whom can then easily slip from middle farmer to poor farmer to wage earner.

Furthermore, there are fine gradations between wage earners and farmer owners. Besides pure wage earners there is a chequered field of subcontractors and share-croppers who are essentially wage earners paid by results. Some share-tenants are workers who contribute little more than their labour to operations, while others may own a considerable share of the working capital. Then there are owners of dwarf holdings who also depend largely on earning wages to eke out a living. Thus it was estimated towards the end of the last century that as many as '75 percent of the agricultural workers in France have their own land'.[41]

In the advanced capitalist countries the borderlines between different sections of the agricultural population are more distinct than in backward countries.[42] They are nevertheless still very much less clearcut than in the towns. It does not, of course, follow that the farmer who employs only one or two agricultural workers is less of a taskmaster than the industrial employer of hundreds of thousands. As one scholar has aptly observed, 'A landowner need not possess half a million acres to be extortionate; in fact, slender means may invigorate his greed'.[43]

Even among farmers themselves the small tend much more to petty oppression than the large.

Another indication of the indistinct differentiation between agricultural wage earners and small farmers, pointed out already by Kautsky, is the frequently paltry differences in living standards. As one agricultural economist said:

> I do not know any life in which the worker is more engrossed, more held to his job, as we say, with his nose to the grindstone, than the life of the small farmer...
> The farm worker who is working on regular hours and who is working for a regular wage has a very much easier time of it than the farmer who is working his own farm. The children of the farm worker have a very much easier time of it than the children of the small farmer... I have seen the children in Denmark; I have seen them in Germany; I have seen them in a good many of the European countries; and wherever I go I find the same thing is true of farm life, that the children are robbed of their childhood, robbed of their youth, and that it must be so, otherwise the family farm cannot keep going.[44]

The social boundary between an agricultural wage earner and a poor farmer is even more indistinct than the economic. In the close community organisation of the relatively isolated village, blood relationships gloss over real interest conflicts and produce strong pressures towards social conformity. The tradition of accepting the authority of the rich and 'cultured' is much more difficult to break down in the intimate unity of the village than in the towns.

The organisation of the agricultural workers in trade unions has not developed very highly even in the most advanced capitalist countries, for various reasons. Workers there are more anxious to escape from agriculture than to organise to protect themselves as agricultural workers. Agriculture is not regarded as an occupation for life by many of those who start off in it as wage earners, particularly in the case of the more vigorous and enterprising. The dispersal of workers over wide areas hampers the formation of trade union branches sufficiently large to give them a sense of community. A large proportion live in tied cottages owned by the employer and occupied by the worker only so long as he works for the same employer, and this leads to a lack of freedom and status which makes self-reliance and organisation more difficult. In addition education is considerably below that in the towns, and rural children are generally taken from school at an earlier age.

The backwardness of the wage earners in agriculture and the obscurity of the boundary between them and the small farmers are clearly stumbling blocks in the way of implementing Marx's policy of counterposing the collectivism of the wage earners to the individualism of the petty bourgeois farmers. We therefore find Marxist parties repeatedly deviating from reliance on the rural poor alone to a policy aimed at influencing the whole of the agricultural community, or at least a sizeable section of middle farmers.

Engels shortly before his death found it necessary to criticise the French Marxists for making concessions to small-peasant individualism in their efforts to appeal to the peasantry as a whole.[45]

The Bolsheviks too, during the revolution and civil war, did not in practice differentiate clearly between the agricultural workers and rural poor on the one hand, and the middle or even rich peasants on the other. Lenin declared, it is true, that the Soviet government was 'to help the toiling peasant, not to injure the middle peasant, and to constrain the rich peasant'.[46] But this declaration was hardly translated into deeds. In the act of the expropriation of the landowners, the peasantry as a whole remained largely united. This unity apparently came to an end *after* the expropriation, when the Bolsheviks, seeking grain for the towns, hard hit by the civil war and the hunger it entailed, thought that by carrying out grain requisitions against the rich peasants with the help of the poor peasants they would at the same time split the peasantry into different contending classes.

In May 1918 workers' food detachments were organised by the Commissariat of Supply, whose main function was to assist in the collection of grain. Their allies in the countryside were to be the newly-formed Committees of Poor Peasants (*Kombedy*) to which the whole rural population except rich peasants, landlords, traders and manufacturing employers of hired labour could elect or be elected. The poor peasants were to be rewarded for their services by obtaining allocations of grain from the quantities seized.

Lenin saw in the establishment of the Committees of Poor Peasants and the food detachments the splitting up of the peasantry into antagonistic classes and the beginning of the socialist revolution in the countryside. 'It is only in the summer and autumn of 1918', he wrote at the time, 'that our countryside is itself experiencing its October (ie, proletarian) revolution'.[47] A little later he described the creation of the Committees of Poor Peasants as 'a turning point of gigantic importance in the whole course of development and the building of our revolution', and as a step by which 'we passed the boundary which separates the bourgeois from the socialist revolution'.[48] In the heat of the moment Bolshevik leaders even believed that a firm start on the immediate collectivisation of agriculture was at hand. Thus the same congress at which Lenin made the speech from which the words quoted above were taken (the First All-Russian Congress of Land Sections, Committee of Poor Peasants and Agricultural Communes, December 1918) passed a resolution declaring that the main aim of agricultural policy must be 'the consistent and unswerving pursuit of the organisation of agricultural communes, Soviet Communist farms and the socialised working of the land'.[49]

It was the intention of the Bolsheviks that a sizeable portion of the estates should not be subject to distribution but be retained as model state farms. The annexe to the Land Decree signed by Lenin on 8 November referred explicitly to 'territories where cultivation is of a high order: gardens, plantations, nurseries for plants and trees, orchards, etc' as 'not subject to division', being reserved for 'the exclusive use of the state or district as model institutions'; and similarly, 'studs, state and private cattle breeding establishments, poultry farms'.

However, the peasants encroached deeply into the sectors Lenin intended to keep free from distribution. For example, only 2 to 3 million acres of estates which had been run as beet sugar farms were retained as state farms instead of the 10 to 12 million acres that had originally been intended.[50]

The establishment of the Committees of Poor Peasants as a means of splitting the peasantry into contending classes also proved extremely unsuccessful. The committees were in existence only a few months, when the Bolshevik leaders had to disband them.[51] (Actually the revolution itself, by giving land to the rural poor, turned them into middle peasants and thus helped to obliterate class boundaries among the peasantry.)[52]

By no stretch of strategy or tactics could the Bolsheviks overcome the basic contradiction in the Russian Revolution—that it was carried out by two different, opposed classes, the proletariat and the peasantry, the former collectivist, the latter—including the rural poor—individualist.

The second support in Marx's theory for the socialisation of agriculture—the counterposing of the collectivism of the agricultural workers to the individualism of the peasant—is thus found to be a weak reed.

Plethora of capital and the cooperative organisation of farming

The victory of large over small farming prior to the socialist revolution was the economic factor on which, in Marx's view, the victory of socialism in agriculture was based. The existence of a large and increasingly more independent collectivist class of agricultural wage workers was the sociological factor on which it hinged.

Both these factors were assumed to be active in the countryside. In Marx's scheme there was a third, affecting the socialist organisation of agriculture from the outside: a plethora of capital and technical resources in the towns which could be made available to agriculture.

There is no need to labour the point that the cooperative organisation of farming has been introduced hitherto only in countries that, far from having an abundance of capital and technical resources, have suffered an acute shortage of them—Russia, China and Eastern Europe. In fact, the relation between industry and agriculture in these countries was exactly the opposite of that visualised by Marx: industry had to *draw* resources *from* agriculture to support its own capital accumulation.

The only case where the collective organisation of agriculture was associated with the pouring of resources into agriculture is that of the Israeli kibbutzim (communal farms). In this case the first two assumptions of Marx—the withering away of the small farms under capitalism due to pressure from the large, and the widening of the gulf between agricultural workers on the one hand, and the capitalists on the other—were not put to the test: the Jewish settlers in the kibbutzim were immigrants, who were not agriculturalists previously and who built the collective farms from scratch. The kibbutzim are as if made to order to verify Marx's third assumption of the effect of pumping capital resources into agriculture. And this test, however narrow it may be historically, however limited to singular national and social circumstances, seems to give support to Marx's supposition. Let us make a short excursion.

The productivity of labour in kibbutz agriculture is high, even by comparison with advanced countries. Any international comparison of labour productivity comes up against a number of methodological difficulties due to differences in soil and climatic conditions, kinds of crops grown, etc. The following figures serve therefore only as a pointer.[53]

LABOUR TIME SPENT ON PRODUCTION OF UNIT OF AGRICULTURAL PRODUCT IN THE KIBBUTZ AND ABROAD

	Hours of work per ton grain	Workdays per ton potatoes	Workdays per ton vegetables	Workdays per 1,000 litres milk
Kibbutz	20-30	7	15-20	5
Advanced countries of Western Europe	20-25	12	15-20	12
United States	15	4-5	6-7	7

Thus productivity in the kibbutz falls below the level of American agriculture (except for milk) and is about equal to Western Europe. (Of course it far exceeds the Russian *kolkhoz*.) The same standard is shown by comparing the net output per agriculturist in the kibbutz with the net output per agriculturist in other countries:

VALUE ADDED (INCLUDING DEPRECIATION) **PER PERSON EMPLOYED IN AGRICULTURE**

	Year	Dollars
Kibbutz	1958	2,047
United States	1954	3,277
Britain	1957	2,358
Belgium	1957	2,038
Holland	1957	1,998
Denmark	1956	1,820
Norway	1957	1,307
West Germany	1957	884
Italy	1957	710
Turkey	1955	302
Japan (excluding depreciation)	1957	265
Morocco	1952	207
India	1951	147

These figures show the splendid achievements of the kibbutzim as regards the production of labour.

These successes are above all due to the relatively heavy capital investment in kibbutzim. Kibbutz agriculture is highly mechanised. Towards the end of 1955 there were 16.3 tractors in the kibbutzim per 1,000 hectares of land. As against this, in Denmark and Holland, which are well known for the high level of their agricultural mechanisation, there are 16 tractors per 1,000 hectares; in Belgium 14; in Finland 13; in France nine; at the other extreme, in Greece there are 0.9; in Turkey 0.6 (Britain, West Germany, Sweden and Switzerland are, however, more highly mechanised than the kibbutz sector).[54]

The productive investment per family in the kibbutzim amounted in 1957 to some 21,800 Israeli pounds.[55] Compare this with the capital equipment of an Arab peasant, estimated at 60 to 80 Palestinian pounds in 1937 or, in 1957 prices, some 1,200 to 1,600 Israeli pounds.[56]

Thus, unlike the Soviet *kolkhozes*, or the Chinese People's Communes, the Israeli kibbutz is not being exploited to help other branches of the economy; on the contrary, capital is being poured into it. Even so, it takes a long time until the kibbutz becomes self-supporting. 'In order to reach financial stability, even partially, a period of 20-30 years, if not longer, is necessary'.[57]

Another important and unique advantage accruing to the kibbutz as compared with rural populations elsewhere is the very high cultural level of its members. This is even higher than the average for Israel as a whole, including the towns. As a single indication of this, it was found that 80.3 percent of the men and 79.8 percent of the women members of the kibbutz could read and write Hebrew and at least one foreign language.[58] Technically the kibbutz members are remarkably proficient, on the whole far surpassing farmers elsewhere, and even the average urban Israeli inhabitant.

This high cultural standard is being carried on and handed down. Thus, while only a minority of Israel's youth receives full secondary education, all the youth of the kibbutzim does, with the result that kibbutz children, who make up only 6 percent of the primary school population, make up a percentage three times as great—19 percent—of the secondary school population.[59]

This cultural advantage of kibbutz members compared with the usual rural population—not to speak of the agriculturists of backward countries like Russia in the 1930s and China at present—is of greater moment for the success of the economy than the disadvantages resulting from urban background and agricultural inexperience.

The fact that kibbutz members are on the whole a small, select minority of pioneers (at present about 3 percent of the Israeli population are in kibbutzim) has also been of immeasurable value in the success of the venture.

Lessons from the kibbutz movement for the fate of collectivisation in the world at large

On the whole, and despite some failings, the kibbutz is a very successful venture. As a large-scale unit it carries out very diversified farming. It unites agriculture and industry. It is highly mechanised. It assures a relatively high productivity of labour. Its members attain a comfortable material and cultural standard. It is almost unique in being a collective farm based on voluntary association.

However, despite its undoubted success, the kibbutz does not attract the individual Jewish farmer to join it, nor even does it attract many of the prospective settlers, even though they are or have been, in the main, propertyless people being settled by the state and public organisations. This is very relevant to attempts to apply the experience elsewhere, particularly in poor and backward countries.

As labour in the kibbutz is still a burden, prolonged and monotonous, and scarcities still prevail, the kibbutz does not appear yet as the embodiment of complete individual freedom. For the individual farmer to join it would be not to 'jump from the realm of necessity to the realm of freedom'. It does not even appear to offer a great improvement in conditions of living.

Even where there is quite a generous supply of capital to the collective farm as is the case in the kibbutz, we have seen that 'in order to reach financial stability—even if partial—a period of 20 to 30 years, if not longer, is necessary.' And the kibbutz did not have to struggle with attachments to private farms or a yearning for a private plot. It did not have to deal with an apathetic and ignorant mass of peasants, but with enthusiastic and cultured small groups of individuals!

From a different angle of historical experience, the kibbutz confirms the conclusions arising from other sections of the present study: if the collectivisation of agriculture is to be the result of a voluntary act by the peasants, it is bound to be a very gradual and prolonged process, and demand vast capital resources. It can come into being only where there is general abundance, with the concomitant of high material and cultural standards, and where the predominance of industry in the economy as a whole has already been firmly established. It cannot be the predecessor of industrialisation, but a very late fruit of a successful industrial society.

Without these conditions collectivisation must be forced. And if it is introduced to help forced industrialisation, it cannot be otherwise.

The Israeli kibbutz gives support to the idea that even if the first two ideas of Marx regarding the cooperative reorganisation of agriculture—the withering away of the small farm under capitalism and the sharpening of class divisions in the countryside till they are as clear as in the towns—proved incorrect the third could, under conditions of social wealth, compensate for the other two. If the stubbornness of the small farm and the bluntness of class differentiation between agricultural workers and capitalists in the countryside are impediments to cooperative advance, a plethora of capital could overcome them.

Unfortunately the collective reorganisation of agriculture—Israel excluded—has taken place only in poor, capital-hungry countries. Such circumstances were never considered by Marx, who took it for granted that the socialist revolution would be victorious in the more advanced countries first. Thus the third assumption underlying Marx's conception of the path of cooperative organisation of farming—a plethora of capital in the towns—has not obtained in the largely backward, non-industrial countries that have introduced collectivisation.

In the light of what has been said above, the debate between the three wings of the Russian Communist Party—the right (Bukharin), the left (Trotsky), and the so called 'centre' (Stalin)—takes on a new meaning.

Bukharin

Bukharin argued in 1925 that the development of socialist industry in Russia should be paralleled by the development of private, individual agriculture. To encourage agricultural production, individual farming including kulak development should be spurred on.

> The well to do top layer of the peasantry—the kulak and in part the middle peasant—*is at present afraid* to *accumulate*... If the peasant wants to put up an iron roof, tomorrow he will be denounced as a kulak and that will be an end of him. If the peasant buys a machine, he does it 'so that the communists may not see'. The technical improvement of agriculture is enveloped in a kind of conspiracy.
>
> If we look at the different strata in the countryside, we shall see that the kulak is displeased with us because we *prevent him from accumulating*. On the other hand, the poor peasants sometimes grumble at us for preventing them from hiring

themselves out as batraks to this same kulak… The poor peasant who has no horse and no implements of production, and who sits on his land, is displeased with us because we prevent him 'earning his bread' with the kulak.

Bukharin's recommendation was:

Our policy in relation to the countryside should develop in the direction *of removing, and in part abolishing many restrictions which put the brake on the growth of the well to do and kulak farm.* To the peasants, to all the peasants, we must say: 'Enrich yourselves, develop your farms, and do not fear that constraint will be put on you.' However paradoxical it may appear, we must develop the well to do farm in order to help the poor peasant and the middle peasant.[60]

This would guarantee a balanced growth of agriculture and industry. He argued that 'the essential part of the task of working out a plan of national economy' is determination of 'the conditions for the correct coordination of the various spheres of production, or in other words, the conditions of *dynamic economic equilibrium*'.

He argued that Russia's economic difficulties were caused by the fact that industrial construction was increasing too fast for the conditions of agricultural production—hence the scarcities of foodstuffs and raw materials. This proved, not that industry was too backward for the level of agriculture, but, on the contrary, that the plans for industrial construction were too ambitious for the existing supply of foodstuffs and raw materials. Furthermore, the high rate of industrial investment 'created a record demand for industrial goods', increasing the general goods famine. 'The failure of industry to satisfy the demand of the village' was not evidence of too slow a rate of industrial development. On the contrary:

'Whilst industry develops at a tremendous pace, whilst the population increases rapidly and the needs of this population increase steadily, the amount of grain remains unaltered'; 'further acceleration of the speed of development of industry depends to a considerable extent on agricultural raw material production and agricultural export', and any further capital investment 'must be affected with due consideration for all those factors which guarantee a "more or less crisis-free development" and better coordination'. 'Any overstraining of capital expenditure will lead in time to the stoppage of enterprises already begun; it will react unfavourably on other branches in every direction, and it will finally *retard the speed of development…* Our bow is at a very high tension. To increase this tension still further, and to increase the "goods famine" still more, is impossible.' 'The greatest sustained speed is achieved when industry develops on the basis provided by the rapidly growing agriculture.'

A concomitant to Bukharin's concept of 'balanced growth' was his opposition to any overambitious aims for heavy industry:

We believe that the formula which calls for a maximum of investments in heavy industry is not quite correct, or rather, quite incorrect. If we have to put the main emphasis on the development of the means of production, we must combine this development with a corresponding expansion of light industry which has a quicker turnover and repays within a shorter time the amounts spent on it.

We must attempt to get the optimal combination of both.[61]

Bukharin was therefore against assigning to heavy industry a preponderance in the economy which would involve a temporary stagnation or decline in other sections of the economy. He saw an intimate, unbreakable connection between the 'balanced growth' of light and heavy industry, and industry and agriculture, which latter was to be based largely on the encouragement of individual farming.

Up to a point, in the short term perspective, Bukharin's policies were realistic. But beyond certain narrow limits Bukharin's recipe would have led Russia to an impasse. Unless industry forged ahead far in advance of agriculture the pull of its demand on agricultural output would be too small to raise the output. Without a ready supply of industrial goods the spur for agricultural production would be absent. Without a technically advanced industry—even if the immediate effect on opening up employment opportunities by building such an industry were small—it would be impossible in the long run to eliminate hidden and rural unemployment. Within the international military configuration Russia could not tie its heavy industry to the 'snail's pace' of agriculture and light industry. Doing too little industrially was as dangerous as doing too much.

Trotsky

Trotsky, as against Bukharin, banked on the *gradual*, voluntary collectivisation of agriculture. As stated in the 1927 Platform of the Trotskyist Left Opposition:

> The growth of private proprietorship in the country must be offset by a more rapid development of collective farming. It is necessary systematically and from year to year to subsidise the efforts of the poor peasants to organise in collectives.
>
> At the same time, we must give a more systematic help to poor proprietors not included in the collectives, by freeing them entirely from taxation, by a corresponding land policy, by credits for agricultural implements, and by bringing them into the agricultural cooperatives.
>
> A sharply progressive tax system; state legislative measures for the defence of hired labour and the regulation of the wages of agricultural workers; a correct class policy in the matter of land division and land utilisation; the same thing in the matter of supplying the country with tractors and other implements of production.
>
> The existing system of universal agricultural tax ought to be changed in the direction of freeing altogether from taxation 40 to 50 percent of the poorest peasant families, without making up for it by any additional tax upon the fundamental mass of the middle peasants...
>
> A much larger sum ought to be appropriated for the creation of soviet and collective farms.
>
> The prices of grain and other agricultural products ought to guarantee to the poor and the basic mass of the middle peasants the possibility, at the very least, of maintaining their economy at the present level and gradually improving it.
>
> It is necessary...radically to change the whole direction of agricultural credits towards assuring to the poor and the weak middle peasant cheap and long term credits.[62]

The collectivisation of agriculture that Trotsky counterposed to Bukharin's encouragement of individual farming was only part of a general strategy of modernising Russia, of speedy industrialisation in place of Bukharin's 'snail's pace' advance (to use the latter's own words), of 'combined development' as an alternative to 'balanced growth'. However, this total strategy suggested by Trotsky could not be reconciled in practice with the policy of voluntary collectivisation of resources to help agriculture modernise, while 'combined development'—with its forced advance of industry, and above all heavy industry—has to rely, where available capital resources are small, and unused resources hardly exist, on the syphoning off of resources from agriculture to help industry along. The latter process was called 'primitive socalist accumulation'.

Preobrazhensky, the Trotskyist economist who did more than anyone to advocate this so called 'primitive socialist accumulation', described it thus:

> ...the more economically backward, petty bourgeois and peasant in character is the country making the transition to a socialist organisation of production, the smaller is the legacy which the proletariat of the country in question receives at the moment of the socialist revolution to build up its own socialist accumulation, and the more in proportion this socialist accumulation will be obliged to rely on the alienation of a part of the surplus product of pre-socialist forms of the economy. Only a more developed country can rely on the surplus product of its own industry and its own agriculture.[63]

In opposition to 'socialist accumulation' (defined as an addition to the functioning means of production as a result of the surplus product produced in the socialist economy itself) Preobrazhensky postulated 'primitive socialist accumulation', which he defined as 'the accumulation in the hands of the state of material resources obtained chiefly from sources lying outside the state economic system':

> This accumulation will, necessarily, in a backward agrarian country, play a colossal role... Primitive accumulation will predominate during the period of industrialisation... We must, therefore, term this whole stage as the period of primitive or preparatory socialist accumulation.

By 'sources lying outside the state economic system' was meant agriculture.

> In the period of primitive socialist accumulation the state cannot do without the exploitation of small-scale production, without the expropriation of a part of the surplus product of the countryside and of artisan labour... The idea that a socialist economy can develop by itself without touching the resources of the petty bourgeois, including the peasant, economy is beyond doubt a reactionary, petty bourgeois utopia. The task of the socialist state is not to take from the petty bourgeois producers less than was taken by capitalism but to take more out of the even greater income which will be assured to the small producer by the rationalisation of everything, including the small production of the country.[64]

Just as in the mercantilist period in Western Europe, early merchant capitalists amassed wealth by colonial exploitation, so socialist industry would draw on internal 'colonies'—small individualist agriculture. Preobrazhensky did not advocate following the merchants in the use of violence against the peasants or in elevating any class—in this case the working class—to the position of an exploiting class. He propounded a measure far milder than those used by the mercantilist bourgeoisie: the partial suppression of the law of value by changing the terms of exchange between industry and agriculture in favour of the former and against the latter, so that a unit of labour in state industry would be exchanged for more than a unit of labour in agriculture. He assumed that these terms of exchange would in a short time lead to such a quick rise in the general level of production that not only would the income of society as a whole rise, but also the income, in absolute terms, of the peasantry.[65] The essence of his standpoint was, however, that resources were to be drawn from agriculture to state industry, and not in the opposite direction, which was precisely the condition identified by Marx as the act of socialisation of agricultural production.

Actually the implementation of Preobrazhensky's 'socialist primitive accumulation' would logically have led to a very different state of affairs from that which he visualised. Any attempt to 'squeeze' the peasants is always likely to be met by a deliberate reduction in production, so that if the 'terms of trade' between agriculture and industry favoured the latter, the amount of trade would fall. There would be only one way to deal with such a 'strike'—to use violence, expropriating the peasants, and concentrating them on such large farms that it would be possible for the state to control their work and output. If the state used these methods, it would also have to face serious opposition from the workers, many of whom, in a backward country such as that under consideration, would still have close family ties with the villages, being raw recruits to industry. Moreover, what would prevent the state, resorting to oppression in the interests of 'primitive socialist accumulation', from doing the same as regards 'socialist accumulation' proper, the extortion of surplus value from the workers in state industry itself?

These were, indeed, exactly the results achieved by Stalin's and Mao's agrarian policies (although the author and his title—'primitive socialist accumulation'— were never acknowledged).

More recent theorists

While Bukharin's policies were realistic, although in the long run leading to an impasse, Trotsky's policy was unrealisable, except in the distorted Stalinist totalitarian form. (Of course in the long run forced collectivisation itself becomes an impediment on economic advance—hence the permanent crisis in Soviet agriculture over the last decade and more).

It is no accident that in all post-Stalin debates in Eastern Europe on agricultural policies the only serious criticism of Stalinist forced collectivisation— whether by Tito, Gomulka or Imre Nagy—was a return to ideas first formulated in the 1920s by Bukharin, the brilliant theoretician of the right of the Bolshevik

Party, who staked his case on the 'individual peasant growing into socialism'. This return is of more than historical interest; it throws light on the central issues involved in the collectivisation of agriculture.

Kardelj, in his book *Les Problèmes de la Politique dans les Campagnes* (*Problems of Agricultural Policy*), repeatedly shows the connection between forced collectivisation and the subordination of the economy to the needs of heavy industry, and rejects them both.

Imre Nagy, the ill-fated premier of Hungary during the Hungarian Revolution, reached similar conclusions, which he set out in a document written during his forced retirement in 1955 and 1956. This document was mimeographed and circularised secretly among leading communists in Hungary, and a copy was smuggled out of Hungary and published in book form abroad. He repeatedly protested against state violence directed towards peasants, and the compulsion to join the cooperative farms. He called for aid to the small individual peasant to increase production, and between these two and the emphasis on heavy industry: 'With the too rapid development of heavy industry, the material resources of the country did not prove sufficient to give new impetus to agricultural production'.[66]

Both in Yugoslavia and Poland private individual farming is predominant. In Yugoslavia at the end of 1958 private farms covered 93.86 percent of the agricultural land with over 97 percent of the cattle, over 95 percent of the sheep and over 88 percent of the pigs.[67] In Poland, in the wake of the October 1956 events, peasants were allowed to leave the agricultural producer cooperatives. The peasants immediately turned their backs unequivocally on the agricultural producer cooperatives. Thus, while at the beginning of 1956 there were close to 10,000 agricultural producer cooperatives covering about 4.6 million acres, or over 9 percent of the farmland, by the middle of 1957 less than 1,800 farms remained, with about 650,000 acres, or little more than 1 percent of the farmland.

Tito and Gomulka demonstrate clearly and in practice the weakness of Marx's three assumptions regarding the cooperative reorganisation of agriculture. First, in this case under Communist Party rule, the peasants are free to join or leave the agricultural producer cooperatives, and they show in no uncertain way their attitude to any form of forced collectivisation. Second, it is recognised in practice that the large-scale mode of production is not always economically superior, and that there are deep social and psychological reasons preventing its ascendancy. Third, a negative demonstration is given of the connection between the process of primitive accumulation of capital—the harsh subordination of consumption to accumulation, of light to heavy industry, of agriculture to industry as a whole—and forced collectivisation. Fourth, Yugoslavia and Poland, being the most 'liberal' of Communist countries, demonstrate clearly that the smashing of small farming in conditions of general economic backwardness is associated with totalitarianism, the exact opposite of Marx's vision of socialism as the realm of freedom.

Agriculture on the morrow of socialist revolution

From Marx's conception of the trends towards the collectivisation of agriculture flowed some basic conclusions about the path agriculture would follow after the socialist revolution.

First, immediately after the working class conquered political power the large estates would be cooperatively run. These farms would serve as a point of support, as an example and an inspiration encouraging the general organisation of agriculture in cooperative farms.

Second, the superiority of large over small farms, and especially of cooperatively run large farms over small individual ones, would be so great as to be obvious to all.

Third, with the workers' state relying on a large industrial sector, it could help the reorganisation of the small farms into large ones by supplying them with abundant machinery, fertilisers, etc.

With a firm launching pad in the countryside, abundant resources flowing into it from the cities, and the presumed superiority of large farming over small, the collectivisation of agriculture could be launched easily, speedily and successfully.

Under such circumstances, the voluntary principle could be adhered to without trouble. The voluntary principle in carrying out the 'cooperativisation' of agriculture is part and parcel of the Marxist conception. The essence of workers' rule, according to Marx—consistent democracy prevailing in the working class—cannot coexist with coercion practised against a large mass of toiling peasants.

If the three assumptions underlying Marx's ideas of the collectivisation of agriculture on the morrow of the socialist revolution are found wanting, the ideas themselves must be found wanting. And in fact, the socialist revolution, the coming of the working class to political power, and the socialisation of industry, banking, and trade, even in the most highly industrialised countries, will in all likelihood not tend necessarily to strengthen the collectivist tendencies in agriculture but, on the contrary, will tend to *give a new lease of life* to individual farming.

Let us assume the most auspicious circumstances for the new socialist regime—its establishment in a highly industrialised country or countries, worried by no military threat so that there is no wastage of resources on armaments, etc, and with abundant resources available for agriculture. The new regime, with the abolition of militarism, will grant the peasants a reduction in taxation, mortgages and many other burdens which crush him under capitalism. It will, through trading cooperatives, increase supplies of food, seed, fertilisers and the like. Cooperative land banks and the state itself will make available a greater amount of cheap credit. The supply of rented or cooperatively shared agricultural machinery will be encouraged. Scientific knowledge will be made readily available to the small farms as it is to the large farms under capitalism. Specialists in poultry, spraying and the like, veterinary surgeons and agronomists, will be at the service of all farmers.

The great disadvantages suffered under capitalism by the small farmers in the sphere of trade have been referred to. They must buy their requisites in small quantities, and the output of each product is very small so that the costs of trading are proportionately much larger than on the large farms. This draw-back, however, is already being diminished under capitalism by the spread of trad-ing cooperatives, which buy agricultural products and supply the farmer with what he needs; and under a proletarian regime, with the sources of supply and also the demands for agricultural products more centralised, these may be ex-pected to strengthen and multiply.

Above all, the insecurity of the market, the instability of the demand for agri-cultural products that so often crushes the farmer, will give way to a stable and widening demand for agricultural goods to satisfy the needs of an urban popu-lation with a rising standard of living.

All these factors will probably give *the private farm a new lease of life under the socialist regime.*[68]

Social factors are also likely to strengthen the individual farm. The rural poor, labourers and small peasants alike, will have their cravings for a plot—or a decent sized plot—of their own satisfied in the seizure or distribution of the large estates, and hence many a proletarian will be transformed into a petty bourgeois. This is bound to strengthen the social forces conserving individual farming.

But the socialist revolution in the long run must have the effect of under-mining the private farm.

If, on the morrow of the socialist revolution, the factors which, under capitalism, undermine the individual farm by crushing the farmer are weakened or eliminated altogether, other factors, more important in the long run, will have a contrary effect: they will undermine the individual farm by showing it to be too narrow a mode of existence for the agricultural population, whose appetite for a better, easier and more cultured life would be whetted with improved conditions.

The small farmer works far harder than the agricultural wage earner. Leisure time hardly exists for him. He has nothing in the world but his farm. But even under capitalism it is only the older generation in the main for whom this way of life is sufficient. The younger generation already rebels against it, craving the diversions and wider culture of the towns, to which it flocks in numbers. There the young people will work shorter hours, and have a rest day on Sunday at least, annual holidays, etc. The cinema and other sources of amusement are at hand. The education of children is superior. The only reason for more of the farmer's sons and daughters not leaving home to go to town is that under capitalism the private ownership of the farm, and the feeling of being independent provide a certain security of employment and income, and security in old age.

The socialist regime, by raising living standards all round, assuring security of employment, and comprehensive pensions for old age and sickness, will deflate the value of economic 'independence' represented in the private ownership of the farm. It will also encourage the desire of the rural population, especially the youth, for culture, leisure and better living. Only then will the knell of the small farm toll: not because of the pressure of its poverty, but *notwithstanding* its prosperity.

Thus the organisation of agriculture in cooperative farms is bound to be an extremely slow process, impeded by some factors that are brought into play by the new socialist regime, not gaining much stimulation from the assumed decline of small farming under the technical superiority of the large ones. The process of the transition of agriculture from individual to collectivist methods will thus be the result of the abundance of wealth and culture in highly developed societies. Individual farming will not be overthrown, but sublimated.

Capitalist pressure is not able to eliminate the small farm. Socialist prosperity, by *attraction*, will gradually—in the very long run—persuade the peasantry to give up their individual farms.

So long as the socialist state controls the commanding heights of the economy in societies where industry is advanced and can serve as a firm base for economic progress, so long as the industrial working class is strong and cultured, there is no reason in the world why the new regime cannot wait patiently for a long time, even decades, before the rural population decides to take to the path of agricultural cooperative farming.

Notes

1 K Marx, 'The Class Struggles in France', in K Marx, *Selected Works* (London, 1942), vol II, p233.
2 K Marx, 'The Communist Manifesto', in K Marx, *Selected Works*, op cit, vol I, p44.
3 K Marx, *Capital*, vol III (Chicago, 1909), p16.
4 Ibid, p946.
5 K Marx, 'The Class Struggles in France', op cit, p221.
6 K Marx, 'The Eighteenth Brumaire of Louis Bonaparte', in K Marx, *Selected Works*, op cit, vol II, p422.
7 To avoid misunderstanding, it should be said that the above deals with Marx's concept of the role of the peasantry in the *socialist* revolution. As regards the peasantry's role in the anti-feudal, capitalist revolution, Marx's concept was radically different. Contrary to the conservative, even reactionary, role played by the peasantry in the socialist, anti-capitalist revolution, Marx showed that a peasantry oppressed by feudalism plays an entirely different part in a revolution directed to the overthrow of this social order. Whereas the proletarian revolution characterises the death agony of capitalism, it is the peasant revolution that accompanies the death agony of feudalism and the rise of capitalism—Wat Tyler in England, Thomas Münzer in Germany, Pugachev and Stenka Razin in Russia. And in this revolution the peasantry as a class plays a progressive, revolutionary role.
8 K Marx, *Selected Works*, op cit, vol II, p18.
9 Ibid, p166.
10 Ibid, p541.
11 K Marx and F Engels, *Selected Correspondence* (London, 1942), p434.
12 K Kautsky, *Die Agrarfrage* (Stuttgart, 1902), pp5-6.
13 Ibid, p115.
14 Ibid, p116.
15 Ibid, pp101-102.
16 Ibid, p102.
17 Ibid, p104.
18 Ibid, p92.
19 Ibid, p104.
20 Ibid, p105.
21 Ibid, pp46-48.

22   Ibid, p141.
23   Ibid, p142.
24   Ibid, p141.
25   Ibid, pp151-155.
26   Ibid, p136.
27   Ibid, pp138-140.
28   Ibid, p106.
29   Ibid, p109.
30   Ibid, p112.
31   V I Lenin, *Selected Works*, vol XII, p248.
32   Ibid, p288.
33   *Report of the Committee on Further Education for Agriculture provided by Local Education Authorities*, (December 1958), Cmd 614.
34   J R Bellerby, 'The Distribution of Manpower in Agriculture and Industry, 1851-1951', *The Farm Economist* (Oxford, 1958), no 1.
35   J A Mollett, 'The Size of Farm Staffs in England and Wales in 1851 and 1941', *The Farm Economist* (Oxford, 1950), no 6.
36   Organisation for European Economic Cooperation, *Third Report on the Agricultural Policies in Europe and North America* (Paris, 1958), p18.
37   Ibid, p41.
38   M Sering, 'The Relation of Land Tenure to the Economic and Social Development of Agriculture', *Proceedings of the Fourth International Conference of Agricultural Economists* (Oxford, 1957), p77; *Economist*, 12 March 1960.
39   V W Ruttan, 'The Relationship Between the BAE Level-of-Living Indexes and the Average Income of Farm Operators', *Journal of Farm Economics*, February 1954.
40   E O Heady, *Economics of Agricultural Production and Resource Use* (New York, 1952), p694.
41   V I Lenin, *Sochineniia*, vol III, p146.
42   The obscurity of class differences in the rural population in backward countries—quite often not only between wage earners, tenants and peasants, but even between them and 'landlords'—is well illustrated in the Chinese countryside where, in 1950, the Communist Party tried to define the class status of different people in connection with the land reform. Thus *The Decisions Concerning the Differentiation of Class Status in the Countryside* (4 August 1950) are so complicated, and the boundaries between the classes so blurred, that in many cases it is extremely difficult to determine whether a person is a landlord or a rich peasant; and, more absurdly in some cases, whether he is a middle peasant, an agricultural worker or a landlord. One member of a family may be considered a landlord, another a proletarian. 'In one family, for instance, if there is a person in the rural area who has, for three years, depended on land rent and loan interest as his major means of livelihood, then the said person is a landlord. If there is another person who has for one year depended on the sale of his labour power as his main means of livelihood, then the said person is a worker'—*The Agrarian Reform Law of the People's Republic of China* (Beijing, 1951), pp50-51. How flimsy the boundary between the classes!

     Another aspect of the problem concerns the class status of a landlord who marries a worker, to which *The Decisions* devotes a whole section; but for the purpose of demonstrating the difficulty of differentiating between classes, when they are not in fact very different, the posing of the question alone suffices.

     Where the detection of the widest cleavages, between landlord and labourer, demands such careful scrutiny, how are the much narrower cleavages—between rich peasants and middle peasants, and between them and the rural poor—to be discerned? For a further elaboration of this point, see Y Gluckstein, *Mao's China* (London, 1957), pp85-89.
43   E V G Kiernan, *British Diplomacy in China, 1880-1885* (Cambridge, 1939), p236.
44   J F Duncan, in *Proceedings of the Fourth International Conference of Agricultural Economists* (London, 1937), p286.
45   F Engels, *The Peasant Question in France and Germany* (1894).
46   V I Lenin, *Sochineniia* (third edition), vol XXII, p50.

47 Ibid, vol XXIII, p393.

48 Ibid, p420.

49 Ibid, pp420-429, 588 n135.

50 M Dobb, *Soviet Economic Development Since 1917* (London, 1948).

51 V I Lenin, *Sochineniia* (3rd edition), vol XXVI, p330.

52 One could criticise the Bolsheviks for deviation from agrarian socialism to petty bourgeois policies and Rosa Luxemburg, the great German-Polish Marxist and enthusiast for the October Revolution, did so sharply. She said, 'The slogan launched by the Bolsheviks, immediate seizure and distribution of the land by the peasants...not only is...not a socialist measure; it even cuts off the way to such measures; it piles up insurmountable obstacles to the socialist transformation of agrarian relations'—R Luxemburg, *The Russian Revolution* (London, 1959), p19. And Rosa Luxemburg, as it turned out, correctly prophesied that the distribution of the landed estates among the peasants would strengthen the power of private property in the countryside, which would in the future be bitterly opposed to the socialisation of agriculture: 'Formerly there was only a small caste of noble and capitalist landed proprietors and a small minority of rich village bourgeoisie to oppose a socialist reform on the land. And their expropriation by a revolutionary mass movement of the people is mere child's play. But now, after the 'seizure', as an opponent of any attempt at socialisation of agricultural production, there is an enormous, newly-developed and powerful mass of owning peasants who will defend their newly-won property with tooth and nail against every socialist attack'—ibid, pp20-21. Unfortunately, Lenin and Trotsky had no alternative. It is true that the Bolshevik programme provided for nationalisation of all landed estates, and Lenin had for years argued heatedly against the Social Revolutionaries who were in favour of distributing the landlords' land among the peasants. However, in 1917, when the land problem demanded an immediate solution, he straightaway adopted the slogan of the much-condemned Social Revolutionaries—or rather, of the spontaneous peasant movement. Had the Bolsheviks not done this, they and the urban working class they led would have been isolated from the countryside, and the revolution would have been stillborn (as was the Hungarian Revolution of 1919).

53 H Darin-Drabkin, *The Other Society: The Kibbutz in the Test of Economy and Society* (Hebrew: Merhavia, 1961), p268.

54 Ibid, p261.

55 Ibid, p429.

56 A Bonne, *Palestine: The Country and its Economy* (Hebrew: Tel Aviv, 1938), p94.

57 H Darin-Drabkin, op cit, p341.

58 Ibid, p457.

59 Ibid, p453.

60 N Bukharin, 'The New Economic Policy and our Tasks', *Bolshevik*, 1 June 1925.

61 *Pravda*, 4 November 1927, quoted in R Erlich, *The Soviet Industrialisation Debate, 1924-1928* (Cambridge, Mass, 1960), pp81-82.

62 L Trotsky, *The Real Situation in Russia* (London, 1928), pp68-72.

63 E Preobrazhensky, *Novaya Ekonomika* (Moscow-Leningrad, 1926), pp68-72.

64 Ibid, pp57-58.

65 Preobrazhensky's position must not be confused with that adopted in practice by Stalin. Preobrazhensky opposed any notion of administrative coercion against the peasants and therefore argued that it was 'self-evident that for Russia the entire process [of collectivisation] would be long, incredibly slow'.

66 I Nagy, *On Communism: In Defence of the New Course* (London, 1957), p193.

67 Information Service of Yugoslavia, RN 721/58-E; D Mutapovic, 'Yugoslav Agriculture and its Development', *Review of International Affairs*, 1 October 1959.

68 To repeat, only regions with individual peasant agriculture have been referred to, and not those, such as areas in Latin America, where large-scale agriculture based on wage labour predominates.

Earthquake in the East

Socialist Review, December 1989

We are witnessing the most massive earthquake of the social and political order in Eastern Europe. It is on a scale reminiscent of 1848 and 1917.

In 1848 there was revolution in France, Germany, Austria and Hungary, and a massive impact elsewhere. The 1917 Russian Revolution was followed by revolution in Germany, Austria and Hungary and had an international impact on an even greater scale.

To understand an earthquake you have to look at the pressure inside the system. It is summed up with Marx's statement that when the social system becomes a brake on the development of the productive forces, the epoch of the social revolution starts.

Marx put the emphasis on the word 'epoch'. It is not a question of one day or one year—it is a long process of tens of years, for as long as the social system is a brake on the productive forces.

Why do the state capitalist regimes act as a brake? In the USSR itself the annual rate of growth of the gross national product between 1950 and 1959 was 5.8 percent. In the period 1970-78 it was down to 3.7 percent. In 1980-82 it was down to 1.5 percent. My guess is that over the last three or four years there was a negative rate of growth.

The manufacturing working class in the USSR is nearly a third larger than that of the US. The number of technicians in Russian manufacturing industry is twice that of the US. Yet the output is half that of the US.

Thirty percent of the population of the USSR are in agriculture compared with 4 percent in the US. But the 4 percent produce enough food for the US, plus exports. Russia, by comparison, is a net importer of food, even though the level of consumption is much lower.

The downturn and stagnation of the last two decades seem to be in complete contradiction to the experience of the Russian economy under Stalin, when the rate of growth was absolutely massive.

Stalin achieved such massive growth rates by putting the emphasis on heavy industry, on capital goods. Capital accumulation is the heart of the system— machinery to produce machinery to produce machinery.

The problem is that, despite the success, it also makes the system very rigid, because the emphasis is on volume of production.

Look at the steel industry in Britain. Enterprises are near to the sea because it saves on the cost of transport of coal and iron ore which are very heavy raw materials.

By contrast, the centre of diamond production is South Africa, while the centre of diamond distribution is Amsterdam. The fact that they are thousands of miles apart doesn't make any difference, as a small volume has a high value. The steel industry is different.

The biggest steel enterprise in the world is in the Urals, at Magnitogorsk. There is no coal there, therefore they bring the coal from thousands of miles away over land. The second biggest steel enterprise in Russia is in the Donbass, in the Ukraine. There is a lot of coal but no iron, so they bring the iron thousands of miles.

The cost of transport must be 30, 40 or 50 times higher than the value of the final product. This is a fantastic waste. Steel is kept artificially cheap. The massive subsidy to these industries has become a formidable burden on the whole economy.

Another example of irrationality is that two plants in Russia produce a bolt 12mm by 60mm in size. One charges 10 kopeks for it. The other produces exactly the same bolt and charges 1.40 roubles, 14 times dearer.

In Britain the difference between the price of Daz and Persil is perhaps 5 percent. If there was a difference of 1,300 percent, one of them would go bankrupt.

The problem in the USSR is that, as long as there was expansion of resources, growth could be maintained by employing more people, using more raw materials and building more factories.

However, once you need to increase the intensity of production, or productivity (to increase output per worker or per unit of capital, in other words to shift from extensive to intensive growth) then the picture is completely different. The extensive method simply doesn't work.

Look what has happened in agriculture. Total agricultural output never rose under Stalin. When he died in 1953 the total agricultural output of Russia was a little lower than it was in 1928, before collectivisation. However, collectivisation still worked for Stalin as it transferred millions of people, and with them food, from the countryside to the town.

In order to siphon off the food from the countryside he had to organise the peasants into collective farms. There was no way of controlling 26 million peasant families, forcing them to deliver the grain, because they would have simply hidden it.

It is much easier to control 200,000 collective farms. But Stalin was worried that even the 200,000 couldn't be controlled. The 500 families on each farm could agree among themselves to hide the grain to pretend they hadn't produced 1,000 tons but only 600 tons.

He therefore organised to control the collective farms by setting up Machine Tractor Stations. Each of these state institutions looks after 20 or 30 collective farms. They did the ploughing and the harvesting.

It's much easier to control 10,000 Machine Tractor Stations than 200,000 collective farms.

The problem is that the tractor driver can decide whether to plough a shallow or a deep furrow. If he ploughs a shallow one he can work much quicker and therefore get a bigger bonus. Nobody is going to be able to go and measure what he has done. If the yield is bad five months later no one can prove it was his fault. It could have been the weather.

The net result of the system is that Stalin's attempt to control agriculture failed to improve output.

In 1959 the private plots of the collective farm members accounted for less than 1 percent of cultivated land. On these plots there is no machinery, not even a plough. There are no young workers, therefore they are very primitive. Yet in 1959 these plots produced 46.6 percent of all meat, 49.2 percent of all milk and 82.1 percent of the eggs produced in the country.

If Gorbachev could cut the labour force in agriculture from 30 percent of the population to, say, 10 percent, there would be a massive opportunity for increased production in industry. As he can't do this, his emphasis must be on increasing industrial productivity and here is where the trouble starts.

Perestroika is about rationalising, making the economy lean and strong. Thatcher carried out a *perestroika* in Britain in 1979-81. She cut the labour force in manufacturing by over a fifth. Every capitalist country has *perestroika*. In Japan the capitalists closed factories, they opened new factories and they changed machinery. But because the Japanese economy is much more modern than the British economy, the restructuring can be much less traumatic. The Russian economy needs even more radical *perestroika* than that carried out by Thatcher.

When Boris Kagarlitsky was in London he spoke about the three main groups in the bureaucracy.

One of them says we need rationalisation, we need the market and we have to follow Swedish social democracy.

A second group argue for a much more radical restructuring—they are called Thatcherite marketeers.

However, according to Kagarlitsky, the biggest group, called the Pinochet marketeers, says Thatcher is too soft. They want to introduce measures as radical as those carried out by General Pinochet in Chile.

A recent Channel 4 programme on the Polish economy featured the manager of the steel plant at Katowice. He said, 'We have to learn from Ian McGregor.' He argued for a radical cut in the labour force and said he'll only be happy when there are two workers looking for each job.

This is the logic of what Gorbachev has to do. In Britain they closed 20 to 25 percent of manufacturing capacity. In Russia they will have to do more. The estimate of 16 million unemployed as the result of *perestroika* is probably an underestimate.

The first opposition will come from the bureaucrats in the factories. Secondly, in order to overcome the resistance Gorbachev needs greater openness, *glasnost*. The trouble with *glasnost* is it gets out of control. Rulers rule by force and persuasion, with a whip and a carrot. They run into trouble when the whip is not strong enough and the carrot is not big enough.

When Stalin died Russia was still a graveyard in terms of political upheaval. Then in February 1956 Khrushchev denounced Stalin and started some measure of democratisation. The Hungarian uprising took place eight months later. Workers took the factories. They set up workers' councils. They smashed the Hungarian police and army. Khrushchev gave them a finger and they took a hand. After that, of course, Khrushchev sent the tanks in.

This effect is nothing new. Alexander II came to the Russian throne in 1855 and promised freedom to the serfs, local government and freedom for women to go to universities. Alexander Herzen, the leading revolutionary democrat at the time, called Alexander II the 'Tsar Liberator'. The only trouble is he gave freedom to the serfs but he did not give them the land. He gave local government but he didn't allow the Poles national autonomy. Instead he sent the troops against them.

The result was that the Narodniks formed a large and active movement and Alexander II became the first Tsar in the history of Russia to be murdered by revolutionaries, in 1881.

The problem with *glasnost* today for Russia's rulers is that it is opening the door to fantastic demands. Look at the workers in Vorkuta who have gone on strike against the law.

Glasnost opens the way for a flood of opposition and anger, both in Russia and the rest of Eastern Europe.

The explosion of the crisis is extremely fast. But the solution to the crisis is a long term matter. This is because here again the past lives with us.

Stalin pushed history forward on a massive scale by creating a huge working class. The working class of Russia today is incomparably stronger in terms of size, concentration and power than the working class of 1917. At the same time there has been a massive regression in terms of ideas, workers' organisation and living traditions.

This is why workers are extremely strong, yet are fighting for very elementary things that were raised as long ago as 1848: democratic rights, the right of assembly, the right of elections and the right of trade unions.

Even more important than this retrogression is the lack of a physical continuation of ideas. When Trotsky writes that the revolutionary party is the memory of the class he stresses the memory is not simply something hanging in the air—it is carried by human beings. They transfer their experience, tell one another about the books they read and so on.

One example of regression was the shocking picture of people carrying the banners of the Tsar on the 7 November demonstrations in Moscow and Yaroslav. Even worse than that, in Lvov in the Western Ukraine during the summer they carried the blue and white banners of Petlura, a Ukrainian nationalist who killed 150,000 Jews in 1919.

The problem is that genuine communism, planning, and the red flag are all identified with an oppressive regime.

There is another problem for the revolutionaries, such as Boris Kagarlitsky and the thousands of others like him all over Eastern Europe. They find it extremely difficult to find their way in terms of ideas. They have to start practically from square one—there is no tradition.

The process of clarification will take time. There needs to be a process of political differentiation. Within Kagarlitsky's group there are anarchists and people with a whole number of other political ideas. It took Marx years to break from the anarchist Bakunin. In the West today I don't know of any organisation with both Marxists and anarchists in it. But in Russia they are together as there hasn't yet been a process of differentiation.

In one way, the development of the workers' movement is very speedy and in another way it is extremely slow, because there is a 60-year desert to overcome. Socialists have to win ideas that were taken naturally in 1917 by masses of workers.

There is also an imbalance between the way in which workers can learn about some aspects of struggle extremely fast, but take much longer to generalise. The contradiction in people's brains is the result of a contradiction in their experience.

Russian workers have massive experience of solidarity in the factories. Basic democratic demands could therefore grow out of the situation. Everybody wants democratic and trade union rights.

The problems are that when the issue goes beyond the immediate factory to be more general, then a whole number of things are missing. Here it is important to understand the attraction of the market.

When Russian workers compare their living standards with those abroad, they compare them with those in West Germany.

If they compared the housing situation in Moscow with Calcutta, where there are hundreds of thousands of people sleeping in the streets, they would say the market doesn't work in Calcutta. But when the comparison is made with West Germany, the market seems very attractive.

When Lenin said revolutionary ideas must come to workers from outside, he meant from outside their immediate experience. In other words, to be a worker and fight for higher wages is natural. To fight against racism is not natural if you are a white worker—it doesn't come automatically. You must go beyond the immediate experience.

On 9 January 1905 in Russia the march to the Winter Palace was led by Father Gapon, a priest and a police agent. People didn't know he was a police agent, but they knew he was a priest and a prison priest at that. The demonstrators carried icons, not red flags. Instead of shouting, 'Down with the Tsar,' they cried, 'We love you, our little father.'

The revolutionaries were a tiny minority, a couple of hundred at the most. When the army shot 500 people dead the mass of people began to change.

It was a very quick jump from 9 January to the slogan of the soviet later that year: 'Eight hours a day and a gun.' The fact that people have to go through transition doesn't mean the transition must take 500 years. As Lenin said, in one day of revolution workers change more than in a century.

There are massive problems for socialists in Eastern Europe to overcome. Even those we call revolutionaries will be mixed with centrists moving leftwards. There will not be a clear line of demarcation. We can expect to see centrists moving leftwards and then differentiation.

The experience of Poland shows that every time force is used the force is weakened. In 1980-81 the ruling class was not as confident as in 1956. The Russian army did not intervene. There is no question that they are terrified of using the 380,000 Russian troops in East Germany in the present situation.

Therefore they have to use both reform and repression. The miners went on strike so they rushed through a law which said strikes are illegal in the mines, on the railways, in the power industry. Then the miners broke the law, but they didn't break it completely because only 18 pits in Vorkuta went on strike.

There will be ups and downs in the struggle. It is not a simple one way process. The miners' strike committee in Kusbass in Siberia was against the strike. It was the workers who decided to go on strike. There is already a differentiation there among the militants.

The events in Eastern Europe are also having a massive impact in the West.

People say Thatcher and Kinnock are right to support the market, that planning doesn't work and that socialism is old hat.

One Polish economist defined communism as a transition stage between capitalism and capitalism. From the West it looks as if socialism has no future as the regimes are falling to pieces. This is a massive boost to the right wing.

This is especially important because of the illusions much of the left has had in the Eastern regimes.

But this situation can also change radically if the workers' strikes in Eastern Europe come to the fore. Then it will be clear that the class struggle is still the dominant factor in the whole situation.

State capitalism is vitally important as a theory. Anybody who thinks there is any form of socialism in Russia is in trouble. Even Ernest Mandel argued in 1956:

> The Soviet Union maintains a more or less even rhythm of economic growth, plan after plan, decade after decade, without the progress of the past weighing on the possibilities of the future... All the laws of development of the capitalist economy which provoke a slowdown in the speed of economic growth are eliminated.

Isaac Deutscher said in the same year that Russia's standard of living would surpass that of Western Europe in the space of ten years. Anybody who believed these things is now completely demoralised. The assumption that Russia is more progressive than what everybody accepts as capitalism has fallen to pieces.

The importance of the theory of state capitalism is that it explains why the economy works the way it does. The emphasis on capital accumulation explains both the massive rate of growth and the impediments to future growth.

As I wrote in 1963:

> If by the term planned economy we understand an economy in which all com-
> ponent elements are adjusted and regulated into a single rhythm in which frictions
> are at a minimum and above all in which foresight prevails in the making of eco-
> nomic decisions, then the Russian economy is anything but planned. Instead of
> a real plan, strict methods of government dictation are involved in filling the
> gaps in the economy made by the decisions and activities of this very govern-
> ment. Therefore instead of speaking about a soviet planned economy, it would be
> much more exact to speak of a bureaucratically directed economy.

This explains the dynamic of the system, the capital accumulation, the creation of a working class. This is the strength of state capitalism. At the same
time it becomes an impediment to the development of the productive forces,
the most important productive force being the workers themselves.

Secondly, the theory prevents us being too impressionistic one way or another.

With all the break that Stalin brought in the Marxist tradition, these traditions are still alive. It is very interesting to hear Boris Kagarlitsky talk of the continuation in Vorkuta between the old Trotskyists, who were sent there to the
biggest gulag, and their grandchildren who are miners.

Ideas cannot be smashed by tanks, by force alone. The ideas of Trotsky can
be very much like a stream. The stream disappears from sight and then reappears
miles later. The stream hadn't dried up—it was just obscured from our sight
below the surface.

The same applies to ideas. As Trotsky wrote in 1939, 'The vengeance of history is much more terrible than the vengeance of the most powerful general secretary.' He has been proved right. Trotsky is smiling and Stalin is dead.

Balance of powerlessness

Socialist Review, September 1991

Why did the coup take place? We can only understand it against the calamitous position of the Soviet economy.

When Gorbachev came to power it was against a background of what was called Brezhnev's stagnation. Now we have a situation much worse than stagnation.

Recent figures showed that gross national product (GNP) was down in 1990 by 8.4 percent. This year it's estimated the drop will be 17.7 percent. The *Financial Times* on 16 May reported that oil production was then down by by 9 percent since the beginning of the year. Meat production from January to April went down by 13 percent.

There is no way of returning to Stalin's command economy. That came to a full stop. In the first Five-Year Plan the annual rate of growth of the economy was 19.2 percent. In the period 1950-59 it was 5.8 percent. In the 1970s the growth rate was 3.7 percent annually. And then it went down to 1 percent.

Stalin transformed a very backward country into the second biggest industrial power in the world. But it couldn't go on because his methods were only effective so long as he could mobilise a massive amount of human resources and raw materials.

You reach a certain stage where increases in the productivity per unit of labour begin to decline. So in the USSR today 30 percent of the population are in agriculture, yet there is still not enough food. Compare that to the US, where 4 percent of the population can produce sufficient food.

In the USSR the number of factory workers is a third higher than the US, the number of technicians twice that of the US, bur production is half that of the US.

They have to raise the productivity of labour. That's why all of them accept the need to move away from the command economy.

But they are trapped because the command economy is not yet dead and the market economy is stillborn. So they get a combination of both systems.

Central government says, 'Let's have more free market, let's have more black market, let's cut the element of the command economy.' But it is estimated that this year only 40 percent of the state's orders for goods will be fulfilled. This is catastrophic for the economy.

Under Stalin there was a lot of waste. But if they aimed at 60 million tonnes of steel, then they would know the amount of coal and iron that they would need, and they would get it, more or less.

The market economy operates with what Adam Smith called the 'hidden hand'. If 60 million tonnes of steel is required, then demand for coal and iron will rise and the companies who produce it will try and meet it. There's waste and friction, but somehow it works.

The worst thing in the USSR today is that they have half abandoned one and not got the other. Under such conditions it is moving more and more towards a two-way or three-way barter economy.

But the economy is too complicated for such a system to work. For example, take the oil industry in Tyumen. The USSR is the biggest exporter of oil in the world. But oil production is going down. One reason is that under Stalin they neglected the living conditions of the oil workers. But it is also because they need to buy oil drilling machinery. When there was a command economy, Azerbaijan, which is an oil-producing region, provided the machinery. But now with the collapse of the command economy, the Azeris want something in return for it. The problem is that there is nothing Tyumen can give them that they want. The situation is being repeated throughout the economy and threatens to deepen the paralysis.

Because the rulers find themselves in such a cul-de-sac, they can't go back and they can't go forward. To achieve a real market economy would mean a massive amount of unemployment. Two Moscow economists of the Plekhanov Institute have estimated that between 31 and 38 million will be out of work before the transition to a market economy is over. Gennady Yanayev, who led the coup, estimated that the move to a market economy in the first year would mean 12 million unemployed.

Putting over 30 million people (over 100 million including their families) out of work on top of the 70 million people in the USSR who already live below the poverty line is terrifying.

And in the USSR it isn't only a question of sacking thousands of workers to move towards the market, but of sacking thousands of managers too. That's why there's massive resistance to the changes and why there are not clear lines of division in the ruling class.

The ruling class is split in all sorts of different ways which are always shifting. Gorbachev is the most extreme case. After first endorsing the Shatalin 500-day plan for the market, he then proceeded to smash it last winter. Then he put the knife into the modernisers. He brought in Pugo and sent the black berets into the Baltics.

Every time he did a turn, he lost somebody. He moved towards the modernisers and lost some of the conservatives. He moved to the conservatives and lost some of the modernisers. He is the extreme case of a Bonaparte. He could have some stability for a time. But at the end of the day there are three possible outcomes.

The situation can either fall to the left—that's what the revolutionaries would love. Or it can fall the the right—that's what the capitalists would like. Or it can remain the same—that's what the social democrats would love.

But this third position cannot hold. You can either have one or the other. For as long as it held, Gorbachev became more and more isolated among the mass of the people, the most unpopular man in the USSR.

The problem in the present conflict and why the coup happened is that there was not a balance of power, but a balance of powerlessness. Both sides are extremely weak. The coup showed this.

Nor is it true that the state machine is on one side of the ruling class or the other. There is no abyss between the KGB and Gorbachev himself. Gorbachev came to office thanks to the KGB. It was Andropov, formerly head of the KGB, who selected him.

The KGB is always the most sensitive to the situation. It is always the most informed section of Soviet society because it is everywhere. This means that, although some of them support Gorbachev, some of them support Yeltsin.

The same applies to the army, which is also divided by nationality. The economic crisis and decline brings out those national divisions.

If the coup was a contest between two forces that are very weak, then we have an equation with a whole number of unknowns on both sides.

That's why the coup looked so incompetent. There's three examples of past coups which help to illustrate the present situation in the USSR. Pinochet's coup in Chile in September 1973 killed thousands on the first day and was settled in a question of days.

Hitler came to power on 30 January 1933. But because there was still opposition to him, and because his side was not completely united, it took him until May to smash the trade unions and the social democrats at the same time. In Italy, the March on Rome was in October 1922, but it took three years for Mussolini to really finish the coup. Why? Because his source of power was not as conservative as Pinochet's. Pinochet was in as strong a position as Hitler, and in a much stronger position than Mussolini.

The coup in the USSR was the thin end of the wedge—and this leaves two possibilities. It can become thicker or it can disappear. Yeltsin called on workers to go on strike in support of Gorbachev.

The main weakness of the Yeltsin side was the apathy, the feeling of, 'Who cares about Gorbachev?' The workers could have changed the whole thing. The degree, however, always depends on the existence of an independent workers' organisation.

So some workers are complete marketeers—followers of Yeltsin—while some want to go back to the command economy. Others look to Anatoly Sobchak, the mayor of Leningrad, who called for support for Yeltsin. A few months ago he was calling for a strong state and for banning strikes.

The more you talk in general about the crisis in society, the crisis of state capitalism, the clearer the picture becomes. The more immediate it is, the more messy. If the coup leaders had known all the consequences when it took place they would have arrested Yeltsin immediately. The fact that they did not gave Yeltsin the initiative, but that is not the end of the story. Nothing is settled.

The problems of the economy remain, and the impact of food shortages, rising prices and unemployment will be massive. Empty stomachs can lead to rebellion or they can lead to submission. It depends on the confidence people have. And mostly it depends on how long the stomachs have been empty. If it goes on for too long, the anger can turn to despair. Millions of unemployed people in Germany joined the Nazis because they were hungry.

The coup was not answered by a crushing workers' victory, and that means there can be a worse coup in a year's time. And by then the workers can be so sick they may well say, 'We don't give a damn, whoever promises us bread we join.'

The conditions for another coup will be there as long as the general crisis continues and as long as there's a hierarchical structure in the army and KGB. The eye of the storm—who initiates the crackdown—can be different next time.

The workers will learn quite a lot from the defeat of this coup. They will learn that workers can remove conspirators, and the minority who struck will feel vindicated in doing so. But those people who backed the coup can learn quite a lot too. They can learn for example, as happened in Chile, when the failed coup of June 1973 was followed by a successful one three months later, that the next coup must be ruthless and bloody.

There is only one way to guarantee that such a coup doesn't succeed. The Kornilov coup against the Kerensky government in August 1917 was smashed by the revolutionary military committee of the Petrograd soviet coordinating the soldiers' councils. Smashing the hierarchy of the KGB and the army—the state machine which remains intact—is the key to defeating such attacks in the future.

The family: haven in a heartless world?

Chapter from *Class Struggle and Women's Liberation:*
1640 to the Present Day, first published April 1984

Under capitalism women's oppression is unique in being rooted in the family where child-rearing, food preparation, and reproduction take place in a private world, separated from social production. As the family is part of the superstructure of society, shaping the ideas and emotions of men and women, children and adults, we should look at the impact of the contemporary family on the emotional side of people's lives.

In the previous chapter we saw how in the second half of the 19th century working men and women protected the family as a solace and refuge from the horrors with which industrial society threatened women, children and men, symbolised by the poorhouse. The rehabilitation of the working class family was buttressed by bourgeois ideas percolating down into the working class. The cliche 'The Englishman's home is his castle' was born. 'Home Sweet Home', first heard in the 1870s, became 'almost a second national anthem'. Few walls in lower working class houses lacked 'mottoes'—coloured strips of paper, about nine inches wide and 18 inches in length, attesting to domestic joys: 'East, West, Home's Best'; 'Bless Our Home'; 'God is Master of this House'; 'Home is the Nest where All is Best'.[1] 'Home,' wrote John Ruskin, '...is the place of peace; the shelter, not only from all injury, but from all terror, doubt, and division... So far as the anxieties of outer life penetrate into it...it ceases to be a home.'

Marx, in his *Economic and Philosophic Manuscripts* (1844), noted the schism in the male worker's feelings between home and work outside it:

> The worker...only feels himself outside his work, and in his work feels outside himself. He feels at home when he is not working, and when he is working he does not feel at home... Man (the worker) only feels himself freely active in his animal functions—eating, drinking, procreating, or at most in his dwelling and in dressing up, etc.[2]

For the housewife, even the latter possibility does not exist, for 'home' is itself the focus of her alienated situation. She is expected to provide nurture for others, with no place or scope for herself.

Concentrating on the working class family, the present chapter will try to show that the family is both protective and oppressive, both a haven from an alienating world, and a prison. We shall show, first, how the family is oppressive; secondly, that it is oppressive for both men and women; thirdly, that it is more oppressive for working class people than for other classes; fourthly, that nevertheless it is accepted because it still does provide some sort of haven in a capitalist world; and finally, that the institution of the family imposes the harshest oppression on people such as gays and lesbians who do not fit it.

The prevailing view of the family as an unchanging, eternal institution leads most writers to abstract it from the class structure of society. Of course there are major similarities of form between working class and middle class families—the nuclear household composed of father, mother and children facing issues of work, child-rearing, personal relations and leisure. But beneath the form lie sharp differences of content which are rooted in the class position of each family. The outside world impinges on the working class family in a radically different way from the middle class family.

Most studies of the family today are of middle class, white families. The only two notable exceptions are *Blue-Collar Marriage* by Mirra Komarovsky, whose detailed examination of the American white working class family was completed in 1959, and Lillian Rubin's brilliant book *World of Pain: Life in the Working Class Family*.[3] Nothing like these works has been undertaken in Britain. Their insights, however, are of general importance in understanding workers' families in advanced capitalist societies, including Britain, and such studies as do exist in Britain confirm the main perceptions of the American writers, despite differences of place and time. I have borrowed from them extensively.

In both books the working class women interviewed talk of themselves as wives and mothers—as housewives and not wage workers. The fact that women's own conception of themselves is in contradiction to the *actual* situation, in which they are both earners and housewives, results from two main factors: first, ideas lag behind reality; secondly, so long as the private family remains, men think of themselves not as fathers but as earners, and women by and large think of themselves as mothers, even if they do earn. Even at work the great majority of working class women, unlike women with interesting jobs and career prospects, think and worry about their homes. And of course there are periods in the lives of the majority of working class wives—when they have infants to look after—when they are totally dependent on their husbands financially, and therefore look upon themselves as 'merely housewives'. Even of the women who do have a paid job, two fifths in Britain at present work part time, hence in their concept of themselves housewifery plays a predominant role. And again, the education system also conditions girls to see their future function as housewives—wives and mothers—and not as workers.

Shattered dreams

working class girls accept the traditional feminine role. Sue Sharpe, in *Just Like a Girl: How Girls Learn to be Women*, a study of schoolgirls in Ealing, West London, most of them from working class families, writes:

> In a College of Further Education in London, a teacher noted that the girls who were taking hairdressing, commercial and typing courses...'dress according to *Girl*, *Petticoat*, and 'Brook Street Bureau' ads. They are totally immersed in self-image; nails, eyelashes, platforms and accoutrements.' The girls taking O-levels however...which might eventually lead them to Teachers' Training College or University... Often their whole attitude is different... And this is reflected in their dress which is correspondingly more relaxed; jeans, T-shirts and not so much make-up.[4]

Middle class girls, Sue Sharpe says, 'have...developed individual ambitions in which marriage and children figure as desirable but also intrusive events and ones to which they would reluctantly commit the whole of their lives'.[5] Working class girls, on the other hand, look to 'Marriage as Liberation', and in a chapter with this title, Mirra Komarovsky writes, 'The greater control which the family exercises over the adolescent daughter in comparison with the son no doubt largely explains the greater frequency with which women listed escape from home as one of the benefits of marriage'.[6] Marriage entices the young women also because it is an escape from boring, dreary jobs. Sue Sharpe writes:

> They see many of their relatives and friends doing jobs from which they seem to gain minimal enjoyment. It therefore makes sense to make their priorities love, marriage, husbands, children, jobs and careers, more or less in that order... Work is then not seen as attractive but as an unfortunate necessity of life and therefore the apparent opportunity to avoid it seems one of the advantages of being a woman.
>
> In addition to this there are other inducements. For instance children are more worth spending time and energy on than many boring and alienating jobs, since they actually respond and grow. The apparent choice of whether to work or not after marriage and after children, and the ability to organise life in the home without supervision, gives an illusion of freedom and greater choice of action.[7]

Alas, the dreams are shattered quickly after the wedding. Thus Lillian Rubin writes:

> The economic realities that so quickly confronted the young working class couples of this study ricocheted through the marriage, dominating every aspect of experience, colouring every facet of their early adjustment. The women, finding their dreams disappointed, felt somehow that their men had betrayed the promise implicit in their union. They were both angry and frightened.

She quotes one young working class mother:

'The first thing that hit us was all those financial problems. *We were dirt poor*. Here I'd gotten married with all those dreams and then I got stuck right away trying to manage on $1.50 an hour—and a lot of days he didn't work very many hours. It felt like there was nothing to life but scrimping and saving; only there wasn't any saving, just scrimping.'

Another woman, 26 years old, mother of two, married seven years, expressed her fear and anger with her husband when he was laid off: 'I could hardly ever forgive him for getting fired from his job. We never stopped arguing about that. I felt so frightened. I almost couldn't stand it. I was scared we'd just get into deeper trouble.'

The men, disappointed in themselves and equally frightened as they looked toward an uncertain future, responded defensively and uncomprehendingly to their wives' angry concerns. A 30 year old postal clerk, father of three, married nine years, told the interviewer:

—I couldn't figure out what the hell she wanted from me. I was trying, and I didn't like how things were coming out any better than she did.

—Did you tell her that?

—Tell her? Who could tell her anything? She was too busy running off at the mouth—you know, nagging—to listen to anything. I just got mad and I'd take off— go out with the guys and have a few beers or something. When I'd get back, things would be even worse. Sometimes I'd feel like hitting her just to shut her up. I never could figure out why the hell she did that. Did she think I didn't care about not making enough money to take care of my family?

Instead of marriage as an escape to freedom, home has become a prison. No longer is the young couple free to run around with the old crowd, to prowl the favoured haunts, to go to a movie or party whenever the mood struck. Both wives and husbands were shaken as it quickly became clear that the freedom they had sought in marriage was a mirage, that they had exchanged one set of constraints for another perhaps more powerful. A 28 year old clerk in a cleaning store, mother of three, married 11 years, sums up those feelings: 'One day I woke up and there I was, married and with a baby. And I thought, "I can't stand it! I can't stand to have my life over when I'm so young".' Her 31 year old husband recalls:

I had just turned 20 and, all of a sudden, I had a wife and kid. You couldn't just go out anymore when you felt like it… I'd get so mad at her, at my whole life, that I'd cut out on work a lot, and that would make things worse because then we had more money problems. Even when I worked steady, my paycheck wasn't big enough, then when I missed days, we were really in trouble.

But you know, a guy's got to have some freedom. He's got to feel like he doesn't have to go to that same lousy place every day of his life, like a slave.

The man's self-esteem was on the line every time he brought home a pay packet that was inadequate to meet the bills, or, worse still, failed to bring one home at all. For the woman, whose self-esteem and status, if she was kept at home bringing up young children, was intimately tied to her husband's accomplishments, the issue became one of 'husband esteem'. A woman of 35, mother of four, married 18 years, said, 'A man who can't take care of his family hasn't got the right to come in and order people around. A man's got to deserve it to have people listen to him when he talks. As long as he wasn't supporting us very good, he didn't deserve it.' Lillian Rubin comments:

> Whether overtly or covertly, these feelings were communicated to the man and, quite naturally, heightened the marital conflict. The men began to act out their anger and frustration—sometimes by drinking and staying out late, sometimes by violence, and almost always by assuming a very authoritarian stance within the family. How else could they assert their manliness? How else could they establish their position as head of the household? The women resisted.[8]

Capitalist society forces men to translate social position into terms of personal worth. Spending money and acquiring property (a house, furniture and so on) are weapons for defending workers' dignity. A feeling of powerlessness at work leads to a sense of individual guilt and corrodes the male worker's self-respect in a world based on social inequality. Financial worries affect the most intimate part of the marriage; they invade the marriage bed. Mirra Komarovsky writes:

> Some poor providers felt 'beat' and...the husband himself or his wife traced the decline in the husband's potency to his sense of economic failure. In other cases it is the wife whose sexual response is affected by her disappointment in her husband as a provider. Some wives are quite explicit in making this connection.[9]

Inequality in the family

There is little, even formal, egalitarianism in the working class family, as exists in professional middle class families. Lillian Rubin writes:

> The professional middle class man is more secure, has more status and prestige than the working class man—factors which enable him to assume a less overtly authoritarian role within the family. There are, after all, other places, other situations where his authority and power are tested and accorded legitimacy. At the same time, the demands of his work role for a satellite wife require that he risk the consequences of the more egalitarian family ideology. In contrast, for the working class man, there are few such rewards in the world outside the home; the family usually is the only place where he can exercise his power, demand obedience to his authority. Since his work role makes no demands for wifely participation, he is under fewer and less immediate external pressures to accept the egalitarian ideology.

The worker's wife usually shows sympathy for her husband, she understands his psychological needs and tries to accommodate to them. Lillian Rubin writes:

> On the surface, working class women generally seem to accept and grant legitimacy to their husbands' authority, largely because they understand his need for it.

If not at home, where is a man who works on an assembly line, in a warehouse, or a refinery to experience himself as a person whose words have weight, who is 'worth' listening to? But just below the surface, there lies a well of ambivalence; for the cost of her compliance is high. In muting her own needs to be responsive to his, she is left dissatisfied—a dissatisfaction that makes her so uncomfortable, she often has difficulty articulating it even to herself.

Sadly, probably no one is more aware than they are that the person who must insist upon respect for his status already has lost it.

This understanding and sympathy of the wife for the husband's predicament is seldom reciprocated by the husband understanding the wife's predicament! Often the pressure on the worker in the outside world is so great that he sees his own family as a trap which has forced him to hunt and be hunted out there.

In fact, any five year old child knows when 'daddy has had a bad day' at work... When every working day is a 'bad day', the family may even feel like the enemy at times. But for them, he may well think, he could leave the hated job, do something where he could feel human again instead of like a robot.[10]

Professional middle class families lead far more active social lives than working class families. Mirra Komarovsky writes:

In Glenton,[11] joint social life with friends is far from being the important leisure-time pursuit that it is in higher socio-economic classes. This applies to exchanges of home visits as well as to joint visits to public recreational places. About one fifth of the couples never visit with another couple apart from relatives. An additional 16 percent do so only very infrequently, a few times a year. And these social occasions may include so impersonal an event as a Sunday school picnic or a company Christmas party.

Even those who maintain social relations with other couples have a very small circle of friends. For one half of them this circle consists of only one or two couples. Only 17 percent see as many as four or more different couples in the course of a year (included in this count are couples seen at least a few times a year).[12]

Why the meagre social life? First, there is a lack of money. Secondly there is a lack of common interests between men and women. Also some husbands feel awkward on social occasions. Hence it is a common occurrence for husband and wife to clash when they have to decide how to spend their leisure hours. The men, after monotonous, boring work at the factory, want to stay at home and relax. Women who have been forced to stay at home have different needs.

They're more often bored and restless, feeling locked in by the walls of their houses, ready to get out—any place, just so long as it's out of the house... He, out at work, is...happy to get back into the peace and quiet of the house, while she's desperate to leave it. For him, the house is a haven; for her, a prison.[13]

Lillian Rubin writes:

The professional middle class families…have more active leisure lives on every count. They do more, go more, read more, have more friends, see more people.

This is partly due to financial differences, which mean that for middle class families a babysitter, a movie, a dinner out, a family vacation, a weekend without children, do not feel like major investments.[14]

For working people work and home are worlds apart. Hence there is little husband and wife can talk about. Mirra Komarovsky writes, 'Generally, having neither competence nor interest in the mate's topic of conversation, each complains that the other "goes on and on about boring things" in unnecessary detail'.[15] About his own job, a 36 year old steeplejack said, 'There is nothing to elaborate about my job. I just mix paint all day and put it on. It's monotonous.' Mirra Komarovsky comments, 'Talk about the job carries the connotation, for the husband, of "griping", which is thought to be unmanly'.[16]

Life contains little beyond the immediate daily tasks. It leaves little space for common cultural activities that might broaden the narrow overlap of interests and crushing spiritual poverty:

> Thus are both women and men stuck in a painful bind, each blaming the other for failures to meet cultural fantasies—fantasies that have little relation to their needs, their experiences, or the socio-economic realities of the world they live in… [The] burdens…are especially difficult to bear in a highly competitive economic system that doesn't grant every man and woman the right to work at a self-supporting and self-respecting wage as a matter of course.[17]

In addition there is little social contact between the wife and her husband's mates: 'The great majority of the wives, some 80 percent, have no social contact with their husbands' workmates. The friendships husbands may form on the job do not include their wives.' Things are radically different among middle class spouses. Lillian Rubin writes:

> For the professional…there is not the separation between working and living that so often characterises the working class experience. Work and life—which also means play—are part and parcel of each other. Their friends are often colleagues or other professionals in similar or related fields. Evenings spent with them mean that the ideas that engage them at work also involve them at play. Social life is almost always a coupled affair, a shared experience of husband and wife.[18]

Housework

Housework makes women's lives extremely narrow and oppressive. Not because the working class woman abhors housework, like the woman of the professional middle class. As Mirra Komarovsky writes:

> Unlike some college-educated housewives who detest housework, our respondents never say that they are too good for it, that housework is unchallenging manual labour… They accept housewifery. There is hardly a trace in the interviews of the low prestige that educated housewives sometimes attach to their role, as reflected

in the familiar phrase, 'I am just a housewife'.[19]

Because working class men as well as women accept the traditional segregation of masculine and feminine tasks, the 'wives do not normally expect assistance from their husbands':

> When the wives were asked to rank qualities which characterise a good husband, 'willing to help wife with housework' was low on the list, the 18th among the 21 qualities presented for rating. Only 4 percent of women considered 'helps with the housework' as 'very important'. Even 'helps with care of babies' was evaluated as 'very important' by only 12 percent of the women.

As against this:

> The high school men help their wives with shopping and with infant care more than do the less educated... Forty percent of the less educated 'never or hardly ever help with the babies', against only 10 percent of the high school graduates.

One reason why middle class professional husbands are more helpful to their wives, Mirra Komarovsky argues, is:

> ...the marriages of the high school graduates tend to be happier, and the warmer the relationship, the more likely the husband is to help with the infants. A happily married man tends to be less calculating about the balance of services.

The fact that the working class woman accepts, in principle, her sex-typed function of housekeeping, does not mean that she is satisfied with carrying this burden. Actually working class housewives are generally frustrated and depressed. Mirra Komarovsky writes:

> The homemaker herself attributes her major problem to the lack of sufficient money for necessities of life, for pleasanter living arrangements, for babysitters and fun. But the sharp segregation of the roles of the sex, despite her acceptance of it, adds to her sense of restriction and isolation... Unrelieved responsibility for young children and a feeling of being tied down creates discontent.[20]

Parents and children

Poverty and insecurity quite often push the parents, especially the fathers, to complete withdrawal. Thus one 31 year old steelworker told Lillian Rubin:

> My father was a very quiet man. he almost never talked, even when you asked him a question. He'd sit there like he didn't hear you. Sometimes, an hour later (it was like he'd come out of a spell), he'd look at you and say, 'Did you want something?' Most of the time, he just didn't know you were there.

A 25 year old woman, the elder in a family of two, recalls:

> My father never seemed to talk or be a part of the family. The only thing I can re-member that he enjoyed was working in his garden. He'd come home, eat, and go out in the yard almost every night of the year, even when it was raining. Otherwise,

he'd just sit quiet for hours, like he wasn't there or something.

Lillian Rubin's comment on these statements is:

It's true that fathers in the professional middle class homes may also be recalled as silent, as not 'part of the family'. But none of the adults who grew up in those homes recall the kind of brooding, withdrawn quality that so often describes the experience in a working class home. The child of a professional father may recall that he was 'always working even when he was at home'; that he was 'preoccupied a lot'; or that he 'always seemed to have something on his mind'. But that same person also is much more likely than his working class counterpart to remember some ways in which fathers participated in family life, even if only to recall the dinner hour as a time for family conversation. Preoccupation, then, would seem to be the most remembered quality about fathers in professional families; withdrawal, the most vivid memory in working class families.

Many working class fathers feel inadequate—they know they haven't 'made it'. In a society where money is a source of self-esteem and power, workers lack both. They are not accorded respect. They feel unsure of themselves, of their work. Their children perceive it clearly:

They know when their teachers are contemptuous of their family background, of the values they have been taught at home. They know that there are no factory workers, no truck drivers, no construction workers who are the heroes of the television shows they watch. They know that their parents are not among those who 'count'... And perhaps most devastating of all, they know that their parents know these things as well. Why else would they urge their children on to do 'better', to be 'more' than they are? Why else would they carry within them so much generalised and free-floating anger—anger that lashes out irrationally at home, anger that is displaced from the world outside where its expression is potentially dangerous?[21]

Failing, inadequate working class parents tend to impose authoritarian rule over their children. Komarovsky writes:

Working class parents emphasised what was termed the 'traditional' values of obedience, neatness and respect for adults. The middle class parents...on the other hand, wanted their children to be happy, to confide in them and to be eager to learn... Working class parents do not speak of emotional security or capacity to relate to others. Such concepts are not in their frame of reference.[22]

Economic and cultural deprivation, together with the heavy hand of the father, crush the development and realisation of personality in the children.

For the child—especially the boy—born into a professional middle class home, the sky's the limit; his dreams are relatively unfettered by constraints. In his earliest conscious moments, he becomes aware of his future and of plans being made for it—plans that are not just wishful fantasies, but plans that are backed by the resources to make them come true. All around him as he grows, he sees men who do important work at prestigious jobs. At home, at school, in the neighbourhood, he is encouraged to test the limits of his ability, to reach for the stars.

For most working class boys, the experience is just the reverse. Born into a family where daily survival is problematic, he sees only the frantic scramble to meet today's needs, to pay tomorrow's rent. Beyond that it's hard for parents to see. In such circumstances, of what can children dream?

What about the girls?

Among the women, a few recall girlhood dreams of being a model or an actress, but most remember wanting only to marry and live happily ever after... It's not that the girls from middle class homes dreamed such different dreams. But along with the marriage fantasy, there was for them some sense of striving for their own development... For those middle class women, marriage came much later since it was deferred until after college. Moreover, once these girls left home for college, they had at least some of the freedom and autonomy young people so deeply desire while, at the same time, they were engaged in an activity that brings status and respect from both family and peers.

For working class people childhood is not a rosy memory. Lillian Rubin writes:

Few adults from working class families look back over those early years with the 'Oh to be a child again' fantasy so often heard among middle class adults. Small wonder, too, that the working class young grow up so fast while an extended adolescence—often until the mid-twenties and later—is the developing norm in much of the professional middle class. Such a moratorium on assuming adult responsibilities is a luxury that only the affluent sector of society can afford.

Were there no tales of happy childhoods? The answer: very few. There are always a few good memories, some families less troubled, more loving than others; but happy childhoods: no... I recalled my own impoverished background. Yes, there were happy moments—an ice cream cone, a small toy, an infrequent and unexpected family outing, a rare approving remark from a harassed, frightened, and overburdened mother, a few cents occasionally to spend as I would and the exquisite agony of making a choice. But those were isolated moments, not descriptive of the warp and woof of my life. The dominant memories of childhood for me, as for the people I met, are of pain and deprivation—both material and emotional, for one follows the other almost as certainly as night follows day.[23]

Violence in the family

That the ideal picture of the family as a source of love, understanding and un-limited support is far from the reality, becomes clear when one looks behind the veneer of the family to the physical assaults quite common in it.

In the nature of things there are no reliable statistics on violence in the family. But it is now accepted that violence inside the family is far more common than was previously thought. Suzan Steinmetz and Murray Straus in their book

Violence in the Family write, 'It would be hard to find a group or institution in American society in which violence is more of an everyday occurrence than it is within the family'.[24] In extreme cases the physical violence becomes murder. An official report in 1977 came 'to the conclusion that over 300 children are killed every year in England and Wales alone, and 3,000 seriously injured. Four hundred receive injuries which result in chronic brain damage, while a further 40,000 children suffer mild or moderate damage'.[25]

The more exploited and deprived people are, the greater the violence. Richard Gelles writes in his book, *The Violent Home*:

> While violence occurs in families at all socio-economic levels, it is most common in families occupying positions at the bottom of the social structure… The bulk of conjugal violence and violence towards children occurs in families with low income, low educational achievement, and where the husband has low occupational status.[26]

Similarly Mirra Komarovsky finds a clear association between low education and high family violence. While 33 percent of wives who had less than 12 years education mentioned a physically violent quarrel with spouses, among those with 12 years or more the figure was only 4 percent.[27] Another researcher found that nearly half of the fathers of battered children were unemployed during the year preceding the decisive act, while 12 percent were unemployed at the time the battering took place.[28]

A study of severely ill-treated young children in north and east Wiltshire in the seven years 1965-71 showed that 48 percent of the fathers (or men who were in the role of father) were unemployed, 71 percent of them were unskilled labourers, and 98 percent did not own their own home.[29] Another research project conducted in the Strathclyde region into non-accidental injury to children in 1980 shows that only 10 percent of their mothers were in full or part employment, and two thirds of the fathers were unemployed.

While women are largely the victims of men's violence in the family, the woman is often the main perpetrator of violence on the children. As Richard Gelles writes, 'The most physically aggressive parent is the mother… It is the mother who usually explodes into violence when she runs out of patience'.[30] Two American researchers reported that out of the 57 cases of child battering they dealt with, the mother was the abuser 50 times.[31]

One form of child abuse in which power and sexual oppression are enmeshed is incest. Incest is rare, but not all that rare. One comprehensive three-year study estimated the number of cases annually in New York at 3,000. Other researchers thought this conservative. 'The most frequently named abuser was the father, male relative or mother's boyfriend, all of whom had easy access to the home. The victims' ages ranged from one or two months old to 17 or 18 years.' Incest, like physical violence, 'is more likely to occur where poverty brings loss of privacy together with other handicaps'.[32]

It is precisely because the family is a 'heart in a heartless world', because people in an alienated environment demand of the family more than it can deliver, because in it husband and wife become more and more dependent upon each other for the satisfaction of emotional needs, that it becomes the cauldron of pressures, frustrations and hate. As Richard Gelles writes:

> Prolonged interaction, intimacy, and emotional closeness of family life expose the vulnerability of both partners and strip away the facades that might have been created to shield personal weaknesses of both husband and wife. As a result, couples become experts at attacking each other's weaknesses and are able to hurt each other effectively with attacks and counter-attacks... [Both spouses] become experts as to their partner's vulnerability. Each soon learns what upsets the other. In the course of family squabbles, arguments or confrontations, one or both of the spouses will 'go for the jugular' by attacking weak spots.[33]

The stereotype of husband as provider, and dependent, nurturing wife, survives despite the fact that in Britain in 1979 the 'typical worker'—a married man with a non-working wife and children—represented a mere 8 percent of the male labour force and 5 percent of the total labour force.[34]

The family as incubus of mental illness

Mental illness is no less injurious than physical illness. An important piece of research by George Brown and Tirril Harris into depression among women shows the interrelation between the class to which women belong and the frequency of psychological disorders.

The women interviewed live in Camberwell, south London. It was found that severe events in life such as a dangerous illness of someone close, the loss of a job, an unwanted pregnancy, failure to obtain a house, or an eviction, caused working class women greater psychiatric distress than they did middle class women. This was particularly marked among women with children: 39 percent of working class mothers developed a psychiatric disorder after a severe event as against 6 percent of middle class mothers.

Working class women whose youngest child is less than six years old have a particularly high rate of disturbance—some 42 percent (as against 5 percent among middle class women whose youngest child is less than six). Also:

> ...we found that if a woman does not have an intimate tie, someone she can trust and confide in, particularly a husband or boyfriend, she is much more likely to break down in the presence of a severe event or major difficulty.

Brown and Harris, like Rubin and Komarovsky, found that class sharply affected this sort of intimate support. In working class families, husbands are psychologically less supportive of their wives than in professional middle class families. Only 37 percent of working class women with a child under six at home had a high level of intimacy with their husbands or boyfriends— half the proportion of the corresponding middle class group.

The middle class woman has greater material and psychological reserves to meet severe events in life than the working class woman. She can move into new areas of activity or make new contacts on which she can build. Brown and Harris write:

> The middle class woman can more often travel, visit friends at some distance, or buy a new dress; she has perhaps greater confidence and skills in seeking out pleasurable experience; and also a stronger belief that she will eventually achieve certain goals of importance. Adjustment in adversity may prove to be largely a matter of how to sustain hope for better things.

The most important factor detrimentally affecting the working class woman's psychiatric state is her feeling of being 'cooped in'—the restriction imposed by not going to work. The importance of a job for women's mental health becomes clear from the following figures: of non-employed women with a child at home, but without intimate ties with their husbands, 79 percent were disturbed when a serious life event occurred to them; the corresponding figure for women who were in similar circumstances but who held a job was only 14 percent.

In the conclusion to their book Brown and Harris write:

> In summary: some of the social class difference in risk of depression is due to the fact that working class women experience more severe life-events and major difficulties, especially when they have children; problems concerning housing, finance, husband, and child (excluding those involving health) are particularly important. Incidents of this kind are the only kind of severe event to occur more commonly among working class women and are the most obvious candidates for the 'inner city' stresses which are the focus of much current social commentary.

One of the most important contributions made by the research of Brown and Harris is the light it throws on the intersection of *class and family* as it affects women's mental health. Belonging to the working class does not make a woman liable to a high rate of psychiatric disorder—if she is single. On the other hand a married woman would not be liable to a high rate of psychiatric disorder—if she belonged to the middle class. The dangerous combination is being working class and married.

> Single women have a particularly low rate of psychiatric disorder (one in twenty is a case) and those widowed, divorced, and separated a particularly high rate (one in three is a case), but in neither group is there an association with class. Class differences are restricted to married women.[35]

In conclusion, the high level of mental illness among married working class women looking after young children and not holding a job is a reflection of both capitalist exploitation and of sexual oppression intertwined with it.

How do women compare with men as regards the incidence of mental illness? Many researchers have dealt with this question. An important summary of the research is an article called 'The Relationship between Sex Roles, Marital Status, and Mental Illness' by W R Gove. Gove says that research in all countries has:

> ...shown that married women have noticeably higher rates of mental illness than married men. In contrast, it is shown that when single women are compared with single men, divorced women with divorced men, and widowed women with widowed

men, these women do not have rates of mental illness that are higher than their male counterparts. In fact, if there is a difference within these marital categories, it is that women have lower rates of mental illness.

Gove estimates from the statistics that women are damaged twice as much by marriage as men. He argues that the reason for this is that 'men have two major roles, jobholder and household head, while the women tend to have only one, housewife'. (The large-scale employment of women contradicts this, but—and this is the important point—women, and men, do still conceive their roles in this way.) In support of Gove's contention that the differences between the job roles of men and women largely explain the differences between the rates of mental illness, he looks into what happens when men reach pensionable age and retire, and finds that 'there is at least tentative evidence that the rates of mental illness of married men and women are more similar after the age of retirement'.[36]

The family is not an impregnable sanctuary

The family does not serve as a safe haven insulated from the world of work. Work intrudes into every aspect of the worker's life. Lasch writes:

> The same historical developments that have made it necessary to set up private life—the family in particular—as a refuge from the cruel world of politics and work, an emotional sanctuary, have invaded this sanctuary and subjected it to outside control. A retreat into 'privatism' no longer serves to shore up values elsewhere threatened with extinction.[37]

A Ford worker describes his situation:

> I never thought I'd survive. I used to come home from work and fall straight asleep. My legs and arms used to be burning. And I know hard work. I'd been on the buildings but this place was a bastard then. I didn't have any relations with my wife for months. Now that's not right is it? No work should be that hard.[38]

A study of the effect of the 'Continental' shift system shows that the men cannot sleep properly, their appetite is affected, they feel permanently tired, get constipation, ulcers, rheumatoid arthritis, headaches and rectal complaints. In addition:

> ...the most frequently mentioned difficulties in husband-wife relationships concern the absence of the worker from the home in the evening, sexual relations, and difficulties encountered by the wife in carrying out her household duties... Another area of family life that seems to be adversely affected by certain kinds of shift work is the father-child relationship.[39]

Capitalism has also transformed sex itself into a major commodity, serving a huge market in fashion goods which claim to increase the sexual attraction of women and potency of men, and in pornography. Sexuality becomes a set of physical sensations alienated from the *person*. As George Frankl, in *The Failure of the Sexual Revolution*, puts it: 'The mass manufacturers of dreams...concentrate entirely on sexual performances and sexual situations, and do not allow the personality of their subjects to obtrude'.[40] Long ago, in 1921, Alexandra Kollontai denounced this concept of sex:

> The bourgeois attitude to sexual relations as simply a matter of sex must be criticised and replaced by an understanding of the whole gamut of joyful love-experience that enriches life and makes for greater happiness. The greater the intellectual and emotional development of the individual the less place will there be in his or her relationship for the bare physiological side of love, and the brighter will be the love experience.[41]

A mechanical approach to sex increases anxieties among both women and men. The woman asks herself, 'Am I as attractive, as successful in bed as the women portrayed in magazines, on films and TV?' The man asks himself, 'Am I a potent stud?'

Sexual permissiveness has not challenged the idea that a woman's place is in the home—it has simply added 'and in the bed'.

Capitalism distorts all human beings in society, depriving men, women and children of the capacity to develop their potentialities in every area of life. The family, that part of this society to which people look for love and comfort, reproduces the external relationships, and this turns it into a cauldron of personal conflicts—of anger, jealousy, fear and guilt. Both men and women fail to live up to the impossible ideal stereotype which society gives them of one another.

Why, if the family is less and less effective in securing the emotional, personal needs of people, do people still cling to it? Why, of all institutions, does this one show the greatest ability to survive?

While it is true that the harsher the world, the less effective is the family in protecting the emotional and material needs of its members, at the same time the greater is the need for just such a sanctuary. The satisfaction of almost all personal needs is to be found nowhere else. To be outside the nuclear family, an orphan, widow or widower with no close relatives, or a middle-aged or old single man or woman, is lonelier and worse. Mutual aid is a basic necessity for men and women. Out of loneliness the nuclear family gains strength. The institution of the family oppresses the woman. She, on her part, participates in creating the chains that bind her, decking them with flowers of love.

The family is an opaque wall preventing people from seeing and questioning the harsh, competitive society outside. It makes a person's inhumanity to another more bearable. The horrors of the outside world explain the extreme tensions in the family, but also explain its perseverance. The contemporary family is the product of capitalism and one of its main supports.

The 'deviant' homosexuals

Sex roles are enforced by our society on everyone. Because of the crucial role of the family, any adult who does not marry and raise a family is marked out as deviant. Homosexuals challenge both the *material* base of the present-day family—privatised reproduction—and its ideological superstructure—the stereotypes and ideas which define the sex roles of women and men. And this is notwithstanding the fact that homosexuality is far more common than is usually assumed. Kinsey's research found that 37 percent of his male, and 13 percent of his female, respondents had experienced homosexual relations to orgasm by the age of 45.[42]

Homosexuals are stereotyped as deviants despite the fact that the monogamous family has not been the historical norm. Of 554 societies listed by George Murdock, in only 135 was monogamy the norm.[43] Nor has homosexuality always been viewed as deviant. C S Ford and F Beach found in their study of 190 societies that for 76 for which data was available concerning homosexuality, 49 perceived it as normal.[44]

In our society homosexuals are forced into the closet. When gay people manage to get out of their isolation by meeting other gays, they are forced into a social ghetto away from work, the family and the mainstream of social life. The gay ghetto breaks the isolation for individual gays, but maintains the isolation of gays from mainstream society.

Even relations between gays themselves are not free from the diktat of the traditional roles of men and women. However hard they try, gays cannot escape the pressures and conditioning of capitalist society. Hence the heterosexual world in which man oppresses woman imposes its own divisions on gays too. One writer explains the male role played by gays:

> Playing roles in a society which demands gender definitions, sexual role-playing, masculine versus feminine—what can we do, those whom society dismisses and condemns as half-men? Too often we react by over-playing. The absurd parodies of straight sexuality we see in the bars, ultra-butch, camp bitch, are cold and brittle. Their eyes betray fear and loathing as they compete viciously, to allay the panic of loneliness at the end of the night.[45]

The division between 'butch' and 'femme' is usually used in relation to women homosexuals. Thus Sidney Abbot and Barbara Love, in their thoughtful book *Sappho Was a Right-On Woman*, write:

> Some lesbians use terminology like 'marriage', 'husband', or 'wife', but there is a profound reason for this. These are the only words in our culture that convey love, trust, permanence, and responsibility in a relationship... Presumably role-playing among lesbians exists because lesbians are raised in a role-playing society... Lesbians have spent all their time in a culture that forcefully sells a way of life based on male and female dominance and submissiveness, independence and dependence, aggressiveness and passivity.[46]

In fact the notion of 'male' and 'female' partners in homosexual relationships is inaccurate. As Arno Karlen, in his massive *Sexuality and Homosexuality*, quotes one psychologist as saying, 'A small percentage always take the female role; another small percentage are muscle men, homosexual pin-ups, who always take the active role. But for the most part, they often switch roles'.[47] But however forcefully the contemporary gay movement and the lesbian groupings in the women's movement reject the gender-related roles, they cannot win. Although the *Gay Liberation Front Manifesto* denounces marriage and speaks of the death of the family, gays, in seeking emotional security in a harsh world, imitate the institution their own sexuality denies. However, as Kinsey showed, lasting couples are rare among homosexuals, although many lesbian pairs live together for five, ten or 15 years. Arno Karlen writes, 'Many homosexuals say they are looking for a lasting affair and are quick to shack up, but in fact have a series of brittle, stormy, short-lived relationships'.[48]

Homosexuals do not demand less emotional commitment from their partners than heterosexuals, despite the superficially more liberal attitude to 'extramarital' sex. Living under terrible pressure in a hostile world, they feel their sexuality far more intensively than most heterosexuals, hence the pervading possessiveness—because possession of things, as of people, gives a modicum of security. As Abbott and Love write: 'In lesbian society, where there is no marriage, no social or legal sanctions to help sustain relationships beyond the initial period of romantic love, insecurity and jealousy have a field day'.[49]

The homosexual world, which appears to undermine capitalist notions, is also completely invaded by capitalism:

> The gay subculture is riven with clashes and illusions. The women tend to be split off from the men, butch men from fem, leather queens from drag queens, and so on. Many of these attitudes are themselves reflections of heterosexual values; others of the pervasive cash nexus. In this gay world it is all too easy for people to lose their individualities, sex becomes the aim of life; individuals become things.[50]

In conclusion, capitalism has turned homosexuality into a 'problem'. So long as the traditional family is an economic unit, for rearing children and satisfying the consumption needs of the adults, homosexuals are bound to be considered deviant: the homosexual male is not seen to fit the man's role as provider for wife and children, and the homosexual female is not seen to act the role of mother and wife. The contemporary family is not only a prison for those in it, but also enslaves those who do not fit into the sex-role stereotypes connected with it.

Notes

1   E Shorter, *The Making of the Modern Family* (London, 1975), pp230-231.
2   K Marx and F Engels, *Works*, vol 3, pp274-275.
3   M Komarovsky, *Blue-Collar Marriage* (New York, 1967); L Rubin, *World of Pain: Life in the Working class Family* (New York, 1976).
4   S Sharpe, *Just Like a Girl: How Girls Learn to be Women* (London, 1976), p71.
5   Ibid, p305.
6   M Komarovsky, op cit, p25.

7 S Sharpe, op cit, pp210-211.
8 L Rubin, op cit, pp80-81 and 90-91.
9 M Komarovsky, op cit, p93.
10 L Rubin, op cit, pp99, 113, 160-161, 179.
11 Glenton is a name given by Komarovsky to two contiguous, closely interwoven industrial townships forming a county.
12 M Komarovsky, op cit, pp311-312.
13 L Rubin, op cit, p188.
14 Ibid, p189.
15 M Komarovsky, op cit, p51.
16 Ibid, pp151-152.
17 L Rubin, op cit, p178.
18 Ibid, p190.
19 M Komarovsky, op cit, pp49, 55, 57.
20 Ibid, pp56, 60.
21 L Rubin, op cit, pp36-37, 55.
22 M Komarovsky, op cit, pp76, 78.
23 L Rubin, op cit, pp30, 38, 40-41, 46.
24 S Steinmetz and M Straus (eds), *Violence in the Family* (New York, 1975), p4.
25 I Renvoize, *Web of Violence: A Study of Family Violence* (London, 1978), pp133-134.
26 R J Gelles, *The Violent Home* (London, 1972), pp125, 130, 192.
27 M Komarovsky, op cit, p366.
28 D C Gil, 'Violence Against Children', *Journal of Marriage and Family*, November 1971.
29 J E Oliver et al, *Severely Ill-Treated Young Children in North East Wiltshire* (Oxford, 1974).
30 R J Gelles, op cit, pp55, 77.
31 S Steinmetz and M Straus (eds), op cit, p196.
32 I Renvoize, op cit, p182. The power of males over females, especially young females, combined with sexual exploitation, leads many of the victims of incest to use their oppression as a weapon of power. As Jean Renvoize reports: 'Many girls unquestionably enjoy such a relationship with their father once they have accepted it, even if at the same time they feel guilty about it. It gives them a sense of power, and some even indulge in petty blackmail, demanding gifts as the price of their silence. If their parents' relationship is poor they may get great satisfaction out of playing the role of "little mother", so that as father and daughter act out their private fantasies the real mother is pushed into the background. Inevitably the girl will have mixed feelings about her mother. She will feel both anger that her mother is not protecting her from her father, for she will know the relationship is wrong even if she is actually enjoying it, and guilt that she is depriving her mother of her rightful place.' Ibid, pp184-185.
33 R J Gelles, op cit, pp164-165.
34 Study Commission on the Family, *Families of the Future* (London, 1983), p19.
35 J W Brown and T Harris, *Social Origin of Depression: A Study of Psychotic Disorder in Women* (London, 1978), pp154, 178-179, 291.
36 W R Gove, 'The Relationship between Sex Roles, Marital Status, and Mental Illness', *Social Forces* (University of North Carolina), September 1972.
37 C Lasch, *Haven in a Heartless World* (New York, 1978), pp xvii-xviii.
38 H Benyon, *Working for Ford* (London, 1977), p75.
39 P E Mott et al, *Shift Work: The Social, Psychological and Physical Consequences* (Ann Arbor, 1966), p18, quoted in T Cliff, *The Employers' Offensive* (London, 1970), p71.
40 G Frankl, *The Failure of the Sexual Revolution* (London, 1974), pp116-117.
41 A Kollontai, *Selected Writings*, p231.
42 A C Kinsey et al, *Sexual Behaviour in the Human Male* (Philadelphia, 1948); A C Kinsey et al, *Sexual Behaviour in the Human Female* (Philadelphia, 1953).
43 G P Murdock, 'World Ethnographic Sample', *American Anthropologist* 59 (1957).
44 C S Ford and F Beach, *Patterns of Sexual Behaviour* (New York, 1951), p130.
45 A Walter, *Come Together: The Years of Gay Liberation 1970-73* (London, 1980), p86.

46 S Abbott and B Love, *Sappho Was a Right-On Woman: A Liberated View of Lesbianism* (New York, 1972), pp92, 97.
47 A Karlen, *Sexuality and Homosexuality* (London, 1971), p198.
48 Ibid, p527.
49 S Abbott and B Love, op cit, pp80-81.
50 *Gay Left*, Spring 1976, quoted in J Weeks, *Coming Out: Homosexual Politics in Britain from the Nineteenth Century to the Present* (London, 1977), p223.

Why socialists must support the gays

Socialist Worker, 26 August 1978

In class-infested society there is oppressor and oppressed in all walks of life. Employer oppresses employee; man oppresses woman; white oppresses black; old oppresses young; heterosexual oppresses homosexual.

The true socialist is able to overcome all these divisions. An engineering worker who can only identify with other engineering workers may be a good trade unionist, but he has not proved himself to be a socialist. A socialist has to be able to identify with the struggles of all oppressed groups.

We are all the children of capitalism, so we tend to conceive of the future— even the socialist future—in an ordered and hierarchical way.

It is as though the socialist revolution will be led by the Father of the Chapel in the print union, the NGA working on Fleet Street. Second in command will be an AUEW Convenor Section 1 from the toolroom in a big car factory. The lieutenants of the revolution will all be 40 year old white male shop stewards.

If there is enough space then we'll allow blacks and women and gays to take part—providing they stand quietly at the back!

A lot of socialists still have difficulty believing that gays will be taking part in the revolution at all.

On the contrary we should look forward now to the first leader of the London workers' council being a 19 year old black gay woman!

The system rules by dividing us. This means there is no natural way by which one oppressed group identifies with another. The most racist extremists in the Southern states of America are the *poor* whites—not the rich whites.

In the same way blacks do not *automatically* support women and women do not automatically support blacks. Gays will not *automatically* support other oppressed groups.

The Nazis sent thousands of gays to the concentration camps. In Chile gays were castrated and left bleeding on the street.

But it is not true that, even given these facts, gays automatically become anti-fascist.

Tens of thousands of gays supported Hitler. Many were in the Brownshirts. After Hitler took power he turned on the gay support and slaughtered them in the Night of the Long Knives.

How can we explain gays joining the Nazis?

If you are an *oppressed* gay putting on a Nazi leather jacket and leather boots gives you for the first time a sense of power. It makes it easier to put down Jews, women and anyone else.

For any oppressed group to fight back there is a need for *hope*.

If you are on the way *down* you feel despair. You look for a victim to kick.

If you are on the way *up* you look for a back to pat.

That's why only by building a socialist movement can you unite workers with oppressed blacks, women and gays.

And that's why it is so important for gays to organise for demonstrations like at Brick Lane and to feel able to identify themselves proudly as gays and—where possible—as revolutionary socialist gays.

Karl Marx wrote that capitalism unites the forces of opposition. But it also divides us. We have to strive *consciously* for that unity.

We are one—all of us together—but only when we *fight* together.

Lecture notes on Marxist theory

London, 1961

Introduction

Marxism sees capitalism as a total system in which all the parts are interlinked. So its critique covers all levels of analysis, and tries to link them together. Therefore it is important, even in a basic programme, not to neglect any level, to try to have some discussion on each topic from every aspect in turn. This means that the question of the state is not to be treated *just* as a political question, the question of production as simply an economic question, the class struggle at simply a social level, etc. Every topic should be looked at from every aspect—the historical, social, economic, political, philosophical, ideological, empirical, etc—in order to see how they link up, and in the end how capitalism functions as a total system and how it can be overthrown.

Reading

Everyone doing this course must read the following pamphlets:
(1) Marx and Engels, *The Communist Manifesto*.
(2) Marx, *Wages, Price and Profit*.
(3) Marx, 'Preface' to *A Contribution to the Critique of Political Economy*.
(4) Lenin, *State and Revolution*.
(5) IS, *The Struggle for Socialism*.

Start with *The Communist Manifesto* and *The Struggle for Socialism* and read the others as they crop up.

In addition, to follow up different aspects of the topics which are touched on, we have included a much longer list of books and pamphlets at the end. We hope that this will help individuals and groups as they move towards a deeper study of some of the issues raised in this outline. Even these notes don't really stand on their own. They attempt to highlight points which comrades should look for in their reading and discussion, and leave all kinds of questions open.

Finally, a knowledge of basic Marxism is only part of what any member of a revolutionary party needs to have. It provides a framework which can help make sense of the world, but needs to be applied to every concrete situation. This can only be learnt in one's day to day practice, discussion and debate, and in the real battles of the class struggle. Without this application, the most elegant educational programme becomes totally meaningless.

Why the working class?

The central principle of Marxism is that the working class is the only social group capable, by its self-activity, of bringing about the advent of socialism. This was written into the statement of the First International and has been the basis of all serious socialist activity since then.

What is a social class?

In any society the first necessity is that man produces and reproduces the means of his existence. Inevitably therefore his relationship to the means of production is crucial, and determines every aspect of his life. In production men relate to each other in one of two ways—cooperation or conflict. Men who stand in the same relationship to the means of production share interests in common and are said to form a class which is the basis of collective organisation to safeguard and further their interests. In doing so they come into conflict with other groups with other interests, and hence arises class struggle. 'The history of all hitherto existing societies is the history of class struggle.' Patricians and plebeians in Ancient Rome, lords and serfs in medieval Europe, slaves and slave owners, etc, form such classes. In capitalist society the two classes upon whose struggle the development of society depends are the bourgeoisie (the capitalist class) and the proletariat (the working class). There are also other classes in capitalist society (eg peasants, the middle class) but in the end their importance depends on how they stand in relation to the two fundamental classes.

The problem of change

Some people see history as the product of the actions of great men. Others see it for instance as men becoming progressively more enlightened. However, real history, the history of mankind, can only be understood as the activity of real men struggling collectively to realise their interests. So a revolutionary change in society can only be the product of a social class whose interests are objectively opposed to the present organisation of society.

The working class in production

Production under capitalism is inherently social—everything that is produced depends on a complex process of social cooperation. This is unlike much peasant production, for example, in which each peasant household produces, independently from all others, more or less everything it needs. But this social nature of production doesn't mean that production is to satisfy social need. The aim of production in capitalist society is to expand capital—to make a profit—and this can only be done at the expense of the working class. So what is produced, why it is produced, the conditions under which people labour, are all in the hands of the capitalist class. An exploited working class is the basis for the very existence of capitalism. The bourgeoisie, who at the time of the bourgeois revolution and the destruction of feudalism were progressive, and could with some justice claim to represent the interests of all oppressed groups in society, have now become totally reactionary, *the* barrier to the further development of the productive forces in the interests of the liberation of mankind. The exploitation of the working class in the realm of production is further revealed in the area of distribution—the share-out between wages and profits, the concentration of wealth in the hands of a few, poverty, inadequate and differential provision of education, social services, etc. Reformists have always concentrated on the area of distribution alone—they have left basically untouched the area of production and exploitation. That is, they have tampered with the effects of capitalist production, not its basic structure, so not surprisingly have never been able to deal with even the social issues they have singled out as the ones parliamentary politics can solve.

Bourgeois democracy and the universal interest

Democratic systems claim to represent the general interest, the universal. In fact the political equality (we all have the vote) goes hand in hand with social and economic inequality, and perpetuates these inequalities. The state really represents a *particular* interest, and the 'national interest', or whatever it is called, is really a particular, capitalist, interest. The working class can have no interest in perpetuating their exploitation, nor can there be a genuinely universal interest which is opposed to the interest of the majority of the population. The working class, unlike the bourgeoisie, represents a genuinely universal interest—the freedom and satisfaction of the needs of all mankind, on the basis of a free, democratic organisation of production to satisfy these needs.

Thus, because of their position in society, the working class as the necessary basis of production, but unable to satisfy their interests within the capitalist social system, represent the *negation* of capitalism. In the society but not of it, their organisation and pursuit of their interests represents a constant threat to the very existence of capitalist exploitation. Because the basis of existence of the working class is cooperative social production, not exploitation of some other class, the proletarian class struggle represents the potential liberation of *all* oppressed groups.

The problem of organisation

The working class is the only social group capable, through its own self-activity, of liberating society, of bringing about socialism. For this to be possible involves the development of a clear awareness of what the working class interest really is—the development of a socialist consciousness. How this can be realised involves questions of strategy, tactics, organisation, programmes, etc, and will be dealt with under the question of the party.

Working class history

That it is possible in practice is shown by the whole of working class history and struggle. The potentiality of the working class is seen most clearly in the Paris Commune and the October Revolution in Russia, and also for example in the Spanish Civil War, the Hungarian Revolution of 1956, etc. British working class history shows a tremendous richness in workers' abilities to organise themselves in resistance to all kinds of capitalist attack. It has not yet shown a direct, conscious, revolutionary challenge to the existing order, except perhaps in the first years of the Communist Party of Great Britain.

Reading: Marx and Engels, *The Communist Manifesto*.

Marx's view of history

The starting point for Marx is always real living men, as they produce their own means of subsistence. What he is concerned with is the double relationship of man to nature and of man to man. That is, man, through the labour process, transforms nature to satisfy his needs. He does so in certain relationships (of cooperation and/or conflict) with his fellow men. These activities make up the *forces of production* and the *relationships of production*, or what Marx calls the *economic base* of any society.

(a) Corresponding to this base, this form of social existence, are certain forms of consciousness (eg religious ideas, political views, etc).

(b) At a certain point in time the harmonious relationship between the forces and the relations of production aiding the development of the productive forces become fetters on this development.

(c) No social order ever perishes before the fullest development of the productive forces possible within it has occurred.

(d) In broad outline the Asiatic, the ancient, the feudal and the modern capitalist modes of production have been historically progressive epochs in the formation of society.

(e) With the capitalist formation and its overthrow the prehistory of mankind comes to an end. 'Men make their own history, but not in circumstances of their own choosing.' The aim of theory is to understand why not in circumstances of their own choosing, and linked to practice, to liquidate these limitations on men's free activity. Under socialism, simply, men will make their own history.

Forces of production

This does not just mean technology and machinery, or the physical level of output.

(a) At first it means nothing more than the real labour power of working men.

(b) Anything which increases this productive capacity is also a productive force. So:

(i) The application of science and technique to industry is a productive force.

(ii) Cooperation of workers in production is a productive force.

(iii) Force itself is a productive force, eg the violence involved in forcing the peasantry off the land in the early stages of capitalism.

(c) In a special sense the term productive force may be applied to the proletariat itself, which by its revolutionary action can set free the forces potentially existing in the social labour on which capitalist society is based. 'Of all the instruments of production, the greatest productive force is labour power.'

Relationships of production

This refers to the social organisation of production, the mode of cooperation under which production is carried out. In legal terms this is expressed by the property relations. (Though NB legal terms, as part of the superstructure, can conceal as much as they express the existing reality—as the Russian constitution shows.)

The conflict between forces and relations of production

As the conflict in the base heightens, there are three possibilities:

(a) The productive forces (embodied in the activity of a rising social class) break through, eg the bourgeois revolutions in France and England.

(b) The productive forces fail to break through, eg the decline of Roman slave society.

(c) There is a stagnation, eg the Oriental (hydraulic, irrigation) societies of Ancient Egypt, Babylon and the Chinese Empire.

The motor of social development, of the change from one form of society to another, is the class struggle. This is crucial, for the end of capitalism is not something which will happen one day when the system just grinds to a halt, and is then replaced the next day by socialism. Capitalism, which is a dynamic system constantly rationalising the means of production, has shown that *given time* it can recover from any crisis and start up again. The cost of this has already been catastrophic—in the 20th century alone there have been two world wars, fascism, imperialistic exploitation of the underdeveloped world, massive unemployment of the industrial working class in the 1930s especially, gigantic waste of resources on armaments since the Second World War, and so on.

The system won't perish until there has been the fullest development of the productive forces possible within it. Now the working class is the crucial productive force. In its full development in terms of consciousness and organisation will lie the great development of the productive forces capable under capitalism—only then can the system be destroyed once and for all. This subjective factor, arising on the basis of the objective contradictions within capitalist production, completes the development of the conflicts within the economic base.

Base and superstructure

On the economic base arise the superstructures of society—the legal, political, aesthetic, religious and philosophical realms. These are attempts to make sense of man's activities in the world—and, like all attempts at understanding, they may be true or false. That is to say, the 'economic base' refers to man's conscious productive activity which aims at creating and preserving the conditions of human life; the 'superstructure' attempts to justify, legitimise, understand, etc the forms this activity has taken.

In general, to date such attempts at understanding have been partial, one-sided, limited attempts. Such attempts become specifically *ideological* when they 'forget' to relate their perspective (eg a religious or philosophical one) to man's real activity, and try to build systems of interpretation in their own right—eg an attempt to write history in terms of what great men (eg kings of England) thought and did; or to write the history of the growth of freedom in terms of the development of law so as to apply to everyone equally—forgetting that because men are not socially and economically equal, that such 'freedom' is often purely academic. As the writer Anatole France put it, 'The law in its majesty forbids both rich and poor to sleep under bridges.' Or again, the social-democratic view that separates economic and political struggles, and fights each separately, 'forgets' the relationship between the two and becomes ideological in theory, leading to disastrous betrayals in practice.

Bourgeois political economy wasn't ideological because it at least attempted to understand the effective basis on which society moved and developed—Marx criticised it for its *inadequacy*. Modern economics has given up this concern and has become mere apologetics in the main.

In the area of political theory, modern democratic views are partial, one-sided views of what actually happens—they cover up the reality of class society by saying that there can be effective political democracy (we all have the vote) while there is still no economic and social democracy. So too in the Communist states, they say that there is socialism because the means of production are owned by the state. They forget to ask who 'owns' the state, and it certainly isn't the working class.

These superstructural elements must all be criticised and undermined, but it isn't enough to do so just in theory. For instance, there have been lots of criticisms of religion as an illusion, but it still remains. Such a criticism, if it is correct, can only be tested by also overthrowing a social condition which requires illusions.

By building socialism and showing that the 'kingdom of heaven' is nothing but a metaphor for what mankind can accomplish by its own efforts here on earth, one will destroy the need for religion.

Reading: Marx and Engels, *The Communist Manifesto*, Marx, 'Preface' to *A Contribution to the Critique of Political Economy*.

Production and exploitation: the economics of capitalist society

The commodity

Commodities are goods produced for sale on the market, and the wealth of societies in which the capitalist mode of production prevails appears as 'an immense accumulation of commodities'. Such a society is characterised by *general commodity production*.

Use value and exchange value

The *use value* or utility of a commodity is its ability to satisfy a person's wants or needs (eg to wear a coat, to eat a cabbage, etc). The *exchange value* of a commodity is its ability to exchange with other commodities, or to be bought and sold for money, on the market. Objects have different use values because they are qualitatively different—their ability to exchange with each other on the market presupposes that they have something in common, that they can be compared quantitatively with each other. What is this common factor? It is the fact that they are all products of human labour in the abstract.

The labour theory of value

This value of commodities which enables them to exchange with each other is measured in terms of the amount of value-creating substance which goes in to make them up, ie in terms of the amount of socially necessary labour time spent in producing them. This *law of value* is the only law which can regulate the exchange of commodities.

So, for instance, if the productivity of labour rises because new machinery is introduced and each shirt made can now be made in half the time it took before, the value of each shirt will be halved.

Two kinds of labour—concrete and abstract

Corresponding to the use and exchange value of a commodity are two kinds of labour—concrete and abstract. *Concrete labour* is the labour which goes into making a particular useful article. Exchange value, however, is measured by making an abstraction from the useful nature of the labour and from the form it takes, ie it is *labour in the abstract*. It might be said that this can't be done—yet capitalist society does it all the time, whenever a commodity is bought or sold.

Circulation of commodities

The capitalist puts money into circulation (eg buying machinery, raw materials, hiring workers, etc) with the aim of getting more money out at the end of the process than he started with. Where does this surplus value come from? It can't come from selling commodities above their value—although one capitalist would gain, it would be at the expense of others and the total amount of value in the system would remain unaltered. In the same way it can't come from buying commodities below their value. Of course *prices* will fluctuate with supply and demand (eg the soaring price of candles during the electricity workers' strike). But price is not the same as value—it necessarily differs from it, and is an expression of how value is shared out in society. Prices don't explain how value is created.

Labour power as a commodity

Additional value can only be created by the capitalist buying some commodity at its value, and creating value by the 'consumption' of this commodity. What peculiar commodity is capable of creating more value than it itself is worth in the very process of being consumed? There is under capitalism such a commodity—man's capacity to labour. For man's capacity to labour to become a commodity, two conditions must be satisfied—it must be 'free' labour in a double sense:
(1) Its owner must be freed from owning any means of production.
(2) He must be free to sell his labour power.

For example, the handloom weaver in the early stages of textile manufacture often owned part or all of the means of production he used. The slave is not allowed to sell his labour power—he is 'owned' by his master.

Equal values exchange, yet the worker is robbed

The principle of capitalism is that equal values exchange. So when the worker sells his labour power he must be paid for it at its value. This value, like all value, is measured by the amount of labour time socially necessary to produce the labourer or, on a society-wide scale, by the amount of labour socially necessary to produce and to reproduce the working class. This will be measured in terms of the amount that has to be spent in clothing, feeding, housing, etc the workers. This subsistence level always has a social aspect and can't be measured absolutely once and for all. For example in certain parts of America, because public transport is so bad, a worker's ability to find a job will depend on him having his own car, and this will have to be taken into account in measuring the value of his labour power.

When the worker sells his labour power what happens? The person who buys it gets the 'right' to consume it, just as if I buy a pair of shoes I have the right to wear them. So the capitalist, in buying labour power, will consume it, ie put it to work perhaps an eight-hour day, and in the first three hours will produce goods whose value is equal to the value of his labour power. The next five hours he works will be creating more value than his labour power is worth—this is called *surplus value*.

Now observe that under capitalism:

(i) What the worker produces belongs rightfully to the capitalist.

(ii) The surplus value he creates belongs rightfully to the capitalist.

(iii) At the end of the process the worker retains his labour power and can sell it afresh.

Capitalism is fair on its own terms, yet the system robs the worker. This process of extracting surplus value, which belongs 'rightfully' to the capitalist, is called *exploitation*.

Exploitation versus oppression

These terms should not be confused. Peasants in Vietnam, black people in South African 'native reserves', women in every society may be terribly oppressed and downtrodden, and of course their struggles to throw off this oppression must be supported without reserve. But they are not necessarily exploited—eg a starving peasant family, unable to grow enough rice to live off, let alone a surplus to sell on the market, is not being exploited at all. It is generally the most skilled, most productive workers who are most exploited, in their ability to produce vast amounts of surplus value.

Capitalism as a total system

Such a system of producing wealth in the form of exchange value, not in order to satisfy social need but to make a profit, is inherently torn by crises and contradictions. Competition between different units of capital leads to the necessity for each capital constantly to rationalise its means of production, eg if one car firm introduced a new technical process others will have to do the same or find a substitute process, otherwise the first firm will undercut all its competitors on the market. So this competition leads to the constant necessity for capital to be accumulated.

Now (1) the rate of accumulation is determined by the rate of profit. As industry becomes more capital intensive (ie as more and more machinery is introduced to replace workers, which is forced on capitalists because of the competition between them), or as Marx puts it, as the organic composition of capital rises, there is less and less living labour from which surplus value can be extracted, there is a *tendency* for the rate of profit to fall. This can offset in many ways (eg by increasing the rate of exploitation through productivity deals) but remains a fundamental tendency of capitalism. (2) Further there is a tendency for production to grow faster than the available outlets. A high rate of accumulation means that there is less available to spend on consumption goods, ie on buying the commodities which the system can produce.

Were it not for the tendency for the rate of profit to fall, one could solve the second problem by raising wages. Were it not for the tendency for production to outstrip the market, one could solve the first by cutting wages (eg fascism).

But these dilemmas arise at the same time from the very nature of capitalist production—it can find temporary solutions to its problems but it cannot resolve them.

These notes outline the basis of Marx's scientific critique of capitalist production. This 'economic' analysis has other aspects which must be brought out briefly.

Philosophical

From the capitalist viewpoint the only aspect of the worker the system takes into account is his ability to labour. Man, with all his abilities, creative powers, emotions, etc, is reduced in the day to day functioning of capitalism to a one-sided abstraction, to his exchange value. From the exploitation of the working class in the process of production arises man's *alienation*—for in the way production is organised he loses control over what he produces, over how it is produced, and gets cut off from his fellow men and from social relationships with them, eg through the competition for jobs which forces groups of workers to be prepared to undercut their fellow workers. In a fundamental philosophical sense man gets cut off from what he really is—or at least could be—the creator and controller of social life.

Human relationships take the form of relationships between things, for although production is already inherently social, independent commodity producers only become aware of their social relations through the exchange of commodities on the market, ie through the intermediary of what they produce. This is the *fetishism of commodities*, the substitution of relationships between things for the real, human relationships which underlie them.

Social

The social aspect of capitalist production is the class struggle. There is a constant struggle by the capitalists to extract surplus value, by the workers to protect themselves and their conditions of work, and the rate of exploitation depends on this balance of class forces. Depending on the extent to which the capitalists feel threatened they are prepared to use ideology (eg 'the national interest', witch-hunting), the state (eg parliament and the anti trade union legislation, or even the police and the army) or war even to safeguard their profits and their class rule.

Historical

Marx's critique of political economy also shows how the capitalist mode of production arose and how it will pass away, ie it treats the system as only one transient historical form of the organisation of production and society. Its origins are violent—in primitive accumulation, in the forcible creation of a working class who had nothing left to sell except their labour power. Its functioning is torn by crisis, contradiction, gigantic waste production (eg arms) side by side with great want and deprivation, and by social conflict. Its great expansion of the productive forces in pursuit of profit goes hand in hand with the creation and re-creation of the working class. In the self-activity, consciousness and organisation of that class lies the future system of production and social organisation for need and not for profit—ie socialism.

Political

The role of the state in the development and protection of capitalism is also crucial, both in how it helps the capitalists to deal with the anarchy of the international market, and to combat threats from the working class at home. It will be dealt with separately.

Reading: Marx, *Wages, Price and Profit* (sometimes published under the title *Value, Price and Profit*)

Reform or revolution

'Reformism' classically refers to theories of the creeping abolition of capitalism by the gradual socialisation of sectors of the economy one by one, or by the use of established political channels.

The word is also used sometimes to refer to the struggle for individual reforms within capitalism. We are here concerned with the first aspect, ie with the whole question of how capitalism can be abolished.

'The emancipation of the working class must be the act of the working class itself.'

The essence of socialism is the conscious direction of society by all its members. The working class is the unique carrier of this consciousness, and in freeing itself it provides the basis for this conscious control. Thus the change from capitalism to socialism is achieved by the working class *as a class* taking control. This is a total process in which the working class becomes conscious of its own position under capitalism and of the possibility of reorganising society as a whole, and builds its own institutions which make this possibility real.

Reformism is incompatible with this for two reasons:
(1) A step by step takeover ignores the nature of capitalism as a total system, and the resistance which will be offered to such a change.

(2) Both step by step reformism and the 'parliamentary road' deny the possibility of the working class acting as a class, and the possibility of real working class democracy. They are elitist and generally concerned with efficiency ('we could run the system better') not freedom ('we could run society in *our* own interests'). Of course running society in our own interests would be running it 'better', but the opposite is not necessarily true. The Labour government which came to power in 1964 pledged to run the system better than the Tories. By this they meant running *capitalism better*.

The working class revolution would be a conscious act. Reformist struggle is very important on the way to revolution, but from a socialist point of view it is to be judged by the extent to which it helps to develop a revolutionary consciousness, and revolutionary organisations of the working class.

Class power

The capitalist class holds power in all kinds of ways—in any capitalist society political, social, economic and ideological power interlock, no matter how different and diverse they may appear to be in different countries. The ideological aspect is very important. 'The ruling ideas are the ideas of the ruling class.' This doesn't mean that the government has to hit the newspapers and television companies over the head with a big stick in order to get support—the papers, etc are generally run by large corporations which share the interests of the large corporations in general, however much they may disagree with this or that government action.

Similarly, ruling class ideas filter down to all levels in society, and become part of the common sense with which we all operate (eg 'a fair day's work for a fair day's pay', or 'we live in a real democracy because we all have the vote').

And unless this were so no tiny exploitative ruling class could survive for more than a few days except by sheer terror. So the struggle for socialism necessarily includes a constant battle against ruling class ideas at all levels.

Reformism ignores this, eg it accepts the ruling class idea that the state is somehow 'above society', neutral, and can be used by whoever wins an election to implement any policies, whether capitalist or socialist (see notes on the state). In general it sees political power as separated from other forms of power.

Production under capitalism

The essence of capitalist production is the domination of capital (dead labour) over living labour, and the continual need to accumulate capital. Exploitation can't be abolished bit by bit, though workers' struggles can limit it. Capitalism is continually trying to increase accumulation as against wages, and this is continually resisted by working class struggle. This struggle for reforms, far from ruling out the necessity of revolution, creates conflicts which can only be resolved by revolution—the capitalists can't give more, the workers can't demand less. Quantitative demands give rise to the necessity for qualitative changes, and either the working class seizes power or it is smashed (eg the 1926 General Strike).

Reformists argue that all the workers need is *more*, that somehow all we mean by exploitation is that there are inequalities in the sphere of distribution. It fails to understand how these inequalities arise from the very nature of capitalist production. For instance many left reformists supported the Labour incomes policy, and said it would be a way of helping the lower paid workers. But under capitalism you can't have controls over profits and dividends, or the very motor of the system—accumulation in order to invest—is undermined. So it was no surprise that the incomes policy became a wage freeze. All that such a policy could conceivably do is to alter the way in which the working class share of the 'national cake' is distributed among workers. It can't conceivably alter the balance between labour and capital (except in the interests of capital).

Furthermore reformism ignores the tendency of a capitalist economy towards crises. So time after time the Labour Party in Britain has found itself in power during just such a crisis, and all its promised reforms are shelved while it solves the crisis—but solving the crisis means making capitalism work better, increasing accumulation, increasing the rate of exploitation! So reformist solutions always end by making the working class pay so that capitalism can be strengthened.

Decreasing relevance of reformism

The classical reformist method of struggle is becoming increasingly less relevant. Power *within* the ruling class is less and less centred on parliament, as shown by the growth of the giant corporations at the national level, and by the increasing internationalisation of such firms. Capitalist economic power is becoming increasingly independent of any particular national base.

The classical power base for reformist action—the national parliament—is thus undermined even for immediate reform struggles. As a result reformist politics comes to demand and to fight for less and less in the way of real reforms and to become more and more openly the agent of capitalism in the heart of the working class (eg the last Labour government compared with its predecessors). Equally as it fails to deliver the goods reformism becomes less and less linked to the grassroots of the working class movement.

The locus of the struggle for reforms, for the protection of workers' living standards, has shifted from the traditional political organisations of the working class to the shop floor struggle.

The future

This local grassroots reformism, unlike the old-style political reformism, is based on workers' self-activity, and as such can become the basis of a new *revolutionary* movement to challenge capitalism. The separation of economic and political struggle is being ended by the ruling class itself. Incomes policy, productivity deals and anti trade union legislation have brought politics back to the shop floor, for even these limited reformist struggles on the shop floor have become a threat to the continued existence of capitalism. The struggle to defend the shop stewards becomes the struggle for a new revolutionary socialist movement, for the construction of a revolutionary party.

Reading: Lenin, *State and Revolution*, Cliff, *The Employers' Offensive: Productivity Deals and How to Fight Them*.

The state and revolution

A clear understanding of the nature of the state in capitalist society is crucial, for on this question more than any other, many sections of the revolutionary movement have gone wrong—leading either to a serious underestimate of the crucial importance of this political level in the workers' struggle for socialism, or else to all kinds of reformist (and often disastrous) strategies and tactics.

What is the state?

The state is a power above society and expresses the existence of irreconcilable class antagonisms in capitalist society. It consists of special bodies of armed men who have prisons, etc, at their command. It is used as an instrument to maintain the exploitation of the working class and to destroy any challenges made against the power of capital.

How the state controls

In the last resort the state uses open violence—troops, etc. In conditions when class conflict is not so open, this violence is usually not so naked, eg use of police to protect scabs, to prevent demonstrations 'getting out of hand', but even here the exercise of force is clearly apparent.

By and large control is usually exercised by ideological means—through control of education, regulation of the press, radio and television, etc. That is, ruling class ideology fosters the illusion that we really have a free press, freedom of speech, and so on. Finally the state presents itself as being neutral, above the petty struggles of the different groups in society, representing what they have in common (the 'national interest', etc).

Forms of state

The state can take many different forms depending on the needs of capital in any given period, eg:

(1) In 19th century Britain, with a strong bourgeoisie and secure capitalist relations of production, the state claimed to play a non-interventionist, night-watchman role. Regulation of many areas of society was opposed, because capital didn't need such regulation.

(2) In 19th century Germany, where the bourgeoisie was very weak, it was the state which unified the nation by means of war in order to provide a secure framework for capitalist development.

(3) In France from 1851 to 1870 Napoleon III governed. There was a relative balance of class forces which allowed Napoleon III, based on the independent peasantry, to control the state apparatus.

(4) Again, under fascism, the threat to the continued existence of capital was so strong that Hitler was able to take power and smash working class organisations by means of open violence of an undreamt-of ferocity. Many capitalists didn't like Hitler but saw no other solution to their problems.

(5) In Russia since the 1930s the ruling class and the state bureaucracy have been fused—political and economic power are in the same hands, and these aren't the hands of the working class.

What these examples show is that under a system of private capitalism the bourgeoisie can rule, but needn't govern, ie need not control the state apparatus directly. But the state always supports their class interest, which is the expansion of capital by means of exploiting the working class—exactly as in Eastern Europe and Russia the governing bureaucracy (which is the ruling class) is based on the pursuit of its own class interest, the expansion of capital production.

There are three views on the left about the state:

(a) Preserve and use the bureaucratic state—the view of reformists and Stalinists.

(b) Abolish it immediately after the revolution—the anarchist view.

(c) Smash the bourgeois state and create in its place a semi-state which will wither away—the dictatorship of the proletariat. This is the Marxist view.

The errors of the first two views become clear when we look at the proletarian state which will be established after the revolution.

The dictatorship of the proletariat

The class struggle does not cease after the revolutionary seizure of power by the working class. All the historical evidence shows that even then the bourgeoisie and other groups who had a vested interest in the capitalist system will fight by every means to destroy the new workers' state. So the new ruling group—the working class—will have to organise itself to destroy all reactionary opposition. There will be a new state—a workers' state.

This state will be fundamentally different from any form of state under capitalism. It will be based on:

(1) The armed people—in place of the 'special bodies of armed men'.

(2) No bureaucracy—all officials will be elected and subject to recall, receiving workers' wages.

(3) Parliament will be replaced by soviets—workers' councils—which will join together control over political and economic decisions, and will control production.

(4) Control of the means of communication—newspapers, etc—will be in the hands of the soviets.

So, against the anarchists one argues the need to defend the gains of the revolution by whatever means necessary. While the class struggle continues some form of state is necessary.

Against the reformists and Stalinists one says that the old state machine has been fashioned to maintain the separation between those who rule and those who are ruled. It must be smashed and new forms of organisation be established.

Some people say they are against any form of dictatorship—even by the working class. To them we say the proletarian dictatorship right after the revolution will be more democratic than any existing system. In fact the proletarian dictatorship is the most democratic conception possible straight after the revolution—the word dictatorship signifies that while there are still classes in society one of these must rule or another will seize power—the conscious rule of a whole social class, the majority class in society. In freeing themselves the working class will free all other oppressed groups in society, for exploitation will be abolished and replaced by production under the conscious control of all those on whom cooperative social life depends.

The withering away of the state

It is important to stress that there will be a state after the seizure of power. The working class must protect itself and its rule, and while there are class antagonisms there will be a state. But this state, the workers' state, will in reality be so different from any bourgeois form of state, so democratic and closely tied to its social base, so unbureaucratic, that it will already be a partial negation of what we mean by a state. The active involvement of millions in its affairs will prevent it 'floating off', prevent it from becoming the private property of a few who might wish to use it to further their own private interests. A high level of economic and cultural maturity of the working class will ensure that they continue to control the state. The overcoming of class antagonism and the international spread of the revolution will rapidly make even this state unnecessary. With the withering away of the state a completely new form of society will be built. It would be arrogant of us to specify the forms it will take—this would be a restriction on the free, conscious activity of those who will be making this new society, who will be making their own history. But it is clear that the separation of political, social and economic control will be overcome: the struggle of man against man will be ended, to be replaced by free cooperation, and the freest possible development of man's potentialities. As Leon Trotsky put it:

> The forms of life will become dynamically dramatic. The average human type will rise to the heights of an Aristotle, a Goethe or a Marx. And above this ridge new peaks will rise.

Reading: Lenin, *State and Revolution*.

Index

117, 129
conflict between production and consumption: 114
consumption: 110-112
contradictions: 93
crisis: 58, 63, 93-94, 106, 108-109, 112, 139, 140, 171, 298, 304, 307
distribution: 22, 24
production: 306-307
Castro, Fidel: 192
Centralisation of capital: 18, 116
Chartism: 182
China: 157
  cult of the individual in: 208-209
  economic backwardness of: 204, 207, 209, 212
  exploitation in: 205-206
  people's communes in: 213, 215-216, 248
  People's Liberation Army: 221-225
  police dictatorship in: 207
  strikes in: 226-227
  students in: 223
  wage levels in: 206
  working class: 229
Chinese Communist Party: 190, 191, 218
Chinese People's Republic, establishment of: 190
Chinese Revolution (1925-27): 190, 196, 203, 226
Chu Teh, 191
Ciliga, Ante: 44, 126
Circulation: 88, 91
Clark, Colin: 131
Class, definitions of: 63
Class division: 19
Class struggle (see also Russia, class struggle in): 125-130, 304
Collectivisation (see also agriculture) in Russia: 46-49, 55-56, 129, 228, 248
Commodities
  production of: 301
  circulation of: 302
Communism: 20, 21, 23, 26, 58, 93
Communist Manifesto, The: 21
Communist parties (see also China, Russia): 196
  Indian: 195-196
  Polish and Yugoslav: 255
  Russian: 39, 166
  in West: 167
Competition (see also international competition, military pressure): 59, 82-83, 87, 89, 92, 97, 125
Condition of the Working Class in England, The (Engels): 157

Consumption (see also capitalist consumption): 21, 31, 32, 89, 100, 102-105
Control of production (see also workers' control): 31
Counter-revolution: 75-76
Credit: 100-101, 107-108
Cuba: 192-196
  revolution: 192
Cultural Revolution (China): 211, 223-227
Cycle of war and booms: 112
Czechoslovakia: 15, 128

Deflected permanent revolution: 196
Degenerated workers' state: 1-4, 10, 17, 18
Democratic dictatorship of proletariat and peasantry: 2, 78, 187-188
Department I/II: 86, 91, 102, 104-105, 110, 114
De Wolfe, Bertram: 129
Dictatorship of the proletariat: 50, 309
Differentials: 39, 45
Directors: 40, 43
Directors' Fund (Russia): 40, 41
Division of labour: 19, 28, 63, 81-82, 84-86, 90

Eastern European crisis impacts on West: 266
Economic cycles: 97, 98, 100-101, 107, 140, 147, 171
Economics and politics, fusion of: 73-74
Economics of capitalism: 301-305
Economist: 141
Egypt: 73
Engels, Frederick: 18-137, 159-168, 177-187, 233-260
Employment, level of (see industrial reserve army)
Exchange, process of: 80
Exchange value: 81-82, 86
Exploitation of workers: 302-303
Export of capital: 115-116, 119, 179, 181-182
Expropriation of Russian peasantry (see collectivisation)

Family (see also mental illness, violence)
  as haven: 273-274, 287
  as prison: 289
  fails to be secure haven: 286
  inequality within: 277-279
  part of superstructure: 273
  role in women's oppression: 273-274
Fascism: 72
Feudalism: 8, 26, 69, 94, 115
Financial Times: 141
First World War: 169-170

Relations of distribution: 9, 22, 31, 55-56, 111, 114
Relations of production: 6, 9, 12, 18, 21, 28, 60, 69, 111, 114, 298-299
and law of property: 68
socialist: 29
transformation of capitalist into socialist: 18
Revolution: 305, 307
Revolution Betrayed, The: 4
Revolutionary party: 5, 130
Ripeness for socialist revolution: 25, 26, 74
Romania, 15
Russia:
army: 1, 51-55, 74, 271
army commanders: 52-55
backwardness of: 18
bourgeoisie: 29
and capitalist crisis: 94ff
capitalist restoration in: 2, 5, 11, 12, 13, 68-69, 75-76
class struggle in: 125-130
compared with Nazi economy: 58
compared with US economy: 261, 269
dependence on agriculture: 27
development of productive forces: 94, 114
economic development of: 261, 269
economy: 2
laws of motion in: 18
industry, scale of: 17
new proletarian revolution in: 3
obstacles facing contemporary socialist movement: 264-266
perspectives for economy: 113
planning in (see also Five-Year Plans): 12
population: 44-45
recent economic problems: 262-263, 270, 272
relation of forces between proletariat and bureaucracy: 126-127
as single workshop in capitalist society: 85-86
state as employer: 65
state capitalism in (see state capitalism)
state controls process of reproduction: 95
state property in: 11
strikes in: 38, 44, 266
totalitarianism: 14
trade unions: 4, 21, 38, 127
unemployment in: 270, 272
war, impact of: 45
war victories: 17, 128
as workers' state: 13
and world economy: 90-92
Russian Revolution (1917): 196
Russian working class: 10, 11, 12, 25, 35, 163,

164, 165
atomised: 127
crystallisation of: 129
lack of democratic rights: 129
lack of legal freedom: 31, 43-44, 55
no control of state property: 68
numbers of: 126, 128
poverty of: 33, 34
recruited into bureaucracy: 128
suppression by state: 107, 127-128
wage levels: 28, 36, 37, 39, 40, 41, 42, 107, 129
will overthrow Stalinist bureaucracy: 130
working hours: 34
Schumpeter, E: 117
Second World War: 1, 12, 120, 170
Self-emancipation of working class: 1, 15
Self-esteem
men and women's differ: 276-277
men feel inadequate: 281
Separation of mental/manual labour: 19, 20, 24
Sex, made into a commodity by capitalism: 286-287
Shachtman, Max: 11, 13, 90, 155-168
Siberia: 12
Slavery: 77, 296
and bureaucratic collectivism (see also bureaucratic collectivism): 159-160, 162, 164, 165
Smith, Adam: 58
Social life, difference between working class and professional: 278-279
Socialisation of labour process: 18, 20, 30
Socialism: 30, 112
Socialism in one country: 56, 189, 228
Socialist economy, production of use values: 112
Socialist mode of production: 19
Soviets: 5, 21, 265, 272
Specialists: 39, 42
Stalin: 73, 155, 203-210
defeats Left Opposition: 38
Stalinism:
as barbarism: 77
as gendarme in distribution process: 9-10
counter-revolutionary role of: 198
is it progressive?: 78-79
Mao's: 203
Stalinist bureaucracy: 4, 5, 9, 10, 14, 38, 42, 48, 50-56, 74, 79, 92-93, 121, 126
adopts price system: 87
campaign against bureaucratisation: 37
as a caste: 63-64
as a class: 63